REBEL
CITIES

REBEL CITIES

Paris, London and *New York*
in the Age of Revolution

MIKE RAPPORT

Little, Brown

LITTLE, BROWN

First published in the United States of America in 2017 by Basic Books
First published in Great Britain in 2017 by Little, Brown

1 3 5 7 9 10 8 6 4 2

A CIP catalogue record for this book
is available from the British Library.

Hardback ISBN 978-1-4087-0291-8
C-format ISBN 978-1-4087-0523-0

Typeset in Garamond by M Rules
Printed and bound in Great Britain by
Clays Ltd, St Ives plc

Papers used by Little, Brown are from well-managed forests
and other responsible sources.

MIX
Paper from
responsible sources
FSC® C104740

Little, Brown
An imprint of
Little, Brown Book Group
Carmelite House
50 Victoria Embankment
London EC4Y 0DZ

An Hachette UK Company
www.hachette.co.uk

www.littlebrown.co.uk

For Helen . . .
. . . it's her book in many senses

CONTENTS

CONTENTS

INTRODUCTION:
THREE CITIES IN AN
AGE OF REVOLUTION

O N A CHILLY winter's day, 23 February 1763, sceptical Parisians watched a huge equestrian statue slowly being lowered onto a pedestal at the centre of a vast square on the western edge of their city. The massive artwork, by sculptor Edmé Bouchardon, was a masterpiece (or so critics would soon say) and depicted King Louis XV, still with eleven more years to reign, triumphantly on horseback. It was to be the centrepiece of the cobbled expanse of the elegant Place Louis XV – now Place de la Concorde – which spread out at the bottom of the Champs-Elysées. The kingly horseman and square alike were to be monuments to the glory of France's Bourbon monarchy, celebrating Louis XV's triumphs in the War of Austrian Succession (1740–1748). The designer of the square was the king's favourite architect, the great neoclassicist Ange-Jacques Gabriel, who trumped fierce competition with his choice of location and plan.

The most imposing sight on Place Louis XV was Gabriel's two colonnaded, symmetrical palaces built in Greco-Roman style in warm golden sandstone, overlooking the square from its northern side. Russian historian Nikolai Karamzin would react just as the designers had intended. In April 1790, as his coach rumbled towards the end of the Champs-Elysées, rolling past its idyllic mix of ornamental groves, restaurants, kiosks and music stands, Karamzin leaned out of his carriage window: 'Your gaze runs on ahead to where a statue of Louis XV rises on a large octagonal plinth surrounded by a white marble balustrade. Approach it and you will see before you the densely shaded paths of the famous garden of the Tuileries, belonging to the great palace: a beautiful view!'[1]

As their carriages emerged onto the square, horses' hooves and rolling wheels resounding across the open space, visitors were always impressed by the unavoidable sight of Louis on horseback, an expression of royal power designed to be admired. Even Thomas Jefferson, though a republican to the marrow, was able to find fulsome praise for Bouchardon's work. It was, he wrote, 'probably the best in the world . . . [I]t is impossible to find a point of view from which it does not appear a monster, unless you go so far as to lose sight of the features and finer lineaments of the face and body'.[2]

Yet in February 1763, the Parisian spectators were not so sure. As the equestrian mass swung from the taught cables of four wooden cranes, the workmen straining at the ropes and pulleys, they bitterly repeated the remark that their king was being held up by four *grues*, a double entendre meaning both cranes . . . and 'whores'. This Parisian grumbling was aroused by a painful awareness that, just thirteen days previously, the monarchy had signed one of its most humiliating peace treaties. The Treaty of Paris had ended the Seven Years' War, one of the most devastating global conflicts of the eighteenth century. For France, it was above all a shattering defeat at the hands of its archenemy, Britain. Most of its empire in India and the Americas had been engulfed by the

British, the French army and navy mauled and the honour of the monarchy battered. Louis XV himself, it was widely known, had not led from the front: he had scarcely left the sprawling royal palace and grounds of Versailles, enjoying the company of his intelligent mistress, Madame de Pompadour, and frequenting his selection of courtesans – hence the hostile witticisms about *grues*. The official opening of the Place Louis XV on 20 June that year was timed to coincide with the formal proclamation of the peace. The idea was that Louis XV could be presented as both powerful and a peacemaker, but when set against the scale of the nation's military disasters, the statue's pretensions rang hollow.[3]

Parisians had another, practical, reason for their irritation. The very origins of the Place Louis XV rested in a competition set by the city authorities for a new square that would break open the tangled knot of medieval streets that strangled traffic in the centre. 'Our towns', complained Marc-Antoine Laugier, author of the famous *Essay on Architecture* in 1753, 'are still a mass of houses crowded together without system, planning, or design. Nowhere is this disorder more noticeable and more shocking than in Paris'. For this reason, some of Gabriel's competitors had suggested locations in the very heart of the city, but the cost, the legal complications and the logistics of the demolition stymied them all. The king intervened as Parisians pondered their quandary, donating some of his own land on the westernmost edge of Paris, and, unsurprisingly, it was Louis's own architect Gabriel who won the renewed competition. So while the end result was undoubtedly magnificent, it missed the initial point of the project: for most Parisians, it was in the wrong place. The Place Louis XV represented the triumph of kingly prestige over the day-to-day needs of the crown's subjects, of royal power over urban reform.[4]

THIS FRICTION REVEALS an important part of the history, and the present, of great cities. They are at one and the same time places where individuals, social groups and communities live, work and socialise, but they are also centres of authority and power – economic, political and social. As such, they are not only places where rulers, governments, corporations and institutions actually reside, but also where they inscribe their presence in a visual sense on the cityscape. The buildings and spaces of a city are used by governments, civic institutions and social movements for practical purposes, and they are built, taken over and adapted to suit. In times of political turmoil, public buildings are embellished, vandalised or even destroyed to convey political messages. In times of stability, they become the settled, even mundane, symbols of authority, power, public welfare, freedom – or the benevolence and glory of the ruler. In periods of great transition or revolution, transformation in the use, look and even existence of buildings and spaces is one way in which people experience or 'live' the change. Moreover, a physical place may shape the course of an historical event, in the way that terrain affects the outcome of a battle.

For all these reasons, a city's spaces and places are contested, either in the sense of who actually has control of the bricks and mortar or in terms of what these places signify, as the Parisian reaction to the grandiose statue of Louis XV showed. As the royal likeness was eased into place in 1763, it would be wrong to view the coarse jokes among the onlookers as an early stirring of popular, revolutionary hostility (it would take more than a generation for such grumbling to develop into anything resembling that, in 1789). It does show, however, that, try as it might, no regime can entirely control the political messages that a place, a building or an embellishment is meant to transmit. And the political conflicts that arise from the control, adaptation and use of buildings and open spaces – the palaces, squares, parks, churches, taverns, coffeehouses, streets, prisons and so on – are never more intense and violent than in times of revolution.

This book is about how three cities, Paris, London and New York, became such sites of struggle in a revolutionary age, that of the American and French Revolutions. It explores, in particular, how, in all the political ferment of the later eighteenth century, the spaces and buildings in these cities both symbolically and physically became places of conflict, how the cityscape itself became part of the experience of revolution and may even have helped shape its course. Revolutionaries in New York and Paris and radicals in London used particular locations and buildings to mobilise their supporters, to demonstrate or debate and to move against the existing order.

Yet the upheavals were not just political revolutions but *cultural* ones as well: through their ideological struggles and attempts to create new political orders, or reform the old one, radicals and revolutionaries used the cityscape to convey their messages, hopeful, threatening and stirring. In the American and French Revolutions, this certainly involved a hefty dose of iconoclasm: pulling down statues, chiselling away political symbols from public buildings, changing street names and, in the French case, destroying religious emblems. Yet it also involved constructing, embellishing and creating: converting old buildings for new political purposes; carving new mottoes and motifs onto older sites, or, in the cut and thrust of revolutionary politics, hastily painting them on; surmounting buildings with emblems such as liberty caps; raising liberty poles; and using the open spaces of the metropolis to hold revolutionary festivals or public meetings to demonstrate political unity and transmit political messages to the massed ranks of citizens. These were all ways in which revolutionaries and radicals sought to rally people to their cause and to implant the values of the new civic order in the hearts and minds of people as they went about their daily lives. In the words of one historian of the cultural history of revolutions, it was an exercise in 'regeneration through the everyday', in which the city became the canvas for the cultural revolutions and the scene of the bitterest confrontations between the supporters of the old order and the new. To a large extent, the eighteenth-century battle for political emancipation hinged on control of these spaces, not only in a strategic sense, important though that could be, but also because it determined whose ideas, whose messages, whose authority was disseminated among the people of the metropolis.[5]

The role of the 'people', in fact, is also essential to this story, since in our three cities the struggle for democratic change unfolded in the neighbourhoods and streets of the urban community. Most obviously, when revolutionary or radical symbols and messages were inscribed on buildings, or when the new civic order took over once familiar public places for new purposes, it was a visual, physical way in which the political battles of the era reached into the most local of levels. Thus, 'space' in this book has two meanings: it can mean a precise place where people meet and interact, but it can also signify distance and the challenges that the sheer size of the eighteenth-century metropolis, particularly Paris and London, posed to revolutionaries and radicals trying to mobilise the people of the city. So part of this story is the dissemination of political activity and initiative across urban space, a geographical shift from the privileged halls of elite power to the taverns, political clubs, local revolutionary committees and streets that in themselves represented the attempts by the democratic movements to open up politics to wider participation.

Revolutionaries in New York and Paris and radicals in London all found ways of reaching into the neighbourhoods and communities of their cities, through political networks or by encouraging the active role of the man and woman (sometimes quite literally) in the street. The artisans, labourers, shopkeepers, men and women who lived in the tenements, queued at food stalls and socialised in the cafés and taverns were not the passive recipients of these experiences. They took an active part in the upheavals, shaping, adapting or challenging on their own behalf the ideas and claims that the revolutionary or radical leadership was trying to convey. Who acted and why, and which communities were the epicentres of popular action, are part of the story of the revolutions in these cities. This spatial urban experience can be seen as one where different, conflicting visions of the future – between those of the middle-class revolutionary politicians and those of the working, artisanal population, for example – were often played out in the struggles for control of the spaces and places of particular neighbourhoods.

Britain, France and America were not, of course, the only places to have experienced, in different ways, the revolutions of the eighteenth century; regions of the world as diverse as the Low Countries, Haiti and Latin America all had upheavals of their own. Nor were New York, London and Paris the only cauldrons of struggle; all three were set in countries where there was an energetic, even frenetic, political life right across the smaller towns and countryside, where people did not simply grumble and follow the lead of the metropolis. Yet the three cities, as seats of authority, as economic hubs and as centres of culture and leisure, were replete with the institutions of the old order, the buildings that housed them and the symbols, motifs, effigies that represented royal or imperial power: parliaments and assemblies, high courts and churches, barracks, fortresses and prisons, but also statues, palaces and triumphant, ceremonial spaces. So they became the most dramatic arenas in which people who wanted political change would challenge the regime – and leave their mark on the cityscape in doing so. The cities also had a concentrated sparkle of the places and spaces in which reformers, revolutionaries and their opponents organised, mobilised, debated and fought: law courts, legislatures, coffeehouses, cafés, taverns, squares and parks. In America and France, it also made them the logical places for the organs of the new order to establish themselves, taking over the old structures that were once held by the former governors, adapting, embellishing and, sometimes, demolishing them.

In a broad sense, the citizens of all three cities were immersed in a shared political culture that bound their experiences together. This was an Atlantic world in which ships powered by nothing more than wind, currents and human muscle criss-crossed the ocean, carrying with them goods, ideas and, above all, people (including the enslaved, whose experience in New York will be part of the story). In this maritime space, concerned eighteenth-century citizens of all three countries looked to the ideological legacy of the political upheavals of the seventeenth century, in the British Isles, particularly the civil wars of the 1640s and the revolution of 1688–1689. These disruptions bequeathed what was known in the English-speaking world as the 'Whig' model of freedom from arbitrary power and civil liberties such as religious toleration, freedom of speech and assembly, habeas corpus and representative government that were jealously defended by British subjects on both sides of the Atlantic and enviously coveted by educated, progressive Frenchmen and -women. Politically engaged people in the eighteenth century also drew on their classical education for inspiration, especially their knowledge of Greek democracy and the Roman Republic. They enveloped themselves in eighteenth-century Enlightenment debates about reason, religious freedom, sovereignty, citizenship, civil and political rights, the social contract, representative government, 'the people' and the 'nation'. Energised by these cultural currents, reform and revolutionary movements made energetic, sometimes heroic, efforts to persuade or to force existing governments to open themselves up to wider, even democratic, participation. France, after all, was ruled by a king who – in theory, at least – wielded absolute power, although there were in practice some important practical and legal limitations to what he could do. Britain, though a parliamentary monarchy, was far from democratic, since the suffrage was limited primarily to male property owners (although, as we shall see, it was a little broader in metropolitan London). Britain's American colonists exulted in their representative institutions, and because property ownership was more widespread there, the male voting population was proportionately larger than it was in the mother country.

In challenging the limits of the political order, revolutionaries and reformers laid great store in what historians now call forms of 'sociability': clubs and societies, festivals, ceremonies and mass meetings that used the spoken and printed word and political symbols, such as the tricolour flag, the liberty pole, the cap of liberty, to transmit their messages to as wide an audience as possible. There were, of course, major differences to ensure that these great movements diverged at important points, not least of which were the intensity and scale of the violence that ensued, the strength and stubbornness of the opposition and levels of support. There were some key cultural and ideological variations, too, conditioned by historical memory that reminded people of past triumphs and tragedies (the civil wars in the British Isles of the seventeenth century, for example) and by cherished myths of a heritage of rights and liberties. Britons and pre-revolutionary Americans spoke of the 'rights and liberties of freeborn Englishmen', while French citizens before 1789 looked back to an age when they had once been free under 'fundamental laws'. These influences were among those that combined to ensure that, in the end, the three peoples emerged from the revolutionary crucible with very divergent results.[6]

The eighteenth-century Atlantic was a highly mobile region, in which people, goods and ideas moved in multiple directions, interacting and producing the vibrant, fertile world of commercial expansion, cultural exchange and political contention, along with such repressive institutions as slavery. It was a world in which the social elites, and the expanding segments of a burgeoning 'public' (a word that was assuming increasingly political overtones in the eighteenth century), could aspire to a cosmopolitan view of the world, learning about it, engaging with it and critiquing it through letter writing and the wide availability of print, including newspapers, journals, books, prints and maps. Travel was undertaken in storm-tossed wooden ships and bone-shaking coaches, but people did it in great numbers, in the pursuit of migration, business, politics and, increasingly for the well-heeled, tourism. The myriad transatlantic connections and how they operated are fascinating subjects, but they are not the subject of this book. Riskily, perhaps, the story here generally takes these connections for granted and concentrates instead on the lives of the cities themselves. So the Atlantic world spans the deep background, but does not figure in the story, which here is the fabric of Paris, London and New York and how their peoples saw their cityscape being used and changed in the process.[7]

The cityscape as a backdrop, as a place where revolution and radicalism inscribed and transmitted their messages, the buildings as sites of political conflict and the reach of political mobilisation into communities across the metropolis, all of this makes the city itself part of the narrative. This book weaves the story of the cities' peoples – intrepid individuals, angry or hopeful communities – into the history of the urban fabric in these momentous, tumultuous years. It aims to show how the city itself figured in the drama. It seeks to evoke a sense of *place* in narrating the experience of this revolutionary age, but it is not a bloodless story about bricks, mortar, stone, fabric and paint. It is also populated by men and women, bewigged aristocrats and lawyers, articulate yet rough-handed artisans and craft workers, quill-wielding blue-stockings and doughty fishwives.[8]

Recently, some historians, very wisely, have begun to think of revolution not just in conceptual terms (although dogged attempts to nail down a universally accepted definition of 'revolution' continue to be pursued by the stouthearted) or in seeking to explain their causes, processes and results by references to great human forces like class, ideology and culture. Rather, they are exploring how groups and individuals lived through the revolutionary upheaval with all its anxieties, its stirring visions of the possible, its wrenching fear, its abject despair and seething hatred. The key point is that revolution is a human *experience* in all its exhilaration, terror and squalor. Part of that experience was seeing – or perpetrating – acts that touched the urban environment in which they lived as different parts of it were adapted, embellished, defaced or even destroyed by revolution and scarred and damaged by conflict. So while this book puts the cities centre stage, that stage is shared with men and women who underwent the lived experience of those triumphant, turbulent and fearful days.[9]

AS THE FOCUS of the narrative to come, Paris, London and New York shared some important characteristics, but there were significant differences, too. They were places where political authority, commerce and money, art and intellectual life intersected and from where, for better or worse, these melded forces then transmitted their energy across the surrounding country. Sprawling London and Paris were so large and were such centres of human activity that they were each referred to as a 'metropolis' by contemporaries. A rivalry had in fact emerged between London and Paris: in the early 1780s, French writer Louis-Sébastien Mercier (later a revolutionary and member of the French Institute) remarked that 'to consider London, neighbour and rival, is unavoidable when one speaks of Paris, and the parallel suggests itself. They are so close and so different, even though they are similar in many ways, so that to complete the portrait of one, it is not out of place, I think, to rest one's gaze a little on several features of the other'. Both were capitals of great European powers, and both were the imperial centres of two sprawling and competing overseas empires. They were among the world's largest cities: only Beijing, at a teeming 1.1 million in 1800, topped London, which nearly hit the million mark, while Paris contained 600,000 people.[10]

This translated into a breathtaking, and, for many, intimidating, urban sprawl. London had a nucleus consisting, first, of the City of London (the 'Square Mile' being the area within the old city walls) and its 'dependencies' in the outlying wards; second, of Westminster, where the centres of political power were located and home to the 'West End', the swanky, airy new residences of the wealthy escaping from the congested, noisy bustle farther to the east; and, third, of Southwark, with its pungent tanneries, breweries, warehouses and workshops on the opposite bank of the River Thames. Yet London was far greater than that, enveloping no fewer than 140 parishes, from east to west, and on both sides of the river. In 1724 Daniel Defoe had already asked with alarm, 'Whither will this monstrous city then extend?' By 1787 one observer likened the amorphous expansion to a fever, a 'building influenza', with London as the 'centre of the disease'.[11]

Paris, though more compact, inspired no less astonishment in first-time visitors. Karamzin was awestruck when he first visited in March 1790: 'Our avid stares turned towards that immense mass of buildings and were lost within it, as if in the vastness of the ocean'. At the centre was the Île de la Cité, the island in the River Seine that for centuries had been the political, legal and religious heart of the kingdom, with its royal fortress turned prison in the Conciergerie, its supreme courts of law and the cathedral of Notre-Dame. Around that were the central districts, called the *ville*, or the town proper, by locals, delineated by the traces of the medieval walls that had encircled old Paris and, demolished by King Louis XIV (the Sun King) in the seventeenth century, had given way to an internal ring of elegant, breezy boulevards. Beyond that were the 'suburbs', or faubourgs, which spread outwards, their tenements and workshops less densely packed than in the city centre, offering glimpses of the grounds of convents and hospitals, of market gardens, their beans twisting around poles, their cabbages lined up in rows and even leafy vineyards undulating over gentle slopes. The boundary of the city, beyond the faubourgs, was marked by a palisade built in 1786 to help the collection of the *octroi*, the hated tax on goods entering Paris.[12]

Although the king himself was absent from the city, Paris boasted the pinnacle of the French legal system (as we shall see); the most senior official in the Catholic Church in France, the archbishop in Notre-Dame Cathedral; and the town houses of many of the richest and most powerful nobles in the kingdom. It was also a diverse centre of manufacturing, mostly carried out by its thousands of artisans and craft workers in small workshops.

London, of course, was unambiguously the capital of the British Empire, with its seats of political power in Westminster, which Abigail Adams, arriving for the first time in July 1784, called 'the Court end of the town' because it included the royal residence at Saint James's Palace and the houses of Parliament at the Palace of Westminster. The economic might of the metropolis, however, was seated farther east, in the City of London, which with its banking, finance, heaving quaysides and artisans organised into guilds (or 'livery companies') was already becoming one of the world's great financial dynamos.[13]

Eighteenth-century New York, by contrast, was diminutive

in scale (in 1790 the first-ever US census showed that its population just edged over 33,000) and, before independence in 1783, a colonial city looking to London as the capital. Its extent, marked by the reach of the four- to six-storey brick-built houses and tenements (their roofs covered in cedar tiles, glistening with varnish and painted in all colours), occupied the southern tip of Manhattan and stretched no farther than a mile along the Hudson River, while on the banks of the East River it stretched upstream for two miles at the very most. Yet New York was a metropolis in the New World context. For one, its strategic importance made it the military headquarters of British forces in North America: it was located at roughly the midway point of the Atlantic Seaboard of British North America. Poised at the mouth of the Hudson, control of New York gave access to the river, which was a natural barrier that divided New England from the middle and southern colonies, and gave inland access to Canada. New York, too, had its own political institutions – the royal governor, a garrison and the colonial legislature that made it the capital of the 'province' of New York. And for a few years after independence was won, it would be the capital of the nascent United States. Moreover, by the time of the American Revolution, the city was shaking off the aura of a colonial outpost and finding its intellectual and cultural voice, with a fine library, theatre and its own university (King's College, later Columbia University).[14]

In the later eighteenth century, too, New York's thriving commerce, its harbour a forest of ships' masts, never failed to impress visitors, who likened it to London or Liverpool, which in the eighteenth century was already a great port facing the Atlantic world. The hubbub of the wharves on Lower Manhattan struck visitors. A British traveller, John Lambert, stared amazed at the 'bales of cotton, wool, and merchandize; barrels of potash, rice, flour, and salt provisions; hogsheads of sugar, chests of tea, puncheons of rum, and pipes of wine; boxes, cases, packs and packages of all sizes and denominations, were strewed upon the wharfs and landing-places, or upon the decks of the shipping'.[15]

All this maritime activity, focused on the East River rather than the Hudson (New Yorkers then called the latter the North River), would turn New York into the country's financial and business centre after independence. It also meant, however, that New York was the main port of entry for a polyglot mix of immigrants, either passing through or there to stay. The waterfront and the jumble of streets behind it bubbled to the sound of different accents and languages, as cartmen, peddlers and birds of passage shouted, warned, cursed and called out in English, Dutch, French and German. To the linguistic babel was added a striking ethnic diversity, including Irish, Jews and African Americans: all of this made New York, already perhaps, one of the most cosmopolitan cities on earth.[16]

Visitors to all three cities were also struck by their tallest structures – their churches. Even diminutive New York had 22 spires puncturing the sky, representing an impressive array of denominations. Catholic Paris had even more, its skyline bristling with the spires, towers and domes of some 200 churches belonging to its parishes, monasteries and convents. The London skyline, too, was pierced by the steeples of its 140 parish churches, but dominating was the soaring charcoal-grey dome of Saint Paul's Cathedral in the City, while the towers of Westminster Abbey and Southwark Cathedral also contended for attention. Some of these churches had symbolic importance for Londoners, who took great pride and comfort from their parish bells, placing bets as to how far their chimes could be heard. The existence of so many ecclesiastic buildings would prove important to the urban experience in both the American and the French Revolutions, as we shall see. For now, the prevalence of churches on the urban landscape meant that the pealing of their bells was one of the prevalent noises, marking the passage of time, calling the faithful to worship and ringing out in times of alarm.[17]

Yet this regular tolling was, in these teeming cities, drowned out by the noise of the crush of life in the streets, an underlying cacophony of rumbling carriage wheels, the clopping of horses' hooves across paving stones, the shouts of drivers and the cries of street vendors selling their wares. Louis-Sébastien Mercier wrote of Paris in the 1780s that 'the water-carrier, the sellers of old hats, of ironware, of rabbit skins, the woman selling fish, all sing about their merchandise in a high and penetrating fashion. All these discordant cries form a chorus which one cannot imagine unless one has actually heard it'. London was so busy that approaching travellers heard all the noises together as a constant distant roar. A German visitor, Georg Christoph Lichtenberg, described a London street in the evening: 'chaise after chaise, coach after coach, cart after cart. Through all this din and clamour, and the noise of thousands of tongues and feet, you hear the bells from the church-steeples, postmen's bells, the street-organs, fiddles and tambourines of itinerant musicians, and the cries of the vendors of hot and cold food at the street corners'. Even in New York, residents complained of the clutter of carts, carriages and goods in some neighbourhoods and of the raucous noise of stall holders competing with 'much noise and strife . . . boisterous conversations and . . . unpleasant disputes'.[18]

Along with the crush of people and the accompanying aural experience, residents and visitors alike remarked on the smells that enveloped the cities. 'You inquire of me how I like Paris', Abigail Adams wrote to her niece shortly after arriving in August 1784. 'Why, they tell me I am no judge, for that I have not seen it yet. One thing, I know, and that is that I have smelt it . . . It is the very dirtiest place I ever saw'. London, particularly the manufacturing dockside East End, hung with the smoke from tens of thousands of hearths and the sickly sweet smell of the breweries that blended with the fumes from the city's tanneries, dyers, blacksmiths and potters' kilns. French traveller and historian Pierre-Jean Grosley complained in the mid-1760s that 'this smoke forms a cloud which envelops London like a mantle; a cloud which ... suffers the sun to break out only now and then, which casual appearance procures the Londoners a few of what they call *glorious days*'. In the early 1780s, French writer, and future revolutionary, Jacques-Pierre Brissot de Warville commented on 'that thick fog, so burning, so filthy, in which part of each day is enveloped' in London. New York was probably less pungent: smaller, cleared by the breeze from the ocean, it nonetheless had certain districts, particularly on its northern outskirts, that had their share of industrial and effluvial stench, not least the slums around the so-called Freshwater or Collect Pond that lay just beyond the urbanised part of Manhattan. Yet for all the pungency, the olfactory experience of walking down the street of an early modern city might also be one of assault by kinder smells – of the flowers, herbs, fruits and vegetables piled on their vendors' stalls; of warm bread from the ovens of local bakeries; of hot coffee being delivered in great urns from the cafés (in Paris); and (in New York) of the sea.[19]

The crush of people, the transaction of business in the street, the noise and the smells stemmed from the fact that all three cities were 'walking cities' – places where, in the absence of the mass mechanised public transport that came later, people mostly went about on foot between home, work, shopping and leisure. Hackney cabs – horse-drawn carriages for hire – existed in Paris and London, but they were expensive, and only the very rich few could afford their own coaches or to stable and maintain a horse. High rents also meant that people made more use of the space that they had, cramming larger families into apartments, making use of the street outside. So much life – selling, buying, meeting,

discussing, playing, even lovemaking (or, more crudely, rutting) –
was transacted in the streets of these crowded cities that there
were very close bonds of community in some neighbourhoods,
particularly in Paris, where people from a cross-section of social
backgrounds sometimes lived not just near each other, but sometimes – almost literally – one on top of the other.[20]

In Paris the rich, the middling and the poor still lived close
together in many central districts, literally stratified according to
the floor upon which they lived. Usually, the ground level and
courtyard of a Parisian house would be occupied by workshops
or retailers. The first storey, or sometimes the second, since it was
farther removed from the noise of the street but not too far to
climb, was taken over by the well-appointed apartment of a noble
or wealthy bourgeois; the upper storeys held the lodgings of the
artisan and his family; and the higher up one went, the poorer the
accommodations and the occupants – journeymen, apprentices,
labourers, servants – until one reached the leaky, dank garrets of the
poorest migrant workers and paupers. By the time of the American
Revolution, distinct neighbourhoods differing in wealth and poverty were emerging in New York, but in this compact city the streets
inhabited by the rich were never far from those of the working
population. What this meant was that, in both cities, the better
off had daily, or near-daily, contact with their poorer neighbours.
This familiarity could make the difference between survival and
despair: in Paris there are many documented cases of the elderly, the
infirm and the unemployed being given small gifts of food, money,
linen and clothing by their neighbours, helping them keep body
and soul together. People of different social backgrounds, but from
the same street or quarter, passed by each other regularly, chatted,
did business and socialised, all of which may have forged a sense of
solidarity that carried weight in the political upheavals to come.[21]

It was perhaps no coincidence that in the one city of our three that did not experience a revolution in this period, London, the segregation of neighbourhoods along varying degrees of wealth and poverty, was the most advanced. In truth, both Paris and London saw the development of wealthy districts swelling with aristocratic mansions and elegant town houses in the West of the metropolis. In both Paris and London, the rich and the fashionable fled the noise, clutter and filth of the old districts and moved westwards, into the prevailing wind, increasingly leaving the East and the centre to the middling sort, the artisans and labourers. In Paris metropolitan nobles were abandoning the great town houses of the increasingly passé Marais in the East to take up residence in the West, in the great mansions of the Faubourg Saint-Germain on the Left Bank of the Seine or, in the later eighteenth century, the even more fashionably aristocratic Right Bank district of the Faubourg Saint-Honoré. Yet the process was far more pronounced in London, where noble landowners made fat profits from developing their estates into spacious, elegant housing often arranged around the airy, green space of a square. In 1752 novelist and magistrate Henry Fielding playfully described this movement of the rich – the 'People of Fashion' – as a flight from a relentlessly advancing working-class 'enemy' or foe. In the 1780s Prussian visitor Johann Wilhelm von Archenholz observed that London's East End, 'especially along the shores of the Thames, consists of old houses, the streets there are narrow, dark and ill-paved; inhabited by sailors and other workmen who are employed in the construction of ships and by a great part of the Jews. The contrast between this and the West end is astonishing: the houses here are mostly new and elegant; the squares are superb, the streets straight and open'.[22]

This development, accelerating London's overwhelming sprawl, made the British capital, perhaps more than anywhere else in the Atlantic world, a place where one could find anonymity – certainly more so than in Paris and New York. In 1780 the public-spirited *London Magazine* published a short list of 'Rules of Behaviour, of General Use, though much disregarded in this Populous City', the title itself speaking volumes. Among its admonishments was 'to be cautious of staring in the faces of those that pass by us, like an inquisitor general; for an over-bearing look has the air of a bully, and a prying one that of a bailiff. If we do it by mistake for a friend, ask pardon'. The same was true of people entering the city's public places, like taverns and coffeehouses, as such staring risks 'shocking his modesty, and dismounting his assurance'. And (here the point was spelt out) it was best 'not to be officiously forward in our discourse or ceremonies to strangers, who, perhaps, desire to be unobserved, or *incog*[*nito*]'. This 'atomisation' of individuals in the anonymity of the British metropolis may have had political significance in the age of revolutions. During the great upheavals of the French Revolution after 1789, Parisian radicalism would be to a great extent rooted in the neighbourhoods and communities of the city first, before finding the overarching metropolitan organisation to direct the whole popular movement. London radicalism in the same years, by contrast, would succeed in forging a metropolitan organisation very quickly, but may have struggled to put down deep, permanent roots in the multitude of the city's neighbourhoods.[23]

Yet all three cities had a vibrant social and cultural life that drew visitors seeking to taste the intellectual and sensory delights that an eighteenth-century metropolis could offer. Taverns, cafés, coffeehouses, theatres, clubs and societies, educational associations, music societies, subscription libraries and reading rooms were all venues where people could gather for company and argument and to consume culture, high and low, in voracious quantities. This was made possible by the very expansion of a consumer society among the industriousness and commerce of the metropolis. Despite the grinding poverty so much in evidence, families with relatively modest incomes worked harder and smarter to raise the extra income for the small luxuries that a consumer society offered – tea, coffee, printed fabrics, finer clothes, decor for homes and also printed literature. This last was becoming more widely available, energised in part by new printing processes, laxer censorship (in Britain and America, certainly, but even in absolutist France) and more efficient forms of distribution, helped by better roads and faster coach services. This was accompanied by the expansion in the layer of literate, educated people outside the aristocratic and bourgeois elites who were finding new ways of spending their leisure time, aided and abetted by the expansion of literacy.[24]

All this was like a shot of adrenaline into the print culture of the age: newspapers, journals, pamphlets, books and engravings (particularly caricatures). A critical, independent public was emerging, which was one of the most striking cultural and political developments of the century. Eighteenth-century Parisians, Londoners and New Yorkers (and, of course, citizens elsewhere) had come to see themselves as independent, active participants in shaping taste and cultural expression. They found their own diverse, vibrant and even clamorous forms of engaging in public debate, which outstripped and even drowned out the voices in the salons and the more formal cultural institutions. Where this activity was focused on art and literature, this was relatively unproblematic and indeed, during the second half of the eighteenth century, commonplace. Far more controversial at the time was the politicisation of this 'public opinion', meaning its elevation as the ultimate source of comment, direction and legitimacy in politics, passing judgement over kings and ministers. This process was already happening in Britain (and its American colonies) by 1700, while in France, groaning somewhat under the weight of its absolute monarchy, public opinion had staggered towards this political application

by midcentury. This concept of 'public opinion' was potentially
dangerous to more authoritarian governments, a potential identified by one of the most progressive Enlightenment thinkers of
the age, Guillaume-Thomas-François Raynal, who wrote in 1770
that 'in a nation that thinks and talks, public opinion is the rule
of government, and government must never act against it without
giving public reasons nor thwart it without disabusing it'. Paris,
London, New York, all had their coffeehouses, their taverns, their
theatres, their assembly rooms, reading clubs, music societies,
museums, educational associations, academies and their parks,
squares and avenues in which citizens could meet, converse, debate
and demonstrate. This made the control of such public spaces a
critical point of conflict in the upheavals to come.[25]

THE INITIAL TREMOR was the Seven Years' War, which ended in
1763 (it is known as the French and Indian War in America, where
fighting had first erupted along the frontier in 1754). Long, bloody
and draining, the conflict had been truly global, raging in Europe,
on the oceans and along the imperial frontiers of the Americas and
Asia. The pressure on the governments and peoples who waged it
was intense, through the recruitment of soldiers and sailors, the
raising of taxation and the requisitioning of supplies. Above all, its
costs imposed enormous financial burdens, particularly on those
who paid the taxes. With peace, everyone hoped for an injection
of fresh life into commerce, manufacturing and trade. Yet there
were daunting challenges: all the belligerents had poured blood
and treasure into the conflict, the most brutal in terms of violence,
scale and expense in more than a half century. All states, even the
victorious British, emerged from the crucible staggering beneath
hefty burdens of debt, as governments struggled to retain credit
in the great financial markets of London, Amsterdam and Geneva

or even to avoid bankruptcy. The French monarchy's borrowing increased by two-thirds during the war, and, by the end of the 1760s, some two-thirds of its annual revenue was being swallowed up just on paying the interest on the debt. Britain's national debt doubled. In both countries, the governments began looking for ways to claw back this eye-watering expenditure and, to do so, to strengthen their authority. The length and the bruising nature of the conflict had stretched the existing administrative and financial systems to breaking point; the weaknesses and limits of all such systems had been alarmingly exposed.[26]

These attempts at overhaul provoked domestic political conflict in all the countries concerned, but particularly tumultuously in Britain, the American colonies and France. In all three countries, the responses of governments and peoples proved to be momentous, unleashing a roar of debate and bursts of political violence that gave rise to claims to freedom, to rights and to more open forms of government, all clashing with more established ideas of what the relationship between the rulers and the ruled should be. In Britain the heat was turned up beneath the habitual sparring between the king's ministers and the opposition, until it burned in a fiery series of controversies that injected politics with a radical new vigour. In Britain's American colonies, protests and imperial countermeasures created a friction that became white-hot and a decade later ignited in the American War of Independence. In France the monarchy and the aristocratic elites collided in a series of political battles that, with the benefit of hindsight, presaged the slide of the old regime towards the French Revolution. In terms of its impact on internal politics, the Seven Years' War may have been one of the most decisive moments in the history of eighteenth-century Europe and America.

These collisions proved to be all the more seismic because they were energised by the entry of the people into politics, and no more so than in the great cities. The return of peace in 1763 did not bring prosperity for everyone. The winter of 1762–1763 had been a bitter one (in Europe there was a freeze in December and January), biting into food supplies and pushing prices up, while slowing down trade in the handicrafts and so depressing the incomes of workers and artisans. With the war coming to an end, demobilised soldiers and sailors added to the armies of labourers seeking honest work, pushing down wages even further. In France, a country where a fifth of the population was dependent upon charity to survive, begging, vagrancy and indigence were permanent features on the landscape, but it is no coincidence that 1764 saw the king – the same benign Louis XV commemorated in stone by Bouchardon – issue a new law against 'vagabonds', distinguishing them from 'real' beggars who were well known in their communities. Those who were rootless, who had no one to vouch for them and who could offer the authorities no convincing explanation as to how they scraped together a living were punished by three years' hard labour in the galleys (for men) or confinement to the poorhouse (for women and children). Three years later, the government established special depots for beggars and vagrants, where, under a regime that was intended to be, in the words of one official, 'better than prison, worse than the army', the poor were set to work in return for a small wage, food and shelter. There were five such depots outside Paris alone – deliberately removed from the populace. The dread of such places, particularly among the approximate third of the capital's labourers who lived on the very margins of indigence, was such that it is scarcely surprising to learn of army veterans stepping forward to prevent the arrests of beggars, claiming that they had once served together.[27]

One might have expected such dire conditions in a city digesting military humiliation, but London seems to have been as badly affected by the post-war dislocation. Paul Sandby's engravings of London life captured the grimly ironic juxtaposition of, on the one hand, the city's triumphant position as an imperial capital and, on the other, the evidence of distress among those who did not prosper with the peace: one depicted a demobbed sailor, still in his uniform, eking out an existence by peddling stockings at Charing Cross, the very heart of the metropolis. As early as 1761, magistrate John Fielding (who with his half brother, novelist Henry, had founded the Bow Street Runners, London's first modern police force) gloomily predicted that a crime wave would cascade across the city when the war came to an end. He directed his officers towards preventing crime and disorder by keeping an eye on taverns, street lighting, brothels and so on, rather than devoting all their energies to just hunting down malefactors after the crime had already been committed.[28]

Fielding's forecast proved to be only too accurate because the economic distress was real enough, with a wave of industrial conflict that boiled on through the 1760s, as the discharge of large numbers of sailors along the Thames in the spring of 1763 sent thousands of seamen thronging to the East End in search of work. The depression in wages led sailors to form committees that led a strike wave in the dockyards and along the quaysides. Mariners prevented ships from casting off by climbing the rigging and reefing up the sails while demanding honest pay. The watermen (the boatmen who plied the Thames with their small craft), coal heavers (who unloaded the fuel from the ships tied up at the docksides), shoemakers, hatters, hosiers, weavers, sawyers, glass grinders, coopers, tailors and silk weavers all petitioned Parliament, protested by marching through the city, broke machinery or pressed their claims on their employers. The threat of violence was never far beneath the surface. 'Sir' (began one message from striking cobblers to their employer in February 1763), 'Dam Your Blood if You do not Ryes Your Works Too 2 Pence a Pair moor We Well Blow Your Braines out ... You slim Dog We shall sett You Houes on fier'.[29]

The confrontations crackled on almost for the rest of the decade: in one violent clash between bludgeon-swinging coal heavers and an employer in 1768, the latter shot two of his attackers dead before fleeing over the rooftops. That year also saw the climax of the silk weavers' attacks on mechanical looms that threatened their livelihoods, and their pain was all the deeper because French silks had been pouring onto the British market since the war's end. Their assaults on workshops became so aggressive that troops were garrisoned in Spitalfields in the East End: in September 1768, one of these soldiers was killed by weavers, and in turn the redcoats shot dead two weavers. The authorities struck back hard: two ringleaders of the weavers' strike were hanged in Bethnal Green, while seven of the coal heavers were executed in Stepney in front of a crowd said to number fifty thousand, under a guard of three hundred soldiers.[30]

New York City was especially hurt by the economic woes that came with the peace because of its position as a colonial port of the British Empire. It had prospered in the war: as the headquarters of British forces in North America, it had seen a lot of business, thanks to the passage of thousands of what one grateful merchant called 'the Tipling Soldiery' who patronised the city's taverns and shops. The maritime community of New York's docks enjoyed a boom time as the Royal Navy anchored in the harbour and as American privateers – vessels licensed to attack enemy shipping – sallied forth and returned with the fruits of their escapades on the high seas. At the war's end, the British soldiers and sailors departed, and so shopkeepers and tavern keepers saw a sudden drop in sales. British traders, taking advantage of the security offered by the peace, dumped manufactured goods onto the colonies at slashed prices. New York artisans making shoes, clothes, furniture and iron goods simply could not compete with the flood of cheaper products. At the same time, the demands of the mother

country for American grain to feed its burgeoning population
brought exports of American wheat soaring but in the process
drove up domestic food prices. To make matters worse, British
merchants, seeking to recoup losses caused by the wartime disruption, demanded the repayment of advances made to their New
York counterparts, while terms of future loans and credit became
tougher. 'Every thing is tumbling down, even the Traders themselves', cried out one New York merchant in early 1764. 'Trade in
this part of the world is come to so wretched a pass', noted another
with understandable sourness, 'that you would imagine the plague
had been here, the grass growing in most trading streets'. In turn,
the American merchants called in the debts of the craftsmen and
shopkeepers whom they had kept afloat during the war. So the
working people of New York were squeezed in a particularly heavy
pincer, between a credit crunch, on the one hand, and a surge of
British competition, on the other.[31]

The result was utter despair. Merchants went bankrupt; workshops and retailers closed down; unemployment spiralled upwards;
the Almshouse on the northern side of the Common filled up with
the indigent and the desperate. The labouring population was hit
the hardest, including artisans, whose small savings were quickly
eaten away as they tried to stay afloat. Amongst the inmates of the
New Gaol (not far from the Almshouse), eighty were inside for
debt in 1766. While the authorities and voluntary organisations
did what they could to help, in the next year a tradesman wrote
of the 'dismal Prospect before us! A long Winter, and no Work;
many unprovided with Fire-wood, or Money to buy it; House-rent
and taxes high; our Neighbours daily breaking; their Furniture at
Vendue [that is, for sale] at every Corner'.[32]

As people of all social backgrounds were experiencing social distress, their governments were confronting the impact of the Seven
Years' War. It was now that they embarked on policies to ease the

recovery from the fiscal haemorrhaging of the long conflict and, to do so, to consolidate their control over their subjects. In France Louis XV and his ministers set to work salvaging national strength and honour through an ambitious programme of reform. This aimed to reinvigorate the French state by modernising the armed forces, investing in infrastructure and securing the finances. For a while, these efforts were energised by a patriotic backlash against the national humiliation, a patriotism that the government itself had whipped up during the war and connected the prestige of the monarchy with that of the country at large. That patriotism, writers and pamphleteers suggested, was a virtue that could restore the kingdom to greatness. The king and his ministers worked with the French aristocratic elites, but this sense of common purpose did not last. Ultimately, their interests collided, resulting in a political conflict that seemed to expose the monarchy at its despotic worst – and one of the epicentres of this collision was, of course, Paris.[33]

In Britain the Seven Years' War provided the background to the passing of King George II in 1760 and the accession of his grandson George III. Although not the nefarious tyrant that American patriots would soon claim him to be, the young king seems to have been determined to have a more direct, though benign, relationship with his subjects. That meant asserting his authority over the landed oligarchy that dominated Parliament and appointing ministers who, George believed, would govern in the best interests of his people. Yet he appointed his favourite – his tutor Lord Bute – as his prime minister and announced his determination to make peace. While this last was undoubtedly popular in some parts of the war-weary country, it was not universally so. The new pacific policy claimed the political scalp of William Pitt (the Elder), who resigned from the British government in 1761. Popular for his patriotic determination to prosecute the war, Pitt was especially well liked in the City of London, whose merchants and financiers saw in the conflict the opportunity for the British to drive the French and the Spanish from their colonies and from the seas, thereby opening up lucrative opportunities for British business. The City – wealthy, proud and politically active – would be particularly fractious in its opposition to royal authority in the coming years.

The political conflict was aggravated by the post-war financial shock. While in Britain the government's response to the debt incurred by the global war was to levy a desperately unpopular tax on cider, in the overseas empire it went further, seeking to consolidate its political and financial control over an expanse of territory that, thanks to the war, had grown much larger, both in North America and in Asia. Successively, the British government banned colonial settlement west of the Appalachian Mountains (in order to avoid provoking further conflict with Native Americans), enforced duties on sugar imports into the colonies and passed the Stamp Act of 22 March 1765 through Parliament. This measure was the most controversial because it was the first time the British government had imposed a tax directly on the American colonies. So it was that, of the three cities, New York would be the most inflamed of all.

CHAPTER ONE

THE REVOLUTION COMES TO NEW YORK, 1765–1775

ON 18 OCTOBER 1765, Cadwallader Colden, the royal governor of the Province of New York, wrote a firm warning to the captain of the naval vessel *Edward*, which had made the Atlantic crossing bearing one of the more controversial cargoes to make the journey: the stamped paper that would be used when the stamp duty imposed by the British Parliament on the colonies came into force. From the governor's mansion within Fort George, the bastion of British power on the southern tip of Manhattan, Colden – seventy-seven years old, irascible, vigorous and intellectual – addressed the 'Master or Commander' of the ship in no uncertain terms:

> From the repeated public Declarations that have been made in
> this place & throughout the Provinces that the Stamp'd Papers
> which are expected from England ... would be destroyed on
> their arival [*sic*] here: which Declarations have been back'd in
> some Places with most violent & riotous proceedings, it has

become necessary for me to take every precaution in my power to preserve them, and to prevent if possible even an attempt to execute a Scheme so unlawfull & ruinous . . . And having given you this notice of the great danger your Cargoe will be in unless the Ship is protected until the Stamped Papers are Secured, I must desire you to put your ship under the protection of his Majesty's Ships of War, and to remain under their Protection till you shall have further directions from me.[1]

Colden, clearly, was expecting violent resistance from the New Yorkers. He asked New York's naval commander, Archibald Kennedy, to assist in the protection and landing of the bales of paper and, over the coming days, had Major Thomas James, the garrison's artillery commander, and military engineer Captain John Montresor bolster the defences of Fort George as best they could.

Yet the colonial protests had begun as New York's law-and-order-loving colonial elites had at first hoped. While almost all colonists hated the Stamp Act, their traditional leaders – the great landowners, the senior lawyers and the prosperous merchants – had channelled the protests into legal forms of opposition. This was supposed to be led by the very people who, they thought, should determine the course of the relationship between Britain and the empire – namely, themselves. Yet in the autumn of 1765, the resistance, as Colden and plenty of others had come anxiously to anticipate, would finish with a full-blown popular uprising that the old elites could scarcely control and posed a revolutionary threat to politics as usual in New York. Once dominated by a handful of powerful, well-connected families, city politics would instead be driven – for a time – by the man and woman in (quite literally) the street. It would become a 'dual revolution', the one a broad coalition of colonists against British rule, the other a revolt of the people against the elites. It was a dual revolution that blended imperial, local and popular politics in an explosive mix. In New York, it was expressed in the very topography of the city's resistance, first to the Stamp Act and then to British imperial rule.[2]

This radical development arose up and down the American colonies. In New York, it was mirrored – and was in some ways shaped – by the political and social geography of the city. On the one hand, when the initiative spilled from the hands of the colonial elites to the New York crowd, this was reflected in the very sites of resistance, a spatial shift that moved from the debating chambers of New York's City Hall and more upmarket coffeehouses to the more open and accessible public spaces of the city, such as the Common, the taverns and the streets themselves. This reflected the direction of the protests in the sense of how they developed politically – who joined them and why. At the same time, New York's particular social geography also helped to determine the course of the resistance in a literal geographical way, by which parts of the city were directly touched. From these dynamics came a more militant, popular form of politics that challenged the domination that the colonies' elites had enjoyed for a century. As would happen in revolutionary Paris a generation later, when the artisans and labourers mobilised and spoke of liberty, they had goals in mind that were different from, and conflicted with, those of the elite leadership who were otherwise using similar political language.

THE STAMP ACT was loathed throughout Britain's American colonies. It imposed a duty on all legal and printed documents, including title deeds, wills, licences to sell alcohol, contracts, apprenticeship papers, dice, playing cards and publications such as newspapers, pamphlets, almanacs, advertisements and calendars. These items would be stamped by an official to show that the appropriate duty had been paid. Those accused of dodging the new taxes would face not a sympathetic colonial jury, but a judge in the vice-admiralty courts.[3]

The stamp duty materially affected a wide cross-section of colonial society, namely, anyone who engaged in any kind of public or legal activity. One could forego gambling and, at a push, quaffing spirits in taverns. Not everyone had property to buy and sell. It was much harder, however, to avoid the stamp duty in the normal passage of life, including marriage or buying a newspaper. The impact on commercial transactions, moreover, threatened to filter down to anyone who made their living from the life of a commercial city such as New York. To make matters worse, the duty had to be paid in the hardest currency there was – sterling, which was in short supply in the colonies, especially among the pressured artisans, craft workers and farmers. Yet quite apart from the material and financial pain inflicted in a time of severe economic downturn, the Stamp Act also rankled with colonists' strong sense of the privileges and liberties that they thought they enjoyed as freeborn British subjects.[4]

New York's resistance opened amongst the colony's genteel representatives in the colonial assembly. In common with other American colonies, New York already enjoyed a considerable degree of self-government. In New York's case, there was an assembly of twenty-seven members (four from New York City). The franchise was broad, though not democratic: voters included all freeholders owning fifty acres of land or more and freemen – those who, by paying a few shillings in tax, secured political privileges. In New York City, this translated into an electorate that was far more inclusive than that in Britain: some two-thirds of all free adult males could vote, and they included a cross-section of the working population, among them the occasional cart man and stevedore from the streets and docks, who cast their votes alongside blacksmiths, masons, bricklayers and well-to-do goldsmiths. These electors chose not only the city's delegates to the colonial assembly, but also the Common Council – the fourteen aldermen and assistants, seven assessors and sixteen constables elected by New Yorkers to run their city. Yet this was neither rampant democracy nor parliamentary rule triumphant, for the power of the elected assemblies had their mighty counterweight in the shape of the governor, appointed by the king, and his own council, effectively an upper house populated by a further twelve royal appointees. The governor's councillors were made sweet by the security of a ten-year tenure of power, grants of land and control of patronage, government contracts and political connections with the mother country. They could reject legislation passed by the assembly, while the governor selected New York City's leading officials, including the mayor, recorder and clerk for the Common Council, as well as the colony's attorney general.[5]

Apart from the governor himself, this political system had been dominated by two competing factions from among the colonial elites, whose differences were not ideological but, in true eighteenth-century fashion, revolved around their sectional interests and their religion, with the main goal being to secure access to office and to the patronage dispensed by the governor. These rival tendencies gathered around two warring dynasties. On one side, the Delanceys were descended from the Huguenot (French Protestant) James Delancey, who had arrived in New York in 1686 and made his fortune in the city's vibrant commerce. To integrate better with the English elites, he joined the Church of England (or Anglican Church). His family became one of the colony's wealthiest within a generation, drawing into their political and social sphere through marriage, business connections and patronage the leading mercantile Anglican families, whose interests they represented the best.

Against the Delanceys stood the Livingstons, whose wealth flowed from their vast landed estates that stretched for miles in

Dutchess County up the Hudson River. They also attracted the cream of New York law, including the 'Whig Triumvirate' of William Smith Jr., John Morin Scott and Robert R. Livingston, a justice of New York's supreme court. The trio's label – 'Whigs' – was a British term that applied to anyone on either side of the Atlantic who supported the results of the 1688 ('Glorious') Revolution, which toppled King James II, asserted parliamentary sovereignty and legitimised a political system in which authority was shared between the monarch and Parliament. Whigs emphasised civil liberty and opposed any shift in the political balance in Britain's unwritten constitution towards the monarchy. In New York, the Livingstons were a natural rallying point for the colony's landed gentry against the city's mercantile interests. As staunch Presbyterians, they could gather support from non-Anglican Protestants ('dissenters') who resented the social and political preeminence of New York's Anglicans.[6]

The bitter rivalry between the Delancey and Livingston factions, which would become particularly inflamed during the revolutionary crisis, played out in New York's City Hall, which stood where Broad Street intersected with Wall Street (now the site of Federal Hall). City Hall accommodated both the colonial assembly and the municipality's Common Council. It also lodged the mayor's court (called the Court of Common Pleas) and the colony's supreme court, while in the cellars lurked the town's festering old gaol. Completed in 1700 to replace the Stadhuis, the municipal seat of New Amsterdam's Dutch masters, City Hall stood in its dominant position facing down Broad Street, surmounted by a cupola bearing the city's clock, which had been donated in 1716 by Stephen Delancey, as if to underscore his family's pivotal place within New York society. The building itself was meant to express the harmonious relations between the colony and the British Crown. Indeed, this political balance was represented by the fact that the governor's council met in the same chamber as the city's Common Council when the latter was not sitting. City Hall, in other words, was meant to be 'British' New York embodied in wood, bricks and mortar. To emphasise the authority (and no doubt the fearful majesty) of the law emanating from this building, in the street outside there were a whipping post, a pillory, stocks and a cage.[7]

That New York's colonial elites chose this building to launch their opposition to the Stamp Act may be significant for two reasons (apart from its being a natural meeting place). First, it sent a clear message of the essential legality of their protests: they were simply the colony's representatives presenting their grievances to the British Crown. Second, it showed a determination by the colony's established leadership to control and direct the opposition. So it was that New York's colonial assembly employed the quill pens of the 'triumvirate' – Livingston, Scott and Smith – to rehearse what were well-known Whig arguments against taxation without consent. Because the colonies did not send members of Parliament (MPs) to Westminster, they argued, the Americans could not consent to taxation enacted in Parliament. Instead, only the colonial assemblies had the right to levy taxes in the colonies: this was not a privilege, they added, but a right. In London, the government retorted that imperial authority rested with king and Parliament, in which the colonists were 'virtually' represented in the same way as the vast majority of disenfranchised Britons. A dismayed William Smith Jr. fretted that 'this single stroke has cost Great Britain the Affection of All her Colonies'.[8]

As 1 November 1765, the day that the stamp duty was to come into force, approached, colonial protests were followed up by a Stamp Act Congress, consisting of delegates from nine colonial legislatures. They too gathered in City Hall to discuss how safely the protests could be further pushed. The congress's resolutions reinforced the principle of trial by jury and declared that taxation

by consent was 'the undoubted Right of *Englishmen*'. This was to
no avail. The congress was just finishing its business on 23 October
when the hollow boom of a cannon resounded from the harbour:
the vessel *Edward*, escorted by two ships of the line, had arrived
carrying two tons of the hated stamped paper.[9]

This was the moment that the initiative began to shift decisively
away from the gentrified lobbies and polished flagstones of City
Hall to the streets of the city itself. With *Edward* ploughing across
the expansive waters of the harbour, it was clear that the finely
crafted prose of the Whig Triumvirate could do nothing against
the stamps: the time had come for direct action. Yet the anxious
lawyers, merchants and landowners of the Stamp Act Congress,
who might have looked out over the streets from City Hall and
contemplated the industrious people going about their business,
saw in the labouring population a reminder that their disorderly,
potentially violent forms of resistance, once unleashed, would not
be easily controlled. It had already happened in Boston, where
in August a crowd had forced the government's stamp distributor from office and wrecked the town house of the governor of
Massachusetts. Now, when *Edward* dropped anchor alongside the
protective guns of Fort George, a crowd of some two thousand
people assembled at the nearby Battery, hoping to prevent the
landing of the controversial cargo, but 'they were secretly landed
in the night and deposited in the Fort', wrote military engineer
Montresor.[10]

So the protests grew more violent, more threatening: 'A mob
in 3 squads went through the Streets crying "Liberty,"' recorded
Montresor in his diary, 'at the same time breaking the Lamps &
threatening particulars that they would the next night pull down
their Houses. Some thousands of windows Broke'. Confronted
with the dangers of social upheaval, New York's merchants
placed themselves in the vanguard of the American opposition

by cramming into the City Arms Tavern, also known as Burns' Coffee House. Here they agreed to import no British goods from 1 January until the Stamp Act was repealed. Montresor sardonically noted 'several people in mourning for the near Issue of the stamps and the Interment of their liberty. Descended even to the Bag-gammon Boxes at the merchant's Coffee House, being covered with Black and the Dice in Crape'. The merchants' actions at the City Arms demonstrated that New York's elites had taken the protests – in both constitutional and physical senses – away from the legal structures of colonial government and into the realm of wider public debate.

The Coffee House had an enormous assembly room that it let out for cultural and social occasions, so in a practical sense it served the purposes of organising the boycott well. Moreover, as a gathering place for the city's businesspeople, it was also the natural conduit by which all New York's merchants could be informed of what was now expected of them. Yet its location, a mere five addresses up Broadway from the fort, at the site now occupied by No. 115 Broadway, also speaks loudly of one of the intentions behind nonimportation. The City Arms was located in the richest quarter of New York – the so-called court end of town, close to the fort and to where the colony's political and social leadership had made their homes in a series of magnificent mansions marching up Broadway. The choice of the Coffee House, in other words, was not just practical; it also demonstrated that the merchants hoped to control the pace and direction of the protests and to avoid encouraging the looming threat of popular insurrection.[11]

Yet if Burns' Coffee House was the seat of elite protest, the streets were the battleground for plebeian resistance. The popular action that followed was not just a reaction to economic distress. From now on and over the next decade, men and women of all social backgrounds were bombarded by a barrage of print that cascaded from the presses in newspapers, pamphlets, broadsheets and engravings, by angry and stirring words bellowed out in taverns and in mass meetings on New York's Common. No New Yorker could avoid politics in these sometimes heady, sometimes terrifying days.

So it was no surprise that so many of New York's working people heeded the calls of an as yet mysterious group calling itself the 'Sons of Liberty'. These were a new breed of political leader, emerging from the ships, dockyards, workshops and countinghouses of the colonies. They were the self-made, articulate people who could connect the constitutional language of the elite opposition with the daily grind faced by the man and woman in the street. They acted as conduits between the boisterous protests of the workshop and waterfront and the high politics of City Hall – and their choice of venue was not the Coffee House, but the taverns where they could mingle with New York's working population, shaking hands and slapping backs, listening to grievances and channelling them towards political goals. Far more anarchic than the orderly, well-heeled environment of the Coffee House, taverns brought together men (they were strongly masculine places) of all social backgrounds and encouraged them to mobilise together against the Stamp Act. Taverns were the places that brought together the disparate faces of the city's multicultural life, and so they were fertile recruiting grounds for the leaders of the radical, popular resistance. These leaders were self-made men of humble origins: merchants and shipmasters like the plainspoken Connecticut Yankee Isaac Sears and the equally blunt Scot Alexander McDougall, instrument maker John Lamb and upholsterer Marinus Willett. On 24 October 1765, they posted across the city threatening handwritten notices entitled *Vox Populi*: 'The first Man that either distributes or makes use of Stampt Paper let him take Care of his House, Person, and Effects. We dare'.[12]

On 1 November, the Sons of Liberty called on people to assemble on the Common, close to the northern edge of the city. Business in New York's normally bustling slips and wharves came to a standstill, as hundreds of artisans, sailors and dockworkers roamed the streets, gathering on the field as night fell. Hundreds of candles flickering inside lanterns lit up the dark autumn night. A hubbub from the growing crowd grew louder, as artisans, labourers, retailers, sailors and dockworkers converged on the Common. As the protesters set off, a river of candles moved through the darkness, accompanied by the roar of hundreds of determined, excited voices.

To follow the protesters' route today is to take a circuitous journey through Lower Manhattan. If the ultimate objective of the march was Fort George on the island's southern tip, where the stamps were now under lock and key, the crowd did not take the most obvious way, namely, straight down Broadway. This makes little sense until followed more closely. The direction of the protest was in fact driven by custom and by the social geography of the city; it was shaped by the particular arrangement of streets and neighbourhoods in New York, which allowed the demonstrators to fuse political with social protest, which would provide the explosive combination in America's 'dual revolution'. One of those who joined the crowd (and was 'in high spirits full of Old Madeira', as he later wrote his breathless testimony) saw an effigy of the British governor, Cadwallader Colden, being carried on a chair, held aloft by a sailor. 'The Mob went from the Fields [the Common] down the Fly [Market] hozaing at Every Corner with Amassen sight of Candles'. The glow from illuminated windows as the demonstrators marched past expressed the residents' support – and warded off the dangers of window breaking when the panes remained dark.[13]

The marchers first swung eastwards, reaching Queen Street (now Pearl) before heading downtown. In the context of economic distress and political anger, this choice of route made both strategic and symbolic sense. Just beyond Queen Street, towards the East River, were the narrow lanes and alleys leading to the slips and wharves – a choice that was significant because the crowd swelled from the sailors and dockers who worked, slept and caroused here. At first sight (and scent), this neighbourhood was perhaps unpromising as a source of articulate political radicalism. Poverty, squalor and violence lurked along this notorious part of the waterfront. Rainwater washed the filth and garbage from the streets in the heart of the city down towards the wharves and slips clustered along the East River. This pungent effluvia oozed past the slums inhabited by the city's poorest people, who found cheap lodgings close to the docks, which were, contemporaries warned, 'Sinks of Corruption' and 'Nautious and Offensive'. Jammed among the wooden lean-tos and crowded tenements were drinking dives, taverns and cheap brothels catering to a boisterous crowd of sailors. Among these seamen could be seen enslaved African Americans who had slipped away for a few hours of illicit freedom or who, more boldly, were trying to melt away into the floating population of the waterfront. This lively mix of people was, it was alleged, out to spend the nights 'drinking, Tippling, Quarrelling, fighting, gaming, and misbehaving'.[14]

Yet the city's commercial lifeblood passed through here, making the docks a beehive of activity, as was evident to anyone who tried to navigate their way past the East River's many landings, from Whitehall Slip on the southern tip where the Staten Island ferry embarked all the way up to Peck Slip and then beyond Cherry Street to the shipyards to the north. Today, many of these landings, like Coenties Slip, are filled in, surprising, often pleasant, open spaces in the hustle and bustle of Lower Manhattan. In the 1760s, a wanderer in these places would have to weave through the crowds of sailors, stevedores, carpenters, sailmakers, rope makers, chandlers, merchants, retailers and voyagers who gave life to this area. The bowsprits of moored ships arched over the quaysides like the boughs of a tree-lined alley. Now in the post-war economic downturn, the Stamp Act and the mercantile resistance to it threatened the livelihoods of the thousands of New Yorkers who grafted a living on the waterfront.[15]

The reaction of the mariners and dockworkers to the crisis was rooted in a strong sense of solidarity and a long-standing habit of revelry and riot. Calling themselves the 'Sons of Neptune' long before anyone had heard of the 'Sons of Liberty', sailors expressed their collective identity on shore as they drank, rutted and scrapped their way through the haunts of the docklands, asserting their strong sense of egalitarian solidarity with their shipmates, a rejection – however briefly – of the authority of landlubber officials and a subversion of the hierarchies of eighteenth-century society. American sailors had cause to resist authority: merchant seamen on shore leave had much to fear from British press gangs, who fed the perennially undermanned vessels of the Royal Navy by forcing merchant mariners into the service. As recently as July 1764, New Yorkers had incinerated a naval longboat in riots against such impressment. It also helped that two of the Sons of Liberty, Sears and McDougall, were successful rough-hewn shipmasters and privateers who commanded the respect of the denizens of the docklands. They had the popular touch and an aura of gritty heroism, and they were comfortable mingling with the sailors in waterfront taverns. From the start, there would always be a strong contingent of sailors and dockworkers in the protests that bedevilled the authorities throughout the crisis leading to the War of Independence. This maritime community may also have provided a multiracial dimension to New York's revolutionary crowds, since among American sailors were free African Americans. Although not devoid of racism, the egalitarian subculture of the maritime world was an obvious place for men seeking an escape from racial prejudice.[16]

The choice of Queen Street as the southwards route was not only aimed at gathering the maritime workers. Although adjacent to the seamy docklands, the street itself was a world away, home to the shopping district and the brick-built houses of the wealthy merchants showing off their 'refinement'. By marching down Queen Street, the protesters may have been demonstrating their determination and strength to the city's elites, whose elegant homes, imitating the classical 'Georgian style' so much in evidence in Britain, had painted façades so that they shone as resplendently outside as they did within. Decked out as they were in the latest London fashions for decor and furnishings, they were testaments to the wealth of the colonial elites (and to their British imperial identity). This display of luxury was all the more resented by many working people for being so conspicuous at a time of economic despair and financial crunch – and, moreover, the colonial elites were suspected of being too open to the corruption of imperial patronage.[17]

So it was no accident that the protesters' route took them along Queen Street. Then the political purpose of the route became apparent when, on reaching the Fly Market, the protesters turned inland onto Wall Street. There they halted outside the home of James McEvers, the New York merchant who had scrambled for the appointment as stamp distributor in August, only to scramble just as quickly to resign it. He frankly admitted: 'My house would have been pillag'd, my Person abused and his Majesty's Revenue impaird'. Now McEvers's wise retreat was rewarded by the crowd with eight cries of *huzzah!*[18]

Continuing down Wall Street, they marched past City Hall, where they brushed aside the pleas of the mayor, John Cruger, to disperse, before at last turning down Broadway towards Fort George. They were now in the 'court end' of town, where the good sea air, the open prospect offered by this southernmost location and its proximity to the seat of the colonial governor in the fortress ensured that it was here that the city's most fashionable town houses had been built. Among them was the grand house of Justice Robert R. Livingston, one of the Whig Triumvirate who, though he now watched the thousands-strong crowd as it streamed by, remained true to his patrician loyalties and abstained from joining the 'mob' in their protest. This was a political choice that spoke loudly of the gaping social division between the colonial elites and the working population who were otherwise united in their opposition to the Stamp Act.[19]

The demonstrators, now thoroughly fired up, approached Fort George. This was chosen as the ultimate target by the protesters for two reasons. First, it was where the stamped paper was being securely held, and, second, it was the hard military kernel of British imperial authority, one of two places where British troops were barracked in the city (the other was on the Common), its batteries trained on the watery expanse of the harbour and its walls sheltering the governor's mansion. That last fact alone meant that if the crowd could not seize the offending paper, they could at least make their extreme displeasure known to the king's representative in New York.

This was the moment when the mass protest might have tipped over into violence. Fort George was not especially formidable: when the army's chief engineer in America, Captain John Montresor, had cast his professional eye over the fortifications the day before, he found them so wanting that his preparations included taking down a garden fence to allow the troops to give a raking fire, removing stacks of timber that had been allowed to pile up and supporting the entrances with pickets. He also had to fix the chevaux-de-frise, defences consisting of a lengthways pole bristling with rows of spikes. Now soldiers manned the ramparts, the dark muzzles of cannon loaded with grapeshot trained landward, all under the command of the garrison's artillery commander, Major James. This figure proved to be especially provocative. In a moment of aggressive if ill-advised defiance, James had sworn that he would 'cram the Stamps down their Throats with the End of my Sword'.[20]

Now Governor Colden watched as his own effigy was, as he himself reported, 'brought up within 8 or 10 feet of the Gate with the grossest ribaldry from the Mob'. The Madeira-sozzled protester saw Colden's unguarded coach being seized and then 'drawed ... about the town ... and the mob still increasing from thence ... with About 5 or 600 Candles to alight them'. The raucous procession returned to the Common, where it fused with a second mass of people hauling a gallows from which dangled an effigy of Colden holding a boot – a pun on the Earl of Bute, George III's unpopular Scottish prime minister in 1760–1763 (Colden was a Scot) – and sheets of paper representing the stamp duty. The pastiche Colden shared his gallows with the devil whispering into the governor's ear. These were motifs already familiar to New Yorkers, who had for many years 'celebrated' Pope's Day every 5 November in a display of anti-Catholicism, a way of asserting their Protestant, British identity. Here Colden and Bute were taking the place of the usual effigies of the pope and Bonnie Prince Charlie, the ill-fated claimant to the British throne who in 1745 had raised the standard of revolt in Scotland.[21]

The demonstrators returned to the fort, this time taking the direct route via Broadway and hauling the coach and carrying the gallows dangling with the effigies. As they returned to Fort George, Major James shouted, 'Here they come, by God!', while the crowd gave out three cheers, taunting the soldiers and daring them to open fire. Some of the demonstrators, recalled the Madeira-tippling witness, 'placed the Gallows Against the fort

Gate and took Clubs and beat A Gainst it'. The well-disciplined British soldiers bore the insults stoically: 'Not a single return of words or otherwise was made ... while this egregious insult was performing', wrote Colden. Unable or unwilling to break through, the assailants withdrew and 'gave three Whozaus in defyance'. Colden then watched helplessly as the protesters drew his coach to the nearby Bowling Green and incinerated it on a huge bonfire, the effigies crumpling into ash.[22]

As the bonfire blazed, a small group returned to the fortress gates, warning Major James that 'they would knock down his house ... and if he was A Man he should Go and defend it'. This hard core then marched uptown again, heading for an estate on the very edge of the city, Vauxhall, just north of Warren Street, overlooking the Hudson. The protesters ripped up the lawn and plants in the garden and broke into James's genteel mansion. Silk curtains wafted down, mahogany furniture splintered and mirrors, china and glass smashed as they were all hurled out of the windows. The books in the library were tossed out, too, while the major's wine cellar disappeared, mostly down the rioters' throats. The roof and inner walls were demolished until, at four in the morning, all that was left was the sorry shell. The rioters finished their night's work by bursting into the cities' churches – all, that is, except for the Anglican ones, Montresor noted – and pealing the bells simultaneously in celebration as the day broke.[23]

With the night's events so clearly showing that they had lost control of the direction of the resistance, New York's elites took fright. Robert Livingston fretted the morning after the riot that 'every man is wild with Politics ... Last night and the night before we had mobbing ... [T]here was such a one Last night as never was seen before in the City'. The violence – or, at least, the threat of it – continued over the coming days: 'Money extracted from private people or die', Montresor recorded curtly on 2 November. 'Others threatened their public chests, city treasure, Customs House &c'. The following day, Montresor was obliged to spike the cannon on the Battery next to Fort George, as well as those uptown in the artillery yard, for fear that they might fall into the wrong hands. He also did his best with the meagre materials he had to bolster further the fort's defences.[24]

Staring into the abyss of mob rule and anarchy, the 'Whig triumvir' Livingston appealed to the sea captains to calm tempers on the waterfront. Among them was probably Alexander McDougall, a member of the Presbyterian church on Wall Street, like the Livingstons. He 'came immediately into our measures', wrote Livingston of one of the Sons of Liberty, probably McDougall. 'With him we went round to every part of the town', enlisting the support of the shipmasters, captains and labouring people, calming the fired-up denizens of the docks. The Whig oligarchs – Livingston and Delancey factions alike – were determined to defeat Britain's imperial policies, but not at the cost of unleashing a social upheaval endangering their property and influence.[25]

Meanwhile, Livingston's fellow 'Whig triumvir' William Smith Jr. wisely tried to defuse the explosive situation by brokering an agreement with Colden, who transferred the stamped paper to the 'Mayor and Corporation of the City', which restored a tense calm. A crowd some five thousand strong stood, sullen but peaceful, as the offending bales of paper made their short journey from Fort George to City Hall, where they were kept under lock and key.[26]

WHEN COLDEN'S LONG-AWAITED replacement as governor, Sir Henry Moore, took over the reins on 13 November, the new incumbent gloomily reported that, in 'the General Terror which has been spread here', no one could be found to fill the office of stamp distributor. The Sons of Liberty kept up the pressure through the winter, with public meetings, effigy burnings, street protests and, on 26 November, an agreement to trade *without* using the stamps. After more than three weeks of stoppage, this act of civil disobedience had the advantage of getting the wharves and quaysides heaving again, providing work for the now hard-pressed sailors and tradesmen who were the Sons of Liberty's backbone. The Sons of Liberty also formed a Committee of Correspondence to coordinate the resistance with counterparts in other colonies.[27]

At last, on 20 May 1766, the joyful news arrived that Parliament had repealed the Stamp Act, made unworkable by colonial resistance and discredited with a change of ministry in London. Yet there was a sting in the tail: Parliament reasserted that it had the right to make laws for the colonies and to bind them and their people 'in all cases whatsoever'. In other words, the underlying constitutional dispute continued to simmer. Yet for now, the *New York Post-Boy* reported, there was 'a sudden Joy ... diffused thro' all Ranks of People in the whole City, Neighbours ran to congratulate each other, and all the Bells in Town were set to singing, which continued till late at Night, and began again early next morning'. Montresor privately noted more texture: 'Night ended in Drunkeness, throwing of Squibbs, Crackers, firing of muskets and pistols, breaking some windows and forcing the Knockers off the Doors'.[28]

The celebrations produced three new additions to the cityscape. On 30 June, the colonial assembly commissioned an equestrian statue to be erected to King George III to mark 'the deep Sense this Colony has of the eminent and singular Blessings received from him during his most auspicious Reign'. The delegates also voted on a statue dedicated to William Pitt the Elder, a tireless advocate of conciliation between Britain and America in Parliament. The monuments would eventually be unveiled, within a few weeks of each other, in 1770: that of the king on the Bowling Green in

August and that to Pitt on Wall Street in September. They were New York City's first-ever statues.[29]

The third addition was much more controversial. So far, the resistance had used existing social and political places in the city (City Hall, Burns' Coffee House, taverns) and to a great extent had been channelled by the social and political geography of the city (the waterfront, Queen Street, the fort). Now New Yorkers embellished one of their public spaces, and, though the new addition was intended to be a celebration of their rights and freedoms as British subjects, they created a new source of confrontation. The Liberty Pole, erected on the city's Common on 21 May, became a symbol of resistance to British imperial authority and a cause of conflict with the red-coated soldiers whose loyalties were uncompromisingly with the British Crown. The Liberty Pole would turn out to be another faltering step in New York's path from resistance to revolution. The pole was not a *cause* of this process – after all, it would be another ten years before independence was declared – but as the crisis in relations between Britain and the colonies deepened, its very presence helped direct the course of the conflict.

An old pine ship's mast – a fitting tribute to the role mariners played in the resistance – was hauled from the docks by the Sons of Liberty and raised on the Common. At first described simply as a 'flag staff', it was soon called the 'Liberty Pole'. A dozen barrels were hung from the top by ropes, and a board was nailed to the mast, inscribed 'George III, Pitt – and Liberty' (William Pitt the Elder was widely credited in America with securing the repeal). Few Britons would have argued with these slogans, but the Liberty Pole became a provocative symbol because of *who* erected the mast – the Sons of Liberty – and *where* it was sited, all the more so because the location was quite deliberately chosen: whereas in Boston a great elm had been decorated as a 'Liberty Tree', New Yorkers, by raising a mast, could select the site.[30]

The Common, which New Yorkers usually called the Fields, had been the place for citizens to assemble for many years and for many reasons. It was close to the city's then northern limits, but it was still within them, a triangular area wedged between Broadway to the west and the Boston Post Road (now Park Row) that veered off Broadway towards the northeast, forming the triangle. The space remains today as City Hall Park (its northern edge now shorn off by Chambers Street). In boisterous style, the Common was the habitual site of popular gatherings, a fact officially recognised in the 1750s, when the authorities had (in their benevolence) moved the gallows there, the better to edify large crowds. Moreover, along its northern edge rose the Upper Barracks, constructed in 1758 to accommodate British troops stationed in the city during the Seven Years' War. So the Common was not just a public space; it was also a site where the power of the state, in all its ominous brutality, was on display. The Liberty Pole, by celebrating the rights of the people, was therefore a deliberate, defiant, counterpoise.

Almost inevitably, the Common became one of the most politically charged places in New York, the more so as the pole rapidly evolved into a symbol of resistance to imperial authority, a fact that made the British soldiers all the more determined to topple it. This turned the area into a battleground between redcoats and New Yorkers at each jolt in relations between the colonies and the government – the Quartering Act in 1765, which compelled the colonies to find billets for British troops; the Restraining Act, punishing New York for its resistance to the Quartering Act, taking effect in October 1767; and the Townshend Duties on a variety of items, including tea (news of which arrived that same month).

The first Liberty Pole, standing as it did in full daily view of the British soldiers in the barracks on the Common, was hacked down on 10 August 1766 by men of the Twenty-Eighth Foot Regiment, in a calculated insult to their sullen hosts. The Sons of

Liberty, undeterred, simply put up a second mast the following day. This was toppled, in turn, on 22 August, only to be replaced by a third. This was found razed by mysterious hands on 19 March 1767, although everyone suspected the soldiers. The Sons of Liberty raised a fourth, encasing its lower part in iron to protect it and mounting a 'strong Watch' in Montagne's Tavern overlooking the Common from Broadway: in another studied insult to the troops, the inn became the headquarters of their organisation.

On every occasion that the redcoats felled, or attempted to fell, the Liberty Pole, the Sons of Liberty led counterprotests, which brought violent retaliations from the soldiery. Innkeepers were told not to serve the troops, who, Montresor remarked, were 'daily insulted in the Streets'. The governor had six-pounder cannon deployed outside both the Upper Barracks at the Common and the Lower Barracks in the fort 'for the safety of the Troops'. Even the brothels of the sardonically named 'Holy Ground' (the streets running west from the Common towards King's College, the future Columbia University, then sited between Murray and Barclay Streets) gave the soldiers a thorny reception – to which the men, armed with bayonets, reacted by terrorising the 'houses' on the nights of 10–12 October 1766. Shots were fired into taverns, like Montagne's and Bardin's (also by the Common), known to sympathise with the Sons of Liberty, or the soldiers hurled themselves onto revellers, reported one newspaper, 'with drawn swords and Bayonets'.[31]

The most momentous clash occurred against the background of New York's determined opposition to the Quartering Act and to the Townshend Duties, imposed on a wide range of imports. This developed into a new crisis, as a committee of New York merchants (effectively becoming the city's first chamber of commerce) subscribed to a new nonimportation agreement in April 1768. As trade was reduced to a trickle and as New Yorkers suffered the consequences, in December 1769 the Delanceys, who dominated the colonial assembly, managed to push through a compromise. The colony would apply the Quartering Act in return for permission to issue paper money, thereby injecting liquidity into an ailing economy. The Liberty Pole and the Common played a central part in shaping the drama that followed.

With the Delancey stitch-up, one of the leading Sons of Liberty, outspoken veteran privateer and Livingston ally Alexander McDougall, took up his pen in his house on Chapel Street, and his broadside, 'To the Betrayed Inhabitants of the City and Colony of New York', was posted anonymously across the city. Accepting the Quartering Act for the 'support of troops kept here not to protect but to enslave us' was an implicit recognition that British taxation was legitimate. In fact, it was 'enacted for the express purpose of taking money out of our pockets without our consent'. This was a supine capitulation at a time when Massachusetts and South Carolina were standing firm and when New York's own merchants were making sacrifices by boycotting British goods. The fact that the vote was held behind closed doors could mean only one thing: the assembly's decision was driven not by the public interest, but by corruption – and McDougall named names: Governor Colden (who had returned from retirement on Long Island to serve the Crown once again) and the Delancey family. He called for a rally on the Common to press the colonial assembly to reverse its vote. The public meeting at the Liberty Pole drew a large and sympathetic crowd on Monday, 18 December, agreeing that they were opposed to 'giving any Money to the Troops, on any Consideration whatsoever', but this resolution was easily brushed off by the Delancey-dominated assembly the following day.[32] Instead, McDougall was forced to listen in uncomfortable silence as the delegates voted that the anonymous broadside was a 'false, seditious, and infamous libel' and promised a reward of one hundred pounds to whoever identified the writer.[33]

While the Delanceys hunted their prey, redcoats launched a series of determined offensives on the Liberty Pole. First, flitting across the open ground of the Common in the cold obscurity of a Saturday night on 13 January 1770, they sawed through the braces that supported it and bore into it a hole that they filled with gunpowder. They were caught by some of the Sons of Liberty on watch at the nearby Montagne's Tavern, which provoked more violence. Three days later, Tuesday, 16 January, the soldiers hid in a deserted building close by until the small hours, stole through the darkness and blew a new powder charge, toppling the mast. In cathartic revenge, they sawed up the pole and deposited the pieces at the door of Montagne's Tavern.

Over the following days, redcoats and Patriots (as the opponents of the imperial measures were beginning to style themselves) confronted each other, exchanging threats and insults as well as printed broadsides that were pasted on walls across the city. On Friday, 19 January, the hot-tempered Isaac Sears and a friend were strolling among the fruit, vegetable, fish and meat stalls at the covered Fly Market (from the Dutch 'Vly', meaning valley, after the dried-up stream that once ran through here), at the bottom of Maiden Lane, when they came across a group of soldiers posting up their latest literary effort. This remarked that the Sons of Liberty 'thought their freedom depended upon a piece of wood', a caustic reference to the Liberty Pole.[34]

The blunt-speaking Sears rounded on the soldiers and berated them. In the ensuing scuffle, Sears and his companion tried to haul two of the redcoats down the icy streets to Mayor Whitehead Hicks on Wall Street to demand their arrest, while the soldiers' comrades ran off for help. Battle was joined as more soldiers, coming to the aid of their comrades, drew bayonets, while the civilians seized whatever they could, even ripping out the runners from sleighs parked close to the mayor's town house. When Hicks finally appeared, he ordered the troops back to barracks, but their route to the Common took them back past the Fly Market and the narrow, grotty streets that clustered along the waterfront. Here they were pursued by sailors and stevedores who joined the crowd. By the time the twenty-odd British soldiers – breathless, aching limbed and desperate for safety – reached Golden Hill (a name incongruously recalling a rising meadow covered in a sea of yellow celandine flowers – 'Gouewen' in Dutch), the toughs of New York City's working life had closed in, bombarding the soldiers with rocks and striking at the stragglers with clubs and fists. More redcoats, led by an officer who was out of uniform, arrived from the Common, shouting, 'Soldiers, draw your bayonets and cut your way through them!' Reinforced, they slashed at their attackers. Now more confident, they yelled, 'Where are your Sons of Liberty now?'

In the melee, bystanders were sliced, slashed and cut, while one soldier was badly injured. The others escaped, severely battered, bruised and shaken. City officials and British officers dashed to the scene and broke apart the grappling combatants, who hobbled and sloped off. The rage was becalmed after Mayor Hicks ordered all soldiers to barracks. While they were told to offer 'no Insult to the Inhabitants', the latter were ordered 'to preserve Peace and good Order' – in other words, not to provoke the troops. But heated blood still simmered: one New Yorker wrote anxiously to a friend in London, 'We are all in Confusion ... What will be the end of this, God knows'.[35]

New Yorkers remembered 'the Battle of Golden Hill' – which raged in an area today bounded roughly by John, William, Fulton and Cliff Streets – as the first combat of the American Revolution. The violence had resolved nothing. The Liberty Pole had become,

irreversibly, a symbol of New Yorkers' resistance, and it was
not long before another stood tall on the Common. The ever-
determined Sears bought a small plot of land close by – 248 feet
square, fronting the east side of Broadway almost opposite where
it crossed Murray Street. The tiny plot therefore sat in a corner
defiantly close to the barracks. On 6 February, New Yorkers were
treated to a great procession as the new mast

> was drawn through the Streets from the Ship-yards, by 6
> Horses, decorated with ribbands, 3 Flags flying, with the Words
> Liberty and Property, and attended by several Thousands of
> the Inhabitants. It was raised without any Accident, while
> the French Horns played, God save the King. It was strongly
> secured in the Ground by Timber, great Stones and Earth and
> is in height above the ground, about 46 Feet; on the Top of it
> was raised a Top Mast of 22 Feet, on which is fixt a Gilt Vane,
> with the Word LIBERTY.[36]

The beast of a mast could hardly be missed – nor could it be
easily felled: it was supported below ground by a socket twelve feet
deep, and two-thirds of its height was protected by an iron casing,
held by iron rings riveted onto the pole. The upper part had similar
hoops, with the shaft between them hammered with as many iron
nails as it could hold. This Liberty Pole, the fifth, would stand
until destroyed by Loyalists in 1776. It would survive this long
partly because of its near indestructibility, but also because British
soldiers, no doubt under strict orders, stayed clear.

IT WAS ALMOST at this precise moment that the political storm
broke again. The Delanceys finally got their man, after a disgruntled printer identified McDougall as the author of the

inflammatory broadside. The firebrand was arrested at his home early in the morning of 8 February 1770. Refusing to pay an extortionate two-thousand-pound bail, McDougall was committed to the New Gaol on the Boston Post Road, appropriately enough just up from the Upper Barracks on the Common and not far from the Liberty Pole. He spent eighty days imprisoned while waiting to be indicted, until a key witness for the prosecution died, collapsing the case against McDougall and prompting his release.[37]

Although they could no longer pursue him through the courts, the Delanceys still wanted blood. On 13 December 1770, McDougall was ordered to City Hall to face questioning by the assembly. In a stormy session, McDougall stood defiantly with his right fist raised, declaring that he would rather cut it off than 'resign the rights and privileges of a British subject'. The predictable result was uproar: delegates sprang to their feet, shouting for his immediate arrest for contempt. McDougall was marched back to the New Gaol, where he remained locked up until March 1771. During both McDougall's periods of confinement, the Common and the street just outside the gaol became the assembly point for New Yorkers hailing him for his patriotic vigour. The atmosphere at times became positively festive, as the crowds saluted the prisoner as a defender of the rights of the people.[38]

Cracks, meanwhile, had broken open in the nonimportation movement. In March 1770, all the Townshend Duties except that on tea were repealed. While New York merchants welcomed the opportunity to resume trade in British goods, the Sons of Liberty wanted to enforce the boycott on tea. The fragile alliance between the two groups fell apart – and they literally collided on Wall Street on 7 July, all pummelling fists, flailing walking sticks and torn fence slats. At a meeting in front of City Hall on 11 July, Sears roared that any merchant who imported British goods 'would lose his life'.[39]

Along with the anger came the shame, as other Americans reacted by excoriating New York for breaking ranks with those other colonies still standing firm behind the boycott. Perhaps the worst insult of all came at the end of July, when an advertisement appeared in the *New York Mercury*: 'The Inhabitants of the City of Philadelphia, present their Compliments to the Inhabitants of the New-York, and beg they will send them their Old Liberty Pole, as they can imagine they can, by their late Conduct have no further Use for it'.[40]

After a brief period of calm as merchants traded again in British goods, tea provoked the next crisis, the repercussions of which would swell into the surge towards revolution. A near-total collapse in the finances of the British East India Company (EIC) in the summer of 1772 shook the British monetary system to its very core. In New York, the financial crisis was compounded by an iron-hard winter: the freeze was so deep that New Yorkers could walk to Brooklyn across the ice on the East River, and it bit especially cruelly on the city's poor, who crammed desperately into the almshouse for relief. Sickness spread, crime stalked the streets and prostitution boomed. There was also a surge of impoverished migrants from the British Isles, fleeing unemployment and eviction, distressed, angry and seeking new opportunities in America. Into this seething environment came the Tea Act of May 1773. The law tried to rescue the EIC by allowing it to sell its tea directly to the colonies and exempting it from the hefty British tariffs. In other words, tea that the EIC had failed to sell in Britain could be dumped cheaply onto the Americans, who in turn dumped the tea into Boston Harbour on 16 December.[41]

In New York, Sears, McDougall and the Sons of Liberty turned the screws on wavering merchants, establishing a Committee of Vigilance to watch for the contraband, burning offending merchants in effigy and reactivating the Committee of Correspondence (established during the Stamp Act crisis) to coordinate resistance with other colonies. On 17 December, they called a demonstration – attended by three thousand people – against the Tea Act outside City Hall. The determination of the Sons of Liberty, supported by a wide segment of the populace, raised the all too real spectre of violence once more.

On 21 December, Paul Revere rode into the city to tell New Yorkers about the drama in Boston. New York had to wait until April 1774 for its Tea Party, because storms in the Atlantic delayed its two tea ships, *Nancy* and *London. Nancy* never passed Sandy Hook, as it had to be provisioned and repaired after severe damage. *London* ploughed on, tying up at Murray's Wharf on 22 April: New Yorkers imitated the Bostonians and poured the leaves into the East River before jubilantly seeing the ship's captain off.

The New York Tea Party was a pale imitation of Boston's, certainly, but it was nonetheless a sign of determined and mounting resistance. Yet New Yorkers, like the Bostonians, had little time to savour their victory. The British government's response was punitive – the king had roared that 'the colonists must be reduced to absolute obedience, if need be, by the ruthless use of force'. Between March and June 1774, Parliament passed the first of four 'Coercive' (Edmund Burke's word) or 'Intolerable' (the colonists' description) Acts, which punished Massachusetts for its defiance. In addition, the Quebec Act, giving special privileges to the French inhabitants of Canada, including freedom to practise Catholicism, inadvertently provoked the Protestant sensitivities of the colonists. The American response was seismic – indeed, revolutionary. On 15 May, the New York Sons of Liberty responded to an appeal from the Committee of Correspondence in Boston by proposing a general boycott – nonimportation and nonexportation – of all trade with Britain. It was effectively a declaration of economic war on the mother country. But the New York Committee of

Correspondence went further, calling for 'a general congress' to coordinate action.[42]

A general boycott could work only if it reached into every street, block and home, since it demanded lifestyle changes from everyone. In other words, the revolution (as it was now becoming) had to move from the public spaces like the Common, the taverns and the coffeehouses into the privacy of New Yorkers' homes. Politics, in other words, had to reach the colonists not only in a moral sense but in a spatial one, too, because the boycott had to be policed in every New York house.

Here the city's women played a vital role. In the boycott of 1768, women had agreed not to buy or drink tea or to use British fabrics, and they worked with the Sons of Liberty to determine which goods they could and should not purchase. As the people who managed the household, women became the agents of nonimportation at the most localised level. More sinisterly, how watertight the boycott was hinged on surveillance and community pressure: women and men were alert to shopkeepers, tradesmen and merchants who were lukewarm, one such New Yorker complaining of 'political inquisitors' who pried 'into the conduct of individuals'. The refusal to use fabrics woven in the mother country also meant that women made homespun clothing as a political statement.[43]

In 1774 women again played a central role in ensuring the boycott's success: now calling themselves the Daughters of Liberty, they worked in the markets and in their homes to close down trade and consumption of British goods – ensuring, for instance, that coffee rather than tea was now the drink of choice. A teenage New Yorker named Charity Clark wrote to her cousin in Britain that, as she and her friends knitted and spun clothes at home, she dreamt of 'a fighting army of amazones … armed with spinning wheels' who would liberate America from its dependence on British goods and secure it from tyranny. The actions of thousands like Charity would, most important, help to remould the way people thought about women's political action. American revolutionaries would later stress the importance of women to the political order after the Revolution: it was not that women would be given the vote or be encouraged to leave the domestic sphere; rather, women's virtue and modesty would provide the moral fibre on which republican democracy would rest. Women's role would be to work their influence at home, being virtuous wives to bolster the virtue of the male citizen, and to be good republican mothers, nourishing their children in the patriotic values of the new nation. It was accepted that women were the intellectual equals of men, and their contributions to the republican order essential, but it was also held to be natural for women to make these contributions in the home and within the family. These assumptions were given form by the way that women like Charity engaged with the politics of resistance.[44]

One group of New Yorkers for whom the opposition offered little, however, were African Americans. People of African origin, in fact, made up just over 14 per cent of the city's population, according to the last census taken before the Revolution, in 1771. African American sailors from the docklands no doubt formed part of the multiracial crowds who opposed the Stamp Act and perhaps took part in later acts of resistance. Certainly, there were free African Americans who would have engaged determinedly in the boycotts of British goods and engaged in other protests. But the vast majority in New York were enslaved: 'It rather hurts an European eye to see so many negro slaves upon the streets', complained Scottish visitor Patrick McRobert in 1774. These slaves were not held or employed in large groups, as on the plantations of the South or the Caribbean, but one or two was the norm for slaveholding households, so the topography of slavery in New York City was scattered. In the homes of wealthy merchants and lawyers, enslaved African Americans were employed as domestic servants:

cooks, coachmen, butlers, gardeners, stable hands. In a city where one in eight artisans also held slaves, they also hammered, hewed, cut and sewed in New York's workshops, shipyards, sail lofts, ropewalks, tanneries, sugar refineries and breweries. In this tightly packed city, they were usually forced to sleep in leaky attics, dank garrets, dark cellars or outhouses like sheds and stables. Discipline could be just as brutal as it was in the South. Most slaveholders tried to discourage slaves from having children because of the costs of supporting them and the pressures on living space. In a city where some of the largest slaveholders included such notable future revolutionaries as George Clinton, who kept eight, and Aaron Burr and John Jay, who each held five, enslaved African Americans might legitimately have asked how much they might hope from the colonial resistance to British rule. Only the New York Quakers acted against slavery as the Revolution approached – voting at their yearly meeting in 1774 to challenge any of their members who owned or traded in slaves. Otherwise, the closer New York came to revolution and war, the more African American slaves seized the opportunities offered by the upheaval to escape – to the point that in early 1775 Patriot patrols were scouring the environs of the city at dawn and at dusk to arrest any groups of African Americans found about without an explanation.[45]

In the story of New York's final slide from resistance to full-blown revolution, the Liberty Pole would have one more part to play. The rising tide of resistance was not just a mounting revolution against imperial authority, but a fresh, sustained challenge to the political dominance of the patricians. Even the Sons of Liberty could no longer claim undisputed leadership of New York's popular movement: a Mechanics Committee had appeared independently, its membership and leadership alike drawn from the artisanal population and demanding greater democratic involvement in politics. The contest between the 'people of property' and the 'mob', opined the patrician Gouverneur Morris (whose estate, Morrisania, was in today's Bronx), was 'about the future forms of government, whether it should be founded upon aristocratic or democratic principles'. This went way beyond resistance to acts imposed by the British and targeted the internal political order dominated by the colonial elites. Morris added that many among the latter who tried to harness the tide of popular resistance were now longing for 'an opportunity to throw off the mask, to join with the friends of government'. The mob, he warned, 'begin to think and reason ... [T]hey will bite, depend on it ... The gentry begin to fear this ... [I]f the disputes with Great Britain continue ... we shall be under the domination of a riotous mob'. Under the pressure, the Delanceys – Church of England in faith, with strong mercantile ties to Britain – would eventually choose Loyalism, throwing in their lot with the Crown and empire. The Livingstons would swing behind the 'Patriot' cause and try to harness the 'mob' in order to supplant the Delanceys and take power in New York. Cynical as both factions might seem, underlying their choices was an agonising dilemma involving a re-examination of their old assumptions and identities, including their loyalty to the Crown, their 'Britishness' and their place in America's future. It was a dilemma encapsulated by the torment of William Smith Jr., one of the 'Whig Triumvirate' whose loyalties to the Livingstons conflicted with his own innate love of order and the rule of law: after much hesitation, he would join the Loyalists.[46]

For now, the patricians tried to slow the pace of resistance. At a tumultuous meeting held on 16 May 1774 at Burns' Coffee House, most of the Committee of Fifty-One chosen to oversee the boycott of trade with Britain were moderate merchants who defeated a proposal, by Son of Liberty Isaac Sears and backed by the Mechanics

Committee, for universal male suffrage in the coming elections to the Continental Congress, due to meet in Philadelphia on 5 September. When the elections came, they secured a compromise whereby the radicals agreed to a more moderate slate of delegates, provided that they supported the boycott. When the delegates cast off from one of the East River wharves for Philadelphia on 1 September, they were cheered by vast crowds, an eyewitness recording the 'Colours flying, Music playing, and loud Huzzas at the end of each Street'.

The Continental Congress between September and October 1774 denied the right of Parliament to tax the colonies and rejected a compromise for a more equal union between Britain and America. In a Declaration of Rights, Congress proclaimed the sole authority of the colonies to tax and to legislate for themselves, while declaring their essential loyalty to the king. At the same time, the delegates signed up to a 'Continental Association', boycotting imports, exports and consumption of British goods until the Coercive Acts were repealed. When Congress adjourned, it agreed to reconvene in May 1775. Then, surreptitiously at first, the delegates and the local colonial committees prepared for war.[47]

In this torrid political atmosphere, the elites and the moderates in New York lost ground to the radicals. The Mechanics Committee forced the dissolution of the Committee of Fifty-One, new elections on 22 November 1774 replacing it with a Committee of Sixty, half of whose members were radicals. This new committee, in turn, appointed a Committee of Observation, supported by the Sons of Liberty, the Mechanics Committee and the crowds on the streets, to enforce the boycott when it came into force on 1 February 1775.

Under this determination of ordinary New Yorkers to press home their protest, the old government institutions began to atrophy. Having fought for almost a decade to shore it up, the colonial elites were seeing their old hierarchical world collapsing around them. In their homes, streets, shops and docks, most New Yorkers brushed aside the old colonial assembly's attempts to repudiate the Continental Congress: the boycott continued, enforced by the Committee of Observation, by threats of popular violence and by the day-to-day choices made by ordinary men and women not to buy British goods. Effective political authority was seized by the Committee of Sixty, which called on all freeholders and freemen to meet at the Exchange at noon on 6 March 1775, in order to proceed with the election of delegates to the next Congress. That day the Sons of Liberty gathered at the Liberty Pole, hoisting a British flag on a red field. Then, led by Sears and with fifes playing, drums beating and trumpets blowing, they marched – as they had a decade before in the Stamp Act protests – past the docks and wharves to rally as much support as they could. They marched behind another union flag, this one with a blue field, emblazoned, on the one side, with the motto 'George III Rex and the Liberties of America' – a still hopeful attempt to marry loyalty to the Crown with the rights of the colonists – but on the other with the words 'Union of the Colonies and the Measures of the Congress'.[48]

At the Exchange, the assembled voters agreed to elect deputies to a Provincial Convention, consisting of representatives from across the colony, who were to meet in New York City on 20 April and choose the delegates for the Continental Congress, which would meet in Philadelphia in May. When the convention met at the Exchange on the appointed day, the old colonial assembly could only watch helplessly from City Hall nearby. This old legislature would meet for the last time on 7 June. The symbolism of the events of 6 March 1775 was clear: by marching from the Liberty Pole to the Exchange, the Patriots were underscoring the legitimacy of the convention by connecting it – in a literal geographic sense – with the rights of the people as represented by the Liberty Pole.[49]

The Common and the Liberty Pole soon played another symbolic role: it was here that, on 23 April 1775, the city learned about the outbreak of war with Britain. An exhausted express rider from New England came thundering down the Boston Post Road, along the Bowery, galloping to the Liberty Pole. Blaring on a trumpet, he assembled passers-by and delivered his bombshell. On the night of 18–19 April, Massachusetts militiamen and redcoats under General Thomas Gage had fought a running battle between Lexington and Concord. American blood had been spilled, the British forced back into Boston, and the rebels were besieging the city. New York, wrote one anxious witness, was 'in a state of alarm; every face appeared animated with resentment'. This 23 April being a Sunday, word spread as people left church, William Smith Jr. recording in his diary that 'at all corners People inquisitive for News'.

As wild rumours flew around, Isaac Sears and John Lamb rallied the Sons of Liberty, who rushed to the docks, stopping two sloops carrying provisions for the British army in Boston. Then, in the gathering darkness, Sears led his men to City Hall, where they smashed down the door of the armoury, seizing the five hundred muskets, their bayonets and the cartridge boxes. They then marched uptown and posted guards at the city's magazine (near the Collect Pond, north of the Common). Sears and Lamb also wrenched the keys to the Customs House from the collector and locked its doors, declaring the port closed for business. It was, Son of Liberty Marinus Willett declared with satisfaction, a 'general insurrection of the populace'. The American Revolution had come to New York.[50]

The following morning, Cadwallader Colden, acting as governor in the absence of William Tryon, who had been on a trip to Britain since the spring of 1774, gathered the stunned representatives of the old colonial order – judges, councillors and Mayor Whitehead Hicks. Among them was William Smith Jr., who mustered enough humour to admit, 'We were ... unanimously of Opinion that we had no Power to do anything'. The old authority had collapsed, and its place was rapidly taken by the Committee of Sixty, which appealed to all 'Patriots' to subscribe to a 'General Association' recognising the upcoming Continental Congress, enforcing the trade embargo and protecting law and security. It convened an elected Provincial Congress to meet in New York on 22 May and take power in the colony. The city would be run by a Committee of One Hundred (which was elected within days). The Committee of Sixty also warned New York's citizens that they should prepare for a British assault. Now New York was also a city at war.[51]

NEW YORK'S TURBULENT journey from resistance to revolution was the result of a complex swirl of British imperial policy, elite politics and the mobilisation of the people. It was also an experience that was written into the physical spaces of the city, in three senses. First, as the political initiative slipped from the hands of the colonial elites towards the Sons of Liberty and their supporters, so the politics of resistance eventually threaded their way into almost every street, house and shop in the city. This was a spatial expansion of political action that went much further than the usual spheres delineated by civil society in colonial New York, like the coffeehouses and taverns, and into the spaces usually reserved for private everyday life. This surge of political activity helped make the atmosphere in New York positively revolutionary by 1775.

Second, the geography of the city shaped the ways in which New Yorkers actually mobilised, both in resisting British authority and in protesting against the political dominance of the colonial elites: the unusual juxtaposition of one of the wealthiest streets in the city, Queen Street, with the waterfront, the heartland of New York's maritime community, explains the physical direction of the demonstration against the Stamp Act. The topographical fact of the Common being overlooked by the barracks, with the gaol almost adjoining the latter, virtually guaranteed that when New Yorkers chose this as the site for their Liberty Pole, it would provoke the repeated confrontations that culminated in the first drawing of blood in the revolutionary crisis with the 'Battle of Golden Hill'.

Third, it is clear that the shape of New York's revolutionary crisis was also informed by earlier customs: the anti–Stamp Act protests adapted forms of the long-standing and ribald 'Pope's Day'; the Common was a habitual gathering place for large crowds of New Yorkers, and the Liberty Pole was not, in itself, a new symbol, but owed much to traditions of the May Pole. Yet New Yorkers infused these older practices with new meanings symbolising their resistance, meanings that were explicit not only in the symbols and slogans, but also in the choice of location. New Yorkers were not just content to celebrate the repeal of the Stamp Act by hailing the authorities' decision to raise statues to King George III and William Pitt, but they chose their own form of festivity (raising the Liberty Pole) and location (the Common). In these choices, they staked New Yorkers' claims to the rights of British subjects and did so in defiance of the nearby instruments of the repressive arm of the state, namely, the gallows and the barracks.

Right up to 1775, New Yorkers made these expressions of resistance while protesting their loyalty to the king. Yet ultimately, as the parade led by Sears and the Sons of Liberty from the Common to the Exchange on 6 March 1775 demonstrated, New Yorkers connected, in both a symbolic and a topographical sense, these rights to the legitimacy of the Provincial Convention. The two were reconcilable, provided that the king himself accepted the convention (and the Continental Congress to which it would send delegates) as legitimate, but if he did not, then the implicit meaning of the parade was that the colonists would be forced to choose between their loyalties as subjects of the British Crown, on the one hand, and their rights and freedoms, on the other. That moment seemed to have arrived a little more than six weeks later with the news of the battles in Massachusetts, precipitating the fall of the old regime in New York.

CHAPTER TWO

LONDON DEFIANT:
WILKES AND LIBERTY, 1763–1776

WHEN ALEXANDER MCDOUGALL was incarcerated in New York's New Gaol in 1770–1771, he was hailed by his compatriots as the 'Wilkes of America'. John Wilkes was a London journalist and politician who relished controversy and who, like the Scottish-born New Yorker, was chastised by authority for roasting those in power, in Wilkes's case most famously in issue number 45 of his scurrilous newspaper, *North Briton*, in 1763. Wilkes was pursued, prosecuted and persecuted with the same persistence and intensity as McDougall, so it was natural for Americans to hail the fiery New Yorker as *their* 'Wilkes'. Rakish, lanky, cross-eyed, jagged-toothed – once dismissing his own ugliness by boasting that it took him 'only half an hour to talk away my face' – Wilkes was an unlikely but heroic symbol of the rights and liberties of British subjects across the Atlantic world. For Britons, Wilkes symbolised defiance towards the elites and the overbearing authority of the eighteenth-century British state. Yet among the liberties that Wilkes defended, as both journalist and politician, were those specific to his home turf, the City of London. And the freedoms of the City were perhaps best represented in stone by Temple Bar.[1]

Temple Bar was the gateway that stood across one of the busiest spots in the metropolis, where the Strand became Fleet Street. To pass from west to east through Temple Bar was to cross from Westminster into the City of London. In Wilkes's day, Temple Bar presented a startling and grisly sight, as French historian and writer Pierre-Jean Grosley discovered: 'There are three spikes, at the top of which are displayed the heads of three of the principal lords who in 1746, having supported the cause of the [Jacobite] Pretender [Prince Charles Edward Stuart], were captured bearing arms and executed as criminals for high treason. These three poles, of fifteen to twenty feet in height, are planted at equal intervals on *Temple Bar*, which separates old London [the City] from the Strand'.[2]

The hulking gatehouse was designed by the great architect Sir Christopher Wren between 1669 and 1672. Its dense wooden doors swung heavily on their massive hinges, its deep central arch allowing carriages to pass through, one by one, and only in one direction at a time, between Fleet Street in the City and the Strand in Westminster. Pedestrians shouldered past each other through the passageways on either side, watched by the blackened skulls of the executed Jacobite rebels. The display of these grisly trophies of state retribution against the insurgents of the 'Forty-Five' proclaimed the essential loyalty of Londoners to the established Hanoverian dynasty. Yet Temple Bar also represented the point where the freedoms of the City of London now held sway in the metropolis.[3]

These liberties were considerable. First, the Court of Aldermen (the upper house of the City's assembly) had direct access to the king, while the Common Council (the lower house) was entitled to demand redress of its grievances at the very bar of the House of Commons. Second, the king had (in theory) to ask permission to enter the City, which could slam its Temple Bar shut against government representatives seeking admission. While usually the 'permission' was a ceremonial occasion, when the lord mayor presented the monarch with the City's symbolic pearl-studded sword, during the Wilkite controversies the gate would in fact be bolted shut for real, in defiance of the king and Parliament. Third, the City policed itself, employing its own constables: when magistrate and novelist Henry Fielding and his half brother, John Fielding, set up their justice house at No. 4 Bow Street, near Covent Garden in Westminster, they had no jurisdiction in the City. Nor did their famous Bow Street runners, the 'thief-takers' who were a precursor to the modern police force. Fourth, and most important, the City had its own political system, which made it virtually self-governing.

Here, political life rested on the guilds, or the sixty-odd livery companies that kept a watchful eye on who could practise trades and crafts in the City. Each had their headquarters, or Companies' Halls, which were usually built back from the street to show them off to the greatest effect. Those that survived the bombing during the Second World War are historic gems hidden in today's thrusting cityscape. In the later eighteenth century, therefore, the City remained a lively hub of activity of all kinds, not just finance but also highly skilled artisans, printers and merchants plying their trades in the warren of streets whose topography had remained almost unchanged for centuries; even after the Great Fire of 1666, the City was rebuilt on the original ground plan. So London's streets beyond Temple Bar were throbbing with activity, noisy with the traffic of carts, tradesmen and people going about their business, of which there were many types, and punctuated by the hourly chiming of bells ringing out the passage of the day from the scores of church towers and spires that pierced the sky above, the centrepiece of which was, of course, the great, soaring dome of Saint Paul's Cathedral at the top of Ludgate Hill.[4]

To be a liveryman was to be a freeman of the City, although the status was also acquired through inheritance or purchase. A freeman could practise a trade within the lines of the old Roman walls and was involved in an intense round of political activity. Freemen elected the City's four members of Parliament and were the members of the hundred parish vestries that cared for the poor, the sick and the elderly; upheld law and order; and chose officials ranging from the parish constable to the church wardens. They also met in their local wards, of which the City had twenty-six, each with a wardmote court that elected an alderman for life and the ward's common council. Above the wards, the City's political life centred on a two-chamber council and the lord mayor. The lower chamber, the Court of Common Council, had 236 members, freemen elected by all the City's ratepayers. The upper chamber was the Court of Aldermen, who could veto decisions from the Common Council and from among whom the lord mayor was elected each year. With such a punishing round of civic obligations, it was perhaps unsurprising that the construction of the lord mayor's residence, the Mansion House, could be partially funded by fines levied on the merchants who found the obligations of civic service an unwelcome distraction from making money. They increasingly relocated, too, to London's more fashionable, airier West End as the century progressed.[5]

The aldermen tended to be plutocrats, directors of the great joint-stock companies like the East India Company, rich merchants, insurers and bankers. In defence of their wealth and status, they could find common ground with the rich landowning interest in Parliament and the court. Yet the liverymen and freemen in the wards and Common Council were different altogether: as skilled artisans, smaller merchants and retailers, they self-consciously saw themselves as voicing the true interests of the people of the City. Yet if the Common Council and the aldermen frequently clashed, they spoke as one voice when the City and its privileges were under attack.[6]

These liberties mattered in an age when such special rights, whether individual, corporate or local, were an essential part of the liberties enjoyed by subjects. This was, after all, an age in which democracy in the modern sense, with equal political and civil rights for all citizens, certainly did not exist in Britain. Parliament was elected by men who, in the countryside, owned property worth forty shillings or more a year – the independent 'yeomen farmers' – or who, in the towns, met one of several different types of qualification, depending upon locality. In London, as we have noted, all freemen of the City could vote, while in Westminster, a so-called scot-and-lot borough, all males who paid the local taxes had the suffrage, giving it one of the broadest electorates in the country. Voting, in other words, was essentially a privilege, not a right attributed to all Britons, but in the old order privileges were directly associated with 'liberty'. For most people, the freedom of an individual or a community depended less on any belief in inherent, natural or universal rights than on the type of special rights that they enjoyed, including those inherited broadly by all 'freeborn Britons' and, more specifically, those attached to their status, what they did for a living, for whom they worked and where they lived. And the City of London's weighty privileges took physical expression in the impressive bulk of Temple Bar.

Most of the time, it should be said, these liberties were welded together with loyalty to the monarchy, but the City never backed down from defending its freedoms when the king or Parliament trespassed on them. This was not a straightforward question of monarchy against democracy, or of conservatism against radicalism, but a matter of the defence of traditional privilege. So Temple Bar represented this customary way of conceptualising freedom, which was defined by law, tradition and locality. The bruising political contests arising from all this were especially intense in the years after Pierre-Jean Grosley's visit, making his final observation on Temple Bar unwittingly apt: 'The English appear to be convinced that the fall of each of those three heads, would be the sign or perhaps even the signal for some revolution in the state. This popular superstition was given credit by the fall of the middle head which, at the death of the last king, had become detached from its pole'.[7] That was in 1760, when King George II had died and was succeeded by the young George III, whose ministers then unleashed a wave of political contention on both sides of the Atlantic. During the ensuing political struggle in the British metropolis, Temple Bar became a symbol of the City's liberties, the defence of which might have been an essentially conservative movement had it not been for John Wilkes and his capacity to mobilise a broad cross-section of people, way beyond the boundaries of the City and across the entire metropolis.

Wilkes had the popular touch. He was a Londoner, born in 1726 in Clerkenwell, in a house on Saint John's Square, where the remains of a medieval cloister, Saint John's Gate (built in 1504 and still standing), had once been a northern entrance to the City's Square Mile. A firm believer in walking, Wilkes rarely took a hackney cab or coach, but could be seen striding lankily through the streets of the metropolis, accepting the greetings of the working Londoners who doffed their hats: he might arrive at a political meeting mud-spattered, but on his way he had reminded Londoners of his presence, that he was 'one of them'.[8] He was already a member of Parliament when his real notoriety took off in 1763 with the *North Briton*, which assailed the ministry (and Lord Bute in particular, George III's favourite) and even made some thinly gloved jabs at the monarch himself. Over the course of his colourful career, Wilkes clashed repeatedly with the king, his ministers and the government benches in Parliament.

Yet these political struggles were far from revolutionary – and this was especially true in the City itself. Even as it resisted encroachments on its freedoms by king and Parliament, the City had a vested interest in stability. The City's importance within British politics rested on a fusion of power, money and trade, represented by a trio of buildings that faced each other in the heart of the Square Mile: the Mansion House, the Bank of England and the Royal Exchange. The Mansion House was built by architect George Dance between 1739 and 1753, when it received its first mayoral occupant. This no-nonsense neoclassical edifice still stands bulkily opposite the Bank. Inside, in the famous 'Egyptian Hall' – so-called because it was inspired by the designs of the Roman architect Vitruvius, who constructed buildings in Egypt – the guests at the lord mayor's banquets could feast in their hundreds beneath the tall columns that support the great arching ceiling and the galleries above the main floor. The great bastion of British financial might facing the Mansion House, the Bank of England on Threadneedle Street, was not the towering fortress that it is today, but a more elegant design by architect George Sampson built in the 1730s. Next to the Bank stood the Royal Exchange, still bearing the grasshopper on top of its stone tower, the emblem of Thomas Gresham who in the reign of Queen Elizabeth I constructed the original Exchange at his own expense so that (he hoped, somewhat in vain) London's merchants would cease to conduct their business in taverns and on the street. Built after the Great Fire of 1666 by Edward Jerman, the new Royal Exchange had a courtyard surrounded by arcades and shops selling silverware, fabrics, books, jewellery and medicines on the ground floor; in this space merchants from around the world met, bartered and sealed agreements. In the narrow streets that hummed with mercantile life around the Bank and the Exchange, there were coffeehouses (in 1739 historian William Maitland counted 551 in the metropolis altogether). In a fug of pipe smoke, steaming coffee, ale and claret, these watering holes hummed with business talk, dealings and auctions, each catering for a clientele specialising in a different branch of business.[9]

So the triangular arrangement of the Mansion House, Bank of England and Royal Exchange expressed the close connections between the City's freedoms, finance and commerce. This relationship explains why the City's leaders and freemen, for all their bluster, had good reason to want to keep domestic peace, law and order. The Bank and the Exchange were the physical expressions of the City's global reach in commerce, of its prosperity rooted in the British Empire. For many patriotic Britons, trade and finance were the bedrock of the nation's greatness – and that despite the political dominance of elites whose wealth was rooted in land. These lords, gentry and yeomen were well aware that, in times of war (and there were many such times in the eighteenth century), it was the men and women of business, trade and finance who supplied an essential weapon: money. In the mid-eighteenth century, Britain had a third of the population of France, but the government enjoyed the same levels of revenue, much of it deriving from large- and small-scale commerce. This finance was woven into an intricate web of credit, the lifeblood of which was confidence that debts large and small would be honoured, a system reaching right up to the Bank of England itself, which had been established in 1694 precisely to help the government finance its wars against France.

Yet there was more to it than just the pursuit of profit and power: for proud Britons, the lucrative system of taxation, credit, trade and empire was underwritten by a parliamentary government that guaranteed the rights and liberties of the subject and, therefore, further boosted confidence that the fiscal and political system was run for the benefit, if not of the whole people, then at least of the moneymakers and propertied among them. Credit, commerce and freedom meant that the livelihoods of a great many people, from the wealthiest merchants who paced the courtyard of the Exchange down to the shopkeepers who opened up their humble lockups each morning in the surrounding alleys, had an interest in avoiding revolution.[10]

Yet the balance between power and liberty was always a precarious one. The City, though loyal to king and country, also jealously protected its freedoms, strengthened as they were by its financial and commercial sinews. When John Wilkes hurled down his challenge to the government through his inflammatory satire in the *North Briton*, he originally did so for partisan purposes. A supporter of William Pitt the Elder, who had resigned from the government in 1761, and, like many City notables who saw the king's policy of ending the Seven Years' War as prematurely shutting off opportunities for the expansion of British global commerce at the expense of France and Spain, he poured his brand of irony, humour and vitriol onto King George's minister Lord Bute. It was when he was then pursued by the authorities for these attacks that Wilkes could claim that whosoever prevailed in his collision with the king would decide 'at once whether English Liberty shall be a reality or a shadow'. In the political battles that followed, the metropolis would witness a radical departure, as a broad campaign to force Parliament and the king to recognise the rights of voters in particular, and of the people in general, became, for a brief period, interwoven with the defence of the traditional liberties and power of the City, a development that was expressed in the spaces of the metropolis.[11]

How THIS HAPPENED is connected to the career of Wilkes himself. Arrested for his blistering attacks on the government in the
North Briton, he endured a brief spell in the Tower of London in
1763, before being released on the grounds of his parliamentary
privilege as an MP. He also took a pistol shot in the abdomen
during a duel fought in Hyde Park against one of the politicians
he had so outraged. He then stole away to exile in France, where
he remained for just over four years. In his absence, Wilkes
was expelled from the House of Commons and found guilty
by the House of seditious libel. In 1768, when he returned
(partly because he had run up eye-watering debts in Paris), he
was reelected to Parliament in March, this time for Middlesex,
the sprawling historic county that enveloped the outlying parts
of the metropolis along the north bank of the Thames, though
not Westminster or the City. It was this election that ensured
that the Wilkes controversy would mobilise not only the City
of London in defence of its liberties, but also a much broader
cross-section of the metropolitan population who were asserting
their rights as electors and as British subjects. This was because,
although Middlesex's voters were freeholders who owned property worth forty shillings a year, it was unusual for a county
constituency because it was so urbanised. In most counties,
freeholders were yeomen farmers, with an interest in land. Yet
the sprawling encroachment of the metropolis into Middlesex
ensured that many electors were part of the City's mercantile
classes – brewers, manufacturers, merchants – and those whom
people at the time dubbed the 'little freeholders', skilled artisans
and shopkeepers who fulfilled the daily needs of metropolitan
life. These were the grocers, weavers, furniture makers, ironmongers, plumbers, painters, wood turners, apothecaries, drapers,

watchmakers and joiners who were resistant to the influence of great property owners (of whom there were comparatively few in Middlesex anyway) and who, determinedly independent, had no truck with the candidates sponsored by the court and the ministry.[12]

Although Wilkes triumphed at the polls, the following month he honoured an earlier promise to face his conviction for seditious libel. Wilkes's now considerable support from the citizens of the metropolis made itself heard. Zealous Londoners made a rescue attempt as he was being driven to gaol. Unhitching the horses from the carriage, they wheeled Wilkes to a tavern safe beyond Temple Bar, the gateway not only symbolising the freedoms of the City, but also, in a very practical legal sense, marking the boundary over which the sergeants-at-arms – the officers sent out by Parliament in pursuit of Wilkes – could cross only at their peril. After dutifully thanking his rescuers and sharing a tankard of ale, Wilkes, obedient to the law, wrapped himself in a cloak and slipped away, crossing the river and surrendering at the King's Bench Prison in Southwark, where he awaited sentencing. Reserved for debtors and, like Wilkes, political prisoners, the King's Bench was neither the most forbidding of the city's gaols nor the most notorious, but the open scrubland next to it, Saint George's Fields, would soon assume emotive meaning.[13]

The fields, which now include the site of Waterloo Station, occupied what was then an undeveloped, semirural area of Southwark, Lambeth and Newington. Like New York's Common, it became a gathering place for opposition supporters, who now included people from all social backgrounds from across the metropolis – not just freemen of the City – who associated Wilkes's persecution with their own travails in the tough climate of the post-war years. This mobilisation brought thousands of London's working population into politics for the first time, people who had little or no stake in the traditional liberties of the City, let alone a vote in parliamentary elections, but who saw in Wilkes's defiance of authority a mirror of their own daily struggle for self-respect and dignity in the face of the overbearing power of the state and the social dominance of the elites.[14]

Just as the radicalisation of New York's resistance was inscribed in the colonial city's space by the emergence of the Common as a place of political conflict, so a parallel development in London's struggle was being expressed in similarly spatial terms, with Saint George's Fields becoming a site of protest. Of course, the primary reason that Londoners gathered on the fields was because it was overlooked by the King's Bench Prison, where their hero was incarcerated; in this sense, they did not choose their spot in the way that New Yorkers provocatively selected the Common. Yet the very location, however inadvertently, represented a departure from the narrow defence of the City's privileges towards a broader demand for a national politics more responsive to the aspirations of the people at large. The City's freemen, aldermen and lord mayors rested their defence of Wilkes and the City's privileges in its customary symbols and institutions such as Temple Bar and the Mansion House. By contrast, although in fact the City leaders intended to develop Southwark, thereby expanding the City's reach onto the south bank of the Thames, Saint George's Fields was still open common land that had no direct association with the freedoms of the City. This meant that people from across the metropolis – the City, Westminster, Middlesex, Surrey – could rally here without appearing to be making a statement that they were mobilising merely in defence of the City's liberties, but rather that they were doing so for a blend of wider purposes, not least for the rights of the electors of Middlesex whose choice of MP had been repeatedly rebuffed and for the liberties of all British subjects against a political system apparently weighted in favour of the Crown and the landed elites.

The fields soon became laden with tragedy, too. On 10 May 1768, a crowd of people from all social backgrounds – but mostly artisans and labouring poor – jostled with troops outside the prison. They had been anticipating Wilkes's release to take up his seat in the new session of Parliament, whereupon his exclusion would lapse. When it became obvious that Wilkes was not being freed, the hubbub of the crowd became agitated, and then insults and projectiles were hurled at the soldiers drawn up outside the prison gates. In retaliation, the troops opened fire, gunning down seven people – one a passer-by driving a cart, another a stable hand shot dead after being pursued by inflamed soldiers who mistook him for someone else. It was far more lethal than anything the opposition in America had been subjected to before the outbreak of open war. The 'Saint George's Fields Massacre', as the deadly fusillade was remembered, confirmed the darkest fears of Wilkes's supporters. When combined in people's minds with the Battle of Golden Hill in New York and the Boston Massacre (in which five people were killed), both in 1770, the shootings in London seemed to show that the government was out to destroy the cherished liberties of freeborn Britons on both sides of the Atlantic, by force if necessary.[15]

Wilkes was finally sentenced on 18 June 1768 to two years in prison for his 'libellous' publications – the judge studiously ignoring the fact that Wilkes was nonchalantly cleaning his teeth with a toothpick – and was disbarred from his Middlesex seat. Yet in the subsequent by-elections between February and April 1769, the prisoner was chosen three times by the Middlesex voters. Yet three times the House of Commons, urged on by the king himself, quashed the results.

Protests against this blunt refusal to accept the verdict of

property-owning voters were heard nationwide, but it was in
London that the two causes – that of the freedoms of the City
and those of Britons at large – became intertwined. For the freemen of the City of London, Wilkes represented both the rights
and liberties of Britons and their own local privileges. Even while
incarcerated in relative luxury (thanks to the many gifts of well-
wishers) in the King's Bench Prison, Wilkes was elected alderman
of the ward of Farringdon Without, one of the most extensive and
poorest districts of the City, on 2 January 1769. That same month,
his supporters gathered in the London Tavern on Bishopsgate to
form the Society of the Supporters of the Bill of Rights, its aim
being 'to defend and maintain the legal, constitutional liberty of
the subject' and to further 'Mr. Wilkes and his cause'. The SSBR
collected funds to pay off Wilkes's apparently bottomless debts, but
it was also a hothouse of metropolitan radicalism, and it reached
into Middlesex and the county of Surrey on the south bank of the
Thames. It launched a petition demanding that the choice of the
Middlesex voters be respected, for the sake of the freedom of all
Britons. The lord mayor, William Beckford, lent his support to the
SSBR petition, which the king brushed off as 'disrespectful to me,
injurious to parliament'. In May 1769, Beckford boldly confronted
the king at court in Saint James's Palace, provoking gasps among
the assembled courtiers when he warned that the 'false insinua-
tions and suggestions' of his advisers threatened to 'alienate your
Majesty's affections from your loyal subjects in general, and from
the City of London in particular'. Beckford became a hero in the
City: a statue was later erected to him in the Guildhall, alcoved
high up on the wall, supported by a pedestal engraved with his
defiant warning to the king.[16]

Yet there were plenty of voices in the City who were alarmed
by the way in which the defence of their freedoms was interwoven
with an opposition that challenged the Crown and stank of 'mob

rule'. This conservatism had been expressed in a 'loyalist' address of support to the king, which was drafted on 1 March 1769 at the King's Arms Tavern on Cornhill and signed by some six hundred petitioners – merchants, stockbrokers and tradesmen who were obviously well off enough to afford the one-shilling entrance fee. The signed document was to be delivered to the king by a grand procession of carriages – the choice of transport in itself a display of wealth – from the City through Westminster to Saint James's Palace on 22 March. Yet the freemen of London had mobilised as the coaches moved off in the City. The stately cavalcade had degenerated into farce when it reached Temple Bar, where the gates were shut against the addressers by a crowd of liverymen and other working Londoners hurling insults. The king's loyal subjects had been forced to carry their address along the Thames by boat.[17]

This would not be the last time that Temple Bar would be used to defy the king's supporters. The close association – at least in the minds of City freemen and their leaders – between the liberties of the City and the rights of all Britons would find its most practical and symbolic expression in the climax of the Wilkes controversy, remembered as the 'Printers' Case'. This affair was sparked after Wilkes was freed from prison in April 1770 and took his seat with the Council of Aldermen in the City's glorious Guildhall. He naturally wasted no time in gleefully asserting his authority against the tentacles of the central government whenever they reached beyond Temple Bar. Since 1728 a law had prohibited the reporting of parliamentary debates in the newspapers, except in the official journals of the two houses, for (a not-unfounded) fear that the MPs would be misrepresented or ridiculed. Yet by Wilkes's day, this was a regulation that was being repeatedly breached, until in February 1771 Colonel George Onslow, a government MP, sick of being mocked, secured an act for the fresh enforcement of the ban. The *Gazetteer* and the *Middlesex Journal* could not resist heaping more insults onto 'little cocking George Onslow', and the House of Commons summoned the two newspaper printers, who operated within the City of London, to explain themselves. Only one of them attended, and in any case both returned to work far from chastened. The House voted for their arrest, George III promising a reward of fifty pounds each for their capture. Yet as one lady observed, 'The City patriots will not give up the printers and threaten if the sergeant-at-arms should attempt to seize them he shall be sent to Newgate', the main prison for the City of London and its environs. Both sides began to steel themselves for a battle. John Wilkes, with the SSBR behind him, made the first move.[18]

First, other newspapers were encouraged to defy the ban. Onslow took the bait: on 12 March, he moved that six recalcitrant printers be arrested. The motion caused a real stir in the House of Commons, the debate raging on through the night until 4.45 a.m., when Onslow finally got his way. Four of the six printers later appeared at the bar of the House to be reprimanded, but two others, John Wheble and John Miller, remained at large. When the House ordered their arrest, Wilkes and his allies waited to pounce when Parliament's sergeants-at-arms dared to pass through Temple Bar, a boundary that now took on a very real legal significance. As prearranged, Wheble had himself arrested by his apprentice (or 'printer's devil', as they were called), who, his hands still smeared with ink, proudly marched him before Wilkes, who sat in judgement at the Guildhall. Alderman Wilkes simply declared the arrest illegal in the City of London, ordered Wheble's release and gave the delighted apprentice a certificate that would still allow him cheekily to claim his fifty-pound reward from the king. Wilkes even had the effrontery to write to the government, explaining that Wheble's arrest had been illegal, 'in direct violation of the rights of an Englishman, and of the chartered privileges of the citizen of the Metropolis'. The second printer, Miller, was caught by a king's messenger-at-arms brandishing a warrant issued by the House of Commons. This occurred, according to Wilkes's plan, in plain view of a City constable, who arrested the king's man for assault and hauled both men to appear before Wilkes. This time they would appear not at the Guildhall, but in the Mansion House, where Wilkes was with Richard Oliver, another alderman, at the bedside of the gruff, bluntly spoken Brass Crosby, the lord mayor, who was lying in bed in agony with gout. When a barrister from the office of the treasury solicitor (the government's lawyer) arrived, he was told – now predictably enough – that he had no jurisdiction in the City. The same occurred when a sergeant-at-arms named Climentson arrived with a request from the Speaker of the House of Commons for the release of his colleague. Climentson was flatly turned down. Holding court in his colourful, oath-peppered fashion and vaguely comical as he donned his justice's wig while still in his nightshirt, Crosby declared the arrest of the printer Miller illegal within the City of London. Instead, he ordered the offending messenger-at-arms to appear before magistrates at the Old Bailey, the central criminal court of the City. Climentson's protests were brusquely rebutted, and he was reduced to paying bail for his colleague.[19]

The king was furious: 'The authority of the House of Commons', he roared, 'is totally annihilated' unless examples were made of Crosby and Oliver, who should be thrown into the Tower of London. Yet even George III knew better than to risk challenging 'that devil Wilkes', contenting himself with the comment that 'he is below the notice of the House'. Parliament retaliated by summoning Lord Mayor Crosby and Alderman Oliver to appear before the House of Commons. In the drama that unfolded, Temple Bar would, for the last time in this saga, play the role for which it was actually built – as a physical barrier between Westminster and the City. On 19 March, Crosby prised himself out of bed and made his painful way into Westminster, followed by Wilkes in a separate coach, and escorted as a hero by the 'Liverymen, Freemen and Citizens' of the City, who had been urged by a handbill to come out in a strong show of support for their lord mayor. Before the House of Commons, Crosby argued, significantly, that had he acted otherwise, he would have broken his mayoral oath to defend the City's charters. It little availed the defiant Londoners: on 25 March, Oliver was sentenced by a House of Commons vote to be imprisoned in the Tower of London until the end of the parliamentary session. It would be Crosby's turn to face the same punishment two days later. The MPs, ferociously angry though they were, avoided a direct confrontation with Wilkes: they recognised that the situation was already combustible enough. To summon Wilkes to the bar of the House would be to light the match.[20]

Even so, the City was stirred up like a hornet's nest: the aldermen and the Court of Common Council rose as one to salute Crosby, Oliver and Wilkes for standing for the City's freedoms. They organised a fund for the legal defence of the first two as they were being judged by the House of Commons. When it was Crosby's turn to be sentenced on 27 March, the occasion sparked violence in the streets outside Parliament: Lord North's coach was attacked as the crowd tried to drag the terrified prime minister from the carriage before ripping it apart, North bleeding from a wound and still cowering inside the cab. Inside Parliament there was alarm on both sides of the House. From the opposition benches, Edmund Burke scribbled frantic notes to his patron, Lord Rockingham: 'The Mob is grown very riotous. Very few of our friends here. It is impossible to know what to do . . . I am monstrously vexed'.[21]

It was as Crosby was being conducted to the Tower that Temple

Bar played its part. The messenger escorting the prisoner was none other than Climentson, earlier a victim of the lord mayor's taunts at the Mansion House. As the procession reached the end of the Strand, the heavy fortified gates of Temple Bar were slammed firmly shut by some of the freemen of the City. A crowd surged around the carriage and seized Climentson. For a terrifying moment, it looked as though the sergeant-at-arms might be lynched but for the lord mayor, who persuaded his would-be rescuers to open Temple Bar and to allow Climentson to do his duty. To his great credit, Climentson could see that his onetime adversary was truly suffering from his illness, so he had the coach take the lord mayor home to the Mansion House rather than the Tower. Crosby, who felt it his duty to face his penalty, managed to rise from his bed early the next morning and hobble his way to the Tower. He and Oliver remained imprisoned until 10 May 1771, when the king dissolved Parliament, putting an end to the sentence imposed by the House.[22]

When Oliver and Crosby emerged from the Tower and walked across its drawbridge, they were cheered by a crowd who included the members of the City's Common Council, crammed into fifty-three coaches lined up in procession. The guns of the City's Honourable Artillery Company boomed in salute. With acclamations ringing in their ears, the triumphant progress threaded its way to the Mansion House for a banquet. As the splendid Egyptian Hall resounded to the clinking of glasses and raucous laughter, Parliament gave up its fight against the printers and, thereafter, allowed the press to publish debates freely.[23]

THE PRINTERS' CASE stood for the freedom of the press, but it had centred on the defence of the privileges of the City of London against incursion from central authority. Yet one of the most striking achievements of the Wilkite controversies was the political mobilisation of working people across the metropolis. Wilkes drew his support both from the artisans, freemen and liverymen of the City and from the artisanal, shopkeeping and mercantile classes among Middlesex voters. Yet his appeal went even further. He could also count on the raucous, window-smashing and head-breaking support from the mass of the disenfranchised, toiling, labouring population who had turned out in such teeming numbers on Saint George's Fields on the fateful day of the massacre. These were the working poor of the metropolis, who had experienced for themselves the harsh hand of the eighteenth-century state, particularly in the economic distress and strike waves of the 1760s. In July 1768, in a spectacularly grisly series of executions, seven striking East End heavers (the grimily poor labourers who unloaded the coal from ships in the London docks) were hanged, not as usual at the gallows at Tyburn (on the present-day site of Marble Arch in the West End), but at Sun Tavern Fields, off the Ratcliffe Highway, as a deterrent to their fellow residents of the East End. A year and a half later, it was the turn of some rioting weavers, who were executed at Bethnal Green, close to their very homes in Spitalfields, the better (an official explained) to 'strike Terror into the Rioters'. For the working people of London, Wilkes was another victim of a harsh, unforgiving system that seemed stacked in favour of the elites. For the apprentices and journeymen of the wider metropolis, Wilkes was someone who at least seemed to defend the common people from the naked power of the propertied.[24]

Wilkes and his supporters had also injected fresh adrenaline into London's political bloodstream. In the City's defiance of king and Parliament, its magistrates had begun to demand political reform as a way of obstructing what many Britons feared to be the onward march of ministerial power. Wilkes was elected lord mayor of London in 1774 and, that same year, was again chosen to represent Middlesex in Parliament. This time, he was finally allowed to take his seat. Two years later, he delivered a speech in which he demanded that 'every free agent in this kingdom should be represented in parliament', meaning universal male suffrage. 'The meanest mechanic, the poorest peasant and day-labourer, has important rights respecting his personal liberty ... [S]ome share, therefore, in the making of those laws, which deeply interest them, and to which they are expected to pay obedience, should be reserved even to this inferior, but most useful, set of men in the community'. Wilkes did not secure a single vote in support. Only Lord North bothered to respond. He assumed that Wilkes was 'not serious'. Time would soon prove that Wilkes's call had real resonance across the metropolis and the country at large.[25]

Like New York, London in this period experienced an injection of popular energy into politics. It was a development that saw the leadership of the City use the defence of its privileges to make a broader point about the rights and freedoms of British subjects in general and so try to connect the freedoms of London with those of the country at large. Unlike in New York, therefore, where the wider popular mobilisation was a protest against both the British government and the dominance of the local, colonial elites, in London the broader metropolitan movement in support of Wilkes did not seek to attack the privileges of the City, let alone the power of its plutocratic aldermen and lord mayor. Instead, the two coalesced, which may be one reason the resistance to authority in London, though certainly riotous, did not become revolutionary. Instead, the privileges and political institutions of the City were deployed to obstruct the attacks of the king and Parliament against Wilkes, against the rights of Middlesex voters and against the freedom of the press: the closure of Temple Bar during these controversies gave powerful physical expression to this defiance.

Since the City's liberties were robustly rooted in its charters and recognised (however grudgingly) by all sides, including the king and Parliament, Londoners were able to make their protests without challenging the wider structures of politics.

This was in marked contrast to New York – and to the American colonies at large – where the government seemed able to brush aside the political institutions, even the colonial assemblies, in pursuit of controversially divisive policies, and where indeed Parliament claimed the right to do so. This was a further reason that the events of the 1760s and early 1770s in London did not take a revolutionary turn: New Yorkers were eventually pushed into a corner where, in order to defend their rights, they had to do so not just *within* the existing political institutions, but *against* them. Londoners, on the other hand, were able to use the existing privileges of the City to make their points and in doing so appeared to have been defending the liberties of all subjects.

Yet this meant that, in the future, there would be limits as to how far the City's leaders would go to challenge royal and parliamentary authority. Defending privilege and existing freedoms was one thing, but pressing for root-and-branch political change, as Wilkes did, was quite another. For all that Wilkes's appeal for universal male suffrage would resonate with more radical, progressive spirits across Britain, he could not count on carrying the City with him. For that, reformers would have to look further afield – across the metropolis and across the country. In this respect, the gathering of Wilkes's supporters on Saint George's Fields was an important development. It represented the political engagement of people, women as well as men, craft workers, apprentices, journeymen, who were unlikely to have enjoyed the right to vote or to have benefited from the privileges of the City of London but who strongly related to the battles waged by Wilkes. In this respect, Saint George's Fields was an appropriate spot: it had no direct relationship to the privileges of the City, but it was an expanse upon which large groups from all walks of life and all parts of the metropolis could freely gather. Moreover, it was, symbolically enough, across the river from the City, a geographical separation that could be taken to anticipate the parting of ways between the City and the British democratic reform movement in the later eighteenth century.

CHAPTER THREE

THE KING AGAINST PARIS, 1763–1776

IN THE MID-1760S, New Yorkers and Londoners resisted what they feared was the invasion by government power of their rights and liberties as British subjects. In both cities, the resistance made use of places in the cityscape that had recognisable, symbolic resonance, were customary locations for people to gather or had practical purposes in terms of location, size and use. Usually, these buildings and spaces had a combination of these things. New York's Common, for example, was a habitual meeting place, but it also assumed symbolic importance as the site of the Liberty Pole, which in turn was a provocative gesture of defiance towards the British army barracks that overlooked the field. London's Temple Bar was a representation in stone of the separateness and the unique freedoms enjoyed by the City of London, but its strong gates were also used in a physical, tactical sense, barring the way of the supporters of king and Parliament at two critical moments in the Wilkes controversies. Moreover, the movement in the location of political action from the habitual bastions of elite politics such as London's Mansion House and New York's City Hall, into the streets and open spaces of the cities, into the domain of the working people, represented a democratisation of the resistance.

In New York, this development did indeed have revolutionary consequences because the British government, by rebuffing the protests emanating from the existing political institutions of the colonies, seemed to compel its American opponents to mobilise opposition both in the public spaces of the city (the Common and the streets, the waterfront and the taverns) and eventually in the more private venues (the home, the store and the workshop, places where men and women engaged with politics in their daily lives by enforcing the boycott on British goods). In London, because the established political institutions of the City were able robustly to defend themselves against the incursions of the central government, the implications proved to be radical, but not revolutionary. By coalescing around the figure of John Wilkes and others of the City's leadership, the popular mobilisation, writ large on Saint George's Fields, reinforced rather than challenged the privileges that empowered the City to resist the king and Parliament. Even so, the emergence of the wider metropolitan movement had radical implications that would go far beyond the City's defence of its traditional freedoms and mark the beginnings of the pressure for democratic change.

The political situation in Paris in the bitter wake of the Seven Years' War was, at first, more analogous to that of London than of New York. Here also there was resistance to what French subjects regarded as the invasion of their rights by an overbearing monarchy, and here, too, this opposition would mobilise a wide cross-section of the city, but, for now, that opposition, even more so than in London, would focus on the defence of one of the most important legal institutions in the kingdom of France, the Parlement of Paris. Its location, in the Palais de Justice on the Île de la Cité, made this very heart of the metropolis the site of some of the most bruising collisions between the king and his subjects prior to the Revolution of 1789, but at the same time the building itself expressed the close, if argumentative, relationship between the Parlement and the monarch and, like Temple Bar in London, the fundamentally conservative orientation of the Parlement's defiance.

THE ÎLE DE LA CITÉ is the island in the centre of Paris around which the River Seine bends. For centuries, the Cité had been the political, legal and religious heart of the kingdom. From here, the great towers of the twelfth-century Notre-Dame Cathedral dominated the city, proclaiming the authority of the archbishop of Paris across the whole kingdom. The Cité – then crammed with teetering tenements and one of the most densely populated parts of Paris – was also the kingdom's legal centre. On the western half of the island, not only was the elegant Palais de Justice the seat of the powerful sovereign court, the Parlement of Paris, but its airy, classical façades fused with the more forbidding turrets and dark cells of the Conciergerie, the prison where trembling convicts awaited their fate. The complex also housed fifteen other subordinate courts, a veritable 'judicial city' within the city, employing an amazing forty thousand Parisians. So this compact island was a congested, throbbing place of lawyers making their way to court, their black cloaks flapping; of the young and rather anarchic legal clerks darting in the same direction; and of law students ambling on their way to learn from the procedures and oratory of the country's greatest barristers. Among these people of law were the clients and their families, as well as the everyday bustle of city life – carriages, carts, street vendors and the dwellers of the nearby slums in the narrow, labyrinthine streets. There were ecclesiastics, cassocked priests or habited monks and nuns, on their way to observe their religious duties in the cathedral or to tend to the sick in the nearby Hôtel-Dieu, the central hospital in Paris. The existence of this great institution also meant that the island was a magnet for the poor and desperate who shambled towards the hospital to find shelter, treatment or, all too often, a place to die. Always a centre of Parisian life, with the Parlement the Île de la Cité became the most hotly contested political site in Paris before the final revolutionary crisis of the old order, a scene of both legal struggle and popular protest.[1]

This was because the Parlement of Paris was the most powerful of the thirteen 'sovereign courts' whose uneven jurisdictions covered most of the kingdom. It was from these courts that the monarchy met the most determined opposition prior to the French Revolution. The French Bourbon monarchs claimed to have absolute, God-given power, but in fact the king's word did not become law until his decrees had secured the assent of these great law courts. Each of these courts had the right to 'register' royal edicts, a process by which the magistrates scrutinised the king's decrees, making sure that they did not conflict with the different privileges and legal customs within their particular jurisdiction. Then the Parlements entered the royal edict on their statute books: without that registration, it did not become law.[2]

The magistrates relished this role, and in the absence of any elected legislature they cast themselves, not without some sincerity, as the *only* constitutional safeguard that people had against the abuse of royal power. The magistrates cited 'fundamental laws' and an historic 'constitution' against the 'despotism' of the crown. Some judges began to claim that there existed a contract between the king and 'nation', in which the Parlements represented the latter. In doing so, in the middle of the eighteenth century the sovereign courts had begun to look to the wider public – the informed, politically engaged people among the king's subjects – for moral support in their disputes with the crown. Lawyers seeking public reputations had their legal briefs printed – often in runs counting into the thousands – and literate Parisians read them avidly, enjoying the legal drama of causes célèbres and, by the 1780s, relishing the criticism of corruption, privilege and intolerance that many of their authors injected into their arguments. Among those who listened agog to the great barristers and who read their published briefs in the 1770s was a young law student from Arras named Maximilien Robespierre.[3]

Yet the Parlement was as much a part of the old regime as the monarchy itself. The courts accepted that the ultimate say always lay with the king, and they usually kept to their primary role, which was to ensure that his word conformed to the existing laws. When they did object, they rarely attacked the monarch himself, but claimed that he had been misled or 'surprised' by ill-intentioned ministers. The story of the relationship between king and Parlements was not one of unrelenting confrontation, but one of wavering between conflict and cooperation, in which usually the Parlements offered powerful legal support to the monarch's authority. On his side, the king was well aware that, when he ruled through his magistrates, they gave his acts the full sanction of legal authority. Consequently, the Parlements, although prone to indulging in fiery rhetoric and harbouring constitutional aspirations, were bound up with the political and social hierarchies of the monarchy. This was a system that the magistrates had no intention of destroying. Rather, they wanted to strengthen their position within it by ensuring that the king ruled through the law.[4]

The fraught but fundamentally symbiotic relationship between the Parlement and the king was magnificently embodied in the very fabric of Paris's Palais de Justice. The portico at the entrance to the complex, resting at the top of the broad, generous steps leading up from the Cour de Mai, boasted four Doric columns, the whole designed after a fire in 1776. The construction, significantly enough, was paid for by the king, even as he was locked in political conflict with the magistrates, and work continued on it until completion in 1787, another year in which monarch and Parlement clashed. Both sides assumed that the struggle, no matter how bitter, would always be contained within the institutional framework of the old order and that, in the delivery of justice, king and judges would ultimately work together.

Just as important, when the magistrates resisted reforms, they did so in the defence of privilege – their own (all judges in the Parlement were from the aristocracy), that of the nobility at large, the provinces, municipalities and guilds. These were of material importance to French subjects, bringing exemptions from taxation, and it was for this reason that frustrated royal officials and enlightened reformers always had to confront the obstacle course of privilege that stymied any efforts at systematic change. The nobles and upper clergy – the bishops and the great abbots – enjoyed the most privileges, the great mass of peasantry the least, but they were all part of the legal fabric that the Parlements were duty-bound to defend. There was also a constitutional argument: in the absence of the civil rights enjoyed by Britons (as progressive French people were enviously aware), such as habeas corpus and taxation by consent, privilege offered the only legal protection the individual had against the potentially crushing might of the absolutist state. Consequently, when the Parlements resisted reform by fending off attacks on privilege, they could argue that they were protecting the only 'freedoms' that French subjects enjoyed. They were thus reasserting their claim to be the thin red line between 'absolutism' (the legal exercise of royal power) and despotism (unlimited power wielded for the capricious desires of the monarch).

The central importance of privilege to the Parlement – as to pre-revolutionary society as a whole – was scripted in the very name of the courtyard below the entrance steps of the Palais de Justice. Enclosed behind ornate, gilded gates, the Cour de Mai took its name from the special right enjoyed by the Basoche, the order of the procurator's clerks, to raise a tree bedecked with ribbons every May. This jurists' maypole was customarily planted to the left of the broad steps, and, minor though this custom may appear, it was a reminder that all French subjects, like the legal clerks of the Parlement, belonged in one way or another to a corporate body – the nobility, the clergy, a professional order, a guild, a town or a province, for example – that enjoyed its own identity and jealously guarded the special rights that defined the status of its members.[5]

It was as France struggled to recover from the humiliating defeat in the Seven Years' War that the defence of privilege sparked one of the deepest political conflicts between the king and the Parlements before the French Revolution. Louis XV entrusted the salvaging of national strength and honour to the dynamic figure of the duc de Choiseul. In his long tenure of power, juggling responsibilities with energetic shrewdness, Choiseul pushed through an ambitious programme of reform aimed at reinvigorating the French state by modernising the armed forces, investing in infrastructure and securing the finances. For a short time, the monarchy and the magistrates – for the most part – did work together, buoyed and energised in the patriotic post-war backlash, a jingoism reflected in the immense popularity of an Anglophobic play, *The Siege of Calais*, which first played at the Comédie-Française in 1765 and centred around the famous incident of the heroism of the six burghers during the Hundred Years' War. This touched the Zeitgeist in which French people spoke of the good of the country as a whole, the *patrie*, and of patriotism as a virtue that could reinvigorate that state. In this atmosphere, the king's reformist minister Choiseul and the Parlements managed to work together, but it did not last. When the clash came, it began not in Paris, but in Brittany, where in 1763 the Parlement of Rennes flatly stated that the government's recovery programme broke the province's special privileges. The trial of strength between the king's governor in Brittany, the duc d'Aiguillon, and the Parlement of Brittany spiralled into a national crisis when d'Aiguillon had several of the magistrates arrested. This assault on the Breton institution stirred the Paris Parlement into action: according to the magistrates, all the Parlements were in fact the fragmented remnants of a single judicial body that had once advised the king. Thus, they could act together, if need be, to uphold the rule of law in the kingdom.[6]

On this basis, the court in Paris issued 'remonstrances'. In a strict legal sense, such remonstrances were meant to be private criticisms of a royal edict, but they proved to be one of the most important weapons in a Parlement's arsenal, not least because in the eighteenth century the courts began to publish them for public consumption. The king could in theory brush aside the magistrates' objections through a ceremony called a *lit de justice*, literally a 'bed of justice', in which the monarch or his represent-ative appeared in the court and from the royal divan (the *lit*) declared the edict to be law. Yet to do this, the crown had to be sure of its strength, because the Parlements became increasingly adept in mobilising public opinion in their support: to move against them in the wrong circumstances would be to provoke a storm of public fury, at best, and disorder, riot and maybe even rebellion, at worst. This time, however, the king felt strong enough to deliver a powerful rebuke to the Parisian magistrates in the 'flagellation session' of 2 March 1766.

On that day, Louis XV, now ageing but still with all his royal bearing, arrived in his carriage outside the Palais de Justice. On these royal visits, the king's coach traditionally stopped at the

Sainte-Anne portal of Notre-Dame Cathedral, on which there is a statue of an enthroned Virgin Mary with the baby Jesus on her lap: the child is bearing, significantly enough, the Book of the Law. From there, accompanied by his courtiers, he would make his way to the Palais de Justice, where he would enter the Sainte-Chapelle, Louis IX's elegantly magnificent chapel in the heart of the palace, watched respectfully by the cream of the French legal profession. Louis would usually hear Mass in the dazzling Gothic elegance of the upper chapel, lit through its stained-glass windows as if inside a prism, the daylight outside casting its purples, reds and blues across the tiled floor inside. After worship, the king would cross into the Palais de Justice and make his way to the great chamber where the Parlement of Paris met.[7]

But not on this occasion: on 2 March 1766, as Horace Walpole, the British novelist and profuse letter writer who was living it up in Paris at the time, put it with his ironic pen, 'There has been a violent clap of thunder here. Tother [*sic*] morning the King, with all his lightnings about him, appeared suddenly in the parliament'. The monarch's carriage stopped in the Cour de Mai, and he alighted, heading straight up the broad steps before entering the Galerie Mercière, turning right and then emerging into the expansive Salle des Pas Perdus. This 'room of lost footsteps' was a vast lobby whose name evoked the sound of hundreds of footfalls being muffled in the expanse of vaulted space and drowned out by the hubbub of lawyers and notaries as they paced the floor with their clients and colleagues, discussing their business. On a normal day, the people of law would have negotiated through a throng of retailers who displayed and sold their goods and services at stalls clustered around the lobby's great pillars: booksellers, swordsmiths, scribes and pastry vendors. The massive Gros Pilier (fat pillar) had for centuries been the spot around which lawyers clustered, offering pro bono legal advice to the city's poor. All this amounted to an important social and political fact: the Palais de Justice was, for Parisians, *their* place for legal redress, and the Parlement was *their* Parlement. The courts were a public space, one that the king could never entirely control.[8]

Yet on that day the king was going to do his utmost to assert himself against his fractious magistrates. He was escorted across the Salle des Pas Perdus and through the double doors in its northern wall, which gave into the magnificent Grand' Chambre, the great chamber of the Paris Parlement, decorated to underscore the majesty of the law while conceding the ultimate authority of the monarch. At the northern end of the chamber, a raised stage was bedecked with a carpet decorated with fleurs-de-lis, the symbol of the monarchy, and on top of which was the king's seat – the divan from which he pronounced his *lits de justice*. At the foot of the stage was an armchair for the royal chancellor. The judges' places were arranged symmetrically across the room in front of the stage: Louis, Walpole continued, had taken the court by surprise, and he gruffly 'ordered four privy councillors, not peers, to follow him into the chamber' – in other words, his speech was to be delivered not (as was customary) by the Parlement's own magistrates, but by his closest advisers, who were told to sit at his feet and, Walpole explained, 'read a *Discours*, in which he informed the giants, that they were nothing but magistrates and rebels, and that he alone is Jupiter Omnipotent and Omniscient'.[9]

The king's speech was a tirade against the magistrates, who, bewigged and resplendent in their robes, listened in stunned, if angry, silence. Everyone in the room knew that Louis XV had appeared to put the magistrates in their place, but probably no one expected the chastisement that they actually received from the royal tongue. At the climax of this, the 'flagellation session', the king rounded on his judges: 'Sovereign power resides in my person only ... [M]y courts derive their existence and their authority from me alone . . . [T]o me alone belongs legislative power without subordination and undivided . . . [P]ublic order in its entirety emanates from me, and the rights and interests of the nation, which some dare to regard as a separate body from the monarchy, are necessarily united with my rights and interests, and repose only in my hands'.[10]

This was an uncompromising statement of absolute royal power, the idea that all legitimate authority remained with Louis. At the same time, however, he implied that such authority would be exercised through established legal channels and would accord with the 'rights and interests of the nation', which he himself embodied. Thus, the rule of law supposedly distinguished 'absolutism' from 'despotism', which by contrast was driven by the unchecked whims of the monarch. Just as Britons and Americans were acutely sensitive to any dangers to the balance in their 'constitution', so eighteenth-century French people were alive to the dangers that their monarchy could all too easily slip from 'absolutism' into the foul pit of 'despotism'. All the ceremony that a king's visit to the Parisian law courts involved was meant to impress everyone with the sacredness and legitimacy of royal power. And since Louis had skipped the customary Mass in the Sainte-Chapelle before delivering his bludgeoning rebuke, after he left the reeling magistrates he felt compelled to offer some sign of devotion to God. As his coach was rolling over the Pont Neuf away from the Île de la Cité, he ordered the driver to stop so that, in full public view, he could kneel on the carriageway and offer his prayers.

After deliberating for seven days, the magistrates sent a delegation to express their contrition, but added a rider that still protested against the king's treatment of the Parlement of Brittany. From here the spiky relations between Louis and his magistrates deteriorated rapidly. The crisis reached a boiling point when the Parlement of Brittany tried to impeach Governor d'Aiguillon in

1768. D'Aiguillon, as was his right, opted to be tried by his peers, namely, the Parlement of Paris, a gambit that the king's new chancellor, René de Maupeou, actually hoped would exonerate the duke. Instead, the Parisian magistrates turned the trial into an investigation of the inner workings of the government itself. Louis XV decided to put an abrupt halt to the proceedings and in a *lit de justice* in June 1770 formally exonerated the governor of Brittany. This provoked a storm of protest from the Parlements. The king boldly tried to face down this judicial opposition, turning up at the Paris Parlement to repeat his tongue-lashing of four years before and imposing an 'Edict of Discipline' aimed at restricting the capacity of the Parlements to resist royal authority. The preamble was what really struck home. Written by Maupeou, it denied that the Parlements represented the nation and that they had any essential legal role in implementing the king's will. The wording was deliberately provocative – and the Parlement of Paris swallowed the bait. The judges used one of their ultimate weapons, a judicial strike, and refused to cooperate with the crown.[11]

In the new year, the government struck. In the night of 19–20 January 1771, royal musketeers banged on the doors of the town houses of every magistrate and demanded of each startled judge that he categorically state – yes or no – whether he was now ready to return to work: seventy defiantly vowed to continue with the strike, thirty-five refused to respond outright and fifty, isolated and confronting the king's soldiers in the cold darkness, agreed to resume service. Yet their attitudes hardened when, the following night, the king, urged on by Maupeou, issued *lettres de cachet* – arrest warrants issued by the monarch – against those judges who persisted in their opposition and exiled them to the provinces. The rest then rejoined the strike and so were bundled into exile in turn. Maupeou then began the process of smashing the power of the Parlements altogether, remodelling those in the provinces but taking a sledgehammer to the Parlement of Paris. The Parisian court saw its far-reaching jurisdiction broken up into six compact legal parcels, each presided over by its own superior court that, moreover, could register laws, but not remonstrate. The Paris court, now spoken of as the Parlement Maupeou, had a jurisdiction restricted to Paris and the immediate area around. For the remaining years of Louis XV's reign, these measures had the intended effect of taming the magistrates.[12]

Yet Maupeou's coup also provoked public uproar. Two of the greatest enlightened minds of eighteenth-century France – novelist, playwright and historian François Marie-Arouet Voltaire and mathematician and social reformer Antoine de Caritat, the marquis de Condorcet – famously supported Maupeou's reforms because they anticipated that a full-scale reform of the law would follow. Yet they were isolated voices. Anne-Robert Turgot, the great enlightened reformer, fretted that Maupeou had taken a major stride towards 'legal despotism'. For the politically engaged public at large, it was far worse than that: the coup showed that despotism was already a reality. If the king could, at a stroke, remove the most imposing legal brake on royal power, then who or what could prevent him from doing anything?[13]

The 'Maupeou revolution' sent shock waves deep into French public opinion. 'Every thing with regard to Politicks is in great confusion', wrote an English noblewoman, Lady Mary Coke, from Paris in April 1771. 'Everybody thinks the Chancellor a bold man, & 'tis not easy to say what turn things will take'.[14]

Royal edicts and the remonstrances of the Parlements, once meant to be a closed discussion between the king and his magistrates, had by now become a matter for public debate, especially in the social spaces of Paris, particularly the cafés whose clientele could read and discuss the latest news, indulge in illegal and often scurrilous pamphlets (*libelles*) and hear the latest gossip and rumours. Bookseller Siméon-Prosper Hardy saw notices being stuck onto walls around the city, seething with hatred for Maupeou: 'All placards found in various places in Paris prove how far the excitement had gone, and how desirable it was that some angel of light and peace should come and unseal the eyes of our monarch by showing him the height of the precipice from which he was about the cast himself without knowing it, believing that he was increasing his authority'.[15]

The next year, Hardy noted that in carnival week (in early March), there was an exuberant demonstration outside the chancellor's town house on the rue Neuve-Saint-Augustin by 'a very great number of masques, and an even greater crowd of benevolent spectators, foolish individuals such as are picked out of the life of the people, and almost all in the pay of the police'. Hardy assumed that the spectacle was designed by the police to make sure that Maupeou could assure the king that 'never had the citizens of his good city of Paris given so may signs of rejoicing and content', although in reality 'a good many people were saying that all His Majesty's subjects were suffering greatly from the disastrous revolution that has just been brought about'. Horace Walpole accepted that Maupeou, 'with eyes equally penetrating, acute, and suspicious', had ignoble motives: 'Power was his object, despotism his road'.[16]

In a society where people were less accustomed to assemble freely and to express their opposition to the government of the day, Paris had no equivalent of New York's Common or London's Saint George's Fields where people could legally rally in protest. Instead, the Palais de Justice became a symbol of the freedoms of French subjects, the more so because the Parlement seemed in 1771 to be on the verge of extinction. In the mid-1780s, Louis-Sébastien Mercier, a progressive Parisian writer (and later a revolutionary), described the typical response of the people of the city to the exile of the judges: 'When the magistrates are exiled or cast out of the temple of justice by armed force, they are called 'revenants' [spirits] because people are so convinced that they will soon be back ... [E]ven one soldier who, on duty at the gates of the palace, now empty of the guardians of the law, said while patrolling: "I am guarding the sepulchre, while waiting for the resurrection"'.[17]

In 1771 it seemed to anxious Parisians that they would have to wait a long time for that 'resurrection'. For now, what, they asked, would happen after this one obstacle to royal power had been so easily cast aside? The answer seemed all too obvious: there was nothing to protect the privileges and freedoms of the kingdom from the will of the king and his ministers. John Moore, a Scottish surgeon who had studied in Paris, returned in 1772 to find public opinion coming to terms with the shock: 'The security, even the existence, of the parliament of Paris, depending entirely on the pleasure of the king, and having no other weapons ... but justice, argument, and reason, their fate might have been foreseen ... The members were disgraced, and the parliament abolished. The measure was considered as violent; the exiles were regarded as martyrs; the people were astonished and grieved'.[18]

Yet slowly, the monarchy itself was trying to accommodate the public support that the Parlements enjoyed, and calmer heads close to the king understood that the magistrates would be essential partners if he wanted to rally the people behind the throne and give legitimacy to administrative and fiscal reform. So when the well-intentioned yet ponderous Louis XVI succeeded his grandfather Louis XV in 1774, he sensed that a fresh start was needed, and the young king reversed the crown's victory. Maupeou was dismissed before the year was out, his system repudiated and the Parlements restored in the old style – personnel, remonstrances and all. Initially buoyed by a wave of popular affection, Louis thought that dismissing Maupeou would satisfy public hopes for a change of political direction. He also appointed, as controller-general of finances, the enlightened reformer Turgot. Yet the appointment of a new ministry merely fuelled public expectations that the young king would completely abjure the 'despotic' policies of his grandfather. As his new chancellor advised him, 'There is no monarchy without the Parlement'. So Louis XVI and his ministers recalled the magistrates to win back public opinion and popular loyalties. Louis himself wrote that 'it may be considered politically unwise, but it seems to me that it is the general will and I wish to be loved'. The political risk was whether the Parlements would toe the royal line.[19]

RELATIONS BETWEEN THE recalled magistrates and the crown were certainly stormy, but not fruitless, in the first years of the new reign. Between 1774 and 1782, the magistrates registered most of the edicts handed down by Louis XVI without protest.[20] The refreshed relationship between crown and judges was reflected in the king's response to the fire that tore through the Palais de Justice in 1776. Apart from providing the funds for the restoration, including the construction of the new colonnaded entrance on the Cour de Mai, he also provided a relief for the palace interior, which was displayed above the entrance from the Galerie Mercière into the Salle des Pas Perdus. This work depicted Louis XVI crowned with olive branches while holding the shield of Minerva, which, according to a guidebook from the time, 'characterises the wisdom and virtues of that august monarch'. In an equally powerful message, however, the relief was also supported by garlands of laurels that connected the monarch to a fasces, a bundle of rods 'symbolising Strength . . . an emblem of the unity of the Sovereign Courts, which, by the maintenance of the Laws, form the foundation of the State'. The relief projected a hopeful message, that king and judiciary would work together for the good of the country, and an implication that the monarch respected the legal limits to his power.[21]

Yet things between crown and magistrates were far from rosy, even in these years. The Parlement of Paris helped to derail Turgot's reform programme in 1776, which came in the punchy shape of 'Six Acts' that included the abolition of the guilds (as too resistant to economic development and trade freedom) and ending the corvée (the hated compulsory labour on the royal highways imposed on the peasantry). Although Louis XVI imposed them with a *lit de justice*, he was truly alarmed by the howls of protest from all parts of French society. He abandoned his minister, who was dismissed in May 1776. The Parlement's resistance to Turgot's reforms was indicative of its political purpose: its primary goal was to defend the status quo, a society based on hierarchies of privilege, and particularly aristocratic privilege. That the court's conservative impulses were all too real was shown when the Parlement bared its teeth in 1766, the very year of its constitutional collision with Louis XV. It upheld the sentence of a court in the northern town of Abbeville, sentencing the eighteen-year-old chevalier de la Barre, who had been convicted of singing blasphemous songs, to have his tongue ripped out and his right hand cut off before his torment was ended by decapitation. His body was then burnt and his ashes scattered. The barbaric sentence gave Voltaire cause to take up his rapier-like pen, comparing the Parlement with the Spanish Inquisition. The Danish ambassador remarked on the apparent paradox: 'Everyone is surprised to see magistrates who wish to be the protectors of the people and to rein in authority demonstrate such a dark spirit of persecution'. The lesson was drawn by Malesherbes, the government's light-handed censor, who warned that 'the judges can themselves be judged by an instructed Public'.[22]

The public itself would be torn, since the struggles between the crown and the Parlements were evidently not clear-cut battles between reaction and progress. In his colourful pen sketches of Parisian life, Louis-Sébastien Mercier captured the ambiguity: the Parlement certainly 'opposed a salutary dike against dangerous edicts and stopped the all-too-violent blows of absolute power ... but then why do they almost always lag behind the ideas of the century?' Moreover, in the two decades that followed the Maupeou coup, the civic culture of 'public opinion' that had been developing from the mid-eighteenth century among France's better-off, literate subjects was steadily infused with a language that idealised such concepts as nation, fatherland (*patrie*), reason, citizens and natural rights. This development was, in no small part, inadvertently encouraged by the Parlements in their struggles with the king and in their appeals to the public. Yet ultimately, the new political language would collide with the Parlement's own assumptions that society rested on hierarchies of privilege and corporate bodies. The full implications were not yet clear, however, and for now the Parlements, however imperfect, were the *only* institutions that seemed capable of defending what few liberties the public actually enjoyed. Of the Paris Parlement Mercier wrote, 'We owe the enjoyment of those rights which have not yet been snatched off us to its vigilance and courage'. The danger came when the king's subjects, 'seeing nothing between themselves and these fearful blows [of despotism], get alarmed – and rightly so – at this terrifying void'. That was the lesson of the Maupeou coup: the crown could, all too easily, tear out the only institution that, for all its flaws, seemed truly to defend what remained of the liberties of the people. Thomas Jefferson would later comment when he was US minister to France, 'If the king has the power to do this, the government of the country is a pure despotism'.[23]

In Paris the political confrontations that raged during the

recovery after the Seven Years' War arose between the king and the magistrates. When there was conflict, it was by and large waged through the long-established rituals within the great chambers and lobbies of the Palais de Justice: the remonstrances, the *lits de justice* and even the punishment of exile were all part of the customary arsenal of political confrontation between the monarchy and the Parlement. Yet into this alignment of formal legal weaponry was injected public opinion. The magistrates – and, increasingly, the king – were well aware of the growing capacity of Parisians to express their views, but the judges assumed that public opinion would rally behind them in their periodic combative bouts with the king. The cafés and salons might resonate with argument and rumour, but ultimately the politically engaged people of the city would, for the most part, lend their moral support to the Parlement, just as Moore, Walpole, Mercier and other observers noted that it had. Parisians in particular were used to frequenting the Palais de Justice whenever they had legal business: the Parlement was their court, the champion of their rights. This gave the alignment of public opinion with the aristocratic magistrates an essentially conservative direction, since for most French people their 'rights' were their privileges, and the Parlements – as their resistance to Turgot's progressive reforms in 1776 showed – were the staunchest defenders of those. This, in turn, ensured that, as the magistrates and king alike expected and hoped that it would, even the bitterest of political controversies would play out within the chambers of the Palais de Justice. Even when the Parlement was exiled, the empty courts became the symbol of the struggle in defence of the people's rights and the laws of the kingdom against the 'despotism' of the king and his ministers.

So as in London where the defence of the freedoms of the City would prove to have a conservative orientation, so in Paris public support for the Parlement bolstered rather than undermined the hierarchies of privilege that defined the elaborate structures of pre-revolutionary society. Yet when confronted with a new and altogether more intense crisis, this careful balance would shift dramatically, and, when it did, the political initiative would fall to Parisian places that were far removed from the lobbies and chambers of the Palais de Justice.

CHAPTER FOUR

NEW YORK CITY IN
REVOLUTION AND WAR, 1775–1783

I N Paris political conflict had so far been contained within the
institutions of the old order. Public opinion, though it certainly
raged across the city – in cafés, theatres, salons, the streets and
among the hawkers and readers of underground pamphlets – still
focused on the Parlement as the best defender of the people against
the monarchy's despotic impulses. In London the mobilisation
of the wider working population of the metropolis in defence of
John Wilkes had democratic implications, but for now only a few
people – including Wilkes himself – were willing to stand up and
demand radical political change.

By contrast, the rising of New York's citizens in protest, boycott and, in April 1775, insurrection in spaces and places beyond
the established sites of colonial politics had decisively pushed the
city towards revolution. In the tense, often terrifying months that
followed, revolution and war marched in step, marking the city
in ways that were both political and strategic. From April 1775
to November 1783, New Yorkers experienced successively the

upheavals of revolution and the trauma of military occupation, both accompanied by the terrors and privations of war. The first phase prior to the capture of the city by the British was marked by a breakneck whirl of political and military activity, as the Patriots sought to consolidate their control over the city and prepare its defences. Then after the defeat of General George Washington's rebel forces on Long Island, Manhattan was occupied by the British army in September 1776, rupturing the direct connection between New York's war and the American Revolution until the redcoats left in November 1783.

All these experiences left their physical signs on the city, and although these changes were rarely permanent, they meant that New Yorkers experienced war and revolution not only through their personal privations and the ebb and flow of terror, hope and relief, but also, first, by witnessing the ways in which the trauma marked their cityscape and, second, by the ways in which politics in these heady and tormented days invaded the spaces of city life that had once been private. If politics had intruded into the homes and shops of New Yorkers during the pre-revolutionary boycotts, then war, revolution and military occupation intensified this experience, as the city's once familiar buildings were commandeered and altered; its resources requisitioned; its streets tramped over by thousands of soldiers, first American, then British; and as first one side and then the other pursued and persecuted their political opponents.

As with communities across the colonies, the revolutionary experience of New York City was one of bitter, sometimes sorrowful, division. All New Yorkers had to weigh their fears, their economic interests, their partisan loyalties and their principles, so that both sides in the visceral, violent break with British rule – 'Loyalists', who remained true to the king and to British rule, and 'Whigs' or 'Patriots', who supported the revolution – represented a cross-section of colonial society. Loyalists (derisively called 'Tories' by their opponents, after the ultraconservatives in Britain who had once rejected the 'Glorious Revolution' of 1688) ranged from the city's patricians to the retailers and craftsmen. Among the mercantile elites were men and women of the Delancey stripe, immersed in London's metropolitan culture through travel and personal connections. They were dependent on strong commercial ties with the empire, and they were bound by faith to the Church of England. They were fearful and often disdainful of the 'mob'. Yet the vast majority of Loyalists across the whole colony of New York were tradesmen, shopkeepers and farmers who – unlike their social equals who rallied behind the Mechanics Committee and the Sons of Liberty – were worried about the economic consequences of revolt, whose personal ties and social networks may have bound them with each other or with the Loyalist elites and who were repelled by the abrasive methods of the colonial resistance.[1]

Patriots also represented all shades of social background and opinion, from cautiously moderate landowners to zealously radical artisans and mariners. Among the moderates, like Gouverneur Morris, there seemed to be little to choose between the evil of tyranny from the mother country and the anarchy of rebellion, but they were equally certain that to stand against the revolution would be to invite something far worse than a political rupture: a social upheaval that threatened property and order. Some were also convinced, reluctantly, that the best way to preserve their freedoms was to resist their encroachments by king and Parliament, perhaps hoping that some new accommodation or compromise would eventually be made. Which side to take was a matter of political pressure, partisan loyalties, economic interests, community ties and conscience, and the agonising dilemma turned New York City into a political battleground, in which opinions – made all the shriller by an uncompromising press on both sides – became more and more polarised.[2]

As the Patriots took control and prepared the city for the British onslaught, they pursued their Loyalist opponents with increasing ruthlessness, turning the streets into scenes of often brutal political collision. So while in the formal locations of authority – City Hall and the Exchange – the revolutionaries tried to forge a workable system of government to confront the crisis, New Yorkers also experienced the upheaval in more direct ways, as the streets and buildings of their city, and sometimes their very homes, witnessed the political mobilisation of the population and felt the impact of military preparations.

At first, the revolutionary institutions that had taken power in the spring of 1775 reflected the divisions between Patriots and Loyalists: in the city government, the Committee of One Hundred, and in the Provincial Congress, which first met in the Exchange on 22 May 1775, the Sons of Liberty glowered across the chamber at their Tory opponents, with moderate Patriots poised awkwardly alongside the former. These fraught months were also days of desperate political brokerage and diplomacy between the Continental Congress and the British government, as hawkish hard-liners and dovish peacemakers on both sides circled and swooped between compromise and conflict. Both the internal politics in America and the last-gasp efforts at diplomacy encouraged a tortured, moderate course, whereby the colonists resisted the imperial measures but stopped short of open war. More cautious New York heads also wisely counselled moderation because of the looming presence of the British mailed fist: on 26 May 1775, the sixty-four-gun British man-of-war *Asia* dropped anchor in New York Harbour, an awe-inspiring display of firepower trained on the city itself.

It was impossible for New Yorkers, even if many tried to avoid taking sides, to remain unaffected by the revolution. In invading the streets and homes of the city, revolutionary politics in the months before the British assault became – whether the citizenry wanted it or not – a matter of everyday life. The Patriots turned the screws on their Loyalist opponents first by terrorising them through 'mob' action, so that the streets became, once again, the site of politics. Yet unlike the Stamp Act riots of 1765, which at their worst assailed property and physically threatened unpopular figures, the action now turned violent in a very real sense, reflecting the stakes that piled higher as the final rupture with Britain shunted closer with each new crisis. There was still, however, some heavily laden symbolism in some of the Patriot action. The Liberty Pole became the site where people would openly declare their support for the revolution – or be compelled to do so. In early March 1775, a tamer and trainer of wild horses named William Cunningham was dragged to the Liberty Pole by, one newspaper reported, a 'mob above two hundred men'. When he refused 'to go down on his knees and damn his Popish King George', instead roaring, 'God bless King George!' he was dragged across the Common, stripped and forced to flee the city. When he returned to New York with the British army in the autumn of 1776, he would become notorious, some said in revenge. In other cases, the assault on Loyalists represented a revolutionary purging of the city's civic institutions. Late at night on 10 May, a dishevelled Myles Cooper, president of King's College, narrowly escaped a crowd by squeezing through a window and scaling the college fence, still in his night-shirt: he had been woken and forewarned by his former student Alexander Hamilton, who was a moderate Patriot and was soon to become one of the country's great revolutionary leaders.[3]

In other cases, the persecution of Loyalists was driven by the impulse to stifle their voices wherever civil society usually flourished. In November 1775 Isaac Sears rode down Broadway with ninety-six horsemen – muskets slung over their shoulders – and raided the shop of James Rivington, publisher of the abrasive Loyalist newspaper the *New York Gazetteer*, close to Trinity Church, carrying off all his type before remounting and riding out of town singing 'Yankee Doodle' (itself a taunt against the dandyism now associated with British metropolitan elitism).

That Loyalist – or allegedly Loyalist – publishers were particularly vulnerable to the repression of dissent was shown during the visit to New York of pamphleteer and political thinker Thomas Paine in February and March 1776. Paine had won celebrity with the publication, in January, of an explosive tract, *Common Sense*, which may have sold as many as a quarter of a million copies. It urged Americans to embrace what many may already have considered, but that few had dared openly to admit: independence from Britain. Now, a month after this political dynamite had exploded into the debate on America's future, Paine had travelled northwards from his base in Philadelphia to see the impact of the revolution on New York. The author's celebrity was such that during his brief stay, there was an anti-Tory riot in support of *Common Sense*. A crowd attacked the home and print works of Samuel Loudon. The publisher was no Loyalist himself – he would flee New York when it fell to the British and become the official printer of the New York State Constitution in 1777 – but he was open-minded enough to produce a rebuttal to Paine's pamphlet. The offending Tory polemic was written anonymously by Charles Inglis, a rector of Trinity Church, who assailed *Common Sense* as one of 'the most artful, insidious and pernicious pamphlets' ever written. Getting wind of Loudon's enterprise, the crowd of Patriot artisans mustered angrily outside his home and shop at No. 5 Water Street and demanded that he reveal the identity of the author. Loudon, a strong-minded Scot, refused. At that the protesters surged forward, knocked Loudon aside, and tore through his home, reaching his office on the second floor, where they found fifteen hundred copies of Inglis's pamphlet. They emerged with the stacks of stitched paper piled high in their arms and marched uptown into the night and to the Common (reinforcing it as a site for uncompromising loyalty to the revolution), where the entire run was incinerated in a great pyre.[4]

In this climate of hostility, many Loyalists and fence-sitters slowly slipped away, including members of the Delancey dynasty. In October 1775 the governor of New York, William Tryon, abandoned the city for the safety of a British ship, *Dutchess of Gordon*, in the East River. The former Whig triumvir William Smith Jr. wrestled with his conscience and avoided committing to either side by retreating upstate to his country home at Havershaw in March 1776. He eventually chose Loyalism, returning to New York two years later when the city was under British occupation. The danger of being assaulted by the crowd and, later, of arrest at the hands of the revolutionary authorities was so thick in the air that Tory merchant Jacob Walton built an escape passage connecting his country seat (in the present-day Upper East Side of Manhattan) with the East River shoreline (in 1913 work in Carl Schurz Park uncovered some of its remnants). The persecution of Loyalists had the tacit support of the official organs of the new revolutionary order. On 8 July 1775, New York's Provincial Congress appointed an eight-member Committee of Safety to oversee the preparations for war, and, in October, the Continental Congress empowered such authorities to arrest anyone 'whose going at large may … endanger the safety of the colony, or the liberties of America'. When independence was declared, the Provincial Congress, meeting in White Plains, proclaimed that anyone 'who shall levy war against the said State within the same, or be adherent to the King of *Great Britain* … are guilty of treason against the State, and being thereof convicted, shall suffer the pains and penalties of death'. In September 1776, its successor, the New York State Convention (drafting a constitution for the new state) created a committee for 'detecting all conspiracies which may be formed in this state against the Liberties of America'.[5]

These orders could work only with the initiative of the hundreds of ordinary New Yorkers, men and women, so the denunciation, intimidation, ostracism, informal censorship and constant vigilance by a wider active layer of citizens became an essential part of revolutionary action. The committees were therefore at the juncture where the official organs of repression met with popular initiative, ensuring that, in a two-way current, the revolution was carried into every street and block of the city. Thus, although the violence was targeted at known Loyalists, an informal network of surveillance ensured that the threat of such violence hung bleakly over the heads of those who carried their politics more discreetly. So if the more spectacular acts of the persecution of Loyalists occurred at the obvious places in the city – politically symbolic sites, public institutions and within the organs of civil society – there was very real potential for that persecution to reach into the bricks and mortar of every neighbourhood and street in New York. The very possibility of surveillance might have been enough to dissuade many Loyalists from declaring themselves, cowing them into sullen, cautious silence and inactivity. Yet that the web of repression did not reach as far as it might have is shown by the fact that Loyalists continued to operate in the city, including some feisty Tory women who worked against the Patriots. Rachel Ogden, for example, became a British agent and ran a Loyalist spy network from her home.[6]

Even so, the pursuit of Tories had grown in intensity with the arrival of Major-General Charles Lee on 4 February 1776. Lee was a fiery, temperamental former British army officer with a colourful career – the Mohawks called him 'Boiling Water' – and he had thrown himself into the Patriot camp when he arrived in New York at the end of 1773, during the uproar over tea. With the outbreak of war, he became Washington's second-in-command as the army battled in New England, inflicting a heavy toll on the British at Bunker Hill in June 1775. Now he was sent to prepare New York's defences. Lee had already written to the leading 'Son of Liberty' Alexander McDougall, berating New York's 'shilly shally mode of conduct' – meaning its alleged lethargy in pursuing Loyalists – before, gout-ridden, he made his not-so-triumphant entry into the city carried on a stretcher. Lee was uncompromising: on 24 February, he dined with Thomas Paine, writing with characteristic bluntness the following day that 'I hope he will continue cramming down the throats of squeamish mortals his wholesome truths'. Paine, in return, saluted the general's 'sarcastic genius' and his 'military knowledge'. Lee made an immediate impression, warning that, should the British warships fire on the city, he would have one hundred Tories executed, and Loyalists still in New York were taken as hostages. Communications with Governor Tryon on *Dutchess of Gordon* were severed when the last person allowed ashore – a domestic servant on an errand – was arrested under Lee's authority. Patriot persecution of Loyalists was not based entirely on paranoia: on 28 June 1776, a crowd of twenty thousand soldiers and civilians gathered on the Common to watch one of Washington's personal guards, Thomas Hickey, hang for his part in a plot to assassinate the general. The web of conspiracy extended to New York's Loyalist mayor, David Matthews, and to Governor Tryon himself.[7]

Eleven days later, there was another gathering on the Common, one that led to a dramatic act of political iconoclasm. In the early evening of 9 July 1776, the Declaration of Independence was read, on Washington's orders, to his troops mustered on the Common. Washington himself was present, on horseback, faced on all four sides by soldiers formed up in a square and bearing an assortment of weapons that would have made a professional logistician weep. Alongside the commander of the Continental army was an aide, also on horseback, who announced 'the unanimous Declaration of the thirteen United States of America'. His voice carried over the hushed ranks as he began: 'When in the course of human events ... ' The reading explained why 'the political bands' that had connected America to Britain had to be dissolved and, in stirring words, laid the fundamental principles that would guide (or ought to have guided) the new order. The troops roared out three cheers. The 'peace & safety on this Country', Washington's order of the day reminded them, now rested only 'upon the success of our arms'. A plaque now marks the place, close to the entrance of City Hall Park off Broadway, opposite Murray Street, where the Declaration of Independence was read out for the first time in New York City.[8]

That Congress had crossed the Rubicon there was no doubt – those who signed the Declaration had committed treason (which is why their names were not published until 1777) – and the assembled soldiers and the crowd of New Yorkers watching made it clear that they understood this. It was, of course, both practical and politically appropriate that the Continental soldiers should have heard the Declaration read on the Common, but more dramatically still a large number of them, joined by the civilians, then surged down Broadway to the equestrian statue of King George III. Lieutenant Isaac Bangs, an officer in the Massachusetts militia, watched what happened:

Last Night the Statue on the Bowling Green representing George Ghwelph alias George Rex was pulled down by the Populace. In it were 4,000 Pounds of Lead, & a Man undertook to take of 10 oz of Gold from the Superfices, as both Man &

Horse were covered with Gold Leaf. The Lead, we hear, is to be run up into Musquet Balls for the use of the Yankees, when it is hoped that the Emanations of the Leaden George will make deep ... impressions in the Bodies of some of his red Coated & Torie Subjects.[9]

The crowd also hacked off the crowns that surmounted the iron fence that surrounded the green – the crownless fence still stands. The statue had stood for no more than six years. Moreover, if, unlike the later French Revolution, the Americans did not literally decapitate their king, they managed to do so symbolically: British military engineer Montresor heard that 'the Rebels ... had cut the nose off, clipt the laurels that were wreathed round his head, and drove a musket Bullet part of the way through his Head, and otherwise disfigured it'. He later learned that the head was taken to Moore's Tavern, at the northern end of Manhattan, where it was stuck on a pike outside – the same fate reserved for traitors' skulls on London's Temple Bar. Meanwhile, the Patriots transported the rest of the lead to Litchfield in Connecticut to be converted into musket balls, work carried out by local women.[10]

APART FROM THIS act of symbolic regicide, the *political* revolution in New York had, so far, made little impact on the cityscape. Yet the city *was* physically marked in these months, less for political or ideological reasons than for strategic ones, for New York was not only in political turmoil but preparing for war. The storm gathered when an American invasion of Canada had been repulsed at the walls of Quebec in December 1775, and then General William Howe, the new British commander in America, withdrew his troops by sea from Boston in March 1776. Few doubted that the next blow would land on New York. John Adams had told George

Washington that New York was the 'Nexus of the Northern and
Southern Colonies . . . a kind of Key to the whole Continent . . . No
Effort to Secure it ought to be omitted'. The British garrison, so far
confined to barracks on the Common, had evacuated the city on 6
June 1775, but not before they were stopped on Broad Street by the
Sons of Liberty and deprived of their munitions. Next, the Patriots
tried to seize the British cannon still at the Battery: an attempt in
the night of 23 August by the Sons of Liberty provoked a broadside
from *Asia*'s guns, which blasted shot into the Battery walls. From
that summer Alexander McDougall took stock of all the saltpetre
in the city, imported gunpowder from the West Indies, experi-
mented with the casting of cannon and hired gunsmiths to repair
the firing mechanisms on a motley assortment of civilian muskets.
The Provincial Congress recruited four regiments, arming them
with weapons from the armoury at City Hall and billeting them
in the now abandoned Upper Barracks at the Common – revolutionary soldiers occupying what had recently been a bastion of
imperial authority. Appropriately, too, General Lee had taken as
his headquarters the nearby Montayne's Tavern, the repair of the
Sons of Liberty.[11]

The city's social face also changed as the danger of bom-
bardment and military assault thickened: New York emptied of
civilians. At the end of August 1775, Ewald Schaukirk, pastor of
New York's Moravian church, recorded in his diary that 'moving
out of the city continues, and some of the Streets look plague-
stricken, so many houses are closed'. Up to a third of a population
of twenty-five thousand may have fled by September 1775. The
majority of citizens who evacuated were not necessarily Tories, as
one New Yorker explained: 'We are in daily expectation of having
our city knocked down and burned by the Men of Warr. Most of
the effects are moved out of town; and at least half the families are
gone and other agoing so that we are a compleat garrison town'.

Another witness, an American army chaplain, found that he could not write his sermon because of the 'rattling streets', as carts, horses and people passed by his billet. By July 1776, the city may have had as few as five thousand of its original residents; all the other occupants were Continental soldiers and militia.[12]

Thousands of Continental soldiers and militiamen took over, commandeering the city's spaces – and it was this that left its physical mark, as they prepared for the anticipated attack. Lee and his successors oversaw a gargantuan effort to fortify New York and its approaches. New York Harbour and the rivers were studded with forts and batteries; today's Forts Washington and Lee commanding the Hudson stand on the site of Lee's original fortifications, facing each other at opposite ends of today's George Washington Bridge. In the city proper, there were gun batteries on the East River waterfront and barricades on the approaches from the North River. The walls of Fort George were smashed down: for Lee, it was untenable as a defensive position, and he wanted to deny the British cover should they take it. Barricades were built across Broadway, with four cannon trained at the fort. A battery was placed on a rise behind Trinity Church. The northern approaches to the city were defended by a collar of redoubts – one dubbed 'Bunker Hill' – interspersed with gun batteries and roadblocks along a line roughly following today's Grand Street.[13]

Long Island was fortified with a line of forts, trenches and breastworks, sealing off Brooklyn Heights from Gowanus Creek to Wallabout Bay, a backbreaking task performed by work parties supplied by four thousand troops and an army of slaves commandeered from local farms. A year later, Nicholas Cresswell, a British visitor to the city, remarked that 'if one was to judge from appearances, they would suppose the Rebels had intended to dispute every inch of ground with our troops'. So those New Yorkers who remained and walked around their streets would be

confronted not only with the ever-present determination of the
Patriots to imprint their politics on the life of the city, but also
with physical reminders that they were at war, not least of which
were the thousands of soldiers tramping through the streets and
camping on every scrap of open ground and the defences that they
were busy constructing.[14]

New Yorkers could find little shelter from this experience, even
in the privacy of some homes. So many thousands of troops, sweaty
and grimy from the work of digging, heaving and wheeling dirt
and stone, made a deep if not positive impression on New Yorkers.
There were large encampments outside the city, on the site of today's
Canal Street and across the water by the ferry at Brooklyn village.
But troops were also barracked in the empty town houses and
country homes of the departed elites. While McDougall managed
to save the homes of John Jay and John Alsop, two representatives
to Congress, those belonging to others, particularly the Tories,
were suddenly crawling with men soiled with the day's toil – work
that they, including Lieutenant Bangs, aptly called 'Fatigue' duty.
'Oh, the houses in New York, if you could but see the insides of
them!' one New York lady wailed. 'Occupied by the dirtiest people
on the continent . . . If the owners ever get possession again, I am
sure they must be years in cleaning them'. Warehouses, the lecture
rooms of King's College and the hospital were taken over by the
military. Street corners and patches of open ground were piled
with supplies or used as parks for wagons. Fences and trees were
cut down for firewood and building materials. The streets were
clogged with soldiers and tents. By early August the city reeked in
the summer heat, as rubbish and human waste gathered: 'The air
of this whole city seems infected. In almost every street there is a
horrid smell', complained one Continental soldier. Disease spread:
Bangs wrote on 24 July that 'Our Company are now about ½ of
them very low with the Camp Disorder, or Bloody Flux, which is

very prevalent throughout the whole Army, & though it Emaciates them very much yet is not very mortal, as not more than one in our Regt has died with this disorder'.[15]

And then ... the British arrived on 29 June, in spectacular fashion, on board a fleet of thirty men-of-war and four hundred transports under Admiral Richard Howe, the masts so dense that they resembled a forest. 'I thought all London was afloat', declared one aghast American rifleman. This flotilla was the largest single military expedition colonial America had ever witnessed, and it was preparing the greatest amphibious operation that the British had attempted up to that point in time. The vessels anchored in the Narrows between Staten and Long Islands. Within weeks, the British were testing New York's defences: on 12 July, two British warships, *Rose* and *Phoenix*, ploughed across the Upper Bay and up the Hudson River to Tarrytown, sailing blithely past the ineffective barrages from Lee's gun emplacements along the water. The Americans, in fact, harmed only themselves: a team of gunners firing from the Battery succeeded in blowing themselves up with their own munitions. A more enterprising attack on the two British warships was made on 16 August, when the Americans sent fireships – old vessels set ablaze – against them as they made their way back down the Hudson, but the currents were too strong for these weapons to reach their targets.[16]

Meanwhile, the twenty-four-thousand-strong British army, under Admiral Howe's brother General William Howe, had by mid-August disembarked onto Staten Island, where they were greeted with relief by the local Loyalists. Among the men who were camped there was an African American 'Ethiopian Regiment', recruited in Virginia by the governor, John Murray, Earl of Dunmore (and onetime governor of New York), promising them emancipation from slavery. The presence of free African American troops was a magnet to New York's African Americans who still chafed under slavery, but who, urbanised in New York City or dispersed across the surrounding farmland and more skilled and better-educated than southern plantation slaves, were not easily controlled by their Patriot captors. Throughout the war, those African American men who were able to make the hazardous journey to the British lines accepted the promise of freedom in return for serving in special British units such as Captain George Martin's Black Pioneers and Guides, who arrived in New York from the Carolinas later in 1776. The enlistment oath was the first time that these African Americans were able to state that they were acting 'freely and voluntarily' and 'without the least compulsion'.[17]

When the British struck, they did so with ruthless efficiency, launching an amphibious landing on Long Island on 22 August. Then in the night of 26–27 August, they outflanked the American positions strung out in front of their fortifications across Brooklyn, before crashing into them from both front and rear as day broke. Only the suicidal heroism of the Marylanders at the Gowanus Pass held open the jaws of the trap for long enough to allow most of Washington's crumpling forces to escape to the safety of their defences along the East River. The Battle of Long Island was the largest full-scale engagement of the American War of Independence. At the end of the month, quartermaster Hugh Hughes assembled a flotilla of small craft of all descriptions, and, in a well-executed nighttime withdrawal, Washington's army was evacuated from Long Island back to Manhattan.[18]

On 15 September, blanketed by smoke from the mighty broadsides of four British men-of-war, thirteen thousand British troops and Hessian mercenaries landed at the rocky inlet of Kips Bay (now the area between the East River, Second Avenue, Thirty-Second and Thirty-Eighth Streets), broke through the American defences and swung northwards towards the main body of the American army along the Boston Post Road. Washington, roused from his headquarters at the Morris-Jumel mansion (at today's 161st Street), rode furiously towards the gunfire to order the thirty-five hundred troops in New York to withdraw before being trapped. General Israel Putnam and his aide Major Aaron Burr thundered down the Bloomingdale Road towards the city, where they sent riders galloping through the streets, calling on all soldiers to abandon their posts and to move northwards. Burr, a New Yorker who knew the island well, guided this force to the safety of Harlem Heights, a twelve-mile forced march into the night. The column slipped past General Howe himself, who, the story goes, was being entertained at the Murray country mansion (now marked by a plaque at Park Avenue and Thirty-Seventh Street) by the ladies of the house, who kept Howe and his officers merry with wine and cake while Burr's column was quietly threading its way through the woods and farmland along the Bloomingdale Road to the west.

The Americans salved some Patriot pride the following morning in a fierce firefight around the Hollow Way, a valley that dipped between the Harlem and Bloomingdale (now Morningside) Heights at roughly today's 125th Street. The Americans managed to drive the British back to a buckwheat field, now the site of Columbia University. The Americans, however, could not hold on to Manhattan: when Howe landed troops at Pell's Point (now Rodman's Neck in Pelham Bay Park) and threatened to cut the Americans off altogether, Washington abandoned the island, his army falling back to its supply depot at White Plains on 16 October. For the rest of the year, the fighting moved away into New Jersey and Pennsylvania, as well as raging in the Hudson Valley. A Continental garrison held out in Fort Washington until the British and Hessians stormed it on 16 November, Margaret Corbin famously taking her gunner husband's place when he was killed.

IN THE CITY hastily abandoned by the Continental army on 15 September, the stunned rump of the civilian population came out onto streets eerily devoid of troops but littered with their heavy equipment and scarred by their fortifications. Pastor Schaukirk wrote that 'there was a good deal of commotion in the town; the Continental stores were broken open, and people carried off the provisions; the boats crossed to Powles' [Paulus] Hook backward and forward yet till toward evening; some people going away and others coming in; but then the ferry boats withdrew, and the passage was stopped'. Others climbed into a redoubt to the north of the city and hoisted a white flag, declaring the city open. The first British troops to arrive were a hundred Royal Marines, who rowed across from Long Island to be greeted by a small crowd of ecstatic Tories who carried them shoulder-high 'like overjoyed Bedlamites', commented Ambrose Serle, Admiral Howe's secretary. At the abandoned fort, a woman hauled down the rebel standard and hoisted up the British flag. New York would remain under British military occupation for more than seven years.[19]

The occupation of the city by American forces had already left its mark. Now thousands of British and Hessian troops fanned out through the city. New Yorkers would feel the privations of war, the material shortages and the psychological swings of hope and anxiety. The fighting was never far away: Continental forces made forays onto Staten Island, and after the French entry into the war in February 1778, the brief appearance of their ships off Sandy Hook in July threatened the city with a state of siege. If conditions were bad in British-occupied New York City, life was far worse for civilians in the thirty-mile-wide 'neutral ground', the no-man's-land in surrounding Long Island, Connecticut, Westchester County and New Jersey, where the population hovered uneasily between the British forces immediately around New York City and rebel-held territory farther out. Both sides sent raiding parties to steal livestock and horses, to press men into service and ride down political opponents, visiting the full horrors of guerrilla warfare on the people.[20]

One group who braved the 'neutral ground', however, was enslaved African Americans. The British had been consistent in promising freedom to slaves in American-held areas who escaped and made their way to British-held territory, but *not*, pointedly, to the enslaved who were already within it, since the aim was to undermine the Patriot cause, not to alienate Loyalist slaveholders. Even so, Loyalist New York became a beacon for runaway slaves well aware of British policy, the more so because the Patriot side offered far less. The Constitution of New York State of 1777 made no provision for the abolition of slavery; when John Jay and Gouverneur Morris had proposed a very mild article that merely 'recommended' gradual abolition, they had been rebuffed. The porous frontier of the neutral zone offered opportunities for flight to British-held New York for resourceful men and women determined to make a dash for freedom. One such figure was Boston King, who had escaped from a plantation in South Carolina: in 1780 he crossed marsh and rivers by wading, swimming and rowing between Patriot-held New Jersey and Staten Island, where he was given a passport by the British commander for safe passage across to Manhattan. Runaway slave advertisements in the Patriot press show that King was one of more than five hundred who made their way to Loyalist New York, but since only about a quarter of owners may have published such notices, the figure may have been as high as two thousand. Escapees employed all kinds of ingenious ruses to help them across the neutral ground: forging passes, paling their skin with paint or dressing and acting as if they were already freemen.[21]

In the city, New Yorkers could occasionally hear the distant rumbling of guns, but the day-to-day way they experienced the war was primarily through their tense relations with the soldiery. Yet they had to absorb another tragedy first: six days after the return of British troops, a fire engulfed the city. Bursting just after midnight on 21 September at a tavern called the Fighting Cocks near Whitehall Slip, the flames and sparks were blown uptown, engulfing homes and businesses. Schaukirk, who was late in the Moravian Chapel on today's Fulton Street, was struck when he saw 'the whole air red' and people fleeing the inferno. New Yorkers assembled on the Common, watching in despair as, one witness said, 'the heavens appeared in flames'. New York's shale roof tiles were lifted by the heat, still burning, and, blown by wind, spread the fire all the quicker. When the breeze shifted two hours into the conflagration, it burned across Broadway, consuming Trinity Church, its proud spire collapsing in a flaming heap. The fire roared up the west side. 'It spread so violently that all what was done was but of little effect', wrote a horrified Schaukirk. 'If one was in one street and looked about, it broke out already again in another street above; and thus it raged all the night, and till about noon'. The Anglican Saint Paul's Church by the Common was spared because New Yorkers, joined by British soldiers and sailors, formed a bucket brigade to douse the flames. The blaze petered out around the open, undeveloped ground to the north. When the day broke, close to a thousand buildings – a quarter of the city – were in charred, smoking ruins.[22]

The military authorities leapt to the conclusion that the fire was the work of revolutionary arsonists. Continental soldiers watching from the Jersey shore certainly cheered, and Washington, gazing up at the blazing sky, remarked that Providence had done what he and his forces had been reluctant to do. Two hundred men and women were arrested and questioned by the British, but the price was paid by Nathan Hale, one of Washington's agents who was arrested in civilian garb and hanged as a spy in a British artillery park on the Beekman estate (now the crossroads of Third Avenue and Sixty-Sixth Street). His famous last words came from Joseph Addison's play *Cato*: 'I only regret that I have but one life to lose for my country'.[23]

For the few New Yorkers who had remained, the fire had other immediate and sinister consequences, in terms of both politics and the fabric of their city. Politically, Governor Tryon, spooked by the possibility of revolutionary agents, abandoned his original plan to restore civil liberties and, much to Loyalist dismay, determined to keep New York City under martial law. So the places that, Loyalists had hoped, would be restored to the old civic order remained under military control. King's College remained an army hospital and barracks. The Common became a parade ground and artillery park. Perhaps the only consolation for Loyalist New Yorkers was that, on 28 October 1776, a large group of them were at last able to hew through the wooden shaft of the Liberty Pole, saw it into pieces and cart it off, 'a monument of insult to the Government, and of licentiousness to the people', sneered Tryon. Cathartic though the felling of the Liberty Pole may have been, truer to the reality of martial law was the conversion of City Hall into the central Guard House; thus, the building intended for the representative institutions of the colonial regime would instead be filled with soldiers. From December 1777, at least the commandant General Robertson appointed a 'vestry' – the idea was taken from municipal government in England – as a conduit between the civilians and the military authorities.[24]

The fire also depleted the housing stock of a city that had to accommodate British soldiers and thousands of Loyalist refugees from across the colonies. Most British and Hessian troops camped on Staten Island, in and around Fort Hill at Duxbury's Point.

Archaeological excavations here in 1919 unearthed the debris and detritus that they left: cooking utensils, barrel hoops, belt straps and buckles, weapon parts and lost buttons, this last suggesting that at least twenty different regiments stayed here at one time or another during the occupation. Even so, many New Yorkers had lost their homes in the fire and lived among the ruins beneath canvas taken from old ship sails, spread out between wooden spars and the jagged, blackened remnants of walls and chimneys. In this 'Canvas Town', the homeless, later joined by penniless refugees, lived out the war.[25]

Although the Patriots had fled, relations between troops and New Yorkers were still tense because of the stress placed on the fabric of the city. The housing shortage frayed New Yorkers' patience, particularly as conditions would get more cramped as time went on, with wave after wave of refugees fleeing the fighting and the Patriots, swelling the population to its largest yet, thirty thousand by 1783. Yet the needs of the soldiery were put first, and this, in turn, put pressure on the built environment of the town. Themselves struggling to garrison and supply their forces in this relatively compact city, the British ruthlessly exploited its buildings. Residents could even chart the speed with which they were commandeered, because the lintels or front doors were marked with the letters 'GR' – George Rex. Special attention was paid to wharves and warehouses and even to taverns. A Loyalist had just finished restoring a dilapidated pub, calling it the 'Tally-Ho' – one can imagine him proudly hanging up the inn sign, the final touch – when it was immediately commandeered by the army. Private homes, particularly those abandoned by Patriot families, were used for billeting soldiers. This began right at the top of the chain of command – the successive garrison commandants, Generals James Robertson and then James Pattison, took over Washington's former headquarters at the luxurious Kennedy

House at No. 1 Broadway – but the practice percolated everywhere. As early as November 1776, Schaukirk noted that troubles began 'on account of the quartering of the soldiers, of whom more and more come in; as also many of their women and children'. One Anglican minister complained that it was impossible to find a bed to sleep on, such was the 'plundering and destruction' in the city. In the bitterly cold winter of 1781–1782, Schaukirk complained that 'the rents of houses are again raised to extravagant figures'.[26]

What really shocked New Yorkers, however, was the treatment meted out to places of worship. Church bells had been hauled down by the Continentals for their metal, but Pastor Schaukirk's diary is peppered with anxieties about the fate that befell so many of the city's churches under British occupation: they were used as barracks and to accommodate prisoners of war. Although Saint Paul's Church, being Anglican, was spared this punishment, in August 1777 the burnt-out shell and grounds of the once-mighty Trinity Church were taken over. New Yorkers were initially drawn there because there was a daily guard-changing ceremony, but it was soon converted into a pleasure garden, named the 'Mall', after the London avenue. Lanterns were strung from the branches of trees, a promenade with benches was fenced in and guards were posted to keep out the riffraff as British officers strolled with their ladies. When the austere Whig triumvir turned Loyalist William Smith Jr. at last made his way back to New York on 11 August 1778, he was stunned by the sorrowful site of his gutted city. And, Presbyterian though he was, he shook his head disapprovingly at the profanation of Trinity's sacred ground. Schaukirk observed bitterly: 'A paltry affair! A house opposite is adapted to accommodate the ladies or officer's women, while many honest people, both of the inhabitants and Refugees cannot get a house or lodging to live in or get their living'. Later, the pastor was shocked further when the walkway was widened, the supporting posts driven into the graves that lay around the churchyard and a stand built for an orchestra within the wreck of the chancel. This 'gave great offense and uneasiness to all serious and still more to all godly men ... Profaneness and Wickedness prevaileth – Lord have mercy!'[27]

Pastor though he was, Schaukirk's reaction speaks of the gulf that had opened between the British forces, whose officers enjoying a dazzling whirl of social activity, and the city's people forced to eke out a living. As the privations of war cut deep, there was a crime wave: on one New Year's Schaukirk's congregation separated early to avoid walking the streets too late at night. Prostitution boomed: in 1777 British traveller Cresswell was impressed by the women in the congregation at Saint Paul's: 'some of the handsomest and best dressed ladies I have ever seen in America. I believe most of them are Whores'. A black market flourished as New Yorkers struggled to feed and warm themselves, despite the efforts of the military authorities to control supplies. 'Provisions here grow dearer', complained Schaukirk at the end of August 1777, 'and the outlook for next Winter is gloomy'. So it proved, and again in November 1781, when, in an intensely cold winter, there was 'great distress for want of wood, the proclamations of no avail'.[28]

The most sinister aspect of life in occupied New York, however, was quite literally locked away behind the city's bricks and mortar. One of the most urgent tasks facing the British army was how and where to hold its prisoners of war. There were, of course, existing prisons, including the debtors' gaol, the cells beneath City Hall, the recently completed Bridewell alongside the Common and the nearby 'New Gaol'. This last was placed under the charge of Provost-Marshal William Cunningham, the victim of Patriot violence in 1775 who had returned, quite literally, with vengeance. Cunningham administered regular beatings to the prisoners in the 'Provost', as the gaol came to be called, and he used the threat of the noose liberally. Ten men at a time were locked up in cells no more than twenty by thirty feet in dimension, with no other furniture than the slop buckets into which they relieved themselves.

As more American soldiers fell into British hands, churches were commandeered, as were manufactures and warehouses, like the Livingston Sugar House on Crown (now Liberty) Street, which became a grimly oppressive reminder of the war's human suffering. Grant Thorburn, a Scottish immigrant artisan, recalled many years later the forbidding sight of 'a dark stone building, grown gray and rusty with age, with small deep windows exhibiting a dungeon-like aspect'. Each floor of the five-storey building was divided into 'two dreary apartments, with ceilings so low, and the light from the windows so dim, that a stranger would readily take the place for a jail', as it had now become, with Hessian or British soldiers patrolling the track around its walls.[29]

Conditions were appalling. According to General Gage, one-time British commander in North America, rebels were criminals 'destined to the cord', not prisoners of war, so were lucky to be alive at all. Moreover, the challenges of feeding British troops meant that American prisoners received reduced rations: they would have lost one pound of their body weight a week, a gradual wasting away that took a terrible toll. Overcrowded, and underfed, the prisoners were ravaged by disease and malnutrition, 'mere walking skeletons', reported one appalled witness, 'overrun with lice from head to foot'. 'I have had men die by the side of me in the night', recalled one veteran of the trauma, 'and have seen fifteen dead bodies sewed up in their blankets and laid in the corner of the yard at one time, the product of twenty-four hours'. Worst of all, with the city's gaols crammed with so much festering humanity, the British resorted to a solution that they had already tried on criminals back home: prison hulks. These were anchored in the waters around Manhattan, especially in Wallabout Bay in the East River. Conditions were so squalid aboard these vessels that the

filth-smeared inmates were woken each morning by the gaolers'
calls of 'Rebels, turn out your dead'. In all, it has been estimated
that between 24,850 and 32,000 Americans were held prisoner in
and around Manhattan, and of these somewhere between 15,575
and 18,000 died – maybe 11,000 in the prison hulks. This shocking figure dwarfs the American combat dead of 6,824 and even
the 10,000 thought to have died from wounds or disease. The
shallow graves on the shore of Wallabout Bay were still yielding
their bleached bones as late as the 1840s.[30]

THE END TO New York's painful wartime days gradually rose
above the horizon. There was word of peace talks after the Franco-
American victory at Yorktown in October 1781, and on 6 April
1782 the packet *Prince William Henry* from Britain tied up at New
York, bringing the Royal Proclamation of 14 February declaring
the cessation of hostilities. Three days later, this document was
read from City Hall, and the British commander in chief, now
General Sir Guy Carleton, hurried to tell his opponent George
Washington. Many Loyalists now rushed to secure their futures.
Some prepared to leave America for good – heading to all parts of
the British Empire. Others worked on contacts and with family
on the Patriot side in the hope they could ease the transition from
British to American rule. William Smith Jr. would eventually sail
for London and exile in December 1783. Strangely confident was
the nattily dressed dandy James Rivington, whose acerbic *Royal
Gazette* had lampooned and lambasted the Patriot leadership since
his return to New York in 1777. It emerged many years later that,
since 1781, he had been working as a spy for Washington, part
of a ring that used invisible ink on the stationery that Rivington
'sold' to his contacts.[31]

African Americans who had escaped slavery anxiously searched and in many cases found ways of remaining free. An estimated 3,000 left New York with the British when they finally evacuated the city in November 1783. Far worse a fate met many of those slaves who had been held by Loyalist families in New York, and who were not emancipated because they were already on the British side of the lines. Aware that under both English and Scots law slaves who touched British soil were free, slaveholders preparing for exile suddenly tried to sell those they held, an utterly traumatic experience for the victims.[32]

Finally, the transfer of power came. It began at eight o'clock on the cold morning of 25 November 1783, when blue-and-buff Continental troops rose from their positions at McGowan's Pass, a site now in the northeastern corner of New York's Central Park, and marched southwards along the Boston Post Road towards New York City. The British abandoned their advanced posts along the line of Grand Street at one o'clock, marching in good order down the Bowery. Swinging over to Queen Street and thence to the wharves on the East River, the redcoats clambered into rowing boats that nimbly spirited them away from the mouth of the East River into the broad harbour. There Royal Naval vessels waited to sail them back home across the Atlantic. William Cunningham, leaving with the troops, did so with a bloodied face – struck by a broom after he had irascibly ordered a woman to strike the Stars and Stripes that she had prematurely displayed. Sailors from the wharves and slips gleefully tore down the signs from taverns that had entertained British soldiers.[33]

The Americans followed in formation, but from Queen Street they wheeled triumphantly into Wall Street, their springing steps bringing them to Broadway. In the vanguard were some veteran New York revolutionaries, including Alexander McDougall (now a general) and the governor of the state of New York, George Clinton. They were escorting George Washington, who rode through the cheers of onlookers. The celebrations of the British evacuation continued for days, but the most famous gathering was a sober one on the morning of 4 December in Fraunces Tavern on Queen Street, where General Washington said farewell to his officers as he retired from military service. Escorted by a silent column of foot soldiers to a barge on the North River, he was spirited over to New Jersey on the first leg of his journey home.

There was one twist in the tale: when, at the end of their victorious march through the city on 25 November, the Americans reached the fort, they discovered the British flag still flying from the pole. The redcoats had greased the pole and cut the halyards to prevent it from being easily lowered. After three failed attempts by soldiers to shimmy up, a sailor used a ladder and nailed cleats to the shaft, by which he reached the top, tore down the British banner and raised the Stars and Stripes, to a salute of musketry from below. This last prank of the retreating British soldiery was a distant echo of the fierce controversy over the Liberty Pole a few years earlier, but the fact that the banner of the nascent American Republic now flew over what had been a bastion of British authority made the moment all the more triumphant for the Patriots.

Yet for tens of thousands of Americans, 25 November represented not triumph but trauma: some sixty thousand Loyalists fled the country, including some eight to ten thousand African Americans fleeing the prospect of re-enslavement. Meanwhile, those Loyalists who stayed behind, still hoping to come to some accommodation with the new order, were about to be confronted with calls for their punishment by angry Patriots. New York City itself was a bleak sight after the fire of 1776 and the successive occupations by American and British forces. Moreover, its location almost on the very fault line between Patriot and Loyalist, between Continental and British, had meant that the privations and horrors of war had been visited on the city in ways to which it was not accustomed. Between 1775 and 1783, in fact, New York's experience of both revolution and war anticipated that of Paris during the French Revolution. Particularly in 1793–1794, the French capital, like New York before it, would also undergo a political and military mobilisation of people, resources, buildings and spaces for the purposes of prosecuting a war. This would be accompanied by the surveillance and prosecution of internal enemies, real or suspected, and by the mobilisation and political participation of a militant popular movement. In the process, Paris would see its cityscape altered in a myriad of symbolic and practical ways, but the scale and depth of its experience would go even further than that of New York's. This lay ten years in the future. For now, in 1783, New York's war was over: it would be as it recovered from the trauma that the real revolutionary transition in its cityscape would begin. And, across the Atlantic, the most immediate, shocking impact from the American Revolution was felt not in Paris, but in the British imperial capital, London.[34]

CHAPTER FIVE

LONDON BURNS: REFORMERS AND RIOTERS, 1776–1780

I N *COMMON SENSE*, Thomas Paine had predicted that 'the cause of America is in a great measure the cause of all mankind'. The reverberations from the American Revolution were indeed felt across the world, particularly in the public spaces of Europe's cities. The vision of a people rising up against its imperial rulers and trying to forge a republican order based on the very progressive principles that also animated European reformers caused tremors of excitement and boisterous arguments in the coffeehouses, taverns and debating and reading clubs of, among other places, London and Paris. People gathered to read the news and excitedly discuss the implications not just for the Americans, but for their own societies.[1]

In Britain the American Revolution, with its proclamation that 'all men are created equal' and its claims to natural, God-given rights, emboldened reformers to go further than before in their push for political change, adopting a democratic programme that would be the touchstone of the parliamentary reform movement for decades afterwards. The political reform movement across the country would begin to organise nationally, a development that in London had physical, spatial expression in the choices of venues for this mobilisation. In France the war would stir anti-British patriotism after King Louis XVI decided on intervention on the American side in February 1778, but it would also energise public discussions on the kingdom's future. At the same time, the American War of Independence also brought severe shocks. France, though eventually triumphing with its American allies over the old British enemy in 1783, had indulged in such prolific military spending that a subterranean financial cavity had been hollowed out beneath the very feet of the monarchy, of which the king remained blissfully unaware until 1786. The discovery of this black hole would unleash the chain of events that brought about the French Revolution in 1789.

In the medium to long term, Britain would recover remarkably swiftly from the humiliation in America, but the immediate impact of the war was spectacular, particularly in London. Here there was a striking contrast in the use and abuse of the fabric of the city. If the political reform movement constructively exploited the public spaces of the city in pursuit of their goals, the antithesis came in the bludgeon-wielding, fire-setting shape of London's worst-ever experience of civil disorder, in June 1780. Six days of riots, which threatened the government's control of the city, were unleashed, in part, by the demands of the American war. Yet through it all, the political and social order in Britain would hold firm: unlike in America, the stirrings for political reform and the convulsion of public disorder in the imperial capital would not lead to a 'dual revolution' – and that despite the shock of military defeat. Part of the explanation for Britain taking a different path lies in the way in which the diverse forces for change confronted the established regime. The direction of this opposition can be plotted with reference to the history of some of London's places and spaces in the struggle for reform, on the one hand, and riot, on the other, providing a fascinating contrast with the experience of revolution in New York and Paris.

DURING THE WILKITE drama of the 1760s and early 1770s, the alliance of opposition forces had been given spatial, geographical expression by the ways in which it used both the traditional sites of resistance (the City of London's Temple Bar, Mansion House and Guildhall) and the wider public spaces of the metropolis (Saint George's Fields). In London this represented an alignment of established interests, namely, the defence of the City's old freedoms and the established rights of Middlesex voters, with a broader, more popular protest movement that, when combined, gave the opposition to the government the potential to force through democratic change. Yet the Wilkite controversies ultimately yielded moderate rather than revolutionary results. This came in part because, by 1774, the king and Parliament had given way in London, even as they were enforcing their will in America. One of the reasons for this difference in policy was constitutional: the City of London could clearly base its claims on an actual charter, while the right of Parliament to tax the colonies was a matter for debate. It was also a matter of practical priorities: the British government could ultimately afford, however grudgingly, to accept the City's privileges since they were part of the existing political framework, while almost laughing out Wilkes's claim that all adult males should have the right to vote. Granting their colonial subjects political representation when even the vast majority of Britons had no political rights was a different matter altogether. Thus, by mobilising in support of 'Wilkes and Liberty', the wider metropolitan movement had lent its support to the already established freedoms of the City of London and the rights of the already enfranchised voters of Middlesex, but received nothing concrete in return. The result, by the time of the American War of Independence, had therefore been fundamentally a conservative one.

Yet this did not stifle the eighteenth-century movement for democratic reform as it was making its first infant steps. The American Revolution inspired a new, more energised debate among British reformers, but, unlike in America (or, later, in France), the discussions among well-heeled and well-connected progressives did not, in the end, connect with the popular protests of the kind seen earlier on Saint George's Fields. In fact, at the time of the American Revolution, the opposite happened: there was a parting of ways between 'reform' and the 'mob' that unfolded in the very buildings and spaces of the city during the inferno of violence in June 1780. So the story charts two courses: on the one hand, the response of the democratic reform movement to the American Revolution and, on the other hand, popular action that proved to be both alarmingly destructive and profoundly conservative, even reactionary.

British reformers saw in the struggle for American rights an opportunity for argument in favour of political change in Britain, but there were ambiguities in their reaction, which was made no easier when the two countries went to war with each other. Among those who did demonstrate some sympathy for the colonists, in word and deed, was John Wilkes, but even he could be ambiguous. Wilkes had been showered with tributes from his many admirers across the Atlantic, but he did not appear to reciprocate. In 1771 the Reverend John Horne Tooke, one of Wilkes's more abrasive and problematic London allies, claimed that the lanky Londoner 'always hated the Americans, was always the declared foe of their liberties, and condemned their glorious struggles for the rights of humanity'. When the Bostonian Patriot John Boylston visited Wilkes at the King's Bench Prison, he reported painfully that Wilkes sneered when the Londoner asked 'after his Friends in the Howling Wilderness'.[2]

Yet Wilkes's actions spoke loudly, too. Before the war, he had kept up a spirited correspondence with the Boston Sons of Liberty, who hoped that Wilkes's cause would help them advertise theirs in the metropolis. While lord mayor in June 1775, he presented to the Common Council a letter from New York's correspondence committee warning the government that the colony would fight if Parliament did not repeal the Intolerable Acts. When, in August, the king's heralds passed through Temple Bar to read the Royal Proclamation declaring the colonies to be 'in open and avowed rebellion', Wilkes allowed them to read it out at the Royal Exchange, but refused to lend them horses for their journey along Fleet Street (as was customary) and forbade any City official except the town crier from attending. With Britain now openly at war with the colonists and habeas corpus suspended, active British collaboration with the colonists was driven underground. Wilkes played a dangerous game when in the autumn of 1775 he helped Virginian Arthur Lee, one of America's first diplomats, and swashbuckling French playwright Pierre-Augustin Caron de Beaumarchais set up a trading company that was a front for the supply of French arms to the American rebels.[3]

Working actively for the American cause was treason, and the outbreak of open war ensured that most Londoners, like people across Britain, rallied around the king. Yet the war did not stop the political reform movement from gathering pace. For radicals, the American crisis confirmed that royal power, supinely supported by a corrupt Parliament, was a real and growing danger to the liberties of British subjects on both sides of the

Atlantic. The political conflict moved way beyond the issues that revolved around John Wilkes, the electors of Middlesex and the freedoms of the City. No one advocated a revolution or a republic – indeed, American independence and republicanism severed the possibility of any active political relationship between British reformers and American revolutionaries – but the former could still endorse the latter's essential interpretation of the imperial crisis. Like the American Patriots, they rounded on the very idea of parliamentary sovereignty and 'virtual representation' and embraced the idea that legitimacy instead came from the people.[4]

The early stirrings, however, were neither radical nor metropolitan, but arose in Yorkshire, in the cause of a mild reform of Parliament. In this great northern English county, John Wyvill, a freeholding landowner, in 1779 formed a County Association with what were the traditional aims of reducing the king's influence in Parliament through 'economical reform', which meant reducing the number of MPs beholden through royal patronage and pensions, and of redrawing constituency boundaries so that they better reflected centuries of population changes. The significance of Wyvill's Association was his attempt to forge a nationwide movement out of it, and in London the impact was radical, with the founding in 1780 of the Westminster Association. This group pressed the programme for political reform much further. It combined the established figures of the Wilkite movement in the City, such as Brass Crosby, with other, more radical, reformers, such as Major John Cartwright and John Jebb, the one a renegade army officer, the other a clergyman and doctor active in prison and educational reform. Its subcommittee declared, in May 1780, that Parliament did not just represent the landowners of the country, but that even though 'a portion of the soil, a portion of its produce, may be wanting to many . . . every man has an interest in his life, his liberty, his kindred, and his country'. That the Association went this far was due, in part, to the rare condition of Westminster as Britain's most populous constituency with one of the broadest electorates.[5]

The radicalism of the Westminster programme was to some extent driven by political expediency, namely, to ensure the election to Parliament of the opposition's favoured candidate, political giant Charles James Fox, by means of harnessing the radical extraparliamentary movement for electoral purposes. In other words, democratic though its aims may have been, it sought to work within the political system, not to revolutionise it. The venue for the meetings of the Westminster Association's subcommittee, Westminster Hall, betrayed the partisan electoral purposes behind the Association. Part of the complex of the Palace of Westminster, the hall was completed in 1099, its hard Norman stone still reinforcing the six-foot-thick walls supporting the hefty fourteenth-century hammer-beam roof. This was the arena for displays of royal power, both ceremonial and legal: it was where some of the country's highest courts – Chancery, Exchequer, Common Pleas, King's Bench – met behind ornate wooden partitions that would be removed for ceremonial occasions until the construction of the Royal High Courts of Justice in 1882. So, like the Palais de Justice in Paris, Westminster Hall was alive with black-robed, bewigged lawyers conversing with clients, their clerks scurrying on their errands, all mingling with curious members of the public and (until they were expelled) the forty-odd shopkeepers who rented space to display their wares to the public: Samuel Pepys was among those who once flirted with the young ladies who sold books, gloves, shirts and ribbons. This was, therefore, a public space – and it was one where the hustings took place during elections among the candidates competing to represent the city of Westminster, during which the hall attracted a rowdy mix of tradesmen, shopkeepers and artisans jostling with knights and nobles, all intermingling with those who could not vote, but who seized the opportunity to make a few pennies – shoe-shine boys, hawkers, ballad singers offering the latest political doggerel and pickpockets. Yet if the choice of venue connected the Westminster Association with the electoral ambitions of Fox and his allies, some of its members, particularly Cartwright and Jebb, the Association's most radical members, linked it to an organisation that was far more national in purpose. Cartwright and Jebb were also founders of the Society for Constitutional Information (SCI).[6]

Founded with other radicals in April 1780, the Society for Constitutional Information issued its first 'Address to the Public', which reiterated the now familiar argument about the dangers that a violation of the balance in the constitution between king, Lords and Commons posed to British liberty. 'As every Englishman has an equal inheritance in this Liberty; and in those Laws and that Constitution which have been provided for its defence; it is therefore necessary that every Englishman should know what the Constitution IS; when it is SAFE; and when ENDANGERED'. The SCI's purpose was to diffuse information about the constitution and British liberties as widely as possible, 'to revive in the minds of their fellow-citizens, THE COMMONALITY AT LARGE, a knowledge of their lost Rights'. All its publications would be free, written by its members, who had to pay a hefty lifetime subscription of thirty guineas. So elite leadership, disseminating their ideas, would awaken a slumbering nation to its rights, among which were universal male suffrage and a fair and equal representation of the people, including annual parliaments. Although the SCI was playing a long game, well aware that Parliament as it stood would offer little or no sympathy for reform, the aims of the metropolitan radicals would prove to be profound and established the core programme for British radicals until deep into the nineteenth century. These were spelled out by the subcommittee of the Westminster Association on 27 May 1780. Its 'Plan for Taking the Suffrages of the People', penned by Cartwright, Jebb and other radicals, took Fox and other moderate reformers way beyond their comfort zone of 'economical reform' and a mild redistribution of seats.[7]

The 'Plan' did not mince its words, flatly stating that its aims were incontrovertible: 'An equal representation of the people in the great council of the nation, annual elections, and the universal right of suffrage, appear so reasonable to the natural feelings of mankind, that no sophistry can elude the force of the arguments which are urged in their favour'.[8] The six-point programme articulated by both the Westminster Association and the SCI – universal male suffrage, annual elections, equal electoral constituencies, secret ballot, the payment of MPs and the abolition of property qualifications for MPs – became the fundamental radical programme right up to the Chartist movement, which reached its high-water mark in 1848. Charles James Fox, with his more limited electoral aims at the forefront, had helped to unleash forces that he neither fully accepted nor fully controlled. Even so, the SCI itself understood that it had little chance of making headway in a Parliament where the power of the landed elites and privileged was so deeply entrenched. In June 1780, when the six-point programme was put to the House of Lords by the renegade peer the Duke of Richmond, it was dismissed without even a vote.

If, following the example of the Yorkshire Association, the aim of the SCI was to reach out beyond the metropolis and to gradually inform and mobilise public opinion, its methods and membership pointed to the SCI's solidly moderate legal means by which it wanted to achieve its democratic ends. It was primarily a middle-class organisation with expectations to match: reform would come, but with the leadership of the educated, the industrious, the respectable, and it would occur by reasoned debate, through educating the people and by eventually convincing enough parliamentarians of the justice of their demands. The choice of Westminster Hall by the metropolitan Association, moreover, emphasised, as we have noted, the desire of moderate reformers to work within the existing political system. Yet unlike in New York or, later, in Paris, there was no alignment with popular protests in the streets outside, as had occurred during the Wilkite controversies a few years before.

Quite the opposite occurred. In the very month that the Duke of Richmond made his predictably ill-fated appeal to his parliamentary peers, the streets of London erupted into violence, delivering a body shock to the very idea that rational debate was possible among the 'people' and that peaceful reform was feasible. For six terrifying days between 2 and 8 June 1780, the metropolis was convulsed by an explosion of popular violence. At its core was the notion that the very rights and liberties of freeborn Britons were threatened by their nemesis: Catholicism. This was an expression of the dark, violently sectarian side of popular Whig ideology: the idea that the constitution and the liberties that underpinned it were not just 'British' but exclusively Protestant. Yet while anti-Catholicism provided the fuse, the force of the blast when it came was also furnished by an explosive cocktail of economic distress and dislocation, frustrated patriotism and xenophobia and years of pent-up fury against the legal might – or, rather, vindictive authority – of the Hanoverian state. It also drew its actors, targets and victims from the metropolitan environment, all of which shaped its direction.

The catalyst was, in part, generated by the pressures of the American war: the British armed forces were starved of manpower in fighting what had become a global war against the Americans and their French and Spanish allies. Parliament's response was a benign measure and, for men and women immersed in the eighteenth-century notions of reason and tolerance, ought to have been uncontroversial. This was a parliamentary act that eased some of the civil disabilities imposed on Britain's Roman Catholics, who had been barred from voting ever since the 'Glorious Revolution' of 1688 and who faced severe penal laws for practising their faith. In theory, priests could face life imprisonment if caught celebrating Mass. Catholics could not legally buy and own land, and those many Catholics who sought a way out of poverty by joining the army or navy were compelled to take an oath of allegiance to the Crown – an oath that included a condemnation of their own religion. In the summer of 1778, Parliament had passed the Catholic Relief Act to ease some of these restrictions, although it fell far short of full emancipation (Catholics still could not vote, for example). Part of the aim was to make it easier for the armed forces to recruit Catholics, the Irish in particular.[9]

The first explosion of Protestant opposition came in Scotland in 1779 – it was so destructive that the British government promised that there would be no such law applied north of the border. Buoyed by its success there, the religious bigotry spewed southwards, personified by Lord George Gordon. Disturbingly, Gordon, a Scottish peer, was a strong sympathiser with the American cause and in Parliament was aligned with the more progressive Whigs. Yet in eighteenth-century politics, this sat quite easily with anti-Catholicism. Many ordinary Britons believed – and had repeatedly been told by those in authority – that Catholicism was dangerous, seditious and opposed to the Protestant constitutional settlement created by the Revolution of 1688. 'Popery' was associated with 'wooden shoes' and 'enslavement', that is, with poverty and despotism. Educated Britons professed, usually sincerely, distaste for the persistence of these ideas, but they still had real resonance in 1780, when Britain was at war not only with Protestant American rebels, but also against the traditional Catholic and absolutist enemies France and Spain. For Gordon, the Catholic Relief Act actually seemed to challenge the very 'Protestant Liberty' for which, he held, the Americans were fighting.

Gordon became president of a Protestant Association created to campaign for the repeal of the Catholic Relief Act. It soon had branches across England, aiming to demonstrate public opposition to Catholic relief by a hefty nationwide petition, which opened in January 1780. 'Popery', declared the Protestant Association's 'appeal' to the people, 'has long been chained in Britain: the consequences of unchaining it will be dreadful to posterity'. By the end of May, the petition was ready, and the 'cause' was given a powerful boost by the official support of the City of London, though not from John Wilkes, whose attitudes towards matters of faith had always been more relaxed.[10]

On 2 June 1780, a warm and sunny day, some sixty thousand petitioners gathered – inauspiciously, given its recent past – on Saint George's Fields in Southwark. Urged by Gordon, they were all wearing blue cockades or ribbons on their hats or lapels. Gordon's purpose was to so impress Parliament with the scale of opposition to Catholic relief that enough MPs would waver and agree to repeal. The blue-festooned protesters paraded, waving banners, singing hymns and chanting psalms. As prearranged, they split into two separate columns, one crossing the Thames by London Bridge, which took it on a three-mile march through the labyrinthine streets of the City of London, gathering supporters as they went. The second column took the direct route towards Parliament, striking out for Westminster Bridge, preceded by a man shouldering the hefty parchment scroll marked by more than one hundred thousand signatures, sewn together the night before. It was the kind of protest march that, in a different context, the parliamentary reformers might have envied: massive, respectable, peaceful and delivering a petition bearing thousands upon thousands of signatures from people of all walks of life. But the mood would soon change.[11]

It was three o'clock in the afternoon when the divisions met again in Palace Yard before Westminster Hall. Here the crowd, which now included both the original marchers and thousands of people of all social backgrounds, including some on horseback and in carriages, pressed into the yard and jostled in the surrounding streets and alleys. It was here that the atmosphere turned uglier. Some of the demonstrators poured into Westminster Hall and against the doors of the House of Lords, where they were repelled by the gatekeepers. The crowd then hammered at the door of the Parliament Chamber with fists and sticks, roaring, 'No Popery!' It took a brave parliamentarian to work his way through this seething crowd: a rare few who were known to oppose Catholic Relief were cheered, but of the rest, those who were forced to yell 'No Popery!' had the best of it. The coach windows of Lord Mansfield, the chief justice, were shattered by stones, but he was to experience far worse later on. Sir George Savile, who had given his respected name to the relief legislation, was forced out of his coach and had to watch as it was torn apart by the mob. The carriage of Lord North – who must have had a sinking sense of déjà vu – was stopped, and a man opened the door, leapt inside and stole the prime minister's hat, melting away into the crowd with his trophy. The archbishops of York and Canterbury were sworn at, pelted with mud and then had their clerical robes and wigs torn from them. While no one was badly hurt, the atmosphere outside Parliament was dark, intimidating and turbulent.[12]

By the time Gordon presented the petition – it was dumped

onto the floor with a dusty thud – his colleagues in the House of Commons had had enough. A call for military protection had gone out, and Gordon was shadowed by two hostile MPs, including Colonel Holroyd, who thundered to Gordon about the mob clamouring outside that 'the first man of them that enters ... I will plunge my sword, not into his, but into your body'. Gordon hovered between the benches and the Strangers (public) Gallery and harangued his supporters thronging Westminster Hall. Dangerously, provocatively, he not only updated them on the progress of the petition in the House, but also announced the names of those MPs who had risen to oppose it. The Commons debated for six exhausting, tense hours until overwhelmingly – by 192 votes to 6 – it suspended further discussion until Tuesday, 6 June. Announcing this to the petitioners, Gordon implored them to return home peacefully. It was close to eleven o'clock at night, and now regular soldiers, the Guards, arrived to clear Westminster Hall and the surrounding streets.[13]

The crowd dispersed, sullen and with frayed tempers. Some of the protesters, furious at seeing their massed support for the Protestant 'cause' shunted into the sidings, were in no mood to heed Gordon's advice. The turn to violence that followed, from this point late on Friday, 2 June, until Thursday, 8 June, would to posterity represent the terrifying, destructive might of the London 'mob' in its full demonic nature. The first victims of the riots were London's Catholics: in the night of 2–3 June, the chapels attached to the Sardinian and the Bavarian embassies were attacked, respectively, in Duke's Street at Lincoln's Inn Fields and Warwick Street near Soho, because they offered havens where the metropolis's well-heeled Catholics could worship. The Sardinian chapel was fired until it was a black shell, while the Bavarian had its contents ransacked and consigned to a bonfire on Warwick Street. Troops prevented the rioters from setting light to the chapel of the Portuguese embassy in South Audley Street. These three locations – the elegant space of Lincoln's Inn Fields, Warwick Street in the then promisingly refined Soho before it acquired its louche reputation and South Audley Street in glitzy Saint James – brought the destructive power of the 'mob' into the heart of the wealthy elegance of the West End. South Audley Street was not too far from the centres of political power and patronage in Parliament, Whitehall and the royal residence in Saint James's Palace.[14]

Yet sectarian bigotry knew no class boundaries. That same night, a crowd headed for Moorfields, then a northeastern outlier of the City of London known for its large immigrant population of Irish. Here the assailants were beaten back by soldiers, and the local magistrates managed to make some arrests. The next day, the city was tense, but quiet. The violence was rekindled on Sunday, 4 June, and Monday, 5 June, when the rioters redoubled their efforts, surging through the East End districts of Little Moorfields, Wapping, Spitalfields and Hoxton, plundering or burning chapels and smashing up schools and pubs frequented by the Catholics – mainly Irish immigrants – among the city's labouring poor. From 5 June the crowd broadened its attacks to include the homes of leading supporters of Catholic Relief: George Savile's house on Leicester Square – Soho again – had its windows smashed and some of its furniture ransacked. Only the intervention of the Guards saved it from worse. Edmund Burke's home on Charles Street in Saint James was threatened, forcing the politician and writer to gather his most valued papers in preparation for flight. Troops drew up in the street in the nick of time. The homes of those London magistrates who had dared to make the arrests in the night of 2 June were demolished. So the riots enveloped the metropolis, studding the neighbourhoods of its eastern rind and certain wealthy houses in the West End with eruptions of violence.

Soon the unrest would engulf the very heart of the metropolis itself.[15]

When Parliament reconvened on Tuesday, 6 June, to debate the petition against the Catholic Relief Act, the crowd that amassed in Palace Yard brandished cudgels and swords and had to be held back by troops guarding the approaches to Westminster Hall. Edmund Burke, fresh from his narrow escape the night before, was forced to draw his sword to defend himself as he made his way through. Some five hundred of the rioters, meanwhile, had surged across Westminster Bridge to Lambeth, where they laid siege to the palace of the archbishop of Canterbury and battered at the bolted doors. Lambeth may have been targeted because it was a debtors' sanctuary: a network of alleys and courtyards where those pursued by creditors could take refuge from arrest and prison. As we shall see, the crowd may have had some sympathy for the hard-pressed shopkeepers and craftsmen who were forced to live in the squalor inside.[16]

When late that afternoon Parliament once again voted to adjourn discussion of the petition, Justice Hyde emerged at five to read the Riot Act and ordered the crowd in Palace Yard to disperse. To the magistrate's horror, someone in the crowd hoisted a red and black banner and shouted, 'To Hyde's house, a-hoy!' A mob dashed off to the justice's home on Saint Martin's Street, again in the West End, ransacking it and making bonfires of the furniture. This marked a shift in the focus of the rioting. From being a storm of rage against Catholics, they had become a violent assault on the agents of law and order. After incinerating Hyde's worldly goods, the crowd ran a few hundred yards northeast to Long Acre and then onto Bow Street at Covent Garden, where they used iron bars and chisels to prise open the entrance to Sir John Fielding's police headquarters and gutted it. It was in this context that the burning of the notorious Newgate prison took place. Newgate may initially have been targeted because it held some of the rioters' comrades, arrested on 2 June, but the crowd freed *all* the prisoners and burned down the gaol. The assault on Newgate was also the first time that the rioters had chosen a target in the City of London itself, so linking Westminster, the City and the East End in a chain of violence and destruction. Radical dramatist Thomas Holcroft, who in 1794 would be an inmate of Newgate himself, saw the convicts and debtors being rescued from the flames, incarceration and, in some cases, the gallows:

> All the prisoners, to the amount of three hundred, among whom were four ordered for execution on the Thursday following, were released. The activity of the mob was amazing. They dragged out the prisoners by the hair of the head, by legs or arms, or whatever part they could lay hold of. They broke open the doors of the different entrances as easily as if they had all their lives been acquainted with the intricacies of the place, to let the confined escape ... [S]o well planned were all the manoeuvres of these desperate ruffians, that they had placed centinels at the avenues, to prevent any of the prisoners from being conveyed to other gaols. Thus was the strongest and most durable prison in England ... demolished, the bare walls excepted, which were too thick and strong to yield to the force of fire.[17]

The Londoners who assaulted the police offices on Bow Street and who burned Newgate were probably not protesting against law and order in themselves. For one, they were victims of crime more frequently than the well-heeled who actually dealt out the justice. Londoners who were attacked or robbed in the streets could usually count on help from their fellow citizens if they cried out 'Stop, thief!' or 'Murder!' Lightly policed that London was in the eighteenth century, day-to-day order could not have held without some cooperation between the authorities and the people. Nor was it necessarily a protest against the all too frequent use of the noose. Most of the victims of hanging in eighteenth-century London were marginalised people: Just over 60 per cent between 1703 and 1772 were recent migrants into the metropolis, so were unlikely to have patrons and networks of local support who could plead for clemency on their behalf. Moreover, of those incomers, a heavy proportion of the hanged – almost 14 per cent – were Catholic Irish who were highly unlikely to elicit the sympathies of this particular mob.[18]

Rather, what Londoners may have resented was the *unequal* way in which justice was so brutally meted out. The men and women who were crammed into Newgate and who were sprung by the Gordon rioters were tradespeople and craft workers such as printers, weavers, upholsterers, glass cutters, brush makers, tailors, chair carvers, drapers, plasterers, leather dressers, smiths, painters, joiners, whip makers. They came from the kaleidoscope of the working life of the metropolis. Together these were the people who were the lifeblood of eighteenth-century London, the denizens of its streets, workshops and markets who made, supplied and serviced everything that made living in the city possible. They were, in other words, little different from the Gordon rioters themselves. Perhaps most relevantly of all, the Newgate arsonists liberated debtors – many of them tradesmen who may have fallen on hard times when their wealthy, well-heeled clientele neglected to pay their bills. The debtors' prison, and the Lambeth sanctuary, loomed large in the anxieties of the city's hard-pressed artisans. So the shift in focus of the attackers, beginning with the debtors' sanctuary at Lambeth but intensi-fying with the assault on Newgate and other prisons, suggested a deeper popular hostility towards the way in which the violent, coercive arm of the state seemed to be loaded against working people in favour of those who were secure in their property and who usually *made* the law. The violence would probably have resonated with those who had rallied behind John Wilkes on Saint George's Fields a decade earlier, and some may even have participated in both events. Yet the Gordon Riots also represented the moment when British radicalism, once represented by Wilkes and his throngs of boisterous supporters, parted company with crowd action, as we shall see.[19]

If Newgate was the main prize, other prisons were forced open over the next two days: Clerkenwell, the Bridewell at Blackfriars and the New Prison (on the South Bank) were prised open, their convicts and debtors freed. At half past midnight on 6–7 June, the town house of Lord Mansfield – one of the leading figures of the bench, a parliamentarian who supported Catholic Relief and a notorious hanging judge (so the rioters had many reasons to dislike him) – was attacked. Rising elegantly on the northeastern corner of Bloomsbury Square, the large, fashionable park and street outside thronged with people as Mansfield made a hasty escape with his family, just before the assailants splintered the door and rampaged through the house, hurling from the windows books, papers, paintings, a harpsichord, furniture and ladies' dresses. They were piled on the square and burned in a huge bonfire, before some of the rioters, swinging fireballs, hurled them into the building, engulfing it in flames.[20]

These outrages culminated on Wednesday, 7 June, when the Fleet and the King's Bench Prisons – both debtors' gaols, the one in the City, the other in Southwark – were broken open and then fired. In the riots' most Dantesque scene, the gin distillery owned by the wealthy Catholic Thomas Langdale at the corner of Holborn and Fetter Lane was torched and turned into an inferno. The flames heated the vats of gin until some 120,000 gallons of the spirits erupted in a liquid fire that leapt from the distillery, punching upwards into the night sky before cascading downwards like tracer bullets onto the street. Those rioters who had broken into the distillery to plunder the liquor were incinerated. Some twenty surrounding houses were also taken in the blast. Streaks of blue liquid flame ran over the paving stones and down the gutters and gathered in fiery pools. Men, women and children burned and poisoned themselves by drinking from the crude spirits that had poured into the street.[21]

'Black Wednesday' was the high tide of the riots, as thirty-six separate fires turned the night sky red. The authorities were frantically mustering what forces they could. Regular troops were marching in from the surrounding counties and camped on Hyde Park, their tents turning the expanse of West End greenery into a sea of canvas and red coats. One Londoner, Ignatius Sancho, complained like a true Whig – hostile to standing armies – that the area now bore 'the features of French government'. By the end of the riots on 8 June, there were more than ten thousand troops either in London or being force-marched towards the metropolis. The City, after some hesitation, mobilised. The lord mayor offered the services of the Honourable Artillery Company and the London Military Association, a volunteer militia, which guarded the Bank of England and the Mansion House, the latter becoming a place of refuge for the rioters' terrified victims.[22]

One of the volunteers from the Military Association recalled the 'awful but beautiful scene': 'Figure to yourself every man, woman and child in the streets, panic-struck, the atmosphere red as blood with the ascending fires, muskets firing in every part, and consequently women and children sprawling in the streets; all the lower order of people stark mad with liquor, huzzaing and parading with flags'.[23] When detachments of the Military Association and the Honourable Artillery Company were sent northwards to Old Broad Street (running north from London Wall) to defend houses that were being attacked, the crowd, the volunteer continued, 'would not disperse, and bid us fire and be damned. There was soon exhibited a scene of killed, wounded and dying. We were very merciful to them, by firing only one gun at once, instead of a volley, thereby giving time to many to get off'.[24]

Meanwhile, the great and the good of the City had also enrolled in the forces of order. Alderman John Wilkes reported to the Guildhall to take part in its defence. He later excoriated his fellow aldermen, including some of his erstwhile supporters, for their lack of zeal in putting down the riots and some for permitting the constables in their wards to wear the blue cockade. He put his own Farringdon Without ward under martial law, closing all the taverns at ten o'clock and taking a detachment of twenty soldiers from the barracks on Ludgate Hill to organise patrols. Seizing a cache of sixty Spanish muskets, he armed the local citizens to defend their neighbourhood from the rioters. On 7 June, Wilkes was seen leading a detachment of soldiers seeing off insurgents, who had incinerated the toll houses on Blackfriars Bridge and were now trying to set light to London Bridge. That evening, between eleven and midnight, he helped defend the Bank of England from a determined assault led by a brewer's drayman, sitting astride his heavy horse bizarrely decorated with chains taken from Newgate. As the mob tried to converge on the Bank, inside the great Threadneedle Street building, soldiers desperately melted down ink pots to make musket balls. Detachments waited behind the doors and on the roof, ready to let loose a point-blank volley should the assailants have broken through the armed ranks in the street. Among the defenders was Wilkes, who wrote in his diary, 'Fired 6 or 7 times on the rioters at the end of the Bank towards Austin Friars, and towards the middle of the Bank. Killed two rioters directly opposite to the great gate of the Bank; several others in Pig Street and Cheapside'. None other than Samuel

Johnson lauded Wilkes for his part: 'Jack Wilkes headed the party
that drove them away. Jack, who was always zealous for order and
decency, declared that if he be trusted with power "he will not
leave one rioter alive"'.[25]

Wilkes's response is not, in retrospect, surprising: although he
made his controversial name by drumming up the support of the
very 'mob' that he now shot down with such zeal, in the end his
power base was in the metropolis and at its core was the City itself.
Its might, its ability to stand up for its own freedoms, was rooted in
the very institutions that the rioters were trying to destroy. On the
rioters' side, the assault on the Bank and the bridge tolls suggests
that the riots had become a wider attack on the moneyed interests
of the metropolis itself. This was the parting of ways between
the defence of the City's privileges and the riotous expression
of the wider population's grievances, two forces that had in the
1760s lined up behind the charismatic persona of John Wilkes.
In defending the Bank of England, therefore, perhaps Wilkes in
his own mind was protecting not property and money against the
working poor, but rather a place that was at the very centre – both
literally and figuratively – of the City's interests.[26]

The riots finally fizzled out on 8 June as firepower wreaked its
devastating toll. In the end, at least 210 people were killed, and
75 later died in hospital of their wounds. Damage to property
amounted to what was then the staggering sum of £30,000. The
legal retribution was heavy, too, with 450 arrests and 62 death
sentences, of which 25 were carried out. As exemplary punishment,
the victims were hanged not at Tyburn, but at points close to where
their crimes were committed, a topography of retribution that
also illustrated how widespread the violence actually was, but also
demonstrated the authorities' determination to stamp their authority wherever it had been violated. Twelve others were imprisoned.[27]

Contemporaries now tried to digest the significance of Britain's worst riots of the century. For one, it showed that there was a dark side to British notions of freedom when too much emphasis was laid on its religious dimension. Ignatius Sancho, an African born on a slave ship and now a free adoptive Londoner, wrote, 'This – this – is liberty! Genuine British liberty! This instant about two thousand liberty boys are swearing and swaggering by with large sticks – thus armed in hopes of meeting with the Irish chairmen and labourers'. Wild rumours circulated that the riots were the work of French or American agents, with the ultimate objective being to bankrupt the British state, but on calmer reflection these anxieties were dismissed. Sancho, examining the unpredictable fluidity of the crowd, commented that no one could have been in overall control: 'There requires, I think, a kind of supernatural knowledge to adjust their motions so critically'.[28]

For the radicals, however, the Gordon Riots ruptured the Wilkite connection with the London crowd. This break, by default, also implied that for radicals, anti-Catholicism need no longer have been an essential ingredient in support for political reform. The role of Wilkes himself in putting down the insurgents was symbolic of the breach. Calm, reasonable assembly was one thing, riot and tumult quite another. In the analysis of John Jebb of the SCI, rioting of the kind that set London aflame was not the solution to parliamentary corruption, but rather was a symptom of it. The crowds, in fact, were courting precisely the kind of despotism and tyranny that the radicals feared: the repression of the riots demanded the imposition of military rule on the streets of the metropolis.[29]

Yet the riots had shaken the very kind of people – educated, hardworking but disenfranchised – to whom the metropolitan radicals most wanted to appeal. Looking back with hindsight, one Londoner confessed that although 'I was old enough to know better . . . I was at this time contaminated with the mania in which thousands beside myself were infected by Wilkes, the political mountebank of the day; and which kept us all stupidly looking on the mischief that threatened the public, not aware of its full extent till it came to their own thresholds, which they had not the courage to defend ... From that moment ... I became a convert to loyalty and social order'.[30]

Edmund Burke, again with hindsight, similarly connected the violence of the Gordon Riots with the movement for parliamentary reform: there was, he said, 'much intestine heat and a dreadful fermentation. Wild and savage insurrection quitted the woods, and prowled about our streets in the name of Reform'. Thus, the Society for Constitutional Information faced the defection of a potentially large base of progressive, metropolitan support. The City of London itself, until recently a bulwark of the defence of the liberties of the subject, had found itself in one of the cauldrons of violence. Many of its leaders swung decisively away from its flirtation with the 'mob', and even from reform. In March the next year, the Common Council voted to bar a convention of delegates representing the various reform associations across the country from using the Guildhall. It was a drift towards a conservative loyalism that would continue over the coming years. The SCI soldiered on, but for much of the 1780s, the reform movement began to flag. It received a fillip when the US Constitution in 1787 sparked new political excitement and with a morale-boosting series of celebrations during the centenary of the 'Glorious Revolution' of 1688. But the real radical revival would come with the epochal events across the Channel, in 1789.[31]

IN NEW YORK, the coming of revolution had been embedded and in some ways shaped by the spaces of the city, the neighbourhoods like the waterfront, for example, or the ascribing of deep symbolic importance to the Common by Patriots, where once it had been just a practical and habitual place for New Yorkers to meet. Yet New York had also experienced a revolution because popular protest and action in the streets had connected politically with the resistance to British measures by the colonial leadership in City Hall, the Exchange and the Coffee House. There was still friction – and indeed the potential for conflict – but in New York (as elsewhere in the colonies), a significant portion of the political and social leadership was willing to align itself with the popular movement. This alliance across social interests was revolutionary, not only because both sides shared the common goal of resisting imperial authority even if they did not agree on the means, but also because it ensured that the Patriot opposition would secure control – in a real, physical sense as well as politically – not only of the streets, the Common and the taverns (the meeting places of the people), but also of the formal institutions of colonial government (the seats of elite power). From here, the revolutionaries could successfully challenge the representatives of imperial authority, as well as hound and harass their Loyalist supporters from the streets and public spaces of their city.

No such connection was made in London. Wilkes and the City forged an alliance with the metropolitan crowd in the 1760s and early 1770s, but this was definitively ruptured by the Gordon Riots in 1780, the climax of which was the robust defence of the City and its institutions by some of the very people who had once stirred the metropolitan crowd. It may well have been that, had the rioters restricted their destructive ire to their original targets – the Catholic buildings and neighbourhoods of the metropolis – the reaction of the City's leaders would not have been quite so strong, not least because so many of them, including Brass Crosby, had lent support to the petition. It was when the rioters physically invaded the City, assaulting its main prison, Newgate, and turning

their attack onto the Bank of England that the defensive reflex in
the City's authorities was brought out. The whole affair, in fact,
reveals the fundamental conservatism in the City: Wilkes may
have appealed for universal male suffrage, but he was almost the
lone voice of radical reform amongst the City leadership. When the
Bank of England was defended with vigour, it was not to ease the
legal disabilities suffered by Catholics, but to defend the financial
institution upon which the City's power rested.

Meanwhile, the movement for democratic reform, which was
just beginning to organise in 1780, now had a long struggle to
garner support for political change in the metropolis, not least
because it, too, eschewed cultivating crowd politics: the mass
demonstration that Lord Gordon had organised proved to be terrifyingly destructive. So for at least a decade, metropolitan radicals
would swerve from anything that smacked of revolution and social
disorder. They wanted to persuade the political establishment of
the justice of their case by demonstrating respect for the rule of law
and for the wider framework of the British parliamentary system.
Thus, their activities were restricted to the well-established physical spaces of London's civic culture – Westminster Hall (as we
have seen), coffeehouses, print shops, taverns, lecture rooms and
(as we shall see later) the meetinghouses of a progressive Protestant
movement, the Rational Dissenters. All of these venues reflected
the firmly middle-class membership of the movement for parliamentary reform in these years. Unlike the revolutionary leadership
in America, therefore, the metropolitan radical movement would
not connect with the politics of the street, and, indeed, it would
quite consciously avoid doing so: there would be no mass open-air
meetings promoting parliamentary reform until the early 1790s.

One reason that Britain avoided revolution before 1789,
therefore, was that when politics spilled over into the street,
it did so in a conservative, indeed reactionary and alarmingly

destructive direction. No progressive denizen of London's coffee-houses or bookshops would think of connecting their cause with such raging, incendiary violence outside. It was a lesson that would appear to gain even greater urgency in the light of the example of the far more dramatic and far-reaching upheaval that erupted in France in 1789.

CHAPTER SIX

PARIS RISES: THE COMING OF REVOLUTION, 1776–1789

THOUGHTFUL FRENCH OBSERVERS – not without a little schadenfreude – wondered what lessons they could learn from the Gordon Riots. For conservatives such as the abbé Dubois de Launay, they were a sure sign that parliamentary government, 'stormy and bizarre', was 'an inexhaustible source of trouble and revolutions'. Progressive spirits came to the opposite conclusion. Louis-Sébastien Mercier argued that 'the liberty enjoyed by the people of London, who can rise up almost at will, is troublesome and dangerous', but that it was also a source of strength: 'From that turbulent people capable of demolishing houses are recruited intrepid soldiers and sailors, accustomed to fear nothing. Put that people to sleep beneath the iron rule of an over-sensitive police force ... and England will lose that nerve and energy which are grounded in the ideas of licence'. By contrast, the strength of the police and the Swiss and French regiments that garrisoned Paris had made any serious rioting in the French capital 'morally impossible'. The implication was that riot and disorder were the price to be paid for a free society and a powerful nation: the question remained whether it was worth it. As Mercier's musings on the British model suggested, enlightened French people scrutinised with some admiration the British example of a government limited by a legislature, where power was balanced between the king, Parliament and judiciary. This was not an uncritical examination, not least because educated French readers were well aware that the axe of regicide also lurked within Britain's political heritage.[1]

Yet though French people gazed with a mixture of awe and hostility at their British rivals, by the time of the Gordon Riots they, like their British antagonists, were digesting the other, even livelier, alternative emerging across the Atlantic. The American War of Independence was a cause around which almost all Frenchmen and -women could, at some level, unite. It helped that French enthusiasm for the American Revolution combined with a hearty dose of patriotism when France intervened in the conflict in February 1778. Although French government officials fretted privately about the dangers of absolutist France aiding American republicans, the war galvanised public opinion like never before. Conservatives hoped that the patriotic spirit of revenge against Britain for the humiliation of 1763 would rally the people around the king. Progressives like the marquis de Lafayette saw the struggle as one for freedom, in which the Americans were throwing off tyranny and realising the ideas of the Enlightenment in the New World. For radical spirits like Jacques-Pierre Brissot de Warville, journalist, pamphleteer and political activist, the Americans were forging a new republican system based on the enlightened ideas of the separation of powers, civil and political liberties and a parliamentary system based on a broad suffrage.[2]

French enthusiasm for things American even translated into Parisian women's hairstyles. The *coiffure aux insurgents*, piled high with motifs alluding to the revolution against British rule, was produced by the queen's own dress designer, Rose Bertin, and her favourite hairdresser, Léonard Autié. Coming just before France officially entered the war, it was hastily banned. American republican virtues were embodied in the rotund figure of Benjamin Franklin, the sage of Philadelphia and American envoy to France whose scientific genius, rustically plain dress and straightness in speech seemed to Parisians to make him the quintessential American. Yet it was more than a question of style: each twist and turn in the American Revolution was written about and discussed, stirring the clamour of political debate. Enlightened spirits in the cafés and salons of Paris saw the American cause as their own, laced with the heady spirit of patriotism in a war against the old enemy. No one was able or willing, at least publicly, to admit the inconsistency between France's policy in America and its own political system. The youthful French aristocrats who had supported the American cause saw the abyss only with hindsight. The vicomtesse de Fars-Fausselandry later admitted that 'the American cause seemed our own; we were proud of their victories, we cried at their defeats, we tore down bulletins and read them in our houses. None of us reflected on the danger that the New World could give to the old'.[3]

Few reflected on the danger because no one expected a revolution in France, one of the most powerful monarchies in Europe. The opposition to royal power had so far been expressed primarily within the legal framework of the Parlements and among the reading, critically engaged public in the cafés, clubs and bookshops of France's towns, particularly Paris. It was aimed neither at overthrowing the monarchy nor at undermining the hierarchies of title and privilege that ordered society. That the focal point for this opposition had been the Palais de Justice shows that the people of Paris, by and large, accepted the claim of the Parlement of Paris that, in the absence of a British- or American-style legislature, it was the best constitutional brake on the intrusive impulses within royal power.

Yet by 1789, all this would change: the Parlement would lose almost all credibility with the French public, who would turn to more radical solutions to the political crisis. In Paris this revolutionary transformation was reflected in a spatial sense, as the focal point for the resistance moved first from the seat of the Parlement in the Palais de Justice to the great cauldron of public opinion, the Palais-Royal on the Right Bank, and then, most seismic of all, from the Palais-Royal eastwards to the artisanal district of the Faubourg Saint-Antoine. The first represented the Parlement losing control of the political debate to the journalists, orators and their public who intellectually pummelled, ideologically bludgeoned and rhetorically battered the old order, a pugilism of the pen that was centred on the Palais-Royal, a gathering place, watering hole and pleasure palace that had been thrown open to the public by its owner, the duc d'Orléans, in the last years of the old regime. The second shift marked the final crisis of the old order in 1789, when it became a social as well as a political upheaval. French people across the kingdom rose up – peasants and craft workers, bourgeois and liberal nobles – but it occurred with special vigour in the artisanal district of the Faubourg Saint-Antoine in eastern Paris, spread out beneath the ramparts of the hulking fortress of the Bastille.

These three points in the metropolis – the Palais de Justice, the Palais-Royal and the Faubourg Saint-Antoine – are like a topographical representation of the coming of the French Revolution. Moreover, as bricks-and-mortar places, their existence had a material impact on the shape and outcome of events. Why the crisis came about in the first place, however, lies in a tangled net of causes, but first among them was the fatally high price that the monarchy paid for victory in America. Politically, the language of rights, of liberty and of patriotism had been amplified among some of the most influential men and women in France and across the wider public. Far more dangerous, at least immediately, were the financial costs, for the war plunged the monarchy deeper into debt until it reached critical levels. The great black hole in French finances was not fully understood until 1786, when the controller-general of finances, Charles-Alexandre de Calonne, having spent two years going through the morass of paper in the treasury, discovered the shocking truth: France was almost bankrupt. He broke this news to Louis XVI on 20 August 1786. It was from this date that the crisis of the old regime began.

CALONNE HAD A not-undeserved reputation as a gambler. Moreover, his rival and forerunner as finance minister, Genevan banker Jacques Necker, had (for the first time ever) published the royal accounts in 1781, persuading the public that France's finances were safely in the black, despite the costs of the war. So Calonne faced an uphill battle to convince both the Parlements and public opinion that the situation was actually critical and that immediate root-and-branch reform was essential. For this reason, he tried to outflank the sovereign courts by appointing an Assembly of Notables, consisting, Calonne explained, of 'the most important and enlightened magnates of the realm' who, he hoped, would hear him out and be convinced. Instead, the notables, meeting between February and May 1787, insisted that the only legitimate organ to pass such wide-ranging reforms was the Estates-General, the closest thing to a legislature that France had ever had – and it had not met since 1614. Calonne recoiled, was dismissed in April and left his successor, Loménie de Brienne, to disband the notables in late May 1787 and to press the urgency of reform on the Parlements. The scintillated French public followed the political debates blow by blow. The word on the streets and in the cafés now was that no taxation was legitimate without the consent of the Estates-General. Radical pamphleteer Jacques-Pierre Brissot urged that 'French Constitution' should now be the rallying cry of the opposition: 'Everywhere it should be repeated that the basis for this constitution is the right not to pay taxes without having consented to them'. Questions such as those of royal authority, constitutional laws and the rights of the citizen were debated and discussed across Paris, but nowhere did these great questions generate more white-hot fervour than in the Palais-Royal.[4]

The Palais-Royal was an elegant complex of colonnades, arcades, gardens, fountains, apartments, theatres, offices and boutiques on the Right Bank. Its façade looked over what was then the main east-west thoroughfare, the rue Saint-Honoré. Among those who knew this spot well was Thomas Jefferson: when he first arrived in Paris on 6 August 1784, he, his daughter Patsy, and his servant James Hemings spent their first two nights in the Hôtel d'Orléans, on the rue Richelieu, right next door to the complex. Originally built by Cardinal Richelieu in the 1620s, the Palais-Royal was gifted by Louis XIV to the duc d'Orléans, his younger brother, when the Sun King abandoned Paris for Versailles. The Palais-Royal is still graced by a long formal garden behind the main residence. During the seventeenth century and for most of the eighteenth, this was an exclusive resort. 'Straight pathways, pools of water and flowerbeds divided it', nostalgically remembered the baron de Frénilly years after the Revolution. 'It was a promenade of luxury, of celebration and etiquette. Everywhere there were feathers, diamonds, embroidered outfits and red heels; no "caterpillar" (that is, a common bourgeois in tail-coat and a round hat) would dare show themselves there ... [T]he Palais-Royal was the heart and soul, the centre and the nucleus of the Parisian aristocracy: it was there that it took root'. This exclusive aristocratic retreat was, however, transformed on the very eve of the Revolution.[5]

In 1780 the then duc d'Orléans, 'the Fat', left the palace to live with his mistress in his grand mansion in the Chaussée d'Antin, a luxurious new development to the north of the boulevards. He passed the Palais-Royal on to his son, Louis-Philippe-Joseph. The family was staggeringly wealthy, but so encumbered was he with debts that the heir seized a golden opportunity to generate more income. The gardens would be thrown open to the public, and arcades, designed by neoclassical architect Victor Louis, would be constructed on three sides to house shops, cafés and cabarets. Louis XVI, making a decision that he would surely come to regret, gave the duke his permission, although he could not resist wisecracking that his cousin had become a shopkeeper. The new galleries formed a rectangle, within which were the ornamental gardens shaded by chestnut trees and cooled by fountains. Each of the galleries – Montpensier to the west, Valois to the east and Beaujolais (initially, because the duke ran out of money, made of wood and jocularly dubbed the *camp des Tartares*) to the north – had a cornucopia of watering holes and boutiques. The Palais-Royal rapidly became a draw for crowds of Parisians seeking entertainment, relaxation, free discussion and sexual adventure.[6] The duc d'Orléans, Jefferson wrote, had added 'one of the principal ornaments to the city and increased the convenience of its inhabitants'.[7]

Among those who savoured such 'convenience' was Russian historian Nikolai Karamzin on his visit in 1790. The pleasure gardens were virtually his first port of call after checking into his hotel on 27 March. He crossed the Seine from the Faubourg Saint-Germain as the sun set and the lanterns lit the streets, and as the Palais-Royal was getting lively:

Imagine a magnificent square château, and within that château there are arcades beneath which innumerable shops are resplendent with all the treasures of the world, ... displayed in the most admirable fashion, to seduce the eyes and lit up by bright and dazzling lights of different colours. Imagine a mass of people flowing through these galleries, walking up and down for the sole purpose of looking at each other! There too one sees 'cafés', the foremost in Paris, which are all equally full of people, where one reads out at the top of one's voice the gazettes and the newspapers, where one makes a din, quarrels and makes speeches ... My head began to spin. We left the galleries and we sat in the avenue of chestnut trees of the Palais-Royal garden. There calm and darkness reigned. The light from the arcades cast their light onto the greenery of the branches, but that light was soon lost in the shadows. From another avenue wafted the slow, voluptuous sounds of a gentle music; a soft, fresh wind made the young leaves on the trees rustle.[8]

This was not the end to the wonders: in August 1787, Jefferson reported that the centre of the park was being dug out in order to create 'a subterranean circus ... wherein will be equestrian exhibitions &c'. Jefferson would return frequently to the Palais-Royal, perusing its boutiques for books and artwork.[9]

For the snobbish Frénilly, shuddering with hindsight, the transformation in the Palais-Royal was nothing less than a 'social revolution ... which, by turning one district upside down was the prelude to the upheaval of an entire kingdom'. There was an exhilarating permissiveness. There was intellectual edification, with a scholarly club and two theatres. One could visit a wax museum with likenesses of famous people (including the royal family) or go dancing and carousing. The Palais-Royal also became a centre for eroticism and pornography: a small marionette theatre in the Galerie de Valois started off by putting on shows for children, but soon found it more profitable to offer what would now be called 'adult entertainment'. Prostitutes strutted openly among the columns, vying for the attention of potential clients – Karamzin's own reverie was interrupted by such 'nymphes de joie' who 'promised us any number of pleasures before disappearing like ghosts in a moonlit night'. This hedonism was possible because, as the property of the duc d'Orléans, it was (apart from informers who tried to blend in) free of police and censorship. Its arcades housed booksellers and publishers, Desenne's being the most famous; hawkers of pamphlets, news sheets, broadsides and erotica circulated among the crowds; and the cafés provided newspapers. The Palais-Royal offered an extraordinary – maybe unique – mix of sensual pleasures, sociability and intellectual debate and a torrent of the printed word. Only London's Covent Garden, with its arcades, coffeehouses, taverns, market stalls, opera house and prostitutes, came anywhere close to the Palais-Royal for its ability to draw people. The Palais-Royal soon became the central gathering place of Parisians hungry for news, opinion and recreation, so much so that it was popularly called 'the capital of Paris'.[10]

It was here that Parisians read, all agog, about the tumultuous debates in the Assembly of Notables and then of the resistance of the Parlement of Paris to royal authority. After the dismissal of the notables, the Parlement was locked in a fraught political arm-wrestling with the government as it took up the cry for the Estates-General. The long, hard struggle culminated on 3 May 1788 with the exile of the leading magistrates, who were arrested in their homes in the dead of night. Two, including the most outspoken of them, Duval d'Eprémesnil, managed to escape and took sanctuary in the Palais de Justice. When their remaining colleagues rallied to their side, meeting in the Grand' Chambre, they resolved neither to leave nor to yield the magistrates to arrest. In the night of 5 May, the palace was surrounded by troops, which forced the lawyers to surrender their colleagues before they were disbanded. Three days later, the Parlements were remodelled by a *lit de justice*.[11]

This strike against the Parlement would prove to be the last time the king tried to rule as an absolute monarch, and it unleashed a further flurry of pamphlets denouncing royal despotism. As public and judicial resistance stiffened, Europe's nervous moneymen began to withhold credit to the cash-starved government. Faced with imminent state bankruptcy, the king's minister Brienne finally yielded to the hue and cry and promised to summon the Estates-General. When the royal treasury suspended payments in August, he fixed 1 May 1789 for the first meeting of the Estates at Versailles and then resigned, advising the king to appoint in his place the only minister who enjoyed public confidence, Jacques Necker. When this Genevan banker with a reputation for financial genius took the reins, he simply announced that he could do nothing until the Estates-General met. The monarchy had run out of ideas: all it could do was wait until the representatives of the kingdom breathed new life into reform.[12]

The Parlement – exiled since May – was recalled in September 1788, and when the magistrates returned to the Palais de Justice, they were greeted by an ecstatic, riotous crowd crammed onto the Pont Neuf and led by the Basoche, the law clerks, and the local artisans of the nearby Place Dauphine whose luxury trades did so well out of the presence of the high-spending judges and lawyers. They rallied around the statue of Henri IV, still idolised as a good king, on the Pont Neuf, where they built a festive bonfire. The government did not take any chances, however, and had also surrounded the court with five hundred troops, supported by the elite regiment of the Gardes-Françaises. When the crowd began to pelt the soldiers with stones and firecrackers, the patience of the troops cracked, a sergeant roaring, 'Fire some fucking lead into the arses of this rabble!' None of the bullets hit their mark, although a lawyer sneaking gingerly past had his coat punctured by a stray musket ball. It was only when the Parlement itself banned gatherings and bonfires in the vicinity that the streets were becalmed. Although not at all apparent at the time, this was the last moment that the Palais de Justice proved to be a popular rallying point in the struggle against 'despotism', and even then the backbone of these demonstrations was people whose privileges and livelihoods were tied to the fortunes of the court. The political initiative soon moved across the river to the Palais-Royal, a shift inadvertently provoked by the Parlement itself.[13]

The summoning of the Estates-General had been a great victory for the alliance of Parlements and public opinion, among which debate now positively roared with excitement. The government lifted censorship when it threw open to the public the question of how to make the Estates-General 'a truly national assembly'. Booksellers did a roaring trade, and newspapers suddenly flourished: no fewer than forty new journals appeared in Paris; between September 1788 and May 1789, it has been estimated that throughout the country, readers were deluged with no fewer than four million copies of different publications discussing the issue. Political clubs met across the city, including in the rented rooms in the upper storeys of the galleries of the Palais-Royal, now *the* venue for tumultuous argument. The moment that the 'capital of Paris' also became the capital of revolution arose on 25 September 1788, when the Parlement issued its response to the question of how the Estates-General should meet: they should 'follow the form observed in 1614'.[14]

When the meaning of this innocuous-sounding phrase became clearer, there was uproar. In 1614 the three orders – the clergy, the nobility and the Third Estate (representing everyone else) – had met, deliberated and voted separately, and then each had produced a single collective decision, the implication being that the two 'privileged orders', the clergy and the nobles, would usually combine to subordinate the collective voice of the Third Estate. Consequently, the clergy and the nobility would be well equipped to defend their privileges, fiscal or otherwise. The Paris Parlement's judgement of September 1788 seemed to reveal that its purpose was to uphold privilege and hierarchy rather than to defend the interests of the vast majority of the nation. The ferment of debate in the cafés, clubs and the press demanded and expected the Estates-General to be a representative, reformist body, the beginnings of a new constitutional order that defended the rights not only of the highly privileged few, but of the people as a whole.

As the elections to the Estates-General approached in the new year, the ground in the political debate had shifted. Where the Parlement had once been applauded for demanding a 'restoration' or a 'revival' of the traditional 'constitution', the wider public now demanded a complete renewal, a break with the past – nothing less than 'regeneration', which was the word now in the air. While only months before the magistrates had been the popular heroes, the defenders of the nation against royal despotism, they now appeared to have been, all along, struggling only to defend the interests of the elites. Jefferson wrote that if the dispute could be resolved peacefully, the meeting of the Estates-General 'will obtain a fixed, free, and wholesome constitution'.[15]

Events unfolded differently. With the political rupture, people who were now calling themselves 'patriots' – those opposed to both royal despotism and aristocratic privilege – gathered daily in the Palais-Royal. Symbolic of this topographical shift in initiative was a striking fact, noted by Genevan journalist Jacques Mallet du Pan: the *parlementaire* Duval d'Eprémesnil, once 'the avenger of the nation, the Brutus of France', was now 'vilified everywhere' . . . and nowhere more than in the Palais-Royal, where he could not set foot without being hissed at by the crowds. Bertrand Barère, the future Jacobin, noted how political pamphlets were suddenly – and openly – flying off the shelves of Desenne's bookshop. Masse's restaurant in the arcades was the meeting place for the Club des Enragés (the Club of Fanatics), which, according to Abbé Emmanuel Sieyès, was the 'largest, best known and most active' of all the patriotic societies.[16]

Sieyès knew what he was talking about, because it was his pamphlet, his contribution to the torrent of opinion and argument, that made the greatest impact of all. This was *What Is the Third Estate?*, published, at first anonymously, in late January 1789. It stood out from the blizzard of other pamphlets in the war of words because of the utterly ruthless logic of its arguments, articulating public hostility to the limitations on the voice of the Third Estate in the starkest of terms. Greeted with an enthusiastic public reception, within weeks perhaps as many as thirty thousand copies were sold. Public readings were held in cafés, reading clubs and political societies.[17]

The Third Estate, Sieyès argued, contained all the productive parts of society, those who tilled the land, manufactured goods, traded and offered the services of the liberal professions, but its representatives, the true delegates of the nation, were shackled by the self-serving resistance of the clergy and nobility to equal political representation for all citizens. As long as the aristocracy refused to abandon its privileges, it would be 'foreign to the nation ... because it consists of defending its particular interests rather than the common good'. The message was clear: in the new order, there could be no privileges, only citizens sharing the same rights and duties. With crystalline clarity, he offered a vision of a politics based on the one and only source of legitimacy: the nation. 'The nation', he famously declared, 'exists before everything, it is the origin of everything. Its will is always legal, it is the law itself. Before it and above it there is only the law of nature'.[18]

The political struggle around the Estates-General had effectively redrawn the battle lines. It was no longer a question of royal 'despotism' against the kingdom's 'fundamental laws', the ancient 'constitution' and the privileges of the subject. It was now a struggle between the conservative defence of those old aspirations and a new vision of a political order based on national sovereignty, equal citizenship and the natural rights of man.

In March, Jefferson remarked to a fellow American that 'the change in this country, since you left it, is such as you can form no idea of. The frivolities of conversation have given way entirely to politicks – men, women and children talk nothing else; and all you know talk a great deal. The press groans with daily productions, which in point of boldness make an Englishman stare, who hitherto thought himself the boldest of men'.[19]

The political conflict grew more intense when the Estates-General gathered at Versailles in May. The Third Estate took on the two privileged orders from the start. The cable, as Sieyès put it, was cut on 17 June, when the Third Estate renamed itself the National Assembly, the only legitimate representative of the sovereign people. Three days later, the National Assembly found itself locked out of its usual debating chamber. The venue was actually closed for cleaning before a great Royal Session of the Estates-General, but the deputies feared that something more sinister – a royal coup – was behind the closure. Led by their president, astronomer (and Paris deputy) Jean-Sylvain Bailly, the National Assembly stood together in the nearby indoor royal tennis court to swear that they would not part until 'the constitution of the Realm and public regeneration are established and assured'. Gradually, the more liberal minds among the clergy and the nobles wavered, deserted their own order and joined the National Assembly; the first noble defectors were led by none other than the duc d'Orléans on 25 June.[20]

Paris had been watching and discussing the developments in Versailles with almost frenzied excitement. Crowds, anxious, exhilarated, buzzing, thronged into the Palais-Royal, where business was at its briskest ever. British traveller (and agricultural expert) Arthur Young, visiting on 9 June 1789, was astounded:

> I went to the Palais-Royal to see what new things were published, and to procure a catalogue of all. Every hour produces something new. Thirteen came out to-day, sixteen yesterday, and ninety-two last week. We think sometimes that Debrett's or Stockdale's shops at London are crowded, but they are mere deserts compared to Desein's [Desennes], and some others here, in which one can scarcely squeeze from the door to the counter ... [T]he coffee-houses in the Palais-Royal ... are not only crowded within, but other expectant crowds are at the doors and windows, listening à gorge déployée to certain orators, who from chairs or tables harangue each his little audience ... I am all amazement at the ministry permitting such nests and hotbeds of sedition and revolt, which disseminate amongst the people, every hour, principles that by and by must be opposed with vigour, and therefore it seems little short of madness to allow the propagation at present.[21]

The duc d'Orléans's son Louis-Philippe later recalled the role of the pleasure gardens in the onset of the French Revolution. Looking back, he observed that the warm, dry weather had aided and abetted the spirit of resistance in the Palais-Royal: 'It was very hot in 1789, and the marvellous summer proved a valuable ally of the Revolution: frequent downpours would have made excellent agents of repression and would have been an excellent way of dispersing gatherings large and small'. The Palais-Royal was the perfect spot for politics alfresco: it was, revolutionary Joseph Cerutti would later say, the 'birthplace of the Revolution'.[22]

YET A PAMPHLET debate, a war of words, was one thing, a full-blooded insurrection with actual shooting and bloodshed quite another. When the patriotic opposition moved from the one to the other, so, too, for a while, did the centre of action slip from the Palais-Royal to the epicentre of the popular uprising, the Faubourg Saint-Antoine. The special character of the Faubourg Saint-Antoine, the easternmost district of Paris, rested on a unique combination of topography and social makeup. It had grown up around the main road, the grande rue du Faubourg Saint-Antoine, that led eastwards away from the Bastille towards the *barrière* at the Place du Trône (now Place de la Nation). It therefore lay outside the old city, its topography helping to forge a strong sense of community. For one, all streets within the faubourg eventually intersected with either the grande rue or the rue de Charenton, so anyone who had some business found themselves at some point on one of these streets. The same people passed by every day, getting to know each other by sight and speaking with each other, to trade or to banter. The houses were smaller – usually three or four storeys – than the towering tenements of the city centre, and rather than build high, developers had constructed long courtyards and alleyways, combining workshops with residences, with many people living in houses behind those that fronted the streets. Though far from salubrious, the courtyards encouraged sociability: neighbours got to know each other very well. Even today, a stroll around the Faubourg Saint-Antoine and into one of its many courts will provide a sense of this social geography. Moreover, anyone from the faubourg who had business to transact in the city had to pass around the Bastille – the only direct way into the centre for the *faubouriens* – and in the process they walked through a clutter of market stalls and street sellers hawking their wares. People stopped, chatted, bought and sold food, drink and flowers – and got to know each other at this point of exit and entry.[23]

The Faubourg Saint-Antoine had a social solidarity rooted in the fact that it was relatively homogeneous: 87 per cent of its people worked in the skilled trades, most famously the ébénistes – furniture and cabinetmakers – as well as the shopkeepers, bakers, vintners and street sellers who catered to them. There was a semiofficial recognition that the faubourg was indeed somehow distinct. Most of it was part of a single parish, that of Sainte Marguerite – it is perhaps no surprise that the *faubouriens* should rally so readily to the familiar toll of the church's bell during the Revolution's great insurrectionary moments. Most important of all, the faubourg's artisans were allowed to practise their trades without needing a master's certificate from the Parisian guilds or corporations. This gave the district's location outside the lines of the old city walls a real economic meaning. Other districts, such as the Faubourg Saint-Marcel to the south or the market district of Les Halles in the centre, had close bonds of community and neighbourhood that gave them a cohesion that lent itself to political mobilisation during the Revolution. Yet the topography and location of the Faubourg Saint-Antoine probably made it especially militant because it was conscious of being *outside* the city – indeed, its residents could be defensively so when, as happened from time to time, the Parisian guilds made forays into the area to try to force its artisans to give up their trades.[24]

This sense of distinctiveness; the close ties of community; the geography of its streets, courtyards and workshops; and the independent artisanal makeup of its population ensured that the Faubourg Saint-Antoine would be in the vanguard of the popular movement during the French Revolution. The closest equivalent in revolutionary New York was probably the waterfront, but though the maritime culture of its denizens forged close, subversive ties, the population was almost by definition permanently on the move, transient. London's artisans and labourers, particularly in the East End areas like the docks, Spitalfields and Stepney, had strong bonds with their trades and neighbourhoods, all of which may help to explain the determination and even the violence with which they had pursued their strikes in the 1760s. But there was nothing in either English-speaking city to match the Faubourg Saint-Antoine for its geographical cohesion, its homogeneity, its separateness and its defensiveness of it.

Yet the Faubourg Saint-Antoine's economic and social fortunes were, perhaps despite itself, closely interwoven with those of Paris. The fruit, vegetable and flower growers who cultivated the fields and market gardens that gave the faubourg its green spaces carted their produce into the central markets around Les Halles, as did the district's bakers and brewers. Meanwhile, the artisans of the faubourg bought much of their raw material from workshops and wholesalers in the city centre: the tailors, for example, purchased their fabrics, buttons and ribbons from the producers who worked around the rue Saint-Denis. The district's crucial lifeline was the central markets at Les Halles, from where its families bought most of their food. There was, therefore, a lot of to-ing and fro-ing with the city centre, which made the spread of news and rumour rapid and regular. Above all, the faubourg's artisans, craft workers, shopkeepers, men and women would learn very quickly when food was scarce in the central markets and when prices had risen. When economic disaster occurred, the solidarity and the social networks of the faubourg helped to mobilise its artisans in protest.

The summer of 1789 was just such a time, but it was made all the more intense because it was larded with the political crisis. The weather throughout 1788 had been disastrous, producing a desperately poor harvest in the late summer. By November the price of bread had become prohibitive for many labourers. It only got worse as the winter closed in.[25] When spring came, Jefferson wrote to a friend, 'We have had such a winter, Madam, as makes me shiver yet whenever I think of it. All communications almost were cut off. Dinners and suppers were suppressed, and the money laid out in feeding and warming the poor, whose labours were suspended by the rigour of the season. Loaded carriages past the Seine on the ice, and it was covered with thousands of people from morning to night, skaiting [*sic*] and sliding. Such sights were never seen before, and they continued two months'.[26] In December bookseller Hardy estimated that there were eighty thousand unemployed in the city.

On 27–28 April 1789, a crowd of workers in the Faubourg Saint-Antoine utterly gutted the homes of the rich wallpaper manufacturer Jean-Baptiste Réveillon and a gunpowder manufacturer named Henriot. Both had made remarks about the price of bread that were misinterpreted: Réveillon had commented that the high prices put pressure on wages, but this was reported on the streets as a demand to lower the pay of the already hard-pressed labourers. The looters were dispersed only after the Gardes-Françaises and the Swiss Guards, army units charged with keeping order in the city, fired volleys into the rioters, killing as many as three hundred people.

This economic distress melded dangerously with political anger, and not just over the 'high' politics in Versailles. Sieyès's claim that the Third Estate was 'everything' was in practice wide of the mark, for the Third Estate was not elected by all members of that order. In Paris (where voting took place on 20–21 April), to vote one had to pay direct taxes and have a university degree, a post in the civil service or a military commission. Failing that, he (with rare exceptions, women were excluded) had to pay at least six livres in capitation, or poll tax, to qualify. This made an electorate of 150,000 (or about a quarter of the Paris population), across sixty districts. The electoral assemblies of the districts then chose 400 electors who would meet in the Hôtel de Ville to select the Paris deputies from among themselves. Amongst a population already fired up by the tumult of debate, the exclusion of much of the city's working population – journeymen, apprentices, stall holders and domestic servants – caused a storm. 'Our deputies are not going be our deputies', fulminated a draper, because 'we can have no part in choosing them'. In the Faubourg Saint-Antoine, perhaps as many as two-thirds of the male citizens were denied the vote, an exclusion that may further explain the violence that came in July.[27]

This stemmed from the political deadlock at Versailles. The defiance of the National Assembly had so alarmed the king that troops had begun being marched into the area in mid-June. By the end of the first week of July, the buildup of royal forces was sinisterly obvious. On 11 July, Jefferson wrote to Thomas Paine that 'great bodies of troops and principally of the foreign corps [mercenary regiments] were approaching Paris from different quarters. They arrived in the number of 25, or 30,000 men. Great inquietude took place'. A new harder line seemed to be imminent when finance minister Jacques Necker, popular because he believed in close government regulation of the grain trade so as to ensure an affordable supply of food, was dismissed by Louis XVI on 11 July. In so doing, the king accidentally lit the fuse. News of Necker's dismissal reached the Palais-Royal in the afternoon of 12 July. One of those who rose to speak to the alarmed crowds was a young, aspiring journalist named Camille Desmoulins, who leapt atop a table outside the Café de Foy (at Nos. 57–60 in the Galerie de Montpensier, on the western side of the gardens) and urged them to arms. A vast crowd of protesters of all social backgrounds marched through the city, forcing the theatres to close.

The collision happened on the Place Louis XV, where a regiment of German cavalry scattered the demonstrators, forcing them to flee across the turn bridge that led into the Tuileries Gardens and, in their pursuit, allegedly (in a report that appears to have been false) killing or severely wounding an old man. Parisians feared the worse: the government was using force to assert its authority.[28]

That night the customs barriers that surrounded the city were burned. They were, after all, the physical locations where the hated tax the *octroi* was levied on goods entering the city, elevating prices. As order collapsed, the electors of Paris, who had continued to gather unofficially in the Hôtel de Ville, assumed authority from the royal officials in the capital. They hastily formed a citizens' militia, eight hundred men from each of the electoral districts, to defend the city from the king's forces and to protect property from civil disorder. With the city in insurrection, the electors directed the new, as yet unarmed, civilian force towards strictly strategic targets. Meanwhile, the public voice, gathered in the Palais-Royal, gave popular, spontaneous legitimacy to the uprising. Over the following day and into the next, the citizen-soldiers frantically scoured the city for weapons and ammunition, raiding the royal stores in one of the great palaces on the Place Louis XV and, in the morning of 14 July, plundering the military hospital of the Invalides. Later that day, this search for arms provoked the great flash point that turned Paris's collision with royal authority into a revolution. This was the storming of the Bastille.

THE BASTILLE ROSE in the East of the city, a fourteenth-century fortress overlooking the Faubourg Saint-Antoine that once protected the city's eastern entrance. Its eight round towers, joined with thick walls a hundred feet high, loomed symbolically in the minds of French people as a symbol of arbitrary power, the dark side of the absolute monarchy. As the city grew around it and eventually engulfed it, its military purpose fell into lassitude, and it assumed a role that gave the Bastille its sinister reputation: a state prison. It was here that prisoners arrested by virtue of the *lettres de cachet*, warrants issued at will by the king, were locked away: writer Voltaire was twice a 'guest', in 1717–1718 and again in 1726, while the marquis de Sade was held here between 1784 and 1789; he was transferred to the Charenton asylum just ten days before the tumultuous events of 14 July.

The ritual of a prisoner's arrival into the Bastille cloaked the prison in mystery. The captive was always shrouded in anonymity, borne in a shuttered coach. As it rumbled through each gate passing from the outer courtyard into the inner, the soldiers on guard turned about-face so that they did not catch a glimpse of the anonymous passenger. Once inside the fortress, the prisoner was locked away in a cell in one of the eight towers. All captives were meant to be questioned by a commissioner from the Châtelet – the headquarters of the royal police in the city – or, if very important, by the lieutenant of police himself. A report was made with a recommendation to the king. If the prisoner was lucky, the monarch would issue a second *lettre de cachet* ordering his or her release, but of the 240 prisoners held during Louis XVI's reign, only 38 were this fortunate. The turnkeys, who were responsible for the day-to-day treatment of the prisoners, were not allowed to speak to them, and on their release the inmates were sworn not to say anything about their time inside (a promise that many blithely ignored).[29]

So the Bastille seemed to be the very embodiment of the oppression of the old order. Conditions in the Bastille were in fact better than those in prisons reserved for criminals. If, by 1789, the inmates were no longer allowed to bring in their own money, food and (since most of these prisoners were well-heeled) servants, they were still permitted to have other personal belongings, while their meals (the food was said to be good) were provided by the fortress kitchens. The Bastille did have dark, damp dungeons in the foundations – the notorious *cachots* – as well as cells in the very top of the towers, icy in the winter and broiling in the summer, but the former were not used after 1776 and the latter only for short periods to punish rebellious prisoners. From that date, too, prisoners ceased to be bound with chains. Torture to secure confessions had been abolished by the monarchy in 1780, and one of Louis XVI's last ministers, the baron de Breteuil, ordered that any *lettre de cachet* should give some indication as to the length of time the prisoner should be held. The fortress did have its secrets: in the archives held within its walls were the papers of the lieutenant of police, who kept under lock and key the documents that his men had seized, including some of the outrageous, illegal pornographic literature soiling the reputation of Louis XVI's queen, Marie-Antoinette, and the evidence that they had built up in the course of their investigations. It also had an arsenal, which would carry the greatest weight in July 1789. By then, thanks in large part to its not undeserved reputation as a bastion of arbitrary rule, the Bastille was not only feared by Parisians, but also resented, and perhaps the latter more than the former.[30]

To keep the garrison's reserves of gunpowder from falling into Parisian hands, Swiss mercenaries had been employed in the dead of night to cart it the short distance from the arsenal to the Bastille. Now, in the morning of 14 July, the cannon that bristled from the ramparts were trained menacingly over the eastern districts of the city, including the Faubourg Saint-Antoine. Of the 602 people who would assault the fortress, 425 of them came from here. The trouble began after armed citizens had begun to gather in the spaces outside the Bastille, early in the morning of 14 July. Runners were sent out to find the Gardes-Françaises, whose troops – worn down by their task of policing a fractious civilian population and reluctant to fire on a people with whom they had begun to fraternise – were now demonstrably mutinous and ready to support the insurgents.

A delegation from the city's electors, who had formed themselves into a permanent committee, appealed to the Bastille's governor, the marquis Bertrand-René de Launay, to pull his artillery back from the ramparts, but not all the massed ranks of armed Parisians knew about this. So when de Launay, anxious to avoid a confrontation, pulled his guns back from the walls, the people below concluded that the guns were being loaded to fire, and the attack began. The assailants felled the first drawbridge, which allowed them to surge into the inner Cour du Gouvernement. Here the firing began in earnest. The attackers reached the moat of the citadel itself, clamouring on the defenders, Swiss troops and veterans, to lower the drawbridge, which was greeted by a murderous volley from the embrasures at either side. The insurgents made repeated attempts on the bridge, only to be driven back by a hail of musket balls. They set fire to two hay carts to send up a smoke screen, and the flames ignited the governor's house. A further delegation from the city electors, whose meeting room in the Hôtel de Ville just under a mile away to the west along the rue Saint-Antoine, had started to fill up with the wounded, could not make themselves heard above the gunfire.[31]

Eventually, marching in double time, two mutinous companies of the Gardes-Françaises surged down the rue Saint-Antoine from the city centre, along with five cannon being hauled by horses commandeered from cab drivers. Women marched among them, carrying gunpowder and musket balls in their aprons. Two of the guns were wheeled through the debris and corpse-strewn courtyards of the Bastille to the Cour de Gouvernement, from where the drawbridge could be blasted into matchwood. Inside the fortress, de Launay frantically scribbled a note demanding that the attackers accept the garrison's surrender with a guarantee of its safety, or else 'we shall blow up the garrison and the whole neighbourhood'. It was five o'clock. An officer inside the bastion waved the note at the attackers through a gap in the drawbridge, while a white flag fluttered from the ramparts. The insurgents eased a plank of wood across the moat to allow one of them to retrieve the letter. Its contents merely infuriated the crowd, who started to shout, 'Down with the bridges! No capitulation!' The gunners were preparing to fire on the still raised drawbridge when, without warning, its chains clattering, it fell open. It is not clear why this happened. Perhaps the defenders decided that it was better to throw themselves onto the mercy of the Parisians than to be immolated in a storm of explosives and falling masonry, or maybe de Launay had lost his nerve. When the Parisians surged across the bridge, taking the garrison prisoner, the fighting was over, although de Launay would shortly be butchered and his head paraded on a pike. Eighty-three attackers lay dead. Another seventy-five were wounded, fifteen mortally, and thirteen maimed for life. All the prisoners – seven in total – were freed.[32]

Jefferson learned about the battle that evening from Ethis de Corny, one of the Parisian electors who had tried to parley with de Launay that fateful day. He would shortly pay sixty livres to the widows of those killed in the assault on the fortress. In his own account of what followed, in a letter to Thomas Paine on 17 July, Jefferson explained that the king 'went to his States general, and surrendered as it were at discretion and this day he and they have come in solemn procession to satisfy the city ... A more dangerous scene of war I never saw in America, than what Paris has presented for 5 days past. This places the power of the States[-General] abso-lutely out of the reach of attack, and they may be considered as having a carte blanche'.[33] This was the symbolic moment of royal capitulation in Paris, which Jefferson witnessed firsthand:

The king came to Paris, leaving the queen in consternation for his return ... [T]he king's carriage was in the center, on each side of it the States general, in two ranks, afoot, at their head the Marquis de la Fayette as commander in chief, on horseback, and Bourgeois guards before and behind. About 60,000 citizens in all forms and colours, armed with the muskets of the Bastille and Invalides as far as they would go, the rest with pistols, swords, pikes, pruning hooks, scythes &c. lined all the streets thro' which the procession passed, and, with the crowds of people in the streets, doors and windows, saluted them every where with cries of 'vive la nation'. But not a single 'vive le roy' was heard. The king landed at the Hotel de ville. There Monsieur Bailly [the Parisian deputy to the Estates-General, now the first revolutionary mayor of Paris] presented and put into his hat the popular [red, white and blue] cockade, and addressed him ... On their return the popular cries were 'vive le roy et la nation'. He was conducted by a garde Bourgeoise to his palace at Versailles, and thus concluded such an Amende honorable as no sovereign ever made, and no people ever received.[34]

Power now lay in the hands of the National Assembly, which would embark on the revolutionary transformation of French politics and society.

THE PARISIAN EXPERIENCE of revolution in 1789 was not, of course, caused by the urban geography and the cityscape, but they did play a part in shaping its course. It is hard to imagine the insurrection of July 1789 unfolding in the way it did – and even having the revolutionary results that it did – without the existence of the contentious cauldron of the Palais-Royal to give it a political voice. The stormy blend of fear, hope and expectation of change, articulated in a language of nation, patriotism and rights, and of the defence of the people against 'ministerial despotism' gave legitimacy both to the uprising and to the assumption of power by the Parisian electors in the Hôtel de Ville, hundreds of yards to the east of the Palais-Royal. The Revolution of July 1789 of course involved people of all backgrounds and from right across the metropolis. Yet the enormous contribution of the *faubouriens* of Saint-Antoine – the citizens of that special district – is striking. The Bastille fell because the almost unique topography and social unity of that neighbourhood gave a solidarity and organisation to the people who provided the hard, militant core of this climactic moment in the uprising.

What bound the Palais-Royal and the Faubourg Saint-Antoine together was not just that the roar of debate in the one and the armed force of the other drove in the same political direction, but also that both were sites where independent action – of the word or of deed – had become a habit. The Palais-Royal, a once exclusive space now opened to all, was one of those rare public places beyond the reach of the authorities, free from censorship. Yet this alone probably would not have been enough to make it the 'birthplace of the revolution': the crowds were drawn because it offered not only intellectual edification and political debate, but also galleries, shops, cafés and the promise of sensual pleasures of all kinds. Its irresistible combination of news, opinion, debate and recreation ensured the Palais-Royal its unique place in the onset of revolution in Paris.

Similarly, albeit for different reasons, the Faubourg Saint-Antoine presented a singular combination of currents, with its topographical distinctiveness, neighbourhood cohesion and militant independence, even as it was interwoven with the city through a myriad of daily personal and commercial contacts with the central districts. Thus, the historical accident of the Bastille's location could not have been less fortuitous for the absolute monarchy. In the end, the Revolution arose from a powerful alignment of two forces made possible by two parts of the city, both, in their own ways, beyond the complete grasp of the authorities: the one the central political rallying point for Parisian opinion, the other the backbone of the popular uprising. This combination of people from a cross-section of the urban population, mobilised in two different yet complementary locations, was explosive and, it seemed, irresistible: it helps explain the decisive victory of the 'Third Estate' – or, rather, the National Assembly – in the Revolution of 1789.

The question now confronting the stunned representatives of the people at Versailles was what to do with the power that had tumbled from the hands of the king into the debating chamber of the National Assembly. It faced a gargantuan task. Immediately, the assembly had to restore calm and order, not only in Paris but also across the kingdom, where revolutionary authorities – electors and citizens' militias like those in Paris – wrested control from royal officials in the great provincial cities and where an insurrection swept across the countryside as the peasantry rose up against the manorial system. Yet the National Assembly had also inherited the financial and political crisis from the absolute monarchy, and, within weeks, the revolutionaries were tackling it with aplomb. In doing so, they would embark on one of the most far-reaching overhauls of society, law, politics and administration carried out by any revolutionary regime in the modern age.

This dramatic transformation would be written in public spaces and places across the country, but perhaps nowhere more strikingly than in Paris. Parisians would experience their revolution not only in terms of changes in institutions, personnel, ideas and language, but also in their built environment as once familiar buildings that studded their city were taken over by the new regime. This had already begun, in fact, in the most dramatic way possible, with the demolition of the Bastille itself, hunk by hunk of masonry. Yet as we shall see, the most important and far-reaching change in the cityscape would be the adoption and conversion of buildings across the capital by the institutions of the revolutionary order. This would be the visual and spatial change that no one could miss, not least because no area of the formal lives of French citizens would be left untouched by the overhaul. This would go further than the mere occupation of spaces and their physical alteration for new purposes. The Revolution was also an ideological transformation, in which a new language of politics – of citizenship, nation, liberty and rights – would be expressed in the rhetoric, symbols and practices of politics; it was, in other words, a cultural revolution.

To establish itself in the hearts and minds of all citizens, the new regime would exploit the opportunities that the cultural life and sociability of the eighteenth century offered in order to get its message across: the press, theatres, clubs and even the imprinting of revolutionary motifs on fashion, furniture and such everyday items as playing cards. Part of this concerted effort to reach into the daily lives of the people would be the embellishment of buildings with the colours, symbols and slogans of the new civic order. Thus, the revolutionary change to the built environment would be both spatial, as the new regime implanted its institutions and personnel in once familiar buildings in every neighbourhood, and cultural, with the interior and exterior of those buildings decorated with the paraphernalia that expressed the aspirations and principles of the Revolution.

The scale of this revolutionary transformation would be particularly profound in Paris, but New York was undergoing a similar experience, if with less intensity. Indeed, the striking difference in the changes that their respective cityscapes underwent reflects the depth and radicalism of the French Revolution as opposed to the more moderate transition of the American. Yet there is an overlap in the experience: the resistance to authority that occurred in both New York (up to 1776) and Paris (in 1789) was shaped by existing places, spaces and neighbourhoods. From now on, the story takes a new turn, as the new civic order in both cities tried to make new political impressions on the cityscape.

London, meanwhile, would avoid revolution altogether, but the response there to the upheaval in France produced no less a fiery ideological collision and, ultimately, a bruising political clash between the conservative order and the reform movement. Although the great imperial capital would not experience the revolutionary transformations of a Paris or a New York, the battle between British conservatism and radicalism would be rooted no less in places and spaces of the metropolis. Yet since New York offers an interesting point of comparison to Paris in the experience of revolutionary transition, it is to there that the story turns next.

CHAPTER SEVEN

NEW YORK: CAPITAL CITY, 1783–1789

W HEN THE REVOLUTIONARIES took power in Paris in 1789, they inherited the fabric of an ancient city. The public buildings that they would use for their new institutions had been built over centuries for the purposes of the hierarchical and monarchical society that had evolved, like the city itself, organically: churches, abbeys and convents; aristocratic mansions and town houses; royal palaces and the offices of the fiscal, administrative and legal branches of the king's government; law courts and prisons; guardhouses and barracks; and the spaces for the ceremonial display of royal authority, such as the Tuileries Gardens, the Place Louis XV and the parade ground on the western fringes of the city, the Champ de Mars.

When Washington's Continental forces marched into New York in November 1783, they took over buildings and spaces that had been used by the colonial regime. New York's post-war experience of republican transformation foreshadowed, on a smaller scale, the transitions later seen in Paris: it saw its civic sites physically transformed, as the young republican regime sought to establish its presence in a powerful visual and cultural sense, with the embellishments and adaptation of buildings and some name changes. There was even some social upheaval expressed in spatial terms, as Loyalists left their houses and grounds behind and saw them confiscated and parcelled out for sale. Thus, the transformations in New York's cityscape in the years between the British withdrawal and the inauguration of George Washington as president in 1789 anticipated the even more far-reaching experience of Paris in the 1790s.

FROM 1783 NEW York recovered from the years of British military occupation as it adjusted to the republican order, as the districts gutted by fire in 1776 were rebuilt and as it expanded northwards along Manhattan Island again. As it emerged, phoenix-like, from the ashes of war, it also became the battleground for the fiery partisanship of American politics as the revolutionaries grappled with one of the greatest controversies of the epoch – the drafting and ratification of the Constitution.

The issues that Americans had confronted at war's end were legion, but for New Yorkers two tasks stood out. The first was the physical reconstruction of their city after the fire and the dilapidation that had arisen from years of wartime occupation. The second was to forge a stable political order that would bind together the widely divergent interests within the new nation, after a conflict that had torn communities apart. New York's challenges in overcoming the first problem were immense. Much of the city was still a devastated wreck, the burned-out shells of buildings from the fire of 1776 still home to the now notorious 'canvas town'. The ravages of wartime had taken their toll of many buildings, public and private. James Duane, New York's first post-war mayor who had ridden into the city with Washington on Evacuation Day, found his two houses gutted, as if they had been 'inhabited by savages or wild beasts'. Many streets had been utterly disfigured: the trenches dug in 1776 now reeked with stagnant water, and the redoubts were piled high with filth. Garbage was strewn everywhere.[1]

The anger of one Patriot writer dripped from his pen: 'We took possession of a ruined city':

> The most elegant parts of the city were laid in ashes, and what was formerly an ornament now appears a pile of ruins. Dirt, filth, and stench filled the houses and streets; there was daily exercised a shameful and wanton abuse of the houses and property of the exiled ... [T]he quays, wharfs and streets were suffered to forego the ruin for eight long years ... [T]he places of worship and other public edifices, were converted into gaols and hospitals; the dead were not suffered to rest in their graves, the burying yards were laid open, and public roads made through them.[2]

Even allowing for exaggeration, the task was gargantuan, but rebuild the city did, and it began its northward development, too, expanding up Manhattan Island. Much of this was due to the energetic stewardship of Mayor Duane, who appointed five commissioners to oversee the reconstruction of the ruined districts. The process of rebuilding was long and complex, but New York City soon began to show signs of the commercial vibrancy that it had boasted before the war. In fact, there was early evidence that it would surpass its former mercantile vigour. On 22 February 1784, as the ice from a hard winter released its hold on the wharves of the East River, a black-hulled ship cast off. Watched by an excited crowd on the waterfront and the Battery, the crew unfurled the Stars and Stripes from its stern and sailed the great vessel out of the bay into the ocean. Its destination was Guangzhou (Canton), the only port in China open to foreign merchants, and its aspirational name was *Empress of China*. It was, the *Independent Gazette* reminded its readers, 'the first ship from this new nation, to that rich and distant part of the world'. The ship returned to New York on 11 May 1785, laden with tea and chinaware, a fact that John Jay, then secretary of state, celebrated as the 'first effort of the citizens of America, to establish a direct trade with China' when he informed Congress. That commerce would have been unthinkable before independence, when the East India Company jealously guarded its monopoly of all British trade in Asia. *Empress of China* had blazed a trail for further voyages – and more ships followed its long yet profitable voyage around Cape Horn and across the Pacific.[3]

Yet there was a price to be paid for New York City's resurgence. Those who paid dearly – at least in the first years after the evacuation – were the Loyalists. Some Tories in New York had wishfully thought that the incoming regime would bury past differences. They were disabused after the first post-war elections in December 1783, when the radicals won landslides in the votes for the city's Common Council and for the legislature of New York State, whose capital was then in New York City. The triumphant radicals gave full vent to their anti-Tory impulses. The pre-war 'Whig triumvir' Robert R. Livingston had noted that there were three contending parties: 'the tories, who still hope for power' but who in fact were cowed by the atmosphere of Patriot revenge; 'the violent Whigs, who are for expelling all tories from the state'; and 'those who wish to suppress all violences, to soften the rigor of the laws against the loyalists'. Yet the tide was radical, with artisanal voters aroused by the revivified Mechanics Committee, which breathed life into the old alliance of middling merchants, artisans and mariners that had been the backbone of the Sons of Liberty. Radicals took their seats in the city's Common Council and in the two houses of the state legislature created by the New York State Constitution of 1777. With the moderate James Duane chosen as mayor by the Council of Appointment (responsible for naming local officials), there was at least a calming influence at the very centre of city politics, but most of the drift was radical, with the veteran Sons of Liberty Marinus Willett becoming sheriff and John Lamb collector of the port. Moreover, the state governor was none other than George Clinton, a fire-breathing Patriot who had once colourfully remarked that 'I would rather roast in hell to all eternity than . . . show mercy to a damned Tory'.[4]

Buoyed by their electoral triumph, the old Sons of Liberty and the mechanics resorted to their old habits of action in the streets. At the end of December 1783, Loyalist publisher and journalist James Rivington was 'visited' by Willett, Sears and Lamb and forced to give up his rebranded newspaper. The *Pennsylvania Packet* later reported gleefully that 'Jemmy Rivington's political existence terminated last Wednesday, the 31st ultimo'. The journalist's role as an agent for Washington (who, according to one witness, discreetly rewarded him with two bags of gold) still remained a secret. More broadly, a mass meeting was held in May 1784 – naturally, on the Common – to demand that 'every tory or person suspected of toryism should be banished from the state'. Carrying this demand to City Hall, the crowd encountered two visiting British officers, who were seized, unceremoniously bundled into a cart and paraded to the jeers of onlookers. Only the intervention of Governor Clinton saved them from a tar and feathering.[5]

The radical spearhead continued its onward thrust at the old Loyalists: the state legislature banned Tories from holding public office, and election officials were empowered to disenfranchise Tory voters on the testimony of one witness (this law, vetoed by the Council of Revision, was nonetheless carried again by the assembly). Some wits were heard to remark that the Loyalists now had what they had wanted: taxation without representation. A super-tax of £100,000 was imposed by the state on those who had chosen to remain within the British lines during the war. Yet the most radical and, for the future shape of the city, the furthest-reaching measure of all was the sale of Loyalist property confiscated by the authorities. This applied to all estates 'attainted' (the word used at the time) before 30 November 1782. The sales offered the opportunity for the consolidation of the smaller middling class of landowners.[6]

The task of auctioning off Tory property fell to the 'commissioners of forfeitures' who had already been active in Patriot-held areas during the war. Manhattan held rich pickings: 'Two-thirds of the property of the city of New York and the suburbs belongs to the tories', it was claimed. Between mid-June 1784 and the end of 1787, the commissioners made 339 forced sales in the city and county of New York alone – properties held by a mere twenty-six Loyalists, demonstrating the scale of their holdings. By far the largest of these estates was owned by James Delancey, that bitter opponent of the Livingston faction in pre-revolutionary New York politics. The sale of his land netted £120,000 (of the grand total of £200,000 from all auctions). This was an expansive stretch of land, extending for a mile from the Bowery to the East River (along the axis of modern-day Division Street, which runs through what would have been the very middle of the estate). At its heart was the Delancey mansion, brick built with two storeys, accessed by a leafy tree-lined drive from the Bowery. This whole estate was parcelled up and sold in small lots beginning in July 1784 and then in subsequent sales over the next two years. The main beneficiaries were fifteen mercantile, legal and landowning families, already established members of the New York elites, who thereby enhanced their property ownership in the city. Yet some fifty of the purchasers in the later sales were from humbler origins: tenant farmers, carpenters, shopkeepers, cartmen, gardeners, butchers, a mariner and a rigger, many of them formerly Delancey's tenants who up to now had no right to buy the land they rented. So the aims of the radicals to open economic opportunities of the smaller, artisanal classes made an impact, but it is equally clear that the elites managed to strengthen their social and economic dominance.[7]

The other lasting mark on the city was topographical. The parcels of land, small and affordable as they were, would became the familiar urban blocks of what is today the Lower East Side, the boundaries of the lots becoming the streets and cross-streets of the area as the city expanded northwards. Delancey and Rivington Streets (the Delancey mansion stood between them on the present line of Chrystie Street) recall Loyalist New York, and Orchard Street, which crosses them both, evokes the fruit trees that once blossomed on the Delancey estate.[8]

THE RADICAL OFFENSIVE marked the city in other, if modest, ways. King's College had been strongly Tory: its rector, Myles Cooper, had been chased out by a mob at the start of the Revolution. Yet there was academic life in Cooper yet: he had dreamed of King's as the nucleus of a whole network of colleges across the 'province', which would, collectively, become a university for the whole colony. Thus, the idea for the State University of New York had first germinated in the mind of a diehard Tory. The radicals in the legislature seized on this concept when James Duane proposed that King's College be given a new charter to reflect the religious freedom that had come from the Revolution's disestablishment of the Church of England. In 1785 the state assembly renamed the college Columbia University (thereby erasing any monarchist allusions), and for two years it was part of the State University of New York. The wider purpose was to transform an educational establishment that had been a church monopoly into a republican institution that was secular and accessible to all citizens.[9]

With the disestablishment of the Church of England, Trinity Church, now rising again from the ashes, could claim no special rights: the legislature greedily eyed its rich endowment of New York real estate. Although a report published in February 1785 sought to prove, at great length, that the land belonged to the state, the assembly did not move against it and allowed Trinity to hold on to its wealth. This was quite possibly because the church vestry itself had been taken over by Anglicans who now had unimpeachably Patriot credentials, including Mayor Duane and Isaac Sears.[10] The survival of Trinity Church showed that the radical tide against former Loyalists had reached its high-water mark. There was no general expulsion, no banishment, no blanket act banning all Tory businesses. Even the radical legislature held itself back from its more visceral impulses. Indeed, by the summer of 1784, the most violent phase in the storm of anti-Tory rhetoric had passed.

Not all Patriots were happy with the persecution of Tories. In this New Yorker Alexander Hamilton had one of his great moments. The lawyer, who on the evacuation took up fashionable lodgings at No. 57 (later 58) Wall Street, had been deeply troubled by the rhetoric of vengeance. Concerned for the financial and economic development of the new nation, he watched with deepening anxiety the flight of wealth carried by Tories who escaped persecution through exile. 'Our state', he lamented, 'will feel for twenty years at least the effect of the popular frenzy'. Hamilton turned his words into deeds in the summer of 1784, defending an unpopular Tory merchant, Joshua Waddington, in a civil suit brought by a Patriot widow, Elizabeth Rutgers, whose brewery on Maiden Lane he had taken over during the British occupation.

Rutgers sued Waddington under the Trespass Act, passed during the war, which allowed any Patriot who had fled the British to sue anyone who in their absence had used or damaged their property. Hamilton successfully fended off most, though not all, of the widow's compensation and back-rent claims when Mayor Duane delivered a sage compromise ruling. Moderate Whig that he was, Hamilton may have hoped that the radical tide could be stemmed by reconciliation among the nation's wealthy and influential.[11]

Yet he was also concerned for the international image of the young Republic. In his 'Letters from Phocion', he challenged the Tory haters, whom he accused of breaking the Treaty of Paris that had ended the war, quoting it verbatim as saying that there could be no further confiscations of property nor any prosecution of individuals for their part in the war. Breaching the treaty would make America, from the very start, 'the scorn of nations, by violating the solemn engagements of the United States'. Moderation was the best policy: 'Abuse not the power you possess, and you need never apprehend its diminution or loss'. Misuse it and 'you furnish another example, that despotism may debase the government of the many as well as the few'.[12]

Yet the radicals also pulled back from the brink. With their urban artisanal backbone, they were acutely aware that New York's prosperity depended upon good commercial relations and a thriving mercantile community. Moreover, they reached beyond mere vengeance and aimed at forging a more equal democracy, in which the overmighty power of the wealthy and the privileged would be cut down to size, allowing artisans and 'mechanics' to enjoy the democratic freedoms that they had done so much to secure. Yet this did not involve 'levelling', or social equality. New York radicals, no less than the moderates and Tories, had a vested interest in the financial and commercial prosperity of the city. Perhaps symbolic of the turning of the punitive tide was the fact that, on a stay in New York City between 30 May and 5 June 1784, as he travelled to Boston from which he would embark for France to become US minister in Paris, Thomas Jefferson, the uncompromising republican, managed to stomach two visits to the erstwhile Tory Jemmy Rivington's bookstore at 1 Queen Street.[13]

One of the great issues that vexed all sides was slavery. Owing to the flight of many African Americans with the British in 1783, and the influx of European immigrants, the proportion of African Americans in Manhattan's population had fallen from 14 per cent in 1771 to 10 per cent in 1790, or 3,096 in number. Yet beneath this statistic lay the unsavoury fact that, for all the emancipating rhetoric of the Revolution, some two-thirds were still enslaved: one in five white households in the city kept at least one slave. It was as anti-Tory rage began to subside that the New York Manumission Society was established at the Coffee House on Broadway in February 1785, the venue advertising its elite, patrician membership – and its rather cautious, conservative aims. Spurred by the state's reluctance to address abolition, and alarmed by the kidnapping of free blacks into slavery, some thirty-two citizens representing a cross-section of political opinion, from Tories to radical Whigs and including Mayor James Duane, Governor George Clinton, Melancton Smith (a radical Whig and New York representative in Congress), Alexander Hamilton, John Jay and some Quakers, the society agreed to work for the gradual emancipation of the slaves held in New York, so that they could 'share, equally with us ... civil and religious liberty'. Its measured approach was driven in part by its unwillingness to alienate potential supporters who themselves were slave owners, as indeed Jay and Clinton were. Within months, the Manumission Society used its influence in the legislature to have a bill for gradual emancipation passed, only for it to be vetoed by the Council of Revision (albeit on the grounds that the law would not have given free blacks the right to vote).

So the society had to be content for many years with other victories: in 1788 it persuaded the legislature to stop the sale of New York slaves outside the state and to ban their importation. Mild as the Manumission Society was, the very presence of abolitionism was enough, in the later 1790s, to spur an organisation of slaveholders to complain that 'a Suspicion seems to prevail among many of the Negro Slaves that the Legislature of the State has liberated them and that they are now held in service by the arbitrary power of their Masters', which stirred 'uneasiness and disquietude' among them.[14]

Perhaps the Manumission Society's greatest success came in its sponsorship of the first African American school in New York City. A committee to explore the possibility was created by the society in February 1786, and the school opened in a one-room building on Cliff Street in November 1787. The children, it was hoped, would 'by an early attention to their morals ... be kept from vicious courses and qualified for usefulness in life'. For these white elite abolitionists, education was the key to their goal of gradual emancipation: instilling African Americans with the values of Christian morality would, they opined, prepare them for life as fully fledged citizens and as productive members of a well-ordered society. At the same time, well-trained, earnest and upright graduates of the school would demonstrate to whites nervous about emancipation that African Americans could be good citizens just like anyone else. Ultimately, the boys (and girls were admitted from 1793, boosting class numbers to a bursting-at-the-seams one hundred) would become the moral leaders of the African Americans in New York. There were stringent restrictions on the behaviour of the pupils and their families alike: children were screened before being admitted, and families were then registered with the society, being told in no uncertain terms to 'maintain good characters for sobriety and honesty and peaceable and orderly living'. The puritanical regulations also warned 'against allowing fiddling, dancing or any noisy entertainment in their houses whereby the tranquillity of the neighbourhood may be disturbed'.[15]

The Manumission Society showed that former Tories and Whigs could at last reach across the old political divide: among the city's elites at least, consensus was possible. This consensus was also reflected in the creation of New York's first bank after a meeting in the Coffee House – that province of the mercantile and legal elites of the city – in February 1784. This was the Bank of New York, spearheaded by Hamilton, and its board included moderates, radicals and Tories alike. When it came to petitioning the state legislature for a charter, people of all political tendencies came together to sign it – though not, significantly, the Mechanics Committee, which objected to Tories sharing in the 'advantages of trade and commerce' and was creating its own, more modest, loan fund for its members. Equally, the resuscitated Chamber of Commerce brought together Tories, moderates and radicals. The pendulum, in fact, began to swing so far that Hamilton was able to forge a tactical alliance with New York's artisans and mechanics. He was helped by the intransigence of Governor Clinton, who at the end of 1784 joined with the radical majority in the assembly to slam out-of-state imports with a duty, doubled for British goods. It was partly a bid for rural support, where farmers applauded the measure because it kept taxes low, but it alienated many city dwellers of all social backgrounds for whom commerce was their economic lifeblood. The elections of 1785 therefore saw a swing over to the moderates. With the Mechanics Committee, now styled the General Society of Mechanics and Tradesmen, campaigning against the radicals, the latter were hammered: Sears, once the idol of street politics, polled the fewest votes. The tide of legislation against Tories was reversed: in 1786 they were given back their full citizenship, and by 1788 almost all laws against former Loyalists had been repealed.[16]

HAMILTON AND OTHER moderates had been dismayed by Governor Clinton's economic policies because they hoped to see a strong federal government put some order into the financial chaos of post-revolutionary America. Hamilton hoped that a central government would be able to assume all the wartime debts of the separate states and to issue one single currency. Owing to their pivotal maritime position, New Yorkers, in particular, had to deal with a bewildering array of notes, especially from New Jersey and Pennsylvania, but also a shower of coins from a treasure trove of sources: Spanish doubloons, French livres, British guineas, Portuguese *moidores*. New York retailers had to keep up with the exchange rates of each. All this was bad enough, but then Clinton had embarked on issuing a New York currency and set up a fund to assume the state's war debts. Admirable though the latter may have been, for Hamilton it was a step in absolutely the wrong direction, for it seemed to be nothing less than a declaration of financial independence from the emerging union of states. Concerned though Hamilton was for the prosperity of New York, he suspected, with good reason, that Clinton favoured it too much over the need, as he saw it, for national unity.[17]

These divisions within New York politics were reflected in the delegation that the state sent to the Constitutional Convention in Philadelphia in May 1787, but they would also provoke one of the greatest public demonstrations on the streets of New York, one that made full use of its civic spaces. Hamilton, the staunch Federalist, had to share the honour of representing New York with two fervent Clintonian states' righters, John Lansing and Robert Yates. The latter two, fully expecting the convention merely to tinker with the Articles of Confederation (which had been adopted back in 1777 and created a very loose form of unity among the separate states), were disgusted when Hamilton and others were clearly pressing for a closer union, with a federal government that wielded far more power than they ever hoped to see. The growing authority of the federal government, critics – soon called 'Anti-Federalists' – feared, would swagger over the sovereignty of the separate states, swathed in its power over foreign policy, the armed forces, taxation, justice and commerce. Ultimately, the proposed constitution, they feared, would lead the country back to tyranny. 'Federalists' countered that the existing confederation was too weak to restore the commercial prosperity of the country and to ensure financial stability, let alone to defend the new nation from external threats.

The young Republic, in fact, seemed on the cusp of succumbing to a swarm of political diseases – financial insolvency, crippling debt and even internal rebellion. In 1786 impecunious Massachusetts farmers under Daniel Shays, crushed by post-war debt, had risen up against the government and were put down, prompting Thomas Jefferson's notorious remark that 'the tree of liberty must be refreshed from time to time with the blood of patriots and tyrants'. A strong national government, it was argued, would offer political and financial stability, encourage commerce and ensure the security of all.[18]

The Constitutional Convention finished its work on 17 September 1787, when, as a relieved George Washington, who presided over the proceedings, wrote in his diary, 'Met in Convention, when the Constitution received the unanimous assent of 11 States and Colo. Hamilton's from New York'. The qualifying reference not to 'New York' but specifically to 'Colonel Hamilton' (his wartime rank) reflected the fact that Yates and Lansing had left the convention early in disgust. They could do so because behind them was a well-organised and deeply entrenched Anti-Federalist opposition in New York. Nowhere else, other than Virginia, did Federalists face such an uphill battle to secure the ratification of the Constitution. The agreement was that nine of the thirteen states had to accept the new political framework in order for it to take effect, but Virginia was the most powerful state in the confederation and New York its emergent commercial hub. The assent of both was essential if the Union as a whole was to stand any real chance of holding together. So it was that, while the debate raged up and down the country, it was particularly brutal and bitter in New York, where the presses of six newspapers worked themselves into a political frenzy as they struggled to keep up with the tempo of the debate. Thomas Greenleaf of the *New-York Journal* remarked that 'the RAGE of the season is, Hallow, damme, Jack, what are you, boy, FEDERAL or ANTI-FEDERAL?'[19]

Yet the controversy also produced one of the most sophisticated and tightly argued political works of the eighteenth century, originally written as a series of letters for the express purpose of arming New York's Federalist delegates at the meeting in the state's ratifying convention at Poughkeepsie. Hamilton wrote the first number, and it appeared in New York's *Independent Journal* on 27 October 1787. The author had put pen to paper in a schooner on his way back from Albany with his wife, Eliza, no doubt the smooth glide of the vessel through the New York highlands stirring his thoughts. Most, however, would have been written in Hamilton's New York home on Wall Street. In all, there would be eighty-five *Federalist Papers*, of which fifty-one have been attributed to Hamilton, five to his fellow New Yorker John Jay and the rest to the Virginian James Madison, a remarkable political and intellectual collaboration, in which sectional interest was, temporarily, subsumed for what the Federalists saw as the good of the nation.[20]

With the support of the Mechanics Committee, New York City was strongly Federalist, although much of the countryside appeared to range behind Governor Clinton and the Anti-Federalists. News of the ratification by other states – beginning with Delaware in December 1787 – was greeted with exuberant celebrations on the streets. New York City's delegates boarded their schooners, which took them up the Hudson to the convention at Poughkeepsie on 14 June. They were locked in acrimonious debate for weeks, with Hamilton leading the Federalist charge against the well-entrenched, and majority, Anti-Federalist phalanxes marshalled by Clinton. Yet slowly, painfully, the Federalists managed to turn the convention around. With the Constitution already ratified by eight states, it would take just one more to dissolve the old confederation and activate the new order. On 25 June, a dispatch rider galloped into Poughkeepsie with the electrifying news that New Hampshire had ratified. The Constitution was now enacted, but this did not break New York's Anti-Federalists. If anything, the debates became even more acrimonious, as Clinton and others sought to keep New York out of the new Union. News then arrived on 2 July, this time from a rider who had galloped seventy-five miles from New York City, that Virginia had ratified. New York would stand on its own if it did not join the new federation. As the stakes mounted, Hamilton at one point thundered that New York City would secede and join the United States if the convention failed to ratify, a threat for which he was called to order.

It was now that the people of New York City, making full symbolic use of their public spaces, entered the fray with a 'Grand Federal Procession'. At eight on the morning of 23 July, Federalists assembled on the Common, a choice of location that was both practical (despite the spitting rain) and symbolic, connecting the struggle for the Constitution with the earlier battles around the Liberty Pole. Massed ranks of New York's artisans – all costumed in their work gear, such as aprons, smocks and tool belts, and carrying a symbol produced by their trade – marched to show their support for the Constitution. There were foresters carrying axes, cabinetmakers drawing a cradle and table, blacksmiths an anchor, sailmakers their canvas sails, bakers a ten-foot 'federal loaf' beneath a banner depicting the current stagnation of trade and printers a press complete with type, which was actually operating during the march to run off copies of an ode to the Constitution and distributed among the crowd as the parade progressed. The carnival moved down Broadway to Great Dock Street, through Hanover Square and up Queen and Chatham Streets and back past the Common, its route following the main thoroughfares of the city, but also passing through its great commercial districts and those inhabited by the wealthy and the powerful. It was, in other words, a tour of artisanal force, one that connected the Constitution with the commercial prosperity upon which the city and its working people depended. It was also an expression of the consciousness of the trades as a pillar of both the city's wealth and the new political order, a reminder to the city's elites that the revolution had not just secured independence, but mobilised and empowered the people. It was, as one observer noted, a way of heralding the new era that had arrived, 'great, glorious, and unparalleled, which opens a variety of new sources of happiness, and unbounded prospects of national prosperity'.[21]

There were five thousand artisans representing no fewer than sixty trades and professions, but the centrepiece was the 'Federal Ship Hamilton', a twenty-seven-foot scale model of a frigate, complete with billowing sails and full rigging, ploughing its way through blue canvas waves that covered the wheels of the carriage that bore it. The ship – like many of the motifs and banners borne by the artisans – explicitly linked the new Constitution with the prosperity of New York's commerce and trades:

> *Our merchants may venture to ship without fear,*
> *For pilots of skill shall Hamilton steer.*
> *This federal ship will our commerce revive.*
> *And merchants and shipwrights and joiners shall thrive.*[22]

Hamilton basked in the popular adulation, and, on 27 July, wavering Anti-Federalists, led by Melancton Smith, switched their votes, giving ratification a wafer-thin majority, the narrowest of any state. That evening, another hard-pressed horse, bearing a breathless express rider, hammered down the road into New York City and, to jubilation, announced that the state convention had at last ratified the Constitution. After years of revolution, war and social upheaval, there was hope at last that the country could look forward to a new era of stability and prosperity.

New York City, in particular, could celebrate this future because by 1788, its very fabric was evidence of the post-war recovery. In January 1788, a few months prior to the acrimonious debates over the Constitution, Governor Clinton told the state legislature that 'the country is in a great measure recovered from the wastes and injuries of War'. The city now staked out its intention to thrust its development towards Greenwich Village when Mayor Duane had the Greenwich Road widened and paved. The decaying wharves and docks that were threatening to slide into the river were slowly but surely being rebuilt anew.

In 1788 the city also tackled some long-standing problems. The filthy, muddy, stinking low-lying streets between the Freshwater Pond and the East River ran past subsiding wooden houses. The streets were unpaved, and there was no drainage or sewage system, so this slum area, crammed with the city's poor and most recent immigrants, became a breeding ground for disease (as it would during the murderous yellow-fever epidemic in 1797). The city could address this area from March 1788, when New York's legislature gave it permission to restore and build new causeways and bridges and – crucially – to 'cause ditches from such public roads or highways to be made and cut through any person's land ... for conveying the water from, and keeping the same roads and highways dry and in good order'. The cost of drainage and other improvements would be carried by the owners of the lots who benefited the most. In September 1788, a law ordered the paving of all streets around the waterfront, the better to encourage commerce.[23]

NEW YORK'S RECOVERY was especially sprightly because Congress had been meeting in its City Hall since January 1785, making it the capital city of the newly independent Republic. Now, with the state's last-gasp ratification of the Constitution in July 1788, Congress designated New York to be the temporary capital of the new federal government. So the city prepared itself to receive the new institutions of the United States. The old fort was levelled in 1788. The plan was to build in its place a grand residence for the president, although the mansion that rose on the site of the old colonial governor's house was never used for that purpose. More strikingly, City Hall on Wall Street was redesigned beyond recognition to lodge both houses of the new Congress, the Senate and the House of Representatives. Renamed Federal Hall, it was the creation of the great French architect and urban planner Pierre-Charles L'Enfant. After fighting with the Continental army, L'Enfant's commissions in New York had included the canvas pavilion for the banquet at the end of the 'Grand Federal Procession' on 23 July 1788, and he had embellished the setting of the memorial to the fallen war hero General Richard Montgomery (killed in the ill-fated American invasion of Canada in the winter of 1775–1776) in Saint Paul's Church.[24]

When their City Hall was chosen as the seat of Congress, the New York authorities obligingly moved out, and they were rewarded later with a brand-new, built-for-purpose City Hall in the middle of the Common, which was ready in 1812 and is still the seat of the New York City government. The old Congress left for the last time in November 1788, during the elections for the new federal Congress. Meanwhile, L'Enfant got to work, and he and his artisans did so with feverish, fast-moving commitment.[25]

While its maritime setting in the bay was dramatic, New York, unlike many European capitals, did not have any striking *internal* vistas that could really show off a great public building. L'Enfant's original vision was to create just this kind of space, a building from which fanned out eight long arcades, each finished with a small entrance pavilion. This would have the effect of creating a distance between the seat of the federal government and the surrounding city. But where in New York could this be built, and how much would it cost? L'Enfant would get his chance, as he put it, to design a city 'proportioned to the greatness . . . of a powerful Empire' in the marbled avenues of Washington, DC, but in New York he had been given City Hall, crammed as it always had been into the southern end of a growing commercial city whose street layout had been determined for centuries by European roads and Native American trails.[26]

Even so, L'Enfant's architecture captured the spirit of the moment. Federal Hall was the ultimate expression in stone, plaster, paint and gilt of the political transformation that had emerged out of the American Revolution. The flagstone ground floor with its arched ceiling remained and was open to all comers as an arcade 'for the recreation and convenience of the citizens', noted the *Daily Gazette* approvingly. The great balcony above was formed by Tuscan columns, out of which rose Doric pillars supporting a heavy pediment from which 'a large eagle, surrounded with a glory, appears bursting from a cloud, and carrying thirteen arrows, and the arms of the United States'. The apex was topped by a 'small, though elegant' spire.

Entering through the arcade, one reached a marble-floored hall soaring up to the cupola above, which flooded the place with light. On either side of this floor were offices, but upstairs were the two houses of Congress. The Senate met in a wainscoted chamber beneath a ceiling decorated with a sun and thirteen stars and with two public galleries for spectators. The room for the House of Representatives was, it was thought, the 'master piece of the whole, and most entitled to the name of federal hall'. By far the largest space in the building, it took up two storeys, the upper lit generously by tall and wide windows, the lower by oval ones, while the ceilings and two public galleries were supported by Ionic columns. On the north end was a seat reserved for the Speaker (above whom, it was intended, there would be a statue of Liberty), with an enormous table projecting expansively into the middle of the room, around which there were seats for fifty-nine representatives. The wainscoting was emblazed with political symbols, including the arms of the United States. The *Gazette* concluded: 'The whole composition is most admirably contrived for the purpose for which it is intended. It is an object which indicates, that something more considerable would have been executed, had not the artist been confined to such narrow limits. The style is bold, simple and regular; the parts few, large and distinct; the transitions sudden, and strongly marked; and we think the whole has an air of grandeur'.[27]

'Bold, simple and regular', with 'an air of grandeur': in other words, republican? Not everyone, in fact, was happy. Anti-Federalists dubbed the building the 'Fools Trap', a symbol of a new, emerging Federalist aristocracy. Yet overall, Americans and visitors alike reacted positively – perhaps no one more than those same wealthy mercantile elites who were the bedrock of the emerging Federalist party. When L'Enfant applied his neoclassical style – elegant and simple, with clean lines and plenty of light and space – to Federal Hall, it took off. The city's oligarchs who lived in this prestigious neighbourhood, on Wall Street, Broad Street, the lower end of Broadway and the Battery, took the form to their hearts and had their brick two- or three-storey town houses built in this striking style, often painting the bricks red or the more pastel shades of grey and cream, leaving the mortar in its vibrant white for contrast. The fresh, inspiring – and firmly republican – form became known as the Federal style.[28]

By April 1789, the new Congress had gathered in L'Enfant's Federal Hall and counted the electoral votes for the presidency and vice presidency. George Washington, of course, took the presidency, but it was John Adams who had garnered just enough to be vice president. On 21 April, Adams was sworn in at Federal Hall. Two days later, 23 April, Washington, the hero of the war, and now of the hour, arrived in New York City. The harbour was cluttered with ships and craft of all sizes, festooned with pennants and ensigns, the broad expanse of water an effervescence of excitement. Among the ships was a Spanish war sloop, *Galviston*, 'dressed and decorated in the most superb manner', reported the *Daily Advertiser*. In the upper bay, people crowded onto the boats, many of them dressed in their finery, and were looking westwards, towards New Jersey, where a distant barge appeared in the Kills. Its passenger, sheltering under an awning of red curtains, was Washington, accompanied by three US senators, five congressional representatives and three officials of New York State and City, including the supreme court justice Chancellor Robert R. Livingston. The barge sliced through the water, rowed by thirteen New York Harbour pilots dressed in dazzling white uniforms. The harbour erupted in noise: 'The whole water scene was animated and moving beyond description' was all the *Daily Advertiser* could say. One of the congressional delegates, Elias Boudinot, wrote that 'Boat after Boat & Sloop after Sloop added to our Train gaily dressed in all their naval Ornaments made a most Splendid Appearance'. As Washington's barge passed by a large sloop to starboard, under full sail, a choir of men and women sang an ode welcoming the president-elect to the seat of government. As if on cue, porpoises were playing just below the water's surface. The guns of the Battery let off a salute.[29] 'We now discovered', Boudinot continued, 'the Shore crowded with thousands of People – Men Women & Children – Nay I may venture to say Tens of Thousands; from the fort to the Place of Landing altho' near half a Mile, you could see little else along the Shores, in the Streets and on Board every Vessel, but Heads standing as thick as Ears of Corn before the Harvest'.[30] As the barge neared the landing at Murray's Wharf, the Spanish warship *Galviston* unfurled the flags of all nations from its rigging as sailors stood along its yardarms. As the barge slipped past, its guns fired off a thirteen-gun salute.

The general, dressed plainly in his trademark colours of buff with a long blue frock coat, stepped onshore via a set of carpeted stairs, where he was greeted by the mayor of New York, James Duane, and Governor Clinton. The chorus of cheers from the crowd was so great that none of the men could make themselves heard. They escorted Washington up Wall Street, turning right onto Pearl (once Queen) Street and all the way up to Cherry Street, where, at No. 3, on the corner with Dover Street, a lavishly refurbished merchant's mansion awaited him. Soldiers had to keep back the press of the ecstatic crowd in order to allow their hero passage. The house on Cherry and Dover would be Washington's home until February 1790, when he would move to a mansion at 39 Broadway until, in August, he left New York for good.[31]

The joyful reception that New York City gave the hero was more than just an outpouring of adulation. It was also the expression of optimism for the future. The new federal government of the independent Republic was finally being installed after six years of debate, compromise and campaigning. And its central institutions – Congress and the presidency – were housed in New York City, for a brief yet glorious time the capital of the United States.

The final layer on the constitutional cake was eased into place with Washington's inauguration as the first president on 30 April 1789, in the midst of a spectacular round of pageantry. Americans could look forward, it was hoped, to a new era of stability and prosperity, and New York would be at the very centre of it all.

Washington took the inaugural oath at Federal Hall on the gallery overlooking Wall Street, in clothes donated by a mill at Hartford, Connecticut, with (noted Senator William Maclay of Pennsylvania) 'metal buttons, with an eagle on them, white stockings, a bag, and sword'. The best description was left by Eliza Quincy, who in 1821 looked back to when she was fifteen-year-old Eliza Morton:

> I was on the roof of the first house in Broad Street ... and so near to Washington that I could almost hear him speak. The windows and roofs of the houses were crowded; and in the streets the throng was so dense, that it seemed as if one might literally walk on the heads of the people. The balcony of the hall was in full view of this assembled multitude. In the centre of it was placed a table, with a rich covering of red velvet; and upon this on a crimson velvet cushion, lay a large and elegant Bible.[32]

Washington appeared on the gallery, greeted with an explosion of cheers. Chancellor Livingston read the oath as prescribed by the Constitution, with Washington repeating it, with his hand on the Bible. When the secretary of the Senate then lifted the book, Washington kissed it, at which moment Livingston proclaimed him president of the United States. At a signal, a huge Stars and Stripes was unfurled from the spire above as a thirteen-gun salute roared out from the Battery. The air rang with cheers from the spectators. Washington, bowing, then retreated into Federal Hall, 'retiring from a scene such as the proudest monarch never enjoyed',

Eliza commented pointedly. Washington then delivered his inaugural address to Congress before attending a religious service at Saint Paul's Church – once a hub of Loyalism – on Broadway.[33]

When Washington withdrew from the cheering crowd on Broad and Wall Streets, he addressed both houses of Congress in the Senate chamber. One who witnessed the scene was Senator Maclay, who remarked that 'this great man was agitated and embarrassed more than ever he was by the levelled cannon or pointed musket. He trembled, and several times could scarce make out to read'.[34] Washington was a taciturn man and had privately confessed to feeling more than a little awkward at the adulation, admitting that he felt like a 'culprit ... going to the place of his execution'. Yet if his first inaugural address disappointed in its delivery, it wisely appealed to the national interest over sectionalism and partisanship: 'No local prejudices, or attachments; no separate views, nor party animosities, will misdirect the comprehensive and equal eye which ought to watch over this great assemblage of communities and interests'. Washington reminded Congress that 'the preservation of the sacred fire of liberty, and the destiny of the Republican model of Government, are justly considered as deeply, perhaps as finally staked, on the experiment entrusted to the hands of the American people'.[35]

The new Republic was striking out into uncharted political waters. The Constitution had provided the framework for the post-revolutionary order, but it was no more than that. There were still many unresolved issues that lay coiled at its feet, not the least of which was slavery. For now, however, its ratification in 1788 seemed nothing short of miraculous. The joyous celebrations in New York in April 1789 were not unique in America: if anything, they were more extravagant and lavish elsewhere in the country. New York was special, however, because it was for now the seat of the new federal government, as it had been for the confederation since 1784. The ratification of the Constitution had rekindled a public interest in festivities celebrating a *national* political culture, one that would only develop and grow over the coming years, as events of national importance – 4 July, Washington's Birthday and (for one side of the partisan divide) the French Revolution – were celebrated in streets, buildings and spaces across America. Such public displays as the Grand Federal Procession in 1788 and the reception of Washington in New York in 1789 showed that ordinary Americans took a lively interest in what the national government was doing.[36]

This understanding was expressed in sound, light, clothing, decoration, bricks, mortar and ceremony in the last week of April in New York City. The festivities may also have been a deep, collective and very audible outpouring of relief. Uncomfortable though all the adulation made Washington in the spring of 1789, the ecstatic welcome that he received was not just an enthusiastic, adoring expression of gratitude and admiration. It was also a catharsis of relief and hope. That Washington had agreed to be president was the final seal on the new political framework. Although there were so many poisonous issues that festered, in these few days in New York, it felt that things might turn out well.

IN 1789 CONTEMPORARIES on both sides of the Atlantic did not fail to draw comparisons between the American and French Revolutions, yet as we shall see, there were some important differences in the spatial experience of revolution in New York and Paris: in France the depth and scale of the overhaul from 1789 was reflected and expressed in a penetration of the new civic order into a multitude of familiar buildings, so that its physical presence, visible in both the arrival of new personnel such as elected officials and judges and the adaptation of buildings, reached deep into neighbourhoods and communities across the city. In New York the transformation was not so radical, since the American Revolution did not constitute quite such a break with the past: the city government and even the state constitution adapted the institutions from the colonial era instead of hacking them down to the roots and beginning anew. The essential political and legal institutions themselves were altered, but not overhauled, and so the entry of the revolutionary personnel – often the very people who had held positions of influence in pre-war New York – into the existing sites of political and legal authority was not so obvious an upheaval as it would be in revolutionary Paris. Moreover, since the real revolutionary transformation in New York's cityscape – the adoption of colonial buildings for regular constitutional government and the application of the republican and national motifs – had occurred after the war, that change was bound up with the reconstruction of the city over the course of the 1780s and into the 1790s. Revolutionary Paris would not have the luxury of such a peaceful transformation and development.

CHAPTER EIGHT

PARIS IN REVOLUTION, 1789–1793

THE REVOLUTIONARY TRANSFORMATION of Paris began with the erasure of one of its landmarks: within days of its capture, the Bastille was razed, stone by stone. A symbol of 'despotism', it could not remain standing while a free nation was building itself anew. No sooner had the hunks of medieval masonry tumbled into the moat below than they – like the graffitied chunks of the Berlin Wall two centuries later – become 'Relics of Freedom', fashioned into mementos recalling 14 July 1789, decorated with symbols of liberty and disseminated across the kingdom. The ironwork – locks, chains, hinges, bars – was wrought into medals commemorating the insurrection and into a range of souvenirs, including inkwells, snuff boxes, keys, paperweights. The key was sent to George Washington, via the good offices of the marquis de Lafayette, who was now commander of the Parisian militia, formally organised into the National Guard. The masonry's most practical use was in the pillars and arches of the Pont Louis XVI (later naturally renamed the Pont de la Révolution), which connected the Place Louis XV with the Left Bank and was completed in 1791: thus, it was said, the people of Paris would forever trample on the ruins of the Bastille.

The Bastille was not the only architectural victim beneath the collapse of the old regime. Allegorical figures weighed down by chains had clustered around the statue of Louis XIV in the middle of the elegant circle of the Place des Victoires, symbolising the seventeenth-century conquests of France's eastern provinces. This 'humiliating spectacle' was now too much to stomach: no part of France could be represented as a supine captive at the feet of an absolute monarch. On 19 June 1790, the National Assembly ordered that the chained figures be carefully removed and put into storage.[1]

Yet the changes to the cityscape would not just be iconoclastic; they would also reflect the enormous task faced by the revolutionaries as they reformed France at every level and in every aspect of legal, administrative, political, religious and fiscal life. Moreover, the Revolution was far from 'complete'. The insurrection of July 1789 had tossed power from the king to the National Assembly, but the process of shaping France anew helped to bring out some deep divisions within French society, conflicts that destabilised the new, emerging political order and threatened to tear it apart at birth. Both the scale of the formal transformation and the continuing political instability ensured that the French Revolution would, first, have a deep and widespread impact on Paris in spatial terms and, second, continue to mobilise its people. So the character and spaces of its neighbourhoods and communities would still come into play in the events that followed. Two in particular will figure largely in this story, namely, the central markets of Les Halles and the Cordeliers district on the Left Bank. Both the impact on and the role played by the city echoed the urban experience in New York, but was all the more intense.

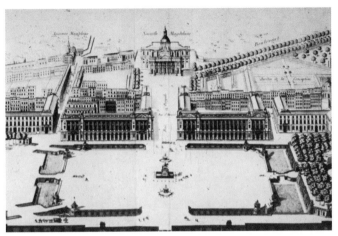

The Place Louis XV, Paris (Introduction): In Ange-Jacques Gabriel's plan, a carriage has just emerged onto the square from the Champs-Elysées (left), heading directly for Bouchardon's statue of the King (centre). The entrance to the Tuileries Gardens is on the right, across the turning bridge, which (Chapter 6) would be the site of the first collision between the Parisians and royal troops during the revolution of July 1789.

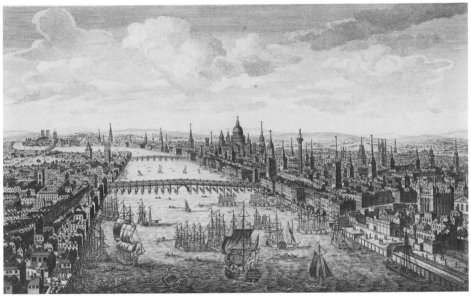

The imperial capital (Introduction): This 1760 engraving captures the thriving sprawl of metropolitan London viewed from the East, with the City (right) as the main focus (from the Tower of London, far right, to the dome of Saint Paul's Cathedral, centre). In the distance (far left, background) are the towers of Westminster Abbey. On the left (foreground) is Southwark. The Thames is cluttered with traffic – a testament to London's importance as port as well as capital city – and the engraving confirms the impression of a city of church spires. (New York Public Library: http://digitalcollections.nypl.org/items/510d47db-9339-a3d9-e040-e00a18064a99)

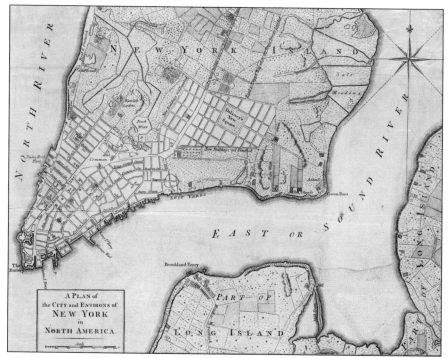

One of its colonial satellites: This plan of New York City (Chapter 1), as mapped in 1766, shows the triangular space of the Common (left, centre) and the star-shaped Fort George close to the southern tip of Manhattan; the Battery, on the tip, is marked. The jagged saw-tooth lines along the East River indicate the throbbing harbour district, while the gently waving line of Queen (Pearl) Street is one block inland. (New York Public Library: http://digitalcollections.nypl.org/items/510d47db-9339-a3d9-e040-e00a18064a99)

Fort George as a bastion of imperial power in New York (Chapter 1) is emphasised by its fortifications and the massive Union Flag flying in the breeze, but the city's church spires dominate the rest of the skyline. (John Carwitham, *View of Fort George with the City of New York from the South West* [1736]. Library of Congress Prints & Photographs Division, Washington, DC: PGA [P&P])

One of the seats of elite resistance in New York: A nineteenth-century sketch of the Coffee House on Broadway, where the non-importation agreement was signed by the city's merchants on 31 October 1765 (Chapter 1). (Benson John Lossing, *Burns' Coffee House.* New York Public Library: http://digitalcollections.nypl.org/items/510d47da-24ab-a3d9-e040-e00a18064a99)

Temple Bar (Chapter 2), eight years before its removal in 1878: This Victorian image captures the same kind of bottleneck of people and traffic that visitors like Pierre-Jean Grosley would have experienced in the 1760s – but, happily, the decapitated heads are long gone. (*Illustrated London News*, 1870/MEPL)

The Bank of England as it was towards the end of the eighteenth century: A pillar of the City of London's economic and political might (Chapter 2), it was defended by, among others, John Wilkes against attack by rioters in 1780 (Chapter 5). One of the essential mechanisms that upheld British social stability and military power, it would help ensure that the City of London would remain loyal to the established order (Chapter 11). (*View of the Bank of England, Threadneedle Street, London* [1797]. New York Public Library: http://digitalcollections.nypl.org /items/510d47db-9292-a3d9-e040-e00a18064a99)

The Palais de Justice (Chapter 3): This 1890 photograph clearly shows the Cour de Mai behind its gilded gates, the great steps and portico (constructed in 1776) of the law courts and the Gothic elegance of the Sainte-Chapelle in the background. (Library of Congress Prints & Photographs Division, Washington, DC: LOT 13418, no. 259 [P&P]

Symbolic regicide (Chapter 4): American patriots on the brink of toppling New York City's first-ever statue, the equestrian monument to King George III, on 9 July 1776. (J. C. McRae, *Pulling down the Statue of George III by the 'Sons of Freedom' at the Bowling Green, City of New York, July 1776*. New York Public Library: http://digitalcollections.nypl.org/items /510d47e3-b9ad-a3d9-e040-e00a18064a99)

New York City ablaze (Chapter 4): Although imagined, Franz Xavier Habermann's engraving captures the scale and speed of the 1776 conflagration. (*Representation du Feu Terrible à Nouvelle Yorck* [1776]. New York Public Library: http://digitalcollections.nypl.org/items /510d47e3-b9b0-a3d9-e040-e00a18064a99)

The burnt-out remains of Trinity Church would become a centre for the whorl of the social life enjoyed by British officers and ladies during the occupation of New York from 1776 to 1783, but such hedonistic uses of sacred ground would scandalise even the most Loyalist New Yorkers, like Pastor Schaukirk (Chapter 4). (J. Evers, *Ruins of Trinity Church as seen after the memorable conflagration of Septr. 21st 1776* [1841], New York Public Library: http://digitalcollections.nypl.org/items/510d47d9-7afb-a3d9-e040-e00a18064a99)

London briefly shared in New York's experience of military occupation, in June 1780 (Chapter 5): As the Gordon Riots were suppressed, the sight of soldiers camping in London's public spaces outraged the Whig sensibilities of Londoners, such as Ignatius Sancho, who were accustomed to viewing standing armies with suspicion. (P. Sandby, *The Encampment in St James's Park MDCCLXXX*. Library of Congress Prints & Photographs Division, Washington, DC: PGA. [P&P])

The 'birthplace of the French Revolution' (Chapter 6): A mid-nineteenth-century view of the Palais-Royal – its elegant, tree-shaded gardens in the middle, so admired by foreign visitors such as Karamzin, its cooling fountain in the centre, its galleries proceeding northwards on either side and finishing, at the top, with the gallery, originally built of wood because the Duc d'Orléans ran out of funds. (Champin and Bayot, *Vue générale du Palais-Royal.* Library of Congress Prints & Photographs Division, Washington, DC: PGA [P&P])

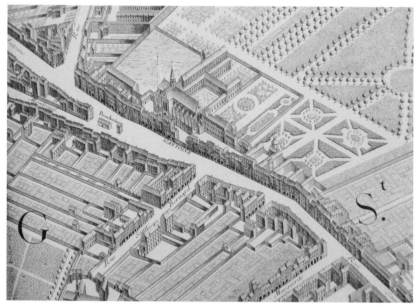

The Faubourg Saint-Antoine where all roads led to the main thoroughfare, the Rue du Faubourg Saint-Antoine (Chapter 6), as if seen from the north-west, and from the air. From the famous Plan Turgot (completed in 1739), the construction of homes and workshops behind the street front can be discerned. At the bottom right, the main road leads to the Bastille and the city centre; at the top left, to the Place du Trône and, in 1789, the customs barrier. (*Plan de Paris, commencé l'année 1734. Achevé de graver en 1739.* Glasgow University Library Special Collections Sp Coll Ax.1.5)

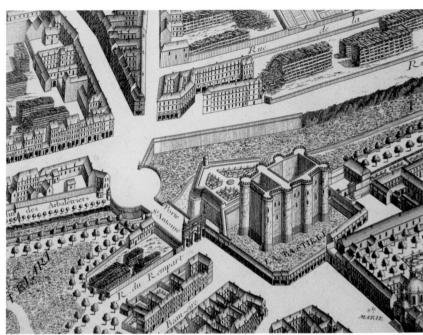

The Bastille, as mapped in 1739: In this image, the fortifications defining the limits of the old city (in the bottom half) from the Faubourg Saint-Antoine outside (top half) can be seen. The only entrance into the city from the Faubourg was through the Porte Saint-Antoine (the gate itself, seen here, was demolished by 1789), guarded by the fortress of the Bastille. On 14 July 1789, the Parisian insurgents attacked the citadel through the courtyards seen in the bottom right-hand corner. (*Plan de Paris, commencé l'année 1734. Achevé de graver en 1739.* Glasgow University Library Special Collections Sp Coll Ax.1.5)

The Bastille falls, 14 July 1789 (Chapter 6): The height of the citadel may be exaggerated in this image (the towers were about 60 feet high), but the engraving intentionally conveys the Bastille as a symbol of oppression and captures the feelings of Parisians who lived beneath the mouths of the guns on the ramparts. On the right, assailants surge across the drawbridge and through the gateway into the inner courtyard, the Cour de Gouvernement, which led to the citadel itself. (P. Berthault & F. Prieur, *Prise de la Bastille, le 14 Juillet 1789* [1804]. Library of Congress Prints & Photographs Division, Washington, DC: LOT 6874, no. 16 [P&P])

Federal Hall in 1789, or rather New York's old City Hall as redeveloped by L'Enfant (Chapter 7): This engraving shows the view from Broad Street, and includes the central balcony on which George Washington took the oath as first President of the United States. Above that, the political symbols of the new order are clearly visible. (*View of the Federal Edifice in New York* [1789] Library of Congress Rare Books and Special Collections Division, Washington, DC: Illus. in AP2.A2 U6 [Rare Book RR])

Les Halles, the central Parisian market district: This map, engraved as if seen from above and looking southeast, shows street names that evoke the merchandise, wares and foods on sale, such as ironware (*ferronerie*) and linen (*lingerie*). At the bottom, the streets for cheese (*fromagerie*) and barrel-making (*tonnellerie*) define the triangle of the all-important grain market (the Halle au Bled) before the rotunda was built in 1762 (Chapter 8). To the north (off bottom of map) stood the Church of Saint-Eustache, where market women would find their economic interests challenged by the Society of Revolutionary Republican Women in 1793 (Chapter 10). At the top, centre, of the image, the Church and Cemetery of the Innocents can be seen; these were demolished between 1785 and 1787 to create the open space of the Market of the Innocents. (*Plan de Paris, commencé l'année 1734. Achevé de graver en 1739.* Glasgow University Library Special Collections Sp Coll Ax.1.5)

Les Halles, the 'belly of Paris' (Chapter 8): This engraving depicts the proclamation of the French Revolution's first Constitution in September 1791, but by illustrating the very scale of the food market (with the Fountain of the Innocents in the centre), it also captures the central importance of the Halles to Parisian life. (P. Berthault & F. Prieur, *Proclamation de la Constitution, place du Marché des Innocens, le 14 septembre 1791* [1804]. Library of Congress Prints & Photographs Division, Washington, DC: LOT 6874, no. 57 [P&P])

The lifeblood of the markets was its women, the Parisian *poissardes* (Chapter 8), in a contemporary German impression (shown here), neither entirely sympathetic nor uncompromisingly hostile. (*Pariser Poisarden* [1794]. Library of Congress Prints & Photographs Division, Washington, DC: PC 5-1794, no. 3 [P&P])

The Cordeliers District (Chapter 8). Top (centre) stands the Cordeliers Convent, where the eponymous club would meet. The turreted house abutting onto the corner of the Rue des Cordeliers and the Rue de Paon was where Jean-Paul Marat would live (and be assassinated in his bath). Further down the Rue des Cordeliers, before one reached the corner of the Rue des Fossés Saint-Germain ou de Comédie (now Rue de l'Ancienne Comédie), stood Danton's house. In the warren of closes and courtyards behind it was the Cour de Rohan, where Marat published his *Ami du Peuple*. (*Plan de Paris, commencé l'année 1734. Achevé de graver en 1739.* Glasgow University Library Special Collections Sp Coll Ax.1.5)

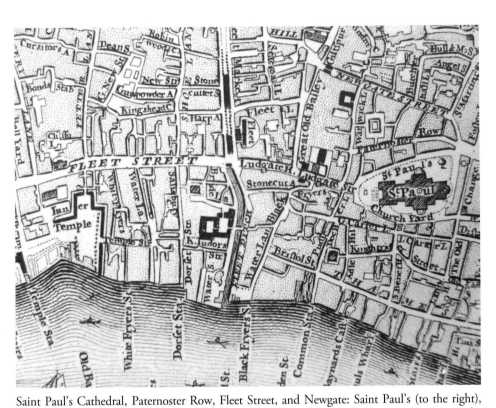

Saint Paul's Cathedral, Paternoster Row, Fleet Street, and Newgate: Saint Paul's (to the right), surrounded by its churchyard, hub of London publishing, along with Paternoster Row, just to the north (Chapter 9). Leading westwards is Ludgate Hill, which becomes Fleet Street (off the map to the left is the Strand by passing through Temple Bar). Perpendicular to Ludgate Hill is Great Old Bailey, leading to the law court of the same name (Chapter 11), and, on its corner with Newgate Street stood the notorious prison (Chapter 5). (J. Rocque, *A New and Accurate Survey of the Cities of London and Westminster, the Borough of Southwark* [1751]. Glasgow University Library Special Collections, Sp Coll HX.93)

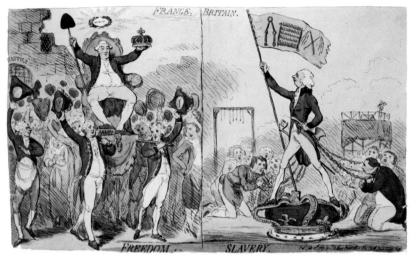

Published two weeks after the fall of the Bastille, Gillray's cartoon captures the initial public enthusiasm in Britain for the French Revolution (Chapter 9): It contrasts Jacques Necker, the popular finance minister borne triumphantly aloft by cheering French citizens emerging from the ruins of the Bastille, with a self-satisfied British Prime Minister William Pitt, who stands atop the British Crown, surrounded by supplicant subjects and the instruments of judicial retribution in the background. (*France. Britain. Freedom. Slavery* [28 July 1789]. Library of Congress: Prints & Photographs Division, Washington, DC: PC 1–7546 [P&P])

The Festival of the Supreme Being on 8 June 1794 in Paris (Chapter 10): The artificial mountain, designed by the artist Jacques-Louis David, stood on the Champ de Mars on the western edge of Paris. A column topped by Hercules – symbol of the might of the French people – stands to the left of the hill. Within days, the guillotine would be moved from the Place de la Révolution (formerly Louis XV) to the eastern entrance to the city, as if to put the greatest possible distance between the reality of terror and the utopian dreams of the festival. (*Vue de la montagne elevée au champ de la reunion* [Paris: Chez Chéreau, No. 257 Rue Jacques, 1794]. Library of Congress Prints & Photographs Division Washington, DC: PC 5-1794, no. 2 [P&P])

A sectional revolutionary committee during the Year 2 (1793–1794) (Chapter 10). Although a hostile, Thermidorian depiction (the man presenting his *certificat de civisme* is being hectored by one of the *sans-culottes* on the committee), the small size of the room and its embellishment with the tablets of the Declaration of the Rights of Man and the Citizen (on the wall in background) show how the revolutionary institutions had to adapt to the spaces of the old regime. The moral and physical exhaustion of revolutionary politics is captured by the expression on the face of the central figure, seated. (Jean-Baptiste Huet, *Comité de l'an deuxième* [1794]. Library of Congress Prints & Photographs Division Washington, DC: PGA [P&P])

A British view of the differences between Britain and revolutionary France at the dawn of 1793 (Chapter 11). Contrasted with Gillray's cartoon of 1789, it shows how far mainstream British attitudes towards the Revolution had changed under the impact of events in France and Britain. Famished French *sans-culottes* fight over a frog, religious imagery (in the background) is disrespected and there are images of revolutionary atrocities on the wall. In a British tavern, by comparison, well-fed British men gorge themselves before a roaring fire while, through the window, farmers work industriously in the fields. One of the revellers toasts the 'King and Constitution' with a bumper of ale. This cartoon, by Isaac Cruickshank, was published and displayed by the famous print-shop owner Fores, whose public showroom was at No. 3, Piccadilly, uncomfortably close to the home of the radical master-shoemaker Thomas Hardy. (*French Happiness, English Misery* [London, 3 January 1793]. Library of Congress: Prints & Photographs Division, Washington, DC: PC 1-8288 [P&P])

A New Yorker's view of the transfer of the capital of the United States from New York to Philadelphia in 1790 (Chapter 12): The devil entices the ship of the constitution (bearing anxious members of Congress) to the Pennsylvanian city, by way of some dangerous rapids. (*Congress embark'd on board the ship Constitution of America bound to Conogocheque by way of Philadelphia* [1790]. Library of Congress Prints & Photographs Division Washington, DC: PC/US-1790. A000, no. 4 [P&P])

The City Hotel on Broadway (Chapter 12): An expression of New York City's thrusting aspirations as an American metropolis, and a new, modern site for political mobilisation during the bitter partisan struggles of the 1790s. (A. L. Dick, *City Hotel, Trinity and Grace Churches, Broadway* [1831]. New York Public Library: http://digitalcollections.nypl.org/items /5e66b3e9-0486-d471-e040-e00a180654d7)

THE PROCESS OF reform began promisingly enough. The revolutionaries' ultimate task – as they had proclaimed at the Tennis Court Oath on 20 June 1789 – was to forge a constitution for the nation. Reflecting this purpose, they now called themselves the Constituent Assembly. They also had to shore up law and order, which had collapsed across the country. Rural France was stalked by fear and convulsed by insurrection as peasants rose up to destroy the hated manorial system that had oppressed them with demands for money, crops and labour. The Constituent Assembly rose to the challenge and, in a tumultuous session on the night of 4 August 1789, abolished what it called 'feudalism' to calm the countryside and, in the process, razed the whole hierarchy of privilege – personal, corporate, municipal, provincial and estate – that had been the source of such contention under the old regime. This meant that the new order had to rest on other principles. These the National Assembly proclaimed on 26 August 1789 in the Declaration of the Rights of Man and the Citizen. Its resonating words boldly stated that 'men are born free and equal in rights'. The central thrust was equality before the law, so the revolutionaries were proclaiming civil – not social or even political – equality. The fundamental rights included freedom of religious worship and of expression, while taxation would be apportioned according to ability to pay. Access to public office would be based only on merit ('virtues and talents') rather than birth. The nation – not the king – was the source of all sovereignty.[2]

These principles were put into practice with a vengeance, and one of the early victims of this overhaul was France's Parlements, once the backbone of legal resistance to royal power. As the revolutionaries began the painstaking process of reforming the whole justice system from top to bottom, the Parlements tumbled with the rubble of the old regime. In Paris the Parlement was little mourned: ever since the bitter struggle over privileges and the Estates-General, the revolutionaries had regarded the old sovereign courts as aristocratic throwbacks to the old regime. They were put on permanent vacation in November 1789, the magistrates quietly filing out of the Palais de Justice for the last time. Then, in August 1790, the courts would be abolished outright. The once-dogged, popular and sometimes principled barriers to royal power had gone without so much as eliciting a whimper of protest.[3]

Few doubted that France would be a constitutional monarchy, but here the revolutionaries encountered their first major obstacle, that is, until the people of Paris intervened. The king would now be called 'king of the French', suggesting that his was an authority drawn from the people, rather than 'king of France', which implied ownership of the country. The deputies in the National Assembly took all legislative initiative, denying the king any right to present bills, but they did accept that their decrees could become law only once they had received royal assent. The question was, should the king have a veto? Some radicals, including a deputy from Arras in northern France called Maximilien Robespierre, insisted that the king have none whatsoever, but they were in a minority. Some diehard royalists, another minority, argued for an absolute veto, but compromise carried the day on 15 September 1789, whereby the king was given a suspensive one, meaning that he could delay laws for the lifetime of two legislatures. The split among the deputies over the issue – between the radicals who sat to the left of the National Assembly's president and the conservatives who sat to his right – has given us the modern political meanings of those previously innocuous terms.

At this stage, however, the Revolution seemed to be stalling, as the king delayed putting the royal seal on the National Assembly's decrees, including the abolition of privilege and the Declaration of the Rights of Man and the Citizen. At the same time, although the harvest was good, its effects were not felt immediately, and by the autumn Parisians were becoming impatient with the lags in the supply of bread and its high price. In the streets and in the political clubs, rumours flew that this was the result of a counter-revolutionary conspiracy to starve Paris. That in turn prompted talk of compelling the king to live in the city, forcing him to sanction the revolutionaries' reforms and compelling the 'aristocrats' to lift their obstructions to the food supply. Not for the first or last time in this great city seething with political passion, bread and revolution fused as one issue. The trigger was a banquet held in Versailles on Saturday, 1 October. Louis XVI had been well aware of Parisian agitation to have him forcibly hauled to the capital, and on 14 September he had ordered the Régiment de Flandres – iron-hard, disciplined and loyal – to Versailles to help protect the palace. On their arrival, the palace guard honoured the regiment's officers with a banquet: when the queen appeared with her four-year-old son, the Dauphin, the drunken officers shouted anti-revolutionary slogans and songs, tore out the compulsory tricolour cockades pinned to their hats and, trampling them under foot, replaced them with the white of the Bourbon monarchy and – alarmed rumours had it – the black of Marie-Antoinette's Austria.[4]

When news of this 'orgy' reached Paris, there was turmoil. On 4 October, crowds of women in the Palais-Royal were demanding a march on Versailles, while in the political clubs and districts speakers called on Lafayette to mobilise the National Guard, for the assumption was that the behaviour of the drunken officers could only presage a counter-revolutionary assault on Paris. As dawn broke in the morning of 5 October, in what appears to have been a coordinated protest, women gathered in both the central market of Les Halles and, of course, the Faubourg Saint-Antoine.

In Saint-Eustache, the market district, the women were summoned to action by a little girl beating a drum and crying out against the shortage of bread. The tocsin sounded in the surrounding churches, the massive bells of Saint-Eustache at Les Halles giving out their sonorous notes, while in the Faubourg Saint-Antoine the women woke up the bell ringer and forced him to ring the lighter but familiar chime of the Church of Sainte-Marguerite. The men and women of the Faubourg Saint-Antoine were once again displaying their ready militancy. Yet the strong presence of the women in the central markets of Les Halles is significant and also rooted not only in their economic interests, for their liveli-hoods were bound up with a plentiful food supply, but also in the character and culture of the neighbourhood. New York had its Fly Market and London had its rich heritage of markets – Smithfield for meat, Billingsgate for fish, Covent Garden for flowers and food, for example – but the Parisian market district of Les Halles was unique in its character, in the ties of solidarity that bound together those who lived and worked there and in its centrality to the lives of almost all working Parisians. It was this combination of the economics, culture and geography of Les Halles that gave the area its revolutionary dynamism.

There had been a market in this central part of Paris since the early twelfth century, when King Louis VI joined forces with the bishop of Paris and bought the lands north of the present-day rue Saint-Honoré. A mosaic of buildings sprang up to accommodate a range of commercial activities, their presence still remembered in some of the local street names, such as the rue de la Ferronerie (ironmongers) and the rue de la Lingerie (linen). The district also boasted a rue de la Tonnellerie (barrel makers), a rue de la Fromagerie (cheese market), a rue des Potiers d'Étain (pewters), a rue de la Poterie (pottery), a rue de la Cordonnerie (cobblers) and a rue de la Petite Friperie (secondhand clothes). Since bread was such a central issue for all Parisians, and was therefore for the government, it was fitting that a new grain market should have been constructed in 1762 just to the west. The rotunda (which was replaced in 1889 by the building that exists today on the same circular site) certainly impressed British visitor Arthur Young, who, in 1787, described it as 'by far the finest thing I have yet seen at Paris'. He marvelled at the throbbing activity: 'Wheat, pease, beans, lentils, are stored and sold'. Flour was sold in bulk from wooden stalls, while there were 'spacious apartments for rye, barley, oats'. The area as a whole changed a little just prior to the Revolution, as the authorities thrust through a new street, rue de Calonne, to improve circulation. The Carreau, the open-air market with stalls not far from the great Saint-Eustache Church, was widened. Between 1785 and 1787, the Church of the Innocents was demolished, the stinking cadaver-stacked cemetery closed (the bones were transferred to the Catacombs to the south of the city) and the site paved over to become the Marché des Innocents, centred on the glorious sixteenth-century fountain that was moved from a nearby corner on the rue Saint-Denis. This market then accommodated the fruit and vegetable sellers of Les Halles.[5]

This district was one of the most teeming in the entire city. A rabbit warren running west from the rue Saint-Denis towards the Church of Saint-Eustache and bounded to the south by the rue Saint-Honoré, it accommodated some 555 people per acre, compared with 360 in the Bonne Nouvelle and in the Ponceau districts to the north. Rents in the poorest lodging houses around the markets were among the cheapest in the city, where a fleapit of a room could be had for as little as a penny a night. Yet the lifeblood of the area, those who gave it its energy, its noises, its smells and its character, was the market people. The *fripiers* – the men and (for the most part) women who sold secondhand clothes – had a fearsome reputation: a customer who lingered amongst their wares was not allowed to escape easily without making a purchase. The streets were clogged with stalls – fruit sellers, bakers, fishwives – all concentrated in their own areas. Eggs, butter, bread and fish were sold on the Carreau. Here, too, thieves, prostitutes and vagrants who had fallen afoul of the law were displayed on the pillory. The streets off the rue Saint-Denis were occupied by grocers selling vegetables and fruit. Some vendors came in from the surrounding villages to sell their produce, including cheese makers, fruiterers and pork merchants who arrived on Wednesdays and Saturdays in the small hours of the morning. They yielded their pitches to the grain merchants at nine or ten. The most colourful figures of all were the market women: the formidable and mouthy *dames des Halles*, who guarded their stalls, selling, chatting and haggling, having day-to-day contact with people – especially other women – from across the city.[6]

The communal solidarity not only of street sellers but also of the market porters (the *forts*) had always been tight, connected by ties of family and occupation and by the simple fact that they knew each other, conversed with each other over their street stalls and in times of need helped each other out. The women of Les Halles spoke a coarse jargon all their own (*poissard*), which involved a blend of rhyme, deliberately mangled syntax and grammar, abuse and threat. It was used in the songs roared out in the drinking dens and market stalls in this district: *parler comme une poissarde* (to talk like a fishwife) was (and still is) to speak with a tough, cutting language in which there is no room for deference. Thus, the term *poissarde* could refer specifically to the fishwives who worked at the stalls on the rue Montorgueil or more generically to the market women at large who also used this way of speaking. Rough and ready though they were, they did play an important, privileged ceremonial role at Versailles: they had enjoyed more or less open access to the queen and were allowed to be in the palace at royal births, with the right to verify the sex of the infant. Thus, Versailles was a natural, familiar objective for the market women when they formed the backbone of the insurrection on 5 October.[7]

As the central food markets, Les Halles was (as Émile Zola would call them a century later) 'the belly of Paris'. This fact was especially important for the city's working people, for whom sparing their families from hunger was a daily struggle and for whom, so far, the Revolution seemed to have made little difference to their material lives. Prosperous families could afford to buy their bread from neighbourhood bakeries, but the city's working population gravitated to the one-thousand-strong bakers who trekked into the city from outlying villages and piled their loaves up on the market stalls of Les Halles. Bread brought in from outside was cheaper because it was often at least half a day old before it was sold, and, legally, it could be put on sale only in one of the city's markets. Once the bread was on sale, it could not be withdrawn, so as the day went on the unsold loaves began to be discounted, and the city's poor hovered, waiting for the right moment. The hard-pressed Parisian workers and labourers therefore always bought their food at the end of the day, when it was often cheaper. They may have frequented one of the neighbourhood markets such as the Marché-Saint-Germain and the Place Maubert on the Left Bank or Saint-Paul in the Marais on the Right Bank, but the busiest, Les Halles, was the largest and most popular. These markets had become a social space for working Parisians, with all-night dances, wine shops and cafés drawing people from all over the city.[8]

They were also at the centre of the insurrection of 5 October 1789 because of a harsh fact of eighteenth-century life: most of the working population of Paris survived because every member of the family contributed to the household economy. Thus, a woman's work was an essential part of the 'family economy', not just because her labour brought in income, but also because her social relationships – with the market sellers, the bakers, the parish priest – could help to keep the bodies and souls of her family together in times of crisis. When food was scarce and expensive, there was a horrifying 'hierarchy of hunger': mothers ensured that their children and husbands ate first, and so they felt the first pinches of hunger. And since women were the ones who went to the markets and bought the family's bread and vegetables, they were the very first to learn that the prices had gone up, yet again, or that there was little or no bread to be had. It was they who carried the news back to their districts and the faubourgs. Unsurprisingly, women had always been at the very forefront of eighteenth-century bread riots, and they mobilised 'their men' behind them. A crisis at Les Halles could therefore send shock waves right across the city.[9]

These hard realities explain why the market women were among the first to seize the initiative in early October and why they were joined by women from all over the metropolis. What may have begun as an economic protest rapidly took a political direction: only by persuading the authorities to change policy would Paris be adequately fed. Their first target was the Hôtel de Ville, the city hall, where the Parisian municipality sat. Somewhere between eight hundred and two thousand (estimates diverge) women from all social backgrounds – fishwives, stall holders from the market, craft workers and well-dressed bourgeoisie – converged here, and, at about nine o'clock, they broke open the doors and surged into the entrance hall and up the great staircase. Any man who happened to stand in their way was unceremoniously bundled onto the steps outside. Remembering that weapons had been distributed here during the July days, the women scoured the vast building, seizing a number of pikes. They then ransacked the offices, gathering papers and hurling them onto a pile in the great hall, where they threatened to burn them. There was nothing here, they declared, that would help secure bread.[10]

At this point, Stanislas Maillard arrived on the scene: he was a veteran of the storming of the Bastille and thus someone whom the women trusted. He dissuaded the women from lighting their paper bonfire and either was persuaded or offered to lead them to Versailles. The women mustered on the Place de Grève outside and set off, seizing two cannon as they marched past the Châtelet. Some were sent back to their own neighbourhoods, drumming up support from as many other women as they could find. In the district of Saint-Eustache – the markets again – a child was sent around the streets blowing on a bugle and ringing a bell.

When the women reassembled on the Place Louis XV in the late morning, their ranks had swollen to between five and seven thousand. While some carried pikes, most were armed with little more than brooms and kitchen knives. With eight drummers and Maillard at their head, they marched off through a drizzle towards Versailles – twelve miles and a six-hour trudge away.

An alarmed Lafayette, meanwhile, had mobilised the National Guard to put a stop to the march, but the militia did not strike out until four in the afternoon, a force twenty thousand strong led by the general on a white charger in pursuit of the women. In the trail of the National Guard came the menfolk, seven to eight hundred craftsmen and journeymen who had downed tools at the end of the day, seized what weapons they could – tools, sticks, pikes and muskets – and set out. The women, drenched from the rain, had already arrived at Versailles by five, where they invaded the National Assembly and gained an audience with the king, who, under intense pressure, finally agreed to give his royal sanction to the revolutionary reforms so far and promised that Paris would be supplied with bread. Lafayette and the National Guard, bent forward in the downpour, tramped into Versailles at ten before spending the best part of the night keeping apart the palace guard and the armed women encamped in the courtyard in front of the royal palace.

In the small hours of the morning, however, just as the Parisian men were arriving, some of the market women broke into the palace and tore around the corridors looking for the queen, who fled in terror, her retreat covered by the royal bodyguard until Lafayette's militia poured in to flush the Parisian women out. To mollify the now crowd of ten thousand thronging outside and chanting 'To Paris! To Paris!', the king sadly bowed to the inevitable and promised that he and his family would return with them to the capital. That day, the king, queen and their children jolted gloomily in their carriages, leaving Versailles forever, followed by rumbling carts laden with flour from the court's own stores. Once in the city, the royal family took up residence in the battered, draughty Tuileries Palace, soon refurbished. The monarchy was now a virtual hostage in a city whose people had by now twice demonstrated their determination to keep the Revolution on track.[11]

WITHIN DAYS, PARIS had become a functioning capital city again. The National Assembly soon followed the king, opening for business in Paris on 19 October. After a brief spell during which it crammed into the assembly room of the Êveché, the residence of the archbishop of Paris next to Notre-Dame Cathedral (which proved disastrous when the public gallery gave out a frightening creak before collapsing under the weight of the spectators), it eventually moved into the Manège, Louis XV's boyhood riding school, on the northern edge of the Tuileries Gardens. Henceforth, both the king and the National Assembly were housed within a few hundred yards of each other. Along with the king and the

National Assembly came the ministries, which took over some of the secondary royal palaces and mansions in the city, an invasion of officialdom that turned the west end of Paris, especially around the Place Vendôme and the Place Louis XV, into an administrative district interlocking with the political axis of the Tuileries and the Manège: in some blocks, there were thirty or forty public officials for every hundred residents. The very character of this central part of the city was transformed.[12]

The Revolution also consciously wanted to reverse the centralisation of authority represented by the defunct absolute monarchy and to disseminate it among the citizenry. This made the real spatial impact, not just in Paris, but across all France. The nationwide political framework was constructed in December 1789 – a uniform system of local government in the shape of eighty-three departments, which are still the fundamental building blocks of French administrative and political life. Cities, towns and villages became 'communes', and the larger ones such as Paris and Marseilles, with a mayor, general council and attorney general, would soon be broken down into electoral wards called 'sections'.

At every level, government would be run by elected councils and officials – and they had to meet somewhere. In the elections to the Estates-General in the spring of 1789, each of the sixty electoral districts of Paris had required spaces in which to meet, and in all of them the only available public buildings that were large enough were parish churches and convent chapels. Yet this was also a perfectly natural choice: churches were public spaces, the habitual and regular gathering places of the community. Over the course of 1789, therefore, many of Paris's 200 churches and chapels had been embellished with political symbols, so that these once-familiar landmarks on the cityscape for a time transmitted dual messages. Alongside the Catholic imagery of the cross, of martyrs, saints, Christ and the Virgin, alongside the coats of arms of long-departed aristocratic and royal patrons, one could now see the secular symbols of the new order. In between religious services, one could hear the boiling sound of debate and, after July 1789, see citizens to-ing and fro-ing down the aisles wearing the tricolour cockade. Political notices outlining the formal business of the assemblies were now nailed up alongside religious ones, and there was usually a guardhouse outside, manned by the National Guard, sporting the ubiquitous red, white and blue in their uniforms. In these early months of the revolution, the existence of revolutionary and Catholic signs side by side was a hopeful signal.[13]

Yet it was not to be: as the revolutionaries grappled with the financial abyss inherited from the absolute monarchy, they made a decision that would secularise these sites altogether and begin to rip apart the delicate consensus that had just about held between the church and the new revolutionary order. To honour the state debt, on 2 November 1789 the revolutionaries nationalised all church land, a sixth of the territory of France, which would be auctioned off to raise money to pay the government's creditors. This was followed up in February 1790 by the abolition of monastic vows, releasing hundreds of Parisian monks and nuns from their orders if they so wished. Yet the revolutionaries had no desire to extirpate Catholicism itself. Having kicked away the economic foundations of the church, the National Assembly remodelled it from top to bottom; the reform came on 12 July 1790 in the shape of the Civil Constitution of the Clergy, which made priests electable by their parishioners and salaried by the state. The pope was not consulted, which troubled many Catholic consciences.[14]

The impact on the city itself was seismic. The city boasted 50 parish churches, 130 convents and monasteries, 12 seminaries and more than 60 colleges attached to the University of Paris, all of them run by the church and its orders. The city's six thousand clerics – cassocked priests, nuns in their habits, tonsured friars – were familiar sights on the streets. With the abolition of religious vows, some monasteries rapidly emptied of their friars, including the Cordeliers on the Left Bank and the Dominicans (Jacobins) on the rue Saint-Honoré. Others chose, almost collectively, to remain true to their order, such as the Carmelites and the Capucins, both on the rue Saint-Jacques.

The effects of the secularisation of church buildings and land ensured that the Revolution penetrated the very fabric of the city. Ecclesiastical buildings were now adapted fully for their political and civic purposes. Most strikingly, the domed neoclassical massif of the Church of Saint-Geneviève, designed by Jacques-Germain Soufflot and still being completed, became the Pantheon, devoted to the interment of the 'great men' (and for a long time it was just men) recognised by *la patrie*, the fatherland.[15] Political clubs also moved into religious buildings. Most famously of all, the Parisian Society of the Friends of the Constitution met first in the refectory and then in the library of the Dominican monastery just off the rue Saint-Honoré (on the present site of the Marché Saint-Honoré), close to the Manège. The remaining friars, still visible in their white robes and black hoods, lent their nickname to the club: the Jacobins. Years later, the monastery's master of novices could claim that 'I can count myself among the founders of the Paris Jacobin Club'.[16]

THE VAST MAJORITY of deputies in the National Assembly – nobles, clerics, lawyers and property owners that they were – cherished the rule of law, the defence of property and the goal of an ordered constitutional government. Outbursts of protests and violence on the streets that had culminated in the women's march on Versailles on 5 October made the deputies fearful of the unpredictable, uncontrollable force of popular insurrection. On 29 October

1789, accordingly, the National Assembly had restricted the right to vote to 'active citizens' – adult males who paid the equivalent of at least three days of unskilled labour in taxes a year. The importance of being an 'active' citizen was not just a question of having the right to vote every two years in national elections. In the new civic order, where every branch of the state, the church and the law was being overhauled, they were also expected to choose the mayor and departmental officials, justices of the peace, judges and parish priests. So the right to vote carried daily local consequence. This was especially true in Paris, where the new municipal constitution, voted by the National Assembly in May 1790, introduced forty-eight new electoral wards called 'sections' to replace the sixty districts that had chosen deputies to the Estates-General. In these new sections, only 'active' citizens would have the right to vote.

In imposing these reforms, the Constituent Assembly sought to weaken the Parisian popular movement. The restrictions on the suffrage and the creation of the sections formally excluded many of the artisanal, labouring militants who had played such a central role in the insurrections of 1789. The protests against these attempts to dampen the political energies among the working population were heard especially loudly in one of the heartlands of Parisian radicalism, the Cordeliers quarter, one of the sixty original districts. The neighbourhood was special because of its social makeup, its location and, fortuitously, the quality of its political leadership. Unlike the Faubourg Saint-Antoine and the district of Les Halles, which had a distinctly 'popular' flavour, the Cordeliers was socially more mixed: during the Revolution the area was alive with tradesmen (including butchers who plied their trade nearby), artisans, lawyers and students on foot who jostled and pushed past each other on the narrow streets. The area had its pockets of wealth and comfort that rubbed shoulders with the artisans and retailers who formed the backbone of Parisian political militancy. In this respect, the Cordeliers district was far from unique in a city where the development of residential areas segregated by wealth was not yet as pronounced as it was in London.

The area's revolutionary distinctiveness came from an historical accident: already in 1789, the quarter happened to be the home of the Revolution's most energetic political leaders. The Cordeliers district was drilled through with streets that included the rue Saint-André-des-Arts, the rue de l'Ancienne Comédie, the parallel passage du Commerce Saint-André and the rue des Cordeliers. To stand on the triangular space of pavement where the rue de l'École de Médecine now intersects with the modern-day boulevard Saint-Germain is to be on the site of the house of Jean-Paul Marat, a doctor by training who had penned radical tracts before 1789, but whose journalistic career took off with the Revolution when he began editing his incendiary newspaper, *L'Ami du Peuple*, a moniker that his adoring artisanal readership soon applied to the man himself. From there, it is a very short walk to the magnificent nineteenth-century statue of Georges-Jacques Danton, the fiery, inspiring lawyer who seized the political opportunities offered by the Revolution with both hands: the pedestal marks the spot where his house stood on the (no longer extant) rue des Cordeliers. South along the rue de l'Odéon, at No. 22, is the house where husband-and-wife revolutionaries Camille and Lucille Desmoulins lived, working together on the newspaper *Révolutions de France et de Brabant*. Across the boulevard Saint-Germain to the north of the Danton statue is the entrance to the passage du Commerce Saint-André, still a picturesque cobbled lane: at No. 9, the good Dr. Guillotin tested his scientific, democratic beheading machine on dead sheep. *L'Ami du Peuple* was printed at the end of what is now the gated courtyard called the Cour de Rohan, which runs off the passage. Along this lane is the Café Procope, where some of the great Enlightenment thinkers had fuelled their discussions with caffeine, but which during the Revolution was frequented by the Cordeliers leadership. It was here that the red (Phrygian) bonnet of liberty was first displayed as a sartorial emblem of free French citizens. The passage du Commerce exits onto the rue Saint-André-des-Arts, where Danton's onetime secretary Billaud-Varenne lived at No. 45. A short left turn down this street gains the rue de l'Ancienne-Comédie, where Danton's friend and ally Fabre d'Églantine occupied No. 12.[17]

Moreover, if all areas of central Paris had their artisans and retailers, the people of the Cordeliers district had enjoyed a political reputation from the very beginning. In May 1790, Anarchasis Cloots, a radical Prussian baron who also lived here, claimed to have overheard a group of labourers, blacksmiths, masons and cartmen discuss some of the more advanced ideas of the Enlightenment. Although Cloots was not unbiased, the popular politics of the district flowed from the effervescent combination of an already articulate, politicised artisanal population, combined with the concentration of a sympathetic radical leadership. It may also have helped that its location close to the Sorbonne meant that it was not too far from one of the hubs of the print trade, along the rue Saint-Jacques, while the rue Saint-André-des-Arts boasted the highest concentration of publishers in the city. Until May 1792 the Abbé Royou's royalist newspaper, the *Ami du Roi* (Friend of the King), bravely had its offices at No. 37, so not far, in either a geographical or a titular sense, from Marat's counterpart.[18]

With the Cordeliers district boasting such democratic credentials, and with a social makeup and topography in which middle-class revolutionaries lived close by artisans, the area quickly assumed a radical, critical mass, as its very reputation then drew other democrats to relocate and settle in the area. Its revolutionary dynamism ensured that in 1789–1790, the assembly of the Cordeliers district had been among the most innovative in its adoption of ideas of direct democracy and in meeting the material needs of the people. In October 1789, the district assembly had sent out an armed detachment of National Guards into the countryside to forage for grain to feed its people. In January, when the Parisian municipality had tried to arrest Marat after he had published some particularly inflammatory journalism, the militia had formed a security cordon in the streets, creating a 'no go' area against the authorities. The district assembly tried to press for the right to recall instantly their delegates to the Paris Commune, the central municipality, if those representatives did not carry out the wishes of their electors. In June 1790, the district assembly proposed – against the less than democratic system of 'active' citizens and sections already voted by the National Assembly – that anyone who paid any tax whatsoever, including indirect taxes, which included just about everybody, should have 'active' citizenship.[19]

Across the city, the district assemblies, originally intended merely as the first step for the elections of 1789, had assumed the shape of permanent local government – and many of them had become hotbeds of popular radicalism. They had taken control of a whole range of policing responsibilities – and this was 'policing' in the French eighteenth-century sense of 'administration and regulation', including appointing committees and selecting police commissioners and justices of the peace to maintain law and order. They had also watched prostitutes and gaming houses, taken care of street lighting and cleaning, supervised trading hours for shops, regulated cafés and inns, overseen weights and measures and taken care of firefighting. For the benefit of the poor, they had run soup kitchens, collected financial contributions to help paupers and undertaken the all-important task of searching for supplies of grain and flour at a reasonable price. Each district also had its five-hundred-strong battalion of National Guards.[20]

When the property-owning, order-loving deputies in the National Assembly created the category of 'active citizens' in late October 1789 and replaced the districts with the sections the following summer, they were partially motivated by an impulse to force out the rough-and-ready militants of the city's working population from local politics, for in Paris only half the adult male population, no more than eighty thousand men, would qualify as voters under the new rules. Moreover, the redrawing of the boundaries provided opportunities to break up the political networks – like that which now existed in the Cordeliers district – that had helped to keep popular militancy on the boil since 1789. Assemblies of the sections were meant only to meet for elections, so a turn to regular constitutional government meant an end to the alert everyday activism of local artisanal militants. The sixty National Guard battalions were allowed to subsist as before, but, though they had tended to follow the inclinations of their districts, rather than the orders coming from General Lafayette's headquarters, the direct link between the local assemblies and the militia had been broken.[21]

Unsurprisingly, some of the most eloquent protests against the changes were heard in the Cordeliers district. Writing in their apartment on the rue de l'Odéon, Lucille and Camille Desmoulins published an article in their *Révolutions de France et de Brabant* warning that France was being turned into an 'aristocratic government' and asking pointedly, 'What is this much repeated word *active citizen* supposed to mean? The active citizens are the ones who took the Bastille'. As for the replacement of the districts by the sections, the Desmoulins captured the feelings of the disconsolate citizens of the Cordeliers district when it was subsumed into the larger Théâtre-Français section. On 17 May 1790, the newspaper mourned elegiacally:

Oh, my very dear Cordeliers, farewell then to our handbell, to our president's chair, and to the tribune, resounding and full of illustrious orators. In their place there will be nothing more than a great urn, a pitcher, to which the active citizens, who are never visible, will come to put in their votes and distribute the tricolour sashes to the most adroit intriguer ... Perish, then, even to the name of this district, this formidable name that would remind citizens of their glory, the taking of the Bastille, the expedition to Versailles.[22]

Yet the death of radicalism in this area, as well as elsewhere in Paris, was very much exaggerated. The bonds of revolutionary solidarity and neighbourhood were not broken by the redrawing of electoral boundaries. In the Théâtre-Français section, which had incorporated the former Cordeliers district, the close political relationship between leadership and population remained as firm as ever. With their skills of organisation, oratory and journalism sharpened, the radicals swept the board in the municipal elections in early July 1790, making short work of the *robins*, the 'black flood' of robed conservative lawyers who inhabited the Saint-André-des-Arts area to the north. Moreover, in the new municipal constitution, Parisians were allowed to assemble to draft petitions to the higher authorities: all it took was fifty citizens to request it, and the sectional assemblies could gather for this purpose, a rule that the radicals ruthlessly exploited.[23]

The Théâtre-Français section continued to attract democrats from all over Paris because of its radical track record, but it was also unique in that it extended its political reach right across the city – and indeed nationally. The Cordeliers enjoyed such influence because, in the very heart of the section's labyrinthine streets, a political club had been established. The founding of the Société des Amis des Droits de l'Homme et du Citoyen (the Society of the

Friends of the Rights of Man and the Citizen) in April 1790 was the Cordeliers' reaction to the squeeze on democratic participation. Like the Jacobin Club, this society was more commonly known by its meeting place, the old Franciscan monastery, the Cordeliers. The society gathered in the monastery's sixteenth-century church, the Sainte-Madeleine, which stood where the rue Hautefeuille joined the rue des Cordeliers. The church was one of the largest in Paris, and it connected to a seventeenth-century cloister, behind which was a large garden, planted with trees. So the Cordeliers Club debated beneath the wooden vaulting, darkened with age, and was overlooked by the statues of Saints Peter and Paul that decorated the rood screen.[24] Its first manifesto, dated 27 April 1790, had declared that its goal was to 'denounce before the tribunal of public opinion all abuses by the different authorities and any attack on the rights of man'. It therefore saw its primary purpose as one of rooting out threats to the Revolution (its official papers were printed with the all-seeing eye of surveillance), but also of putting into practice the egalitarian principles of 1789. This meant challenging the limits placed on political rights by the emerging constitutional order.[25]

The club drew its membership from the same people who had made the Cordeliers district such a political hothouse: radical lawyers, merchants, artisans, tradesmen and retailers. Its membership dues were kept deliberately low, far lower than those demanded by the well-heeled Jacobins, who still excluded the poor from membership, such as the pin makers, cobblers, washerwomen, seamstresses, domestic servants, day labourers and others who grifted out a life in the city. With its democratic impulses, the Cordeliers Club encouraged all such people to attend its sessions as observers, and women attended in large numbers. The club therefore kept revolutionary energies simmering in Paris.[26]

Moreover, the new system of suffrage and sections, while far from democratic, was still a radical departure from the old days of royal authority in Paris. Under the absolute monarchy, there had been a mayor of sorts – a *prévôt des marchands* (its nearest English translation would be 'provost') and a city council mostly made up of échevins, or aldermen. Yet this had been far from a model of local representative government, for all these officials had been effectively appointed by the king, and, in any case, their functions had been mostly ceremonial. Since the seventeenth century, most of the council's responsibilities had been hived off by the lieutenant of police in the Châtelet, who commanded forty-eight police commissioners and had his headquarters in the grim hulk of the fortress, prison and morgue of the Châtelet on the Right Bank of the Seine. Along with the military governor who controlled the armed forces, it had been in the Châtelet that real power resided. As contemporary writer (and then revolutionary) Louis-Sébastien Mercier had bluntly put it, 'The authority of the municipality counts for nothing', adding that the *prévôt* and the échevins were mere phantoms next to the real power, which was in the hands of the police.

The Revolution's creation of the sections in the summer of 1790 was therefore a real break with the past: these wards had directly elected assemblies, justices of the peace, police commissioners and National Guard officers. Moreover, the fact that they were often installed in what were once the sedate settings for prayer, worship and contemplation made them the visible reminders that a revolution had taken place and that the transformation had reached into the most localised of levels. The sections, their personnel and their buildings represented the profound revolutionary change that had threaded its way into the very fabric of the city. Once the forty-eight new wards were elected in July, the new Paris Commune, with astronomer Jean-Sylvain Bailly as mayor, was soon installed in the Hôtel de Ville.[27]

The new system of local government had just begun to function when the Festival of Federation took place on the first anniversary of the fall of the Bastille. There was real hope that, after all the explosions of violence, the new administrative system would ensure that peace and security would finally return. At the Festival of the Federation on 14 July 1790, the king, the National Assembly, the Paris municipality and literally hundreds of thousands of people would join with National Guard units from every department in France on the Champ de Mars, the parade ground on the southwestern edge of the city. There everyone, from the king downwards, would take an oath of loyalty 'to the Nation, the Law and the King', intended as a display of national unity and a solemn undertaking to make the new civic order that was emerging in France work. On the day itself, there seems to have been genuine exuberance and pleasure among participants and onlookers, perhaps 350,000 in all. Among those who took centre stage were those who had benefited most from the reforms in Parisian government, namely, Bailly, as the city's moderate mayor, and Lafayette, who as commander of the National Guard was the guarantor of law, order and stability. If the federation was anyone's triumph, it was theirs.[28]

They were buoyed by the genuine exhilaration unleashed by the celebrations, and in the weeks that followed the tricolour as a style item reached its voluntary height: fashion designers on the rue Saint-Honoré produced a 'Patriotic Women's Négligée', which had a blue coat with red collar and white piping, white ruffles edged with red and a white skirt. Even floral-patterned skirts bore the compulsory red-white-blue on the petals; women's bouquets, pinned to the fichu above the bust, were mixes of white-petalled daisies, blue cornflowers and bloodred poppies. Ladies' fans bore revolutionary images: the National Guard, the National Assembly and the champions of the day, including Bailly and Lafayette, were favourite motifs. Medals, jewellery, glass, crockery and china were engraved or glazed with the motto 'The Nation, the Law, the King'.[29]

There was a fleeting sense of optimism, even of relief, but questions nagged. Despite his oath, Louis himself had serious misgivings, in particular about his loss of power, about the safety of his family and about the religious reforms. For many nobles, the threat of violence and the abolition of privilege made exile look more alluring. Eventually, perhaps as many as a quarter of all French nobles fled the country. The king's own brothers, the comtes d'Artois and de Provence, followed by aristocratic army officers fleeing their mutinous soldiers and by clerics appalled by the ecclesiastical reforms, had already fled into Germany, where an army of émigrés began to muster not far from the frontier, dreaming of marching into France with European support, crushing the chattering revolutionary upstarts and restoring the old order.

Yet nothing mobilised broader support for the counter-revolution more than the greatest miscalculation that the Constituent Assembly made in its three-year existence. This was the clerical oath decreed on 27 November 1790, which required all priests and bishops to swear allegiance to the new Civil Constitution. The revolutionaries, stung by some of the royalist criticism of their reforms so far, seem fully to have expected that parish priests would flock to take the oath, displaying overwhelming support for the Revolution. The results were, in fact, horrifying and split the clergy almost down the middle between oath-taking 'constitutional priests', or jurors, on the one hand, and nonjurors, or 'refractories', on the other. In Paris the 56 per cent of ecclesiastics who opted to take the oath could not be said to have represented a resounding endorsement of the Revolution. The weighty importance of this result rested in the fact that priests did not merely consult their own consciences, but reflected the views of their parishioners, so the implication was that the French people as a whole were deeply divided over the Revolution. So in the early months of 1791, the question of who would or who would not take the oath absorbed public attention – and gave rise to violence – in streets and churches across Paris. The clerical oath blew apart the delicate revolutionary consensus and crystallised positions among all French people for or against the Revolution as a whole. The nonjurors gave anyone disgruntled with the new order a cause around which they could coalesce.[30]

At the other end of the political spectrum, the controversy gave a renewed sense of purpose to the radicals in the first half of 1791. During the bitter schisms that followed from the clerical oath, the Cordeliers Club, seeing itself as a 'school' for politics for the men and women of the labouring population, acquired its metropolitan reach. The organisation sent out delegates to encourage the creation of 'popular societies' in all the other sections, political clubs that would welcome people, men and women, of all conditions. Their purpose was to mobilise and politically educate the working population of the city and partly to press the oath on the more reluctant among the Parisian clergy. Louise Kéralio-Robert, a Cordelier journalist, lavished praise on these societies in April 1791: one day a future generation living 'under a form of government more sublime that the one we have now' will raise a monument thanking the popular societies for laying the foundations of a better world. Within a year of Louise writing those words, twenty-six sections had such a society, mostly meeting in buildings that once belonged to the church.[31]

So it was that, when all the frictions, all the conflicts, came boiling to the surface, as they did in the summer of 1791, the old Cordeliers district was one of the epicentres of the metropolitan eruption. There was no other Parisian area quite like it. On the one hand, it bridged the social gap between the radical middle-class leadership of the burgeoning democratic movement and the militants of the city's working population. On the other hand, it made a strong claim to the political direction of the popular movement across the city. The Jacobin Club across the river was more elitist, intended primarily for left-wing deputies in the National Assembly and their like-minded supporters; located close to the Manège, it was rooted less in metropolitan than in national politics, corresponding with hundreds of sister societies across the country. Those were its great strengths. By contrast, the power of the Cordeliers Club rested in its distinctly metropolitan reach and from being rooted in a neighbourhood whose social and political character made it a linchpin binding the axle of the middle-class radicalism to the wheels of popular revolutionary activism. Neither revolutionary New York nor radical London could boast such a district, a difference that may go some way to explaining the different political turns that each of these cities took in the later eighteenth century.

THE CRISIS CAME in the morning on 21 June 1791, when Parisians learned that the king and his family had fled Paris. British American radical Thomas Paine, who was visiting Paris from mid-April, was woken up in his room by Lafayette, who was yelling, 'The birds are flown! The birds are flown!' Paine would join the incipient republican movement, telling Emmanuel Sieyès – famous as the author of *What Is the Third Estate?* in 1789 – that 'against the *whole hell of monarchy* ... I have declared war'. Louis and the royal family left behind not only vacant royal apartments in the Tuileries – which some wit pasted with a notice saying 'House to Let' – but also a gaping void in the constitutional monarchy that the National Assembly had been working so painstakingly to put together. Agonisingly close to the safety of the frontier, the king was recognised in the village of Varennes and drawn ignominiously back to Paris in shame and put under house arrest in the Tuileries, his constitutional functions suspended.

The Parisian reaction was a turbulent mix of despair, anxiety and anger. For some, whatever threads of trust they still had in Louis XVI fell away: across the city, royal symbols were spontaneously hacked, gouged and struck off monuments and buildings. The Parisian sections went into permanent session to deal with the alarm and the possibility of violence in the streets. The National Guard battalions were called to arms by drumbeats, to prevent outbursts of rioting and to keep an eye out for suspicious political activity, whether royalist or radical. The suspicion that the force's commander, Lafayette, was complicit in the king's flight led some Parisians to hurl insults at the militiamen as they patrolled the streets. Maybe, people of all political stripes darkly feared, the royal flight was a prelude to an invasion by an émigré army, backed by Marie-Antoinette's brother Austrian emperor Leopold II and the full might of the Austrian army. A republican movement was stirring.[32]

It was in this turbulent, fearful atmosphere that a decisive response came from the Cordeliers Club. Within days, it had cemented a partnership with a high-brow political society that met in the sunken circus at the centre of the Palais-Royal called the Cercle Social, which included avowed republicans such as Paine, radical journalist Jacques-Pierre Brissot and Enlightenment philosopher and mathematician the marquis de Condorcet. Together, they presented a petition demanding a referendum on the monarchy, for signature by men and women of all social backgrounds on the Altar of the Patrie on the Champ de Mars on 17 July 1791, almost a year to the day that the same site had seen such exuberant demonstrations of hope and unity.

The Jacobin Club, torn apart by a schism between radicals and moderates – the latter broke away to form their own club, the Feuillants, in the monastery of that name almost across the street from the Jacobins – stood aside. Confronted with thousands of petitioners marching through the city and anxious about the danger to public order in the highly charged atmosphere, Mayor Bailly called out Lafayette and the National Guard.[33] When two peeping toms were discovered, allegedly drilling holes in order to peer up the skirts of women petitioners on the platform, they were accused of planting explosives, butchered and then decapitated. The authorities now panicked: Bailly, having the red flag of martial law flown from the Hôtel de Ville, joined Lafayette in leading a column of National Guards to confront the thousands of demonstrators on the Champ de Mars. There were some scuffles, and then a lone musket shot tore through the air, whereupon the militia opened fire and stormed into the scattering crowd, with deadly impact. When the field, embankments and altar were finally cleared, as many as fifty people lay dead, although no firmly accepted count was ever made.[34]

In the short term, the Champ de Mars massacre appeared to have shattered the republican movement, and Cordeliers in particular. In the wake of the violence, some two hundred people were arrested, and the National Assembly moved against the republican leadership: when, that very evening, members of the Cordeliers Club tried to assemble, they found the cloister barred by two cannon. The authorities swooped as Marat, journalist Louise Kéralio-Robert and Camille Desmoulins escaped into hiding. Georges-Jacques Danton, who had been dining just outside the city on 17 July, managed to flee across the Channel to Britain. Leaders of the popular societies were arrested. In a dark foreshadowing of the logic behind the Terror, one National Assembly deputy concluded that in such times of crisis, 'when the survival of the state is at stake, illegal arrests are justifiable'. Thomas Paine had missed the carnage and its aftermath because he had returned to London on 8 July, but he had left behind a bitterly divided city.[35]

In the long run, the great loser from the massacre was the monarchy, although few if anyone foresaw that the coming year would witness its slow, dying agony. Louis was released from house arrest on 6 September 1791 after he had accepted the Constitution, which was promulgated on 14 September. The elections to the new Legislative Assembly took place in a febrile atmosphere of suspicion and uncertainty. The result was a strong return of radical candidates who otherwise fell far short of a majority but included some of the inner ring of the Cercle Social, like Brissot and Condorcet: they and others who had emerged from provincial politics during the crisis included a host of talented, idealistic and articulated deputies, the ultimately ill-fated phalanx of republicans known as the Girondins because some of their most influential and eloquent representatives came from the Gironde in southwestern France. In the new Legislative Assembly and in the Jacobin Club, the Girondins worked doggedly to embarrass the king and force him openly to declare, either as a traitor to the Revolution or as an unambiguous supporter of it. The expedient was war, and Brissot campaigned for military action against the German princes harbouring the émigrés across the frontier. Since the king and his courtiers in the Tuileries quietly calculated that the iron-disciplined armies of the German powers would rout the ramshackle French forces and fully restore the monarchy, they also backed military action. Thanks to this unholy, inadvertent alliance between king and radicals, the political forces in favour of war – over the heroic, lonely opposition of Maximilien Robespierre in the Jacobins – eventually carried the day. It was declared against Austria on 20 April 1792, and Prussia joined battle against France a month later.

It was the start of a conflict that would not end completely until Napoleon Bonaparte was defeated at Waterloo in 1815. In 1792 the war began disastrously. French resistance on the frontiers seemed to crumble as Austrian and Prussian forces edged towards Paris over the summer. Republicanism re-emerged in the capital, the talk on the streets and in the press being that the king and queen were actively working for the Austrians. On 20 June, a massive demonstration of between ten thousand and twenty thousand people, many of them armed, broke into the Tuileries Palace and forced the king to don the red Phrygian bonnet and to drink to the health of the nation. Who organised this near insurrection is still a mystery, but some evidence points to Cordelier involvement. In July the Legislative Assembly declared *la patrie en danger* (the fatherland in danger), a state of emergency in which the revolutionaries tried to mobilise the whole people in defence of the Revolution.

Meanwhile, democratised National Guard units from across France were mobilised and sent to the front, some of them passing through Paris en route, like the famous Marseillais, who marched into the city on 20 July, singing the battle hymn of the Army of the Rhine and so giving the future French national anthem its more familiar name. That same day, the assembly of the Théâtre-Français section, under the presidency of Danton (who had returned from London and then won a seat in the Legislative Assembly during the elections in September 1791), announced that it was thenceforth recognising the political rights of all citizens, whether they were 'active' or not. This example was quickly imitated by other sections across the city. After the allied commander, the Duke of Brunswick, threatened Paris with 'exemplary and forever memorable vengeance' if the king and his family were harmed, the days of the constitutional monarchy were numbered. Rather than be cowed into submission, the more radical of the Parisian sections appointed delegates to meet at the Hôtel de Ville to draft a petition demanding the king be deposed; this meeting became a central organising committee for the sections, now fully mobilised and with their armed wing in the National Guard units now open to all male citizens.[36]

Under the inspirational leadership of leading Cordeliers like Danton, on 10 August the National Guard and armed militants of the Parisian sections took control of the Hôtel de Ville, installing a Revolutionary commune whose members included a large number of leading members of the popular societies, including Cordeliers such as Danton's friend Fabre d'Églantine and two figures who would play a prominent role in Parisian politics in the coming months, lawyer Gaspard Chaumette and journalist Jacques-René Hébert. Then, backed by National Guards from across the country, including the Marseillais, they stormed the Tuileries, their assault coming from the Place du Carrousel. The Swiss Guards showed suicidal courage in defending the palace. As Louis and his family strolled the short distance through the gardens to take refuge with the Legislative Assembly in the Manège, the king kicking up leaves as he went, the Swiss were massacred by the revolutionary assailants. In the Manège, the royal family, crammed into a small, stuffy lodge reserved for journalists, was forced to listen as the Legislative Assembly voted to depose the king and to call elections, based on near-universal male suffrage, for a national convention. The king, Marie-Antoinette, and their children were then imprisoned in the Temple – a grim, turreted keep in northeast Paris once built by the Knights Templar, but now used as a state prison.

Along with the political revolution, the Parisian cityscape was violently altered in an orgy of iconoclasm: crowds gleefully ran through the streets, ripping down, chiselling away and burning symbols and words associated with royalty. As one National Guardsman wrote in a letter home that evening, 'The bronze statues on the Place Royale, the Place Vendôme, the Place Louis XIV and the Place Louis XV were pulled to the ground . . . In this capital city, only the equestrian statue of Henri IV [the most popular of monarchs] was spared'. Among the victims was Bouchardon's equestrian statue of Louis XV. Within months, the king killing on this very spot would be more than just symbolic: the actual regicide took place on a scaffold erected next to the now empty pedestal when Louis XVI, sentenced to death for treason by the new convention, was guillotined on 21 January 1793.[37]

THE FRENCH REVOLUTION took its radical turn because of the multitude of challenges and dangers that beset the revolutionaries almost from the start: the hesitancy of the king in embracing his role as a constitutional monarch, the schism over the religious reforms, the emigration and open hostility of conservative aristocrats, popular anger over the exclusions from political rights in the name of stability and the restiveness of both the urban poor and the peasantry who saw little material improvement to their lives. If political decisions such as the clerical oath and the flight to Varennes were important steps on the road to the 'second revolution' on 10 August 1792, the war was the immediate and most pressing factor of all. All these problems affected the entire country, albeit in ways that varied from one locality to another. Yet the role of Paris, as the capital, was critical. Maximilien Robespierre, the Jacobin leader who was elected to the Revolutionary commune on 13 August 1792, rebuffed moves by the then Legislative Assembly to have it disbanded. He claimed that during the insurrection of 10 August, the commune, not the assembly, 'have been the people'; in other words, the commune (and through it the people of Paris mobilised in their sections) expressed the sovereign will of all French people. The claim that Paris in some way spoke and acted for the whole nation would help tear the young Republic apart in the coming months.[38]

Yet Paris played a central role in other senses. First, as the capital and as an ancient metropolis, it felt the physical experience of the Revolution in multiple ways – in the adaptation of its buildings for

the purposes of the new political organs of the central government
and in the multitude of institutions of the new civic order that
would reach into the most localised of levels in Parisian life. It also
felt the full force of the less constructive impact of the upheaval:
the emptying of monasteries and convents, for example, and the
iconoclasm that followed the flight to Varennes and the fall of the
monarchy. All these changes were daily visual and spatial reminders that this was a city in revolution. In fact, along with language,
ideology, symbols and political practices, they became a material
part of the revolutionary transformation of politics.

Second, the great revolutionary events that shunted the monarchy towards its bloody demise were, as we have seen, shaped
by the urban, social and political geography of some of its most
important neighbourhoods – the Faubourg Saint-Antoine, the
quarter of Les Halles and the Cordeliers district. The responses of
Parisians to the successive crises between 1789 and 1792 were not
caused by the layout and location of these places, which included
cycles of rumour and anxiety, the circulation of political ideas
and language, the movements of royal troops, political decisions
made by the king and by revolutionary politicians, the shortages
of bread and so on. Yet the character of particular neighbourhoods – both in geographical and in social terms – does go a long
way to explain how the events unfolded and where much of the
revolutionary impulse came from: the Faubourg Saint-Antoine
in the storming of the Bastille, Les Halles in the October Days
and the Cordeliers district in the crisis that followed the flight to
Varennes. The makeup of distinct neighbourhoods made Paris a
truly revolutionary city, with a popular militancy that kept politics
on the boil with each new crisis. This combination of geography,
social structure and political activism distinguished the Parisian
experience from that of London and New York in this era. The very
nature of the city, so essential to the revolutionary process if far

from being the only focus of it, may help explain why the French Revolution, as it unfolded in Paris, took the radical turn that the earlier American version just about avoided and that the British managed to avert altogether.

CHAPTER NINE

LONDON DEBATES THE FRENCH REVOLUTION, 1789–1792

'HOW MUCH THE greatest event it is that ever happened in the world! And how much the best!' exclaimed the leader of the opposition Whigs, Charles James Fox, of the French Revolution. Yet Fox's enthusiasm was not shared by everyone: he, after all, had embraced the cause of (moderate) reform in Parliament and so saw the events in France as a vindication of his own devotion to civil rights and religious freedom. In the summer of 1789, many politically moderate Britons were, on the one hand, delighted that the French had risen up against tyranny, seeing in their Revolution a distant echo of their own one in 1688, when they toppled King James II and definitively established a political system balancing parliamentary with royal power. On the other hand, they also looked on in fascinated horror at the atrocities, as they read in the newspapers of heads paraded on pikes. For more cautious Britons, and for Londoners in particular, comparisons with the Gordon Riots only nine years before sprang readily to mind, and on 20 July the conservative *Times* made just such a connection, loftily warning its readers against 'the sad effects of an unlicensed populace'.[1]

There was always going to be a fierce argument about what the stunning, alarming events across the Channel meant for the British people. But the nationwide debate over the meaning of the French Revolution and its relationship to the British future would be explosive, one of the most contentious in modern British politics. And the political passions unleashed in London were no less rooted in its public spaces and the social networks that inhabited them, including, as we shall see, the city's pulsating publishing and bookselling life.

WHEN THE WAR of words erupted in earnest, the spark was provided by the mild-mannered, scholarly Richard Price in the Old Jewry in the City of London, the central meeting place of the community of Rational Dissenters in the metropolis. As 'Nonconformists', Protestants who were not part of the established Church of England, Rational Dissenters had suffered exclusion from political rights, public office and military commissions since the seventeenth century. Parliament itself had slowly eased these restrictions: Nonconformists were not allowed to vote unless they took Anglican Communion, but, curiously, they could stand as MPs, and nineteen of them took seats between 1754 and 1790. Even so, while Anglicans monopolised high municipal office, they were perfectly happy to let Nonconformists do the really hard work in the local government, such as serving as constables, night watchmen and overseers of the poor. For a group that boasted some prosperous and ambitious manufacturers, merchants and financiers, the ban on high position in some of the City's great financial institutions, such as the East India Company and the Bank of England, certainly hurt. In London Rational Dissenters had meetinghouses at the Gravel Pit in Hackney in the East, in neighbouring Newington Green and in the Old Jewry in the City, a short walk from the Bank of England.[2]

The Old Jewry was a chapel on the street of the same name. With its twenty-six hundred square feet of space, its six bow windows catching the light from the narrow confines of the street outside, it was the perfect place for the annual anniversary celebration of the 'Glorious Revolution' of 1688, which held a special place in the hearts and minds of Dissenters. It was for just that event that people from across the metropolis, but particularly the Dissenting communities in Newington Green and Hackney, gathered there on 4 November 1789. And it was then that Richard Price lit the short fuse that detonated the British debate on the French Revolution.[3]

A world-famous mathematician and Dissenting clergyman, Price was also a social reformer, a figure of the cosmopolitan Enlightenment. Among his friends were American revolutionaries John and Abigail Adams, who gravitated towards this small, sombrely dressed but kind and witty character in the years after the War of Independence, when John became the first US minister to Britain. Abigail described Price as 'a good and amiable man', although he was at this time prone to 'lowness of spirits' since his wife suffered paralysis from a stroke in 1784. When Abigail and John's daughter Nabby gave birth to a son in 1787, the delighted grandparents asked Price to christen the baby, which he did in their home in Grosvenor Square. It was while paying his respects to the American couple in their home that the French radical pamphleteer and future revolutionary Jacques-Pierre Brissot, during a brief visit to London in 1788, had a long-awaited meeting with Price. 'His face inspired so much respect', the Frenchman gasped, 'I thought that I was seeing Socrates'.[4]

Price's audience on 4 November 1789 was the London

Revolution Society, established (as the organisation's own minutes explained) 'in order to commemorate the ['Glorious'] Revolution [of 1688] and the confirmation of the people's rights'. Much of the society's leadership was drawn from Rational Dissenters like Price, but it also attracted (its records remarked further) 'a more general attention, and drew to it many persons of rank and consequence from different parts of the kingdom'. With a hefty membership fee of half a guinea, the society could scarcely have had a membership akin to that of the Cordeliers Club: the London Revolution Society included progressive Whig Earl Stanhope, who was (with due deference) its chairman, and several sympathetic MPs. Although Dissent remained at its core, its members harboured a range of religious beliefs, including Anglicanism, and its reformist agenda attracted some leaders of the Society for Constitutional Information, set up in London in 1780 to spread radical ideas among the general population. The London Revolution Society's initial aim was to secure a law making 4 November a legal day of thanksgiving for the 1688 Revolution, but according to its regulations, its members also had to subscribe to three principles, namely, that 'all civil and political authority is derived from the people', that 'the abuse of power justifies resistance' and that civil liberties, including religious conscience, were 'sacred and inviolable'. Its annual red-letter day was the anniversary celebration of the 1688 Revolution, held on 4 November, which could attract up to three hundred of its members. These commemorations would begin soberly enough with a religious service in the Old Jewry meetinghouse at noon, before becoming more bacchanalian when the whole gathering processed through the City to a tavern for dinner, washed down with dozens of toasts.[5]

At the annual commemoration in 1789, when Price rose in the Old Jewry, he reiterated the central planks of the society's programme. The principles underlying 1688, he declared, were the 'liberty of conscience in religious matters', 'the right to resist power when abused' and 'the right to chuse our own governors; to cashier them for misconduct; and to frame a government for ourselves'. Yet, he pursued, religious freedom in Britain was far from absolute, and political representation of the kingdom in Parliament was unequal. Without fair and equal representation, a kingdom was only partially free, or only seemed to be free. The purpose of the Revolution Society, therefore, was to 'contribute all we can towards supplying what [the Revolution of 1688] left deficient' and to transmit it, improved, to posterity. The times for doing so were propitious. Price cast his gaze across to France:

> What an eventful period is this! I am thankful that I have lived to see it . . . I have lived to see THIRTY MILLIONS of people, indignant and resolute, spurning at slavery, and demanding liberty . . . and an arbitrary monarch surrendering himself to his subjects. After sharing in the benefits of one Revolution, I have been spared to be witness to two other Revolutions, both glorious. And now, methinks, I see the ardor for liberty catching and spreading . . . Be encouraged, all ye friends of freedom, and writers in its defence! . . . Behold the light you have struck out, after setting AMERICA free, reflected to FRANCE, and there kindled into a blaze that lays despotism in ashes, and warms and illuminates EUROPE![6]

After the service, suitably stirred, the Revolution Society processed eastwards to Bishopsgate, where they filed into the London Tavern. There, among the evening's other business, they agreed to send an address of congratulation to the National Assembly in Paris, saluting 'the glorious example given in France to encourage other Nations to assert the *unalienable* rights of Mankind, and thereby to introduce a general reformation in the governments of Europe, and to make the World free and happy'.[7]

As for Price, he once remarked that funerals had a tendency to send the mourners after the departed, and so it tragically proved: he caught a bitter chill while attending the burial of a fellow Dissenter and died, still confident that a new future of liberty was at hand, on 19 April 1791. By that stage, his sermon, published as *A Discourse on the Love of Our Country*, had unleashed a debate that was as contentiously spiky as it was intellectually rich. There was a brief period of calm before the storm, because it was not until early January 1790 that an Anglo-Irish Whig politician and intellectual, Edmund Burke, folded his slender frame into a chair in his town house, now at No. 37 Gerrard Street, Soho, and read the *Discourse*, his piercing eyes darting across the page through his spectacles, which perched on a sharp (and much-caricatured) nose. He absorbed Price's words with a mounting sense of alarm. He had already been provoked around New Year's Day by a letter from a young French acquaintance, Charles-Jean-François DePont, who had cited the 'authority of the Revolution Society in England' as evidence that the French may be 'taking the best route to attain Liberty'. Burke violently disagreed, and he took up his pen in response. Do not assume, Burke would tell his young French friend, that the London Revolution Society represented British society at large: 'Half a dozen grasshoppers under a fern make the field ring with their importunate chink, whilst thousands of great cattle, reposed beneath the shadow of the British oak, chew the cud and are silent'. What started as a modest 'letter' would expand into one of the founding stones of modern conservative thought. *Reflections on the Revolution in France*, published by Burke's usual printer, James Dodsley of Pall Mall, appeared on 1 November 1790.[8]

Burke took as his starting point the now standard Whig

interpretation of British political history: the constitution had evolved over centuries since Magna Carta whereby the power of the monarchy was limited by Parliament and an independent judiciary. This carefully balanced constitutional order guaranteed the liberties of all subjects – at least, Burke was careful to argue, as was appropriate to their station in society. Each member had a rank and position, but it was not unchanging: individuals could, through talent, virtue and hard work, rise within it. Political power was exercised by a minority, certainly, but it was done in trust for the protection of the liberties and property of all the people. These liberties were transmitted from one generation to the other as the hereditary birth right of all Britons, 'a people inheriting privileges, franchises and liberties from a long line of ancestors'. They were grounded in Britain's 'ancient constitution' and so were inseparable from the balance of the House of Commons with the hereditary crown and peerage.[9]

Hereditary government was, therefore, no bad thing: the 1688 Revolution merely restored the historically founded Protestant succession, rescuing it from the deviation embodied by James II's dangerous, absolutist pretensions. William III was enthroned by Parliament (not the people) because he had a rightful claim to inherit the crown. The 'Revolution' of 1688 was therefore no expression of popular sovereignty, still less a 'revolution' in the modern French sense. Rather, it was an old-fashioned 'revolution', meaning a turn of the wheel whereby things returned to their natural historical order. For Burke, it followed that just as the monarchy and peerage were hereditary, so too was both the allegiance of the people to them. Parliament, he said, quoting its own declaration in 1689, had bound *themselves, their heirs and posterities for ever*. Those rights that British subjects enjoyed were not, as the French revolutionaries and their British sympathisers argued, 'natural' and universal, embedded within the rational fibre of all human beings, but were prescriptive and rooted in the specific historical inheritance of Britons.[10]

Such a constitutional system based on inherited prescriptive rights, Burke argued, struck the best middle path between the oppression of despotic government, on the one hand, and the horrors of mob rule, on the other – both were, in their different ways, tyrannies. For Burke, change was possible and indeed sometimes necessary – 'a state without the means of some change is without the means of its conservation' – but only after 'cautious and deliberate' consideration. Such change had to be rooted in custom if it was to stand the test of time. An established religion was the essential mortar promoting social harmony, moral compass and civic unity.[11]

The French Revolution, by contrast, had levelled the entire structure of the old regime, disinherited the church and sought instead to build a new order. Since the revolutionaries had ruptured completely with the past, they could be guided only by abstract principles: 'the metaphysics of an under-graduate, and the mathematics and arithmetic of an exciseman', as Burke put it. 'When antient opinions and rules of life are taken away . . . ', he warned, 'from that moment we have no compass to govern us; nor can we know distinctly to what port we steer'. In attacking the French Revolution, Burke took the opportunity to deplore the passing of gallantry, the polished, courtly manners – 'that generous loyalty to rank and sex' – that in the past would have meant that 'ten thousand swords must have leaped from their scabbards' to defend Queen Marie-Antoinette (whom he had once seen 'glittering like the morning star, full of life, and splendor, and joy') against the insults of the Paris crowd and from the outpourings of the gutter press. But, Burke lamented, 'the age chivalry is gone . . . [T]he glory of Europe is extinguished for ever'.[12]

Seven thousand copies of *Reflections* were sold within six days of publication; a French translation appeared in Paris on 29 November, and ten thousand of the tomes flew off the booksellers' shelves. Burke himself was stunned by the response: a long-standing Whig opponent of royal influence in Parliament, the onetime supporter of American rights and friend of Charles James Fox, he found himself suddenly praised by his onetime adversary King George III, who was positively enthusiastic: 'Read it, it will do you good! – do you good!' he burst out to one of his startled courtiers, and he gave bound copies as gifts. Burke found many of his political friendships and antagonisms suddenly – and in some cases irrevocably – reversed. In the Commons on 6 May 1791, Fox had a heated exchange with his friend in the House. When Fox – ebullient, rotund, high-living *bon viveur* that he was – leaned over to seek assurance that, at least, there was no loss of friendship, Burke turned and said that there was. Even the official proceedings of the Commons recorded the tears that trickled down Fox's cheeks. Ultimately, Burke and a host of other opposition Whigs deserted Fox and joined the government benches alongside Prime Minister William Pitt – every bit a contrast to Fox with his sharp, analytical mind and slender, angular frame. The French Revolution had split the parliamentary opposition, leaving Fox to soldier on with a tiny rump of MPs.[13]

OF GREATER LONG-TERM import was the response outside Parliament, and it came in a blizzard of books and pamphlets, as Burke's florid prose provoked replies from all sides. This would have been impossible without the urban environment in which much of the publishing, printing, buying and selling took place.

Provincial publishing and bookselling were vibrant, but the beating heart of the whole enterprise was in London, in the area immediately around Saint Paul's Cathedral. In 1785 there were six booksellers clustered in Saint Paul's Churchyard and sixteen on adjacent Paternoster Row – together accounting for an eighth of all London bookshops. A visitor then dropping westwards down Ludgate Hill, away from the soaring dome of Wren's cathedral, would pass by a further four bookshops on the ground floors of the five-storeyed houses on either side of the street. Continuing onto Fleet Street, the visitor would stroll past no fewer than thirteen other bookstores – complete with awnings and ample bow windows to display the stock to passers-by. On the same itinerary the visitor would have passed by thirty-three, or just over a quarter, of London's 124 printers, more than half of those (eighteen) on Fleet Street, but with an impressive six in that narrow but busy lane for bibliophiles, Paternoster Row. These booksellers and printers, moreover, jostled with a host of other occupations related to the press: stationers, bookbinders, music sellers, card makers, paper stainers, letter founders and more.[14]

The axis from Saint Paul's Churchyard down Fleet Street was therefore extraordinary for its immersion in the world of print: Paris and New York, vibrant though the political press was in these cities, could not boast such an intense concentration of publishers, printers and booksellers in such a small area. This did not shape the British debate on the French Revolution – Burke's publisher, as we have noted, was in Westminster, on Piccadilly – but it was one of the central arenas of the debate and made the appearance of at least two of the most important and influential replies to Burke possible. So if Richard Price, the London Revolution Society and the Rational Dissenters, bound together by their network of chapels and their central meeting place of the Old Jewry, set the political fuse, the world of print around Saint Paul's and Fleet Street supplied much of the explosive.

The location stemmed from a lingering custom from when

the Stationers' Company enjoyed a monopoly on copyright: its gloriously elegant hall still stands on its own square on Ave Maria Lane, a short stroll from Saint Paul's Cathedral. When, in 1710, a new Copyright Act removed this monopoly, the press, publishing and bookselling boomed from Scotland to Cornwall, and the world of print in London became positively labyrinthine in its rich diversity. Print cascaded out in every conceivable format: newspapers, books, pamphlets, plays, broadsides and engravings. London's newspapers pulsated, so that by 1793 there were thirteen morning dailies, eleven evening papers and eleven weeklies, to say nothing of monthly magazines. In the 1780s, Prussian visitor Johann von Archenholz estimated that sixty-three thousand individual copies of newspapers were being printed in London every week. The book trade kept pace. By 1790, forty-six hundred titles – books, pamphlets and plays – were being published each year in England (a figure that would rise if Scotland was included), more than three-quarters of them in London. Britons, and especially Londoners, were accustomed to freely available print. It was not that print was cheap, but its very expense made the vibrancy of urban life all the more central to its dissemination: there were far more *readers* of newspapers and books than there were copies. This was thanks in part to lending libraries, of which there were six in London by 1786. As they charged subscriptions, they were primarily middle-class institutions, which made the coffeehouse all the more important. Coffeehouses not only caffeinated or intoxicated their customers by offering coffee, chocolate and, better still, wine, brandy and punch, but they were the venues for cultural and political debate and discussion. Coffeehouses were often sparse places: they generally had a small bar in one corner, from which drinks were served, but the rest was taken up by booths, wooden chairs or tables, and the atmosphere rolled with a fug of pipe smoke.

Decor and comfort may not have been at a premium, but coffeehouses were places of business, of conversation and reading,
and subscribed to newspapers for their customers to enjoy.[15] 'An
English coffee-house', wrote an impressed Archenholz, 'has no
resemblance to a French or German one. You neither see billiards
nor backgammon tables; you do not even hear the least noise;
every body speaks in a low tone, for fear of disturbing the company. They frequent them principally to read the PAPERS, a task
that is absolutely necessary in that country'.[16] Thanks in no small
part to the habit of coffeehouses providing newspapers to their
customers, it was estimated that for every single copy, there were
anywhere between twenty and fifty readers. The impact was all
the greater because reading aloud was a pastime that was enjoyed
not only at home – for the benefit of children, or to help ease the
passage of domestic chores – but also in the workplace, taverns
and coffeehouses.[17]

Unsurprisingly, the coffeehouse frequented most by writers,
booksellers, publishers and readers was in the hub of London
publishing. The Chapter Coffee House on Paternoster Row, in the
shadow of Saint Paul's Cathedral, had a library of its own, stocked
with the most recent works, whereby publishers advertised their
new volumes. In 1773 a visiting Irish clergyman named Thomas
Campbell was given access to the library for a year for a shilling – a
bargain. Since the collection was a draw for clients, books could
not be borrowed, but were read at one of the coffeehouse tables,
while sipping a coffee or quaffing a brandy. But its low subscription
rate meant that the working people of the City made good use of
the library: Campbell was impressed to see a 'whitesmith' (a tin
worker) who was clearly 'a specimen of English freedom' because,
still in his apron and carrying his tools under his arm, he 'sat down
and called for his glass of punch and the paper, both of which he
used with as much ease as a Lord'.[18]

Pivotal to all this activity were London's booksellers, who also acted as the publishers. They shouldered the risk by purchasing the copyrights from the writers and then bearing the costs of printing, binding and advertising before selling the copies. In particularly large ventures, several booksellers and printers might form cartels ('congers') to share the cost and to spread the risk, or else copyrights were split up and sold in shares to booksellers and individual patrons: in 1746 Samuel Johnson's famous *Dictionary* was sponsored in this way. One of the most important venues for the sale and auction of copyrights was the Chapter Coffee House, where transactions were fortified by heavy eating and lubricated by copious drinking.[19]

Standing at the centre of this world was Joseph Johnson, whose bookshop was at No. 72 Saint Paul's Churchyard, an elegant brick-built building with tall windows on the ground floor that looked across the yard towards Wren's great cathedral. Johnson was short in physique, but a giant in publishing. Poet William Blake called him a 'squat, little' man, but he was attentive and generous towards his authors. His table was the place where progressive intellects could meet and exchange ideas in the angular, cramped, irregularly shaped upper dining room in his house. The conversation hummed as the candles slowly burned down after a dinner with plain, hearty fare – boiled cod, roast venison, vegetables. Johnson specialised in progressive, radical works, and over time his dinner guests included William Blake, William Wordsworth, radical reformers John Horne Tooke and Thomas Holcroft of the Society for Constitutional Information, radical intellectual William Godwin (later father of Mary Shelley, who would write the story of Frankenstein's monster) and Thomas Paine. There was also Mary Wollstonecraft.[20]

Mary Wollstonecraft was born on Primrose Street in Spitalfields (just north of today's Liverpool Street Station) in 1759, into a family grown comfortable and successful from the area's weaving trade. She was baptised in Saint Botolph's Church on Bishopsgate. Although not a Dissenter herself, she enjoyed close ties with the community at Newington Green and developed a strong friendship with Richard Price, many of whose ideas she shared. She also sharpened her political ideas and her skills in debate at the weekly supper club organised by the congregation. Through these circles she met Thomas Christie, a Scot, who recruited the serious-minded and intelligent Wollstonecraft as a reviewer for his new progressive, reformist journal, the *Analytical Review*. It was as she was writing for Christie that she met Joseph Johnson and became part of his circle. In other words, Mary Wollstonecraft was part of the two overlapping networks: of Rational Dissent and of the publishing world centred on Saint Paul's Churchyard and Fleet Street. With her reformist sympathies and friendships in both, and with her work as a reviewer, it was almost inevitable that she would be drawn into the debate on the French Revolution. It was Johnson who found her affordable lodgings in one of the new terraces being constructed in Southwark, at No. 49 George Street, so that she could stroll across Blackfriars Bridge and meet the publisher regularly at his shop in Saint Paul's Churchyard. She told her sister that 'you would respect him; and his sensible conversation would soon wear away the impression, that a formality – or rather stiffness of manners, first makes to his disadvantage – I am sure you would love him did you know with what *tenderness* and humanity he has behaved to me'.[21]

It was as a reviewer that she first read Price's *Discourse on the Love of Our Country*, and so she was quick off the mark to reply to Burke's attack. Her *Vindication of the Rights of Men* was published on 29 November 1790, the first of about forty-five responses to Burke that appeared in the year immediately after *Reflections*. And the publisher was Joseph Johnson.[22]

In 150-odd pages, Wollstonecraft punctured Burke's florid prose style (but, she conceded, 'once a wit and always a wit'), restated the principles of civil liberty and attacked Burke's obsession with tradition: 'We are to reverence the rust of antiquity, and term the unnatural customs, which ignorance and mistaken self-interest have consolidated, the sage fruit of experience'. The French revolutionaries were 'settling a constitution that involved the happiness of millions', so 'why was it a duty to repair an ancient castle, built in barbarous ages, of Gothic materials?' For Wollstonecraft, hereditary property and honours were not bulwarks of freedom, but the opposite, preventing the expansion of civilisation in Europe. Human rights were received 'not from our forefathers, but from God'. Privilege, hierarchy and wealth were no guarantees that the country's leadership would be fit to govern. Rather, the foundations of civic virtue were freedom and human reason, and this, Wollstonecraft argued, was important in the home just as it was in public life. Her feminist blood boiled at Burke's complaint about the treatment of Marie-Antoinette and the demise of chivalry. This ignored 'the distress of many industrious mothers . . . and the hungry cry of helpless babes'. Reason, honesty and virtue were the true foundation of 'manners'; chivalric gallantry assumed that women were weak, merely sentient beings, and this prevented men from seeing women as rational, intellectual equals. All women, not just Marie-Antoinette, faced 'obstacles to surmount in the progress toward dignity and character'. Wollstonecraft would develop these themes in her most famous tract of all, *A Vindication of the Rights of Women*, published in 1792, also by Johnson.[23]

Johnson undertook to publish the most famous of all the responses to Burke, Thomas Paine's *Rights of Man*. Paine had already made a name for himself in America with his groundbreaking argument for independence, *Common Sense*, and his letters on the Revolution, the American Crisis series. He had returned to Europe in 1787, after a glorious, colourful and some-times fraught wartime career in America and a few frustrating post-war years, in which he struggled to find anyone willing to build an iron bridge based on his own design (he travelled with a massive model to display the engineering). He went first to Paris, where he met Jacques-Pierre Brissot and discussed the abolition of slavery with the Amis des Noirs and mathematics with Condorcet, with whom he would soon develop a close friendship. He then crossed the Channel, returning to Britain for the first time since 1774 and heading for London, where he took up lodgings at No. 154 New Cavendish in Fitzrovia. In October 1789, he returned to France, writing to George Washington that 'a share in two revolutions is living to some purpose'. Coming back to London, he brought with him a gift from Lafayette to Washington: the key to the Bastille. 'That the principles of America opened the Bastille is not to be doubted', Paine wrote in sending the hunk of iron to the US president, 'and therefore the key comes to the right place'. Then, stunned by his onetime friend Edmund Burke's florid assault on the French Revolution, Paine had escaped the hurly-burly of the centre of the metropolis to write *Rights of Man* by taking a room in the Angel Inn in Islington (then a suburb), directly north of the City of London. When he finished the manuscript of part 1 in the evening of 29 January 1791, he celebrated with friends, downing a couple of bottles of wine from the Angel's excellent stock before sleeping off the weeks of flat-out writing. Two days later, he walked southwards from Islington into the City, where he strode purposefully through Saint Paul's Churchyard, threading his way around passers-by, carts and horses, and headed for Johnson's shop at No. 72. There he presented the publisher with his work.[24]

Rights of Man was a straight-talking, aphorism-peppered

assault on Burke's *Reflections*, a polemical defence of the French Revolution and a staunch argument in favour of democracy. Paine rejected the weight of the past as a guide to government here and now. Parliament had no right, as it had done in 1689, to bind 'themselves, their heirs and posterity for ever' to submit to monarchy. 'The vanity and presumption of governing beyond the grave', wrote Paine, 'is the most ridiculous and insolent of all tyrannies'. Hereditary government made no sense: 'The idea of hereditary legislation is as inconsistent as that of hereditary judges, or hereditary juries; and as absurd as an hereditary mathematician, or an hereditary wise man; and as ridiculous as a hereditary poet-laureate'. The French Revolution was justified because the old order had been corrupted by despotism 'too deeply rooted to be removed ... by anything short of a complete and universal revolution'.[25]

The rights that the French had recognised in 1789 belonged to the very nature of humanity – they were 'pre-existing in the individual', Paine declared. Everyone, therefore, had a stake in the 'civil power' that stemmed from 'the social compact', not between people and rulers, but among the '*individuals themselves*, each in his own personal and sovereign right'. Out of this contract came a constitution, which is a clear, written document that precedes all government and which no government can alter arbitrarily: Britain, Paine taunted Burke, had no such clear, reasoned framework. Moreover, Paine contrasted the close relationship between church and state that Burke saw as fundamental to a stable political order, with the 'universal right of conscience' recognised by the French revolutionaries and by the Americans. The French Revolution was creating an order that was founded on the sovereignty of the people. 'Sovereignty', Paine concluded, 'appertains to the Nation only, and not to any individual; and a Nation has at all times an inherent indefeasible right to abolish any form of

Government it finds inconvenient, and establish such as accords with its interest'.[26]

Having taken in Paine's manuscript, Johnson promised to have the first edition ready for sale on 22 February, the birthday of Washington, to whom Paine dedicated the work. Yet even as the loose, unbound sheets were still being stacked on the floor, the government was considering how to react. The British authorities were quite happy to see their mighty French antagonists distracted by their own domestic turmoil, but, like Burke, they were truly alarmed when radical writers like Paine appeared to be implanting the principles of the French Revolution in British soil and seemed to be encouraging Britons to imitate the French example. Thus, the debate on the French Revolution was not conducted in an ivory tower. The anxiety that Paine's tract and celebrations such as those of the London Revolution Society stirred amongst supporters of the status quo led them to look for ways of countering radical arguments, by repression if need be.

The government weighed its options before reacting to Paine's treatise: it could use the existing laws against blasphemy, obscenity and 'seditious libel' (promoting insurrection against the established order through writing or speech). Such cases were taken so seriously that they were handled by the government's own attorney, the mighty treasury solicitor. So the danger of prosecution for printing something as bluntly radical as *Rights of Man* was real enough that the government consulted with the treasury solicitor to see if Paine could be prosecuted. Johnson began to sweat as his premises were visited over and over again by agents of the Crown. Arrest and prosecution would bankrupt him, and on the day the book was meant to appear, he pulled it.

Paine frantically searched for another publisher – and he found one. *Rights of Man* saw the light of day thanks to Paine's acquaintances from Johnson's dining table and to the ribbon of publishers stretching from Saint Paul's Churchyard down Fleet Street. Two other radical habitués of Johnson's, Holcroft and Godwin, helped Paine to load the unbound sheets onto a cart in Saint Paul's Churchyard and, with a rumble of wheels and clacking of hooves over the granite setts, or paving stones, *Rights of Man* trundled down the hill to Fleet Street, where another publisher, J. S. Jordan, had agreed to take the legal risk, while Paine covered the finance with a hastily arranged loan. *Rights of Man* finally appeared – triumphantly, as it turned out – on 13 March. The government's lawyers, meanwhile, stayed their hand, convinced that the cover price of three shillings would confine its readership to the better-off.[27]

This assumption was soon proved wrong. Paine's tract, short but sharp, would reach tens of thousands of readers. Within weeks of its publication, *Rights of Man* became a best seller. By May the book had run into six editions and had sold fifty thousand copies, breaking publishing records. *Rights of Man* may have reached at least several hundred thousand in one way or another: Paine's supporters were gratified to learn that the treatise was being read aloud in taverns, workshops and homes. Paine, characteristically, also granted every request for permission to print cheaper popular editions in towns up and down the country, waiving the royalties, so that his ideas could circulate. By 1 April, he had decided to undertake the production of a cheap edition himself, in London, before slipping across the Channel to see how far the Revolution had progressed in France. There, as we have seen, he would lend his good name to galvanise the republican movement that stirred in the wake of the king's flight to Varennes. He would return to London days before the Champ de Mars massacre, and by then his republicanism had boiled over.

He now stepped up his ideological assault on the existing social and political order in Britain. The sequel, *Rights of Man, Part*

Two, would be published in February 1792. Like Wollstonecraft's second *Vindication*, which appeared in the same year, it was more radical than the first: Paine's work was a blistering attack on monarchy, aristocracy and the wastefulness in public expenditure that they engendered. A truly democratic political system would focus on social justice and create a proto–welfare state. The political stakes in the debate on the French Revolution, in other words, piled higher. On the one hand, radical writers stepped up their assault on the existing order in Britain – and circulated their ideas widely among the population at large. On the other hand, the British authorities took greater and greater alarm as the Revolution in France took ever more radical turns, at the very time when the Revolution's British sympathisers seemed to become bolder in their demands for political change in Britain.[28]

Responses to both Wollstonecraft's *Vindication of the Rights of Men* and Paine's *Rights of Man* were mixed. Conservative Whigs and moderate reformers were aghast. Gothic novelist Horace Walpole luridly described Wollstonecraft as a 'hyena in petticoats'. John Wyvill of the Yorkshire Association complained, 'It is unfortunate for the public cause that Mr. Paine took such unconstitutional ground, and has formed a party for the Republic among the lower classes of the people'. The conservative *Gentleman's Magazine* warned that both Wollstonecraft and Paine aimed to 'poison and inflame the minds of the lower class of his Majesty's subjects to violate their subordination'.

Radicals, naturally, took the opposite view. Christie's *Analytical Review* hailed Wollstonecraft, putting her alongside progressive historian Catherine Macaulay (who had also reacted enthusiastically to *Vindication*) and remarking that it must deeply wound Burke, with all his talk of the submission of 'the fair sex', 'that two of the boldest of his adversaries are women!' The Society for Constitutional Information was careful to disavow

Paine's republicanism, but on 23 March 1791 it voted thanks to Paine 'for this most masterly book' and the hope that the British people would read it with the attention that it deserved. The society worked with Paine to produce a cheap edition for working people. In the struggle for reform, the battle for hearts and minds was well and truly on – and the hottest subject of the debate was over what lessons the British could draw from the French Revolution.[29]

THE BRITISH POLITICAL controversy over the French Revolution grew out of the fertile ground of intellectual life and print culture across the country, but particularly in the metropolis. In 1789 there was perhaps no freer place for the press and for writers than revolutionary Paris, since censorship had evaporated. Americans would soon, in 1790, have their rights to freedom of speech guaranteed in the First Amendment to their Constitution. Under colonial rule, New Yorkers had themselves been accustomed to a wide latitude of freedom in the press, a freedom successfully defended in law as early as 1734. In that year, John Zenger, a journalist of German origin, was prosecuted but acquitted for publishing satirical jibes against the governor of the colony. London was not, therefore, unique in boasting of a lively production and access to print, but it did have a long-established business in publishing, one that had flourished ever since the ending of the Stationers' Company monopoly in 1710. The threat of prosecution hung over publishers who crossed the line into blasphemy or seditious libel, and as Johnson himself recognised as his stomach churned with anxiety over *Rights of Man*, it was a line ambiguous enough that it was not always possible to know exactly where it lay. Even so, visitors, as we have seen, remarked positively on the availability of print, the vibrancy of the coffeehouse culture that supported it and the engagement of such a wide cross-section of the population with the press. On such solid foundations, and the accompanying habit of criticism and debate, did the production and circulation of tracts such as *Vindication of the Rights of Men* and *Rights of Man* rest. Politics – even extra-parliamentary politics like these – therefore rested in spaces and places that were long established and habitual for critically engaged Britons. Londoners (and Britons up and down the country) debated the Revolution even as they sat in their familiar, unchanged surroundings: the locations reflected the fact that the arguments about the French Revolution and the criticisms and defence of the British constitution were kept within legal boundaries. It was this habit of free discussion, alongside, first, the commitment to legality among the reformers and, second, the relative caution with which (so far) the government proceeded against them that ensured that London avoided a revolutionary upheaval in these years.

Yet this did not mean that political mobilisation and engagement did not in themselves expand, moving into new public spaces: as we shall see, one of the most important effects of the French Revolution debate in Britain was to draw into politics a wider section of the public, particularly articulate, literate, skilled artisans, who saw democratic reform as the solution to the economic and social pressures they confronted. It was with this development – as the political debate spilled over from the coffeehouses and the well-heeled reform organisations like the London Revolution Society to the workshops, taverns and associations that attracted Britain's working population – that the alarm would begin to ring deafeningly in government ears. Moreover, as events in France took their further radical, republican turn in the summer of 1792, and as war between Britain and revolutionary France began to loom, Burke's gloomy prognosis about the French Revolution seemed all the more convincing to Britons anxious for social stability and for British security. In the ensuing conflicts, the direction of democratic politics in Britain, and in the United States, would be tied closely to the course of the Revolution in France.

CHAPTER TEN

PARIS IN THE TERROR,
1793–1794

LONDONERS AND NEW Yorkers – like all people who read about and discussed the events in revolutionary France – looked on with a mixture of awe, fascination and horror. Observers across Europe and the Atlantic world watched aghast as the French Revolution gradually slipped into what became remembered as the Terror. For foreigners – and for many French people subsequently – this episode was synonymous with the ghastly mechanics of the guillotine, which decapitated the once great and powerful, beginning with the king himself. Yet over the course of 1793, the Terror emerged primarily as a response to a desperate military, political and economic crisis: it was a state of siege in which the new Republic grasped at the means – too often repressive and draconian – to consolidate and defend itself. In its multiple purposes, in fact, the Terror infused through the city, its life and its fabric, but in return Paris, its people and its cityscape helped shape the ways in which the Terror acted at the local level.

The Terror was an experience that was shared across the city, but in a myriad of ways: gut-wrenching fear; a nagging, persistent anxiety; the pangs of hunger; but perhaps most of all just as a struggle to get on with daily life in very difficult circumstances. Moreover, because it reached into politics at the most localised of levels, the sections (the forty-eight wards), the Terror was etched onto the face of Paris. In the advance of the machinery of political control, in the mobilisation of people and material for the war effort and in the economic measures to keep the people and armies fed, not a public building or space in Paris was left untouched.

Yet the Terror was not just politics imposed from the 'top' downwards onto the people. The republican militancy of the sections had never been off the boil since they had marched to overthrow the monarchy on 10 August 1792. The artisans, craft workers and retailers who had mobilised and helped to radicalise the Revolution had strong ideas as to what kind of republic they wanted. So the politics of the Terror was not just a struggle of republicans against their enemies, but also a turbulent relationship within the Revolution itself, one that wavered between grudging cooperation and open violent conflict between, on the one hand, the middle-class leadership in the Convention (the assembly elected to frame a constitution for the newborn French Republic) and in the revolutionary government and, one the other, the popular movement in the sections. This was a fraught relationship that was entangled with the communities and the local fabric of the city, particularly when the sections became the very places where the Terror from 'above' met and fused with the Terror as seen from 'below'.

HOW THIS AROSE is explicable by the intensity of the crisis faced by the new Republic. In early September 1792, just weeks after the overthrow of the monarchy on 10 August, some of the Paris sections – perhaps with the connivance, or at least the knowledge, of the revolutionary leadership in the Paris Commune (the municipality) and the government – had organised the killing of prisoners, including surviving Swiss Guards and nonjuror priests, who had been arrested in the wake of the attack on the Tuileries Palace. The streets outside the city's prisons ran with the blood of some fifteen hundred of these alleged counter-revolutionaries, who, the Parisian militants feared, would be ready to break out and slaughter the women and children of the city while the menfolk, donning their National Guard uniforms, marched out to fight the Prussians and Austrians who were now dangerously close to the capital. The tide on the front, in fact, turned on 20 September when, standing knee-deep in mud in driving rain around the now famous windmill at Valmy, the French beat back a Prussian assault and forced their army to retreat. This was followed by the proclamation of the Republic the following day and, on 6 November, a further French victory against the Austrians at Jemappes, which opened up the Low Countries to a French invasion. A month after the war turned in France's favour, the Convention debated the fate of Louis XVI, tried him and sent him to the guillotine on 21 January 1793. As 1793 bleakly dawned, however, the situation of the newborn Republic very rapidly turned into a desperate struggle for survival.

The Convention declared war on the Netherlands and Britain on 1 February, as French armies pressed on to the Dutch border, and from that point on the list of France's enemies grew longer, so that, by the summer, the Republic was also at war with Spain, Portugal and the Italian kingdoms of Piedmont and Naples. To cope with the expanding scale of the conflict, the Convention introduced conscription in February 1793, but in doing so provoked an explosion of open counter-revolutionary revolt in western France: in the Vendée, Brittany and Normandy. To compound the crisis, food shortages and inflation sent food prices spiralling

upwards, pushing working families to the wall and stirring popular militancy in the Parisian sections. With that came the danger
of further insurrection, this time against the Convention itself, as
it hesitated to do much to improve the material lives of the great
mass of French people.[1]

In this climate of military disaster, counter-revolution, civil
strife and social distress, the Convention began to build the
machinery of political repression: there was no plan, no design, but
the 'system of Terror', as it would be called in retrospect, emerged
contingently, mostly between March and September 1793. In
the spring, a decisive, fast-acting executive was established when
the Convention elected the Committee of Public Safety and the
Committee of General Security, the former to control the war
effort, foreign policy, the armies and the government ministries,
the latter to handle internal security and policing. They became
the effective government of revolutionary France. A Revolutionary
Tribunal was established in Paris to try traitors. 'Representatives
on mission' – deputies from the Convention – travelled across
France to mobilise the people and their resources for the war and to
combat counter-revolution. In August the *levée en masse* introduced
universal mass conscription for the first time and declared that all
of France's resources were subject to wartime use. Committees of
surveillance were established in every rural commune and every
urban section: in Paris they had been set up spontaneously by
the Paris sections as 'revolutionary committees' in the wake of 10
August 1792 to keep watch for suspected counter-revolutionaries.
Now they were given legal recognition, ensuring that the Terror
would reach right across the metropolis.

In 1793–1794, the conversion of churches, convents and once
proud aristocratic town houses reached its climax as every available
public space – buildings, parks and gardens – was commandeered
either for the political institutions of the Terror or for the pressing

demands of the war effort. This process of taking over buildings in every quarter of Paris not only made the Revolution more visible, indeed more intrusive, than ever before, but also represented the physical advance of the revolutionary organs deeper into the neighbourhoods and communities of the capital. At the level of the Paris sections, the committed militants of the popular movement provided the personnel. They had their own perspective on the purpose of the Terror and the direction that the Revolution ought to take.

What this meant was that the converted buildings in which the organs of the Paris sections met – the general assemblies, the committees of surveillance, the guard posts of the National Guard, the justice of the peace – were the very places where the policies emanating from the Convention and the revolutionary government meshed with the more localised interests and aims, anxieties, fears and hopes of the popular movement. This often prickly, tense interweaving made Paris a revolutionary hothouse, where the intensity and the penetration of surveillance, political conflict and wartime mobilisation in these violent uncertain months dwarfed the experience of New York in 1775–1776. So the story of the Terror as it unfolded in relation to the fabric of Paris needs to be told from the interlocking perspectives of the popular movement and of 'high' politics.

Since sometime in the summer of 1791, the artisans, craft workers, journeymen and retailers who formed the popular movement had taken to calling themselves the *sans-culottes*, which literally meant those 'without breeches', since the working people wore trousers rather than the tailored breeches and stockings that they castigated as aristocratic. The term therefore signified a social identity, but it was not for a modern working class or proletariat, because it covered both labourers and men and women of some independence, such as master craftsmen and shopkeepers. It was also a political label for any committed radical patriot. The *sans-culottes* embraced a populist language that implied a common interest across all the working people of Paris, encompassing not just waged labourers, journeymen and apprentices, but also the artisans, master craftsmen and retailers who employed them and provided the political leadership. The *sans-culotte* identity sprang from the world of the Parisian workshop, or rather an idealised version of it: one of solidarity and mutual respect, of the moral qualities of hard work and family and plain, even violent, speaking.

Their political programme was one of direct democracy: the people remained sovereign, so the sections would hold their representatives in the commune and in the convention to binding mandates, and they could be subject to instant recall. This vision of democracy was coloured by the pursuit of social justice: since government was meant to be of and by the people, then it followed that, since the poor formed the majority, their freedom, security and concerns should be the first priority of democratic government. The *sans-culotte* programme – expressed in the popular societies, sectional assemblies and radical newspapers – was blunt, direct and violent. In all these respects, therefore, the *sans-culotte* identity was rooted firmly in Parisian life: its language and its confidence in the independence and usefulness of its workshops; its sense of social solidarity, virtue and justice sculpted by the family and communal life of the city's neighbourhoods; and its capacity to mobilise, organise and then act grounded in the sections.[2]

With their assemblies, committees, National Guard units, justices of the peace and popular societies, the forty-eight Parisian sections had become the basic organising cells of the *sans-culottes*. Now, with the surveillance committees, they bore local responsibility for the security of the Revolution against its enemies, a co-optation that represented the expansion of the repressive arm of the Terror into the most localised level of the city. The surveillance committees were to look out for 'suspects' and foreigners, hear denunciations and issue *certificats de civisme*, which were identity papers testifying to the holder's patriotism and without which no citizen could hold public office, travel or find work. These institutions embedded the physical presence of the Revolution, and of the Terror, in public buildings across the city. Church premises had been converted into the headquarters for the district detachments of the National Guard. Bleachers and rostra had been built inside chapels, installed in clerical refectories and squeezed into convent libraries for the general assemblies or popular societies of the forty-eight sections. Now fitted with benches, public galleries and a speaker's tribune, these once sedate places rang to the fiery, and sometimes bloodthirsty, debates over revolution, war, terror and democracy. Similar venues had become the chambers of the sections' justices of the peace, who heard disputes between neighbours and spouses and – where possible – effected reconciliations. The occupation of empty aristocratic town houses and of old ecclesiastical buildings by the Parisians' sections was the physical symptom of this experiment in radical popular democracy. It represented the spatial diffusion of political activity and authority: they were the homes, in stone and timber, of the *sans-culotte* movement.[3]

The *sans-culottes* proposed brutally simple solutions to the people's woes and anxieties: they advocated political terror as the solution to economic misery, counter-revolution and war. They sought the death penalty for food hoarding and financial speculation, a strict maximum on prices and the use of the guillotine to terrorise real and potential counter-revolutionaries. They wanted to purge the army and the government of 'moderates', replacing them with reliable 'men of the people'. In pursuing these goals, the *sans-culottes* had an overarching organisation in the Évêché Committee, a central assembly of delegates from the sections that met regularly in the archbishop's palace next to Notre-Dame Cathedral (hence its name). Its decisions were to be ratified by the general assemblies of the sections, and its delegates could be recalled immediately by them. Thus, the Évêché Committee bound together the neighbourhoods and localities of *sans-culotte* activism, but at the same time remained independent from the formal structures of both metropolitan and national government.[4]

The target of the *sans-culottes* as the crisis deepened in the spring of 1793 was the Girondins, the onetime radicals who had pressed France into war and who, in the debates over the king's fate in January, had tried to spare him the death penalty. This had split them irrevocably from their former Jacobin friends, among them Maximilien Robespierre, and the internal politics of these early months of the Republic saw the bitterness and hatred turn virtually into a fight to the death between the Girondins, now sitting on the right in the Manège, and the Jacobins, who seized the uppermost benches on the left, earning themselves the lofty nickname of the Mountain. Since neither side commanded a majority in the Convention, each had to convince the uncommitted deputies of the centre – the Plain (or the 'Marsh') – to follow their lead. The Girondins, who held many of the important ministries, seemed unequal to the task of saving the Republic from military defeat and internal collapse. They were tainted by treason after their close associate General Charles-François Dumouriez, the victor of Jemappes, was defeated by the Austrians on 18 March. The general tried to lead his troops against Paris to restore the constitutional monarchy under the orphaned boy king Louis XVII, still imprisoned in the Temple. When his men refused to follow, he defected across the lines on 5 April. For both Jacobins and *sans-culottes*, Dumouriez's desertion showed that the Girondins were guilty of treason, at least by association.

The final push against the Girondins came not from the Jacobins, but from the *sans-culottes*, who had been in a state of

agitation and frenetic activity since the overthrow of the monarchy on 10 August 1792. On 25 February 1793, food and grocery
riots had swept across the city, and on 9–10 March a violent
sans-culotte assault against the presses of the leading Girondin
journalists nearly developed into a full-scale insurrection against
the Convention. The refusal of the National Guard and of some
cooler heads in the Paris Commune to join the revolt prevented
it from doing so. Yet as the Girondins and Jacobins grappled at
each other's political throats, the latter increasingly aligned themselves with the *sans-culottes*, while the Girondins targeted Parisian
radicalism with especial venom: in April Robespierre's erstwhile
friend Jérôme Pétion appealed to 'respectable men of means' to
drive 'these poisonous insects back into their dens'. Even so, both
Girondins and Jacobins had agreed on the benefits of the free circulation and sale of goods, which from the *sans-culotte* perspective
offered nothing to ease the shortages and high prices. On 4 May,
if only for the sake of the war effort and internal stability, the
Jacobins pushed through decrees providing for the relief of poverty
and the first price controls on grain and bread. From now on a
pragmatic, if often tense, political alliance between the Jacobins
and *sans-culottes* began to gel. By mid-May the Évêché committee
was organising the *sans-culottes* in the sections, making plans to
purge the Convention of the leading Girondins.[5]

When the insurrection came, the *sans-culotte* women of Paris
were central to its success. On 10 May, two militant women,
former chocolatier Pauline Léon and flamboyant actress Claire
Lacombe, received permission from the Paris Commune 'to form
a society where women, and only women, could be admitted', the
petition read. The society's purpose was to 'deliberate on the means
of foiling the projects of the enemies of the Republic'. Once it was
up and running (initially in the library of the Jacobin convent on
the rue Saint-Honoré), the Society of Revolutionary Republican

Women numbered at least 170 who were drawn from the city's trades: there were cake and pastry makers, haberdashers, a hosier, a washerwoman, linen workers, a secondhand dealer, dressmakers, a gold polisher, a cobbler and the wives of a saddler and of a gasman.[6]

In the last weeks of May, these women helped the *sans-culotte* men weaken and isolate their Girondin prey in the run-up to the coup. This was an 'achievement' all the more important because on 11 May, the Convention had moved from the old royal riding school at the Manège into a specially prepared chamber in the Tuileries Palace. The new venue, called the Salle des Machines because it had once housed the mechanical equipment for the theatre in the palace complex, was chosen partly at the behest of Robespierre, who had complained that the public galleries of the Manège were large enough to accommodate only several hundred spectators: the representatives of the people should be watched by thousands of their fellow citizens, who would sit as one with their deputies, thus ensuring utter transparency. The Salle des Machines, converted into an amphitheatre with public galleries vast enough to hold four thousand spectators (Robespierre had called for twelve thousand!), was therefore a political cauldron, a place where the debates of the Convention could become, effectively, mass political rallies. To deny one's opponents access to this environment would be to seize an important tactical advantage. The *sans-culotte* women understood that the popular movement's struggle against the Girondins was not just a matter of winning an argument, but about the physical control of the spaces of political action. To this end, the female militants crammed into the public galleries, driving away Girondin supporters and drowning out their orators with their heckling, shouting and booing. Since admission to the public galleries was by passes issued by the deputies, the Girondins reacted to this behaviour by trying to restrict such entry cards to their own supporters, but the Revolutionary

Republican Women reacted by mobbing the entrance to the legislature and turning back anyone armed with a pass. Among their victims was Girondin feminist Théroigne de Méricourt, whom the *sans-culotte* women seized and flailed mercilessly with a whip.[7]

Such brutal 'policing' of the Tuileries inspired other *sans-culotte* women to take control of the streets in other neighbourhoods. In other words, the streets as a site for political activism were in these weeks not an exclusively male domain, a point that was noted with some anxiety by Antoine-Joseph Gorsas, a Girondin journalist, who complained of the 'tremendous agitation' that coursed through Paris: 'Women gathered, doubtless excited by the furies. They armed themselves with pistols and swords, they arrested people and rushed to various city crossroads ... [T]hey wanted to purge the Convention; above all, they wanted to make heads fall and to become drunk with blood'. The women of the *sans-culottes* – armed with pikes, their fists and their brutal tongues – had made it downright dangerous for the Girondins and their sympathisers to move about the city.[8]

When the coup against the Convention came on 31 May, the Évêché Committee, as the coordinating organ of the Paris sections, drummed up the *sans-culottes*, who this time had the backing of both the Paris Commune (which proclaimed itself the 'Revolutionary General Council') and the National Guard, now commanded by the tough, coarse François Hanriot (Lafayette had deserted to the Austrians after the fall of the monarchy in August 1792), who had risen through the ranks. Hanriot's men surrounded the Tuileries and trained their cannon on the Convention, while the *sans-culottes* invaded the chamber and demanded the surrender of twenty-two leading Girondins. Yet even Jacobins balked at this demand: Danton fumed at this attempt to coerce the representatives of the people. By doing so, he roared, the insurgents were committing an outrage against the entire French people. Hanriot's response was characteristically brutal: 'Tell your fucking president that he and his Assembly are fucked, and that if within one hour he doesn't deliver me the Twenty-Two, I'm going to blast it!' After a siege that lasted into the night and through the following day and into the next, the Convention finally yielded; among those surrendered was the journalist and orator Brissot.[9]

The results were shattering. The Girondins were placed under house arrest, which meant that they easily made their escape to the provinces, back to their constituencies, where they organised resistance. In Paris the Convention was now dominated (politically though not numerically) by the left-wing deputies of the 'Mountain', whose hard, pragmatic core was – in contrast to the provincial Girondins – made up of the twenty-four representatives from Paris. Civil war exploded, piling yet more conflict and bloodshed on top of all the other pressures that threatened to shred the young Republic. The embittered Jacobins slated the provincial uprising as a 'Federalist revolt' because, they alleged, it was aimed at breaking France apart. And if the coup of 31 May–2 June had brought the Jacobins to power, the victory was that of the *sans-culottes*, a tide that seemed to set the Revolution on a course plotted 'from below' rather than 'from above'. Over the coming months, the deputies of the Mountain were never allowed to forget that they had not seized that power themselves.

YET WHO REALLY spoke for the whole *sans-culotte* movement? Whoever could claim that title would wield immense political power, with the capacity to channel the Revolution towards more egalitarian social goals. The question became urgent after 13 July when Charlotte Corday, a young, pallid Norman woman of strong Girondin sympathies, gained entrance to the home of Jean-Paul Marat on the rue de Cordeliers and stabbed him to death with a single surgically accurate blow of a knife as he lay immersed in his bath to ease the pain from a skin disease. Marat, the Cordelier leader and one of the Parisian deputies in the Convention, had been the idol of the popular movement. His newspaper, *L'Ami du Peuple*, had called for unrelenting, merciless punishment against the Republic's enemies in a brutal, blood-soaked language that appealed to the rough-and-ready, confrontational style of *sans-culotte* politics.

With Marat martyred, others scrambled to assume his mantle. Amongst the contenders were the Enragés – the 'demented' extremists – a loose group of activists who included 'red priest' Jacques Roux, orator Jean-François Varlet, and the two founders of the Society of Revolutionary Republican Women, Claire Lacombe and Pauline Léon. Vying with them was a group who had emerged from the Cordeliers Club to coalesce around the unlikely figure of Jacques-René Hébert, a former theatre clerk turned author of the newspaper the *Père Duchesne*. Hébert was a fastidious, well-dressed and quiet man, but his alter ego, portrayed on the masthead of the newspaper, was very different: a sturdy, pipe-smoking furnace maker wielding an axe and proclaiming, 'I am the real Père Duchesne! Fuck!' Hébert and his associates had become powerful figures in the Cordeliers Club and in the Commune, where his ally Gaspard Chaumette was the city's public prosecutor. In appealing to the *sans-culottes* for support, both sides competed with each other to commend Terror as the answer to the Republic's ills and to the social stress that bedevilled the working people of Paris.

In the short run, it was the Hébertists who triumphed. Hébert's opportunity came on 4 September 1793, as food prices continued to soar. From his vantage point in the Hôtel de Ville, Hébert harnessed a spontaneous strike and protest march by the city's labourers demanding higher pay and cheaper bread. When they gathered on the Place de Grève – the square lent its name to the

French word for 'strike' – Hébert emerged from the city hall and harangued them, persuading them to protest the following day at the Convention itself. On 5 September, Chaumette led thousands of *sans-culottes* to the Tuileries, where he demanded that the Convention activate 'revolutionary armies' – armed ranks of *sans-culottes* who would surge across the countryside requisitioning grain from the peasantry – and impose the death penalty on hoarders. When the Convention agreed (although it scarcely had a choice), the crowd departed in triumph. Hébert sealed his victory by eliminating his rivals on the radical Left: Roux was arrested on 5 September and Varlet on 18 September.[10]

That left the Society of the Revolutionary Republican Women, which through Pauline Léon and Claire Lacombe had been aligned with the Enragés. It was not long before the Hébertist offensive turned, with Jacobin support, on them, and the storm troopers were the women of Les Halles, the same who had marched on Versailles in October 1789. Why the authors of one of the most celebrated moments in women's political activism should have become the instruments by which another famous milestone in women's political engagement was shut down is explained mainly by a clash of economic interests, but the topography of the city played its part, too. The women's club had moved their meetings from the library of the Jacobin club to the crypt of the Church of Saint-Eustache, at the city's central markets. A flamboyantly Gothic pile, with a neoclassical colonnaded entrance porch at its western end, it was known as the 'cathedral of the Halles', and the men and women of the markets had always seen Saint-Eustache as 'their' church, an apple's throw away from the food market at the Carreau, just to the south. To the west, it was just a few paces from the distinctive rotunda of the grain market. This physical proximity between the new venue for women's political militancy and the stalls and booths of the market women was explosive.

One of the goals of the Revolutionary Republican Women was the implementation of the *sans-culotte* economic programme, but this collided with the concerns of the market women, for whom the maximum on prices, the dangers of being accused of hoarding and the enforced circulation of the inflation-ridden paper currency the *assignat* at face value were all potentially disastrous. The Revolutionary Republican Women, therefore, had invaded 'their' space and were promoting policies that posed a very real danger to the market women. And the militants were easily recognisable, for, on 12 May 1793, the club had ordered all its members to wear the red-white-blue cockade. In the summer months that followed, the markets became the site of confrontation between the warring groups of women, with thrown punches and cockade ripping among grappling posses of club members and the feisty women of Les Halles.[11]

The violence came to a head on 28 October, when the Society of the Revolutionary Republican Women met in their crypt as usual: the members – distinguishable by the tricolour cockades and the red Phrygian bonnets on their heads – were arriving when a crowd of market women surged down the steps shouting, 'Down with the red bonnet! Down with the *Jacobines*! Down with the *Jacobines* and the cockade! They are all villains who have caused the misery of France!' Their shouts grew louder as more of them joined the fray, the sound amplified in the confines of the crypt. When some of the political activists managed to escape and gain the nearby offices of the sectional justice of the peace, he accompanied them back to the crypt only to stun the society's members by announcing, 'The revolutionary *citoyennes* are not in session: everyone can enter'. This left the clubbists at the mercy of the market women, who surged across the room, hurling obscenities and tearing and smashing the society's emblems to pieces as they punched and beat those who tried to stop them. Eventually, the militants fled, their

shoes and clogs hammering the cobbles as they reached the safety
of the sectional offices on the nearby rue Coquillière. Besieged by
the stall holders who were shouting 'Vive la République! Down with
the women revolutionaries!', everyone inside – the women and the
committee of the Section des Halles – quietly left, two by two, out
of the building through an alleyway, the passage de Sainte-Agnès.
The crowd, deprived of its prey, eventually melted away.[12]

Building on their triumph, the market women petitioned the
Convention to ban the Society of Revolutionary Republican
Women. They were pushing at an open door. The Jacobins in the
Convention were already limbering up to close down an organisation that, they claimed, troubled public order. What was left
unsaid was that the closure of women's political organisations,
decreed on 31 October, was the final nail in the coffin of the troublesome Enragés. What was expressed, however, was the standard
eighteenth-century assumption that there were abilities and areas
of activities that were natural to men (politics and public life) and
those natural to women (marriage, child-rearing and the home).
In other words, it was time to put the genie of female political
activism back into the bottle.

With the rout of the Enragés, the Hébertists claimed the sans-
culotte programme as their own. With the sections, the popular
societies, the Commune and the Cordeliers Club behind them,
they were in a formidable position from which they would
confront the Jacobin-dominated revolutionary government and
Convention with their demands for an intensification of the
Terror. 'Suspects' were now defined in the broadest of terms by
the 'Law of Suspects' on 17 September 1793, including 'those
who, by their conduct, relations, utterances or writings have shown
themselves to be partisans of tyranny, of federalism, and enemies
of liberty'. The symptoms of the economic crisis were attacked
aggressively with controls, some enforced with draconian brutality:

food hoarders received the death penalty; the rich were crushed by a forced loan; 'revolutionary armies' were recruited from the sections to scour the surrounding countryside for grain. A 'General Maximum' fixed both prices and wages. The victims of this populism included the queen, Marie-Antoinette, who followed her husband to the guillotine on 16 October, a scapegoat offered by the revolutionary government to Parisian radicalism. Then, just a day before the women's political club was banned, it was the turn of twenty-one Girondins. They went to the guillotine defiantly singing the Marseillaise.[13]

The autumn of 1793 was the high-water mark of the *sans-culotte* tide. The Convention itself recognised that it needed the cooperation of the *sans-culottes* if some of its measures were to operate as intended in Paris, but at the same time it sought to control and channel their energies. The Law of Suspects was partly an attempt to absorb the committees of surveillance – hotbeds of *sans-culotte* activity – into the machinery of the central government by paying their members' salaries and by decreeing that they were to report directly to the Committee of General Security. Thus, buildings right across the city that had once been cloisters, chapels and seminaries became the nexus at which the machinery of repression imposed 'from above' met with the initiative of the *sans-culottes* 'from below'. And since the surveillance committees were rooted in the sections, they were close, terrifyingly close, to the everyday lives of all Parisians: the Terror could not have operated in the streets, workshops and closes of the city without some cooperation from people willing to be the eyes and ears of the committees, to make denunciations and to identify 'suspects'.[14]

The Terror continued to worm its way into every nook and cranny of city life, all the more so because Paris was at war, engaged in a struggle for the very survival of the Revolution. The pressure on France's resources – its people, its agriculture, its manufacturing,

its finance – was intense. The French economy was picked bare as
the revolutionary government made energetic and often draconian
efforts to mobilise the whole country behind the war effort. This
was the purpose behind the *levée en masse* decree of 23 August
1793, which made a deep impact on the Parisian landscape. The
first article grittily ordered: 'From this moment, until the point
when the enemy has been driven from the territory of the Republic,
all French people are under permanent requisition for the service
in the armies. Young men will go into combat; married men will
forge arms and transport food supplies; women will make tents,
uniforms and serve in the hospitals; children will tear old cloth into
lint; old men will be carried into public places, to stir the courage
of the warriors, the hatred of kings and the unity of the Republic'.[15]
It was, in other words, the first modern effort to wage total war –
and it marked the fabric of the city. Paris was transformed into an
armed camp, as blue-coated battalions of regular soldiers, conscripts
and National Guards passed through on the way to the northern
frontiers. Conscripts marching in ranks out of the city through
the Porte Saint-Denis became a regular sight, betraying a nervous
jumble of emotions – fear, anxiety, patriotic zeal and bitter sadness.

Parisians witnessed much of their city being taken over by war
industries. The *levée en masse* declared that the capital would be
the centre of an 'extraordinary factory for weapons of all kinds',
and the Convention charged the Committee of Public Safety
with 'forming any establishment, manufacture, workshop and
factory that it judges necessary'. Parisians witnessed once familiar
buildings and spaces being transformed for wartime production.
People crossing the Seine saw floating factories moored beneath
the city's bridges – broad, flat-bottomed barges with suitably
Jacobin names: *Sans-Culotte, Républicain, Intrépide, Tyrannicide,
Régicide* and *Carmagnole* (this last a popular *sans-culotte* dance).
Aristocratic town houses and palaces became hives of industry:

the Palais Bourbon (today where the National Assembly meets) in the Faubourg Saint-Germain was renamed the Maison de la Révolution and became a powder magazine in September 1793. The Évêché was converted into an arms workshop, its apprentices at one point giving a concert in honour of the Paris Commune in the cathedral of Notre-Dame next door. The Luxembourg Gardens – overlooked by the palace of the same name (now the seat of France's modern-day Senate), which had become the prison for high-profile 'suspects' – was a sea of canvas sheltering a giant open-air workshop that resounded to the hammers and bellows of workers making pikes, muskets, bayonets and sabres. The artisans were housed in old convents and monasteries nearby, along the rue de Vaugirard, in particular. At one point, such workshops were producing up to eight hundred firearms a day: it was truly a gargantuan, even heroic, effort. The once elegant town houses of nobles and the gardens, chapels and courtyards of convents and monasteries became workshops where the lock, stock and barrels of muskets were assembled, or they became stables for the army's thousands of horses and carts and grain stores for the army's food supplies. In former abbeys and convents, dormitories that once housed friars and nuns resounded to the nocturnal snoring of armament workers who now lived on the premises. The uninhabited Île Louviers (now part of the Right Bank, south of the Bastille) was the site for a factory making buttons for uniforms; its manager, a man named Gérantel, had been trained in the workshops of Birmingham. Alongside it was another armament factory, this one powered – a rare sight for the times – by a steam engine. At Chaillot, now the site of the Trocadéro, six huge furnaces in a factory run by Jacques-Constantin Périer rolled out cannon of all calibres. Now that the Convention had moved to the Tuileries Palace, the Manège became a forge.[16]

Yet while these strenuous wartime efforts helped to ensure the survival of the Republic, for those who fell afoul of the regime, the once familiar cityscape of spires and church towers now bore a sombre meaning. Fourteen monasteries and convents were converted into prisons, including the old religious houses belonging to English, Scottish and Irish orders. So, too, were former colleges of the University of Paris, aristocratic palaces, hospitals and poorhouses. Added to the already existing prisons, such as the Conciergerie on the Île de la Cité, La Force in the Marais and the Abbaye at Saint-Germain, there were forty-four in all, so that by 1794 Paris had four times as many gaols as it had under the old regime – a reflection in bricks, mortar and human suffering of the impact of the crisis. The prison population in fact fluctuated wildly, from 1,640 in September 1793 to 7,140 at the end of April 1794 (this last from a police report published in the official newspaper, the *Moniteur*). Conditions were overcrowded, filthy and enveloped in the stench of incarcerated, diseased humanity: certainly, a few months after the Terror, the government received a frank report that 'almost all the gaols are infected with the odour of the latrines' because of their construction and their location. Part of the problem was precisely that so many of the buildings used as prisons had been converted, with stout wooden partitions, grilles and locks fastened hastily into place; the convents and monasteries where friars, nuns and seminarians once paced contemplatively were not originally intended to incarcerate so many people.[17]

The symbolic dimensions of the cityscape were also marked by the political conflicts of the Terror, in the form of iconoclasm. After their defeat of the Enragés in the autumn of 1793, Hébert and his allies not only pressed *sans-culotte* demands but also had a cultural programme. In July 1793, Chaumette had published an essay entitled 'Signs of Royalty to Be Erased': 'Soon a republican will be able to walk through the streets of Paris without running the risk of wounding his eyes with the sight of all these emblems and demeaning attributes of royalty ... We must work tirelessly to make these repulsive images disappear, gothic monuments to the servitude of our fathers'.[18]

Street names were changed to efface any reminders of France's royal heritage: it was now that the Place Louis XV became the Place de la Révolution; the Palais-Royal, the Palais-Égalité; the rue Bourbon, the rue de Lille (and so it remains today); and the Place Royale, the Place des Vosges. The way people addressed each other changed: the polite form of address, *vous*, was discarded in favour of the egalitarian *tu* in a semantic shift that the French still call *tutoiement*: there was to be no deference among citizens of a republic. Strangers no longer greeted each other as 'Monsieur' or 'Madame', but as 'Citoyen' or 'Citoyenne'.[19]

Yet while the 'destruction of signs of royalty and feudalism' had enjoyed the blessing of the Convention, from October 1793 the Hébertist Commune wanted to go further in the cultural war. This was the 'dechristianisation' campaign, an explosion of iconoclasm, forcible defrocking of priests and closures of churches. Catholicism would be replaced by a secular, patriotic religion, a 'cult of reason'. Dechristianisation was given some encouragement from the Convention, which voted on 5 October to adopt a new republican calendar, devised by Danton's friend Fabre d'Églantine, who backdated year 1 to 22 September 1792, the date of the inauguration of the French Republic. Soon the Republican calendar would be posted on office walls everywhere. The Convention also passed a decree that each commune had the right to renounce formally the Catholic religion.[20]

Dechristianisation became official policy in Paris on 23 October 1793. Street names were again altered to reflect the city's secular republicanism: 'Saint' was simply removed from some; others were renamed altogether: the rue Saint-Honoré became the rue de la Convention, and the rue Saint-Denis became the rue Franciade.

To this day, in some old Paris streets, one can still see the chisel marks where workers had struck away the word 'Saint' from the cornerstones. The archbishop of Paris was forced to renounce his faith – 'the superstitious credulity of our forefathers', offensive to 'the reason of free men' – and churches were closed. They were also given secular names: Saint-Eustache became the 'Temple of Agriculture'. The climax was set in Notre-Dame Cathedral, renamed the 'Temple of Reason'. The Commune had ordered that 'the gothic simulacra of the kings of France which are placed at the door of Notre-Dame will be brought down and destroyed' (they were in fact statues of the kings of Judea). The effigies were hurled onto the square below. All religious embellishments from the interior of the cathedral were prised out: the sculptor's invoice runs to a staggering thirty pages.

Then, on 10 November, the Commune held a great festival in the Temple of Reason: young women shrouded in virginal white led the municipal officials towards a 'temple of philosophy' where the altar once was. At the climactic moment, a white-robbed 'Goddess of Reason' appeared on the scene, played by a Parisian actress, who then led the procession to the Convention. When it was all over, gone were the images of saints, of the Virgin Mary, of Christ, the effigies of nobles and priests, the reliquaries, the candlesticks and the incense burners. The bare shell of Notre-Dame – even its spire was melted down for its metal – was a far cry from the cathedral that stands today, which is in many respects a nineteenth-century re-imagining by the great restorer Eugène-Emmanuel Viollet-le-Duc.[21]

The impact of dechristianisation on the cityscape – not to say on the spiritual and cultural life – of Paris was traumatic. The city where monks and nuns in their easily identifiable habits and priests in their flapping cassocks were once a part of the exuberant panorama of street life, this city where the passage of time was marked by the bells of its multiple parish churches, this city where (some) Parisians still paid homage to holy shrines enclaved on street corners, found its very character and atmosphere transformed. Yet without the spaces and places that the revolutionaries were able to convert to their own uses, one is left wondering how the Revolution and its principles would have survived strangulation almost at birth. Their very existence and location helped shape the way in which ordinary working Parisians engaged with politics and experienced the Terror in 1793–1794. The story, moreover, is not all one of destruction, for revolutionaries like Alexandre Lenoir, intrepid director of the Museum of National Monuments, established in 1791, worked hard, even heroically, to save what he could. He risked his life in an attempt to stop the hammer and chisel blows from falling on the tombs of the kings and queens of France when they were attacked at the Basilica of Saint-Denis in August 1793.[22]

The Convention drifted along with the dechristianisation movement, but for Robespierre and his Jacobin allies in the government, the Republic was struggling with enemies enough without gratuitously adding otherwise quiescent but pious peasants to the list. Moreover, Hébertist dechristianisers were the same people who were rhetorically threatening the Convention with insurrection: 'Paris has made the Revolution, Paris has given the rest of France freedom, Paris will maintain it', a delegation from the Commune warned the squirming deputies. Behind this fiery talk, Robespierre suspected the Hébertists of adopting the *sans-culotte* programme in order to take power for themselves, their extremism perhaps even masking counter-revolutionary purposes. Unsurprisingly, the anxious Jacobins and others in the Convention began to backpedal. On 6 December 1793, the Convention declared the freedom of religious belief and worship.[23]

Over the coming months, the Committee of Public Safety

began to recall some of the looser cannon among the representatives sent on missions to the provinces to crush counter-revolution and 'federalism'. These deputies had been ruthlessly effective: the insurgent cities of the provinces had all been retaken and the counter-revolution in western France contained, though not defeated; the armies on the frontiers were holding their own; and even the economy was now being shored up. Yet at the same time, Robespierre and his colleagues in the revolutionary government were concerned that the many bloody excesses committed in the pursuit of this success were creating more enemies than they had eliminated. So the Law of 4 December – or 14 Frimaire, in the new revolutionary calendar (Frimaire being the 'frosty month') – gave the Committee of Public Safety ultimate control over all the levers of authority from the ministries down to the communes. It was an authoritarian, centralised government, the very opposite of the revolutionaries' intentions in 1789. It strengthened the repressive muscle of the central organs of the Terror in Paris and had the aim of controlling the Terror in the provinces and of weakening the authority of the Paris Commune, of absorbing the institutions of the city's sections fully into the machinery of the central government. This infusion of authority into the institutions, spaces and buildings of the Parisian sections did not occur without some resistance, and the scene was set for a murderous political confrontation in the spring of 1794.[24]

Within days of the Frimaire Law, some voices in the Convention and among the Jacobins began to call for more moderation, or even an end to the Terror. These 'Indulgents' included Fabre d'Églantine, the creator of the revolutionary calendar, and Camille Desmoulins, who began to edit a newspaper called the *Vieux Cordelier*. As its title suggested, Desmoulins was claiming the mantle of the Cordeliers of the early Revolution – democratic, republican – in contrast to the club as it existed in 1794: vengeful, bloodthirsty, Hébertist. Soon, Desmoulins and d'Églantine were joined by their old friend and ally the thunderous Georges-Jacques Danton: all were Cordeliers of the old stamp and residents of the same district. Together, the three deputies fought a campaign for clemency in the press, in the Convention and in the Jacobin Club. The ensuing collision with the Hébertists, who on the contrary called for the intensification of the Terror and with whom, as the self-proclaimed voices for the *sans-culottes*, the Law of 14 Frimaire naturally rankled, became a fight for survival.

It was uncertain which way the leading Jacobins on the Committee of Public Safety – Robespierre and his associates Louis-Antoine Saint-Just and Georges Couthon – would leap. Suspecting the Hébertists of preparing an insurrection and the Indulgents of corruption (Fabre had already been arrested in a financial scandal), they struck at both in the spring of 1794. The Hébertists were the first to fall under the blade: Hébert and nineteen of his closest supporters were arrested on 14 March, tried and guillotined on 24 March. The *sans-culottes* whom they had claimed to lead scarcely trembled: the incorporation of the institutions of the sections into the central machinery was only too successful. The popular movement was atomised, its leading militants now salaried by and working for the state and the maximum on prices functioning to keep their families fed. To have backed the Hébertists would have been professional, political and perhaps actual suicide. The remaining Hébertists were purged at all levels, including in the sections and the Paris Commune, which was taken over by Robespierre's acolytes and placed under the direct control of the Committee of Public Safety. The 'revolutionary armies' of *sans-culottes*, the scourge of the peasantry of the surrounding countryside, were disbanded. The turn of the Indulgents came when they were arrested on 30 March. At their trial before the Revolutionary Tribunal, Danton's voice, roaring in his own defence, apparently resonated across the Seine. It was to no avail: Danton, Desmoulins and Fabre, along with thirteen others, were decapitated on 5 April.

The execution of Danton and his friends marked a new direction in the Terror. The Hébertists, at least, had noisily – and impolitically – threatened insurrection and appeared to pose a real danger to the government and the Convention. Yet the Indulgents did not, so why they were sent to the scaffold is less clear. The evidence of Fabre's corruption certainly led Robespierre to suspect their motives, but that they did not threaten an uprising suggests that Robespierre and his allies were beginning to see the Terror as something beyond a mechanism for republican defence. Terror, the Jacobins agreed, would be temporary, but it was also open-ended, since no one could tell for sure when it would be safe to return to regular forms of law and government. In the combat between 'liberty' and 'despotism', there could be no middle ground: 'social protection', argued Robespierre, 'is due only to peaceful citizens [and] there are no citizens in the Republic but the republicans'. So it was not just enemies, but also the corrupt, the indifferent, the indulgent who could not be tolerated.[25]

The purge of the Indulgents probably marked the moment when the Terror moved from being *primarily* a series of draconian, defensive measures to a means of enforcing a more rigid form of political orthodoxy and of suppressing internal dissent. From there, it became an ideologically driven attempt to 'regenerate' French society as a 'Republic of Virtue'.

An official expression of this aim to remodel human morality was the Festival of the Supreme Being, a celebration of a new civic religion, one that recognised the existence of a deity and the immortality of the soul, but also the austere republican values that one now had to embrace in order to be part of the narrowing circle of the virtuous. At a ceremony held on a plasterboard mountain on the Champ de Mars on 8 June 1794, Robespierre, who happened to be president of the Convention on that day, led his fellow deputies in the celebrations. This was part of a programme that aimed to create citizens whose moral universe had expunged the habits of the old order and who were devoted to the self-sacrificing republican morality of the new. Not everyone was comfortable with this. Some, at least, were brave enough to grumble: Jacques Thuriot, a surviving ally of Danton, was heard to whisper about Robespierre as he played the high priest of the new moral order, 'Look at the bugger: it's not enough for him to be master, he has to be God'.[26]

One reason for the unease was the logic implicit in the new cult: once the Terror became an instrument of moral transformation, no one could see when and how it would end. There was also a terrible irony to the Festival of the Supreme Being that no one could miss: during the ceremony, Robespierre opined, 'Even here, on this altar, our feet cannot tread a spot that is not soiled with innocent blood', a reference to the massacre of republican petitioners on 17 July 1791. Yet the ultimate sanction, the final guarantor of the 'Republic of Virtue' itself, was the guillotine, a hideous fact that the Festival of the Supreme Being studiously avoided: the instrument of execution was given a day off and hidden beneath its shroud. Moreover, this irony was given spatial expression when the guillotine was moved first, on the following day, to the Place Antoine (the site of the Bastille) and then, on 14 June, to the easternmost edge of the city, on the Place du Trône Renversé (Square of the Overturned Throne, the modern-day Place de la Nation). So after the Festival of the Supreme Being was celebrated on the westernmost fringes of the capital, the executions would soon take place at the opposite end of the metropolis, as if the utopian dream of the festival could not be tainted by the blood that was being spilled to achieve it.[27]

The relationship between the new morality and the guillotine was soon scripted into law. The decree of 22 Prairial (10
June 1794) accelerated the work of the Revolutionary Tribunal:
defendants were stripped of legal counsel; the definition of treason was expanded dramatically; the jury could convict on the
grounds of 'moral proof' when there was no hard evidence; the
only sentence available was death. These measures routinised the
Jacobins' hazardously narrow conception of 'virtuous' citizenship.
The speed with which the mechanics of the guillotine were put
to work accelerated. In its first fifteen months from March 1793,
the Revolutionary Tribunal passed 1,251 death sentences, with
an average of 3 victims a day being guillotined; more people, in
fact, were acquitted than condemned. After 22 Prairial, which
plunged Paris into the final six bloody weeks of the Terror, 1,376
people were sentenced to death, or 30 each day. The streets had
grown strangely quieter: few people could afford carriages anyway,
but these were also ostentatious symbols of wealth best avoided.
People were reportedly careful about hanging around in groups to
chat and joke with neighbours. Walls were daubed with political
slogans, not least 'Liberty, Equality, or Death'. The entrance to tenements, as the law now required, displayed the names of lodgers,
the better to keep watch on who was moving in, out and around
the city. Parisians avoided displays of luxury, wearing deliberately
unkempt clothing, always with the ubiquitous, compulsory tricolour cockade.[28]

Yet the 'system of Terror' was in the end made up of people with
all their weaknesses. The exhaustion and anxiety, the high stakes
and the ever-present knowledge that the price of failure was death
all took their toll. Pre-existing political differences took on an extra
sharpness in this pressure cooker, even at the heart of the revolutionary government. To be a member of the Committee of Public
Safety was to engage in a punishing, thankless round of political

activity, day in, day out. And perhaps no one was more enclosed in the stifling political atmosphere than Robespierre. A quick walk through the 'Incorruptible's' political topography in the last months of his life reveals how busy, and politically claustrophobic, his existence and that of his colleagues must have become.[29]

Since the Champ de Mars massacre in July 1791, Robespierre had lodged with the family of the prosperous Jacobin master joiner Maurice Duplay at No. 366 (now 398) rue Saint-Honoré. True to his austere form, Robespierre did not live it up in one of the elegant, sparkling town houses for which this fashionable street was so well known. The Duplays were solidly middle class, Maurice a hardworking master craftsman, a self-made joiner who had built up his business with his own hands and now employed journeymen and apprentices, his family prosperous enough to hire servants. When Paul Barras, one of the politicians who later engineered Robespierre's downfall, visited the Duplay house, he passed by long planks of timber leaning against the wall of the coach entrance, the raw materials of Maurice's trade. In the courtyard, one of the daughters was stringing out laundry, while her mother sat with a basket and salad bowl, plucking herbs from their stems. Two relaxed armed guards were engaging the women in conversation. For the comfort-loving Barras, all this was worth hostile comment, but for Robespierre this environment probably represented the idyllic version of the virtuous artisanal family. While the Duplay family lived in two-storey apartments at the end of the short courtyard, Robespierre's rooms were on the first floor of the building to the right, reached by an external wooden staircase. He inhabited a simple, sparsely furnished room next door to a small cabinet for washing. It was a frugal existence that no doubt appealed to Robespierre's sense of republican virtue. Perhaps the most important observation to be made is that, for a brief period, one of the most powerful men in France inhabited a modest room in the home of a working family. The nation had travelled a long way from the ritual and glamour of Versailles.[30]

In one of Robespierre's typical days, he would leave the Duplays (if he had managed to get back there to rest at all) in the morning and walk to the Tuileries Palace, about ten minutes' walk (if that) to the east down the rue Saint-Honoré. In one important and impressive sense, he remained true to his principles, refusing offers of guards to protect him on his rounds: a representative of the people had to be accessible, transparent and modest – not surrounded by armed men. The palace itself had changed dramatically since the Convention had moved in. On the dome above the central Pavillon de l'Horloge, now called the Pavillon de l'Unité, was a massive scarlet Phrygian bonnet supported by an iron frame; rising above that, in turn, was a thirty-three-foot tricolour pennant. On either end, the Pavillon de Marsan was now emblazoned with the word *Liberté*, while the Pavillon de Flore, on the opposite end, overlooking the river, was marked with Égalité.[31]

The Tuileries was not only broadcasting the symbols and slogans of the new order to passers-by, but also (not so subtly) proclaiming that the onetime royal residence, renamed the Palais National, was now the political heart of the Republic, the very seat of the representation of the people. Robespierre, prim in his knee breeches and powdered hair, would have headed for the Pavillon de Flore – or, rather, de l'Égalité. Recognised by the soldiers who manned the cannon guarding the entrance, he would have walked up the old Escalier de la Reine, the queen's staircase, into a room that still luxuriated with Gobelins carpets spread over the parquet floor and the furniture left behind by Louis XVI just over a year previously. Here Robespierre would meet with his colleagues on the Committee of Public Safety for a few hours before the Convention opened, whereupon the committee members would march through the Tuileries Palace into the debating chamber to defend government policy and, if necessary, forestall political rebellion from the deputies.

When not in the Tuileries, in the evenings Robespierre strode back to the rue Saint-Honoré and into the Jacobin Club, on a site now occupied by the Marché Saint-Honoré. There he would sound out his arguments and policies among the faithful, galvanise their support and face down his adversaries and critics. Still there was no rest: Robespierre would rejoin his colleagues in the Pavillon de l'Égalité to draft committee orders, to wait for news from the frontier and the provinces and to respond to the intelligence as it came in. These daily gatherings often ran deep into the night, since the despatches from the front were carried by riders who arrived in the small hours. Camp beds were ordered to allow the hard-pressed committeemen to steal what sleep they could.[32]

So it was that Robespierre's life was confined, in these crucial months, to an axis that was no longer than a third of a mile in length, the site of a gruelling routine of policy making, legislating, policy defending, strategising, organising, mobilising and crisis management. Robespierre's experience was not mirrored to the same extent by his colleagues on the committee, but it gives a sense of the punishment that being in government entailed at the time. It would have been exhausting, and many revolutionaries took to heavy drinking, though not Robespierre. When the outside did intrude into this pressurised world, it came in rasping ways. There was an alleged assassination attempt on Robespierre on 23 May when a young woman named Cécile Renault was found looking for Robespierre, so that she could see 'what a tyrant looked like'. When her basket was searched, two small knives were found. Tried and executed, she shared her fate with a man named Admirat who, armed with two pistols, had waited at the Convention to take a shot at Robespierre. By chance, the Jacobin leader took a different route than usual, so the would-be assassin returned home frustrated. His neighbour, however, was one of Robespierre's colleagues on the committee, Collot d'Herbois, who was saved only because both of Admirat's pistols misfired. The blood-soaked carnage that followed – Renault and Admirat were guillotined with fifty-two others, all dressed in the red shirts reserved for parricides – reflects the violent depths into which the government had plunged in its exhaustion and fear of (as Robespierre put it at the time) 'calumnies, treasons, fires, poisonings, atheism, corruption, famine, assassinations ... [T]here still remains assassination, and then assassination, and then again assassination'.[33]

Both attempts helped bring forth the Law of 22 Prairial that accelerated the work of the Revolutionary Tribunal. Robespierre happened to live on the street that had led to the guillotine. For the victims, the route began with a transfer from whatever Paris gaol they were being held in to the Conciergerie, the prison that festered beneath the Palais de Justice on the Île de la Cité. When arraigned, they would be marched upstairs to the Revolutionary Tribunal, which sat in the old Grand' Chambre once occupied by the Parlement, now stripped of its regalia and finery, a whitewashed shell whose austerity was alleviated only with strips of red-white-and-blue wallpaper. If condemned, they would be executed on the same or following day: their hair cropped at the back, their collars cut away and their hands bound just before being forced to mount carts in the Cour de Mai. These tumbrils would then be driven across the river and pass on the long journey down the rue Saint-Honoré, watched by clusters of – usually – silent people. The slowness of the cortege from the prison, followed by a quick, mechanical death, was all part of the grim theatre of the Republic's retribution against its enemies. Yet as the tumbrils passed by the home of the Duplays (not far from the end of the journey), the sight of Robespierre's lodgings could unleash some powerful emotions. When the Hébertists trundled past the Duplay house in three carts on 24 March 1794, executioner Charles-Henri Sanson alleged that 'the crowd cheered lustily, as if to thank Robespierre for ridding France of unprincipled rascals like Hébert'. On the other hand, when the pinioned Danton was carried past only a few days later, he is said to have rasped, 'I will drag Robespierre with me; Robespierre will follow me!'[34]

Victims were decapitated on a scaffold in the centre of the Place de la Révolution and their bodies taken to mass graves and covered in quicklime in the Cemetery of the Madeleine to the north. When the guillotine was moved to the Place du Trône Renversé, as we have seen, it was because in the hot summer, the stench of blood on the Place de la Révolution had become unbearable. Thereafter, the machine's victims were buried in large common graves in the Picpus Cemetery, which is today a peaceful place for the dead to rest.[35]

In this exhausting, fear-drenched environment, mutual suspicions, political differences and territorial disputes – the aggrieved Committee of General Security accused the more powerful Committee of Public Safety of intruding on its authority over policing – began to tear the government apart. Personal hatreds were amplified. In the Convention, the moderates of the 'Plain' questioned the use of Terror after a triumphant French victory over the Austrians at Fleurus on 26 June 1794: the war had decisively turned. The public mood in the streets, workshops and cafés was a wrenching mix of hope for the future and fear of the present. In this atmosphere, Robespierre's diverse opponents began to gather: representatives on mission recalled from the provinces, vengeful survivors and friends of those already purged, angry members of the Committee of General Security and fearful moderates who wondered if they would be next. In mid-June, Robespierre quarrelled angrily with Lazare Carnot, the committee member in overall charge of the military effort, who had accused him of aspiring to dictatorship. He stormed out and disappeared from the meetings of the committee and of the Convention for five critical weeks, and he barely appeared at the sessions of the Jacobin Club, all symptoms of a physical and psychological collapse that came from months of pressure. When Robespierre finally returned to the fray, the eclectic opposition was mustering its forces. Robespierre's fatal error on 26 July was to speak in the Convention of another purge, without naming names. Overnight, an unholy alliance gathered of deputies from all sides who felt like potential targets.[36]

The following day, when Robespierre tried to speak, the coup was unleashed: in a turbulent session on 27 July (9 Thermidor), the Convention voted to arrest Robespierre and his closest colleagues on the committees. Although the Paris Commune, still controlled by Robespierre's appointees, refused to allow the captives to be incarcerated in one of Paris's crammed prisons, only thirteen of the forty-eight sections bothered to send National Guard detachments to defend the Jacobin leaders, who took shelter in the Hôtel de Ville. The *sans-culottes*, silenced by the earlier purges of their leaders, their sections cowed and rancorous at controls on wages, were at best uncertain as to whom to support. Even those National Guards who had rallied on the Place de Grève drifted away, unsure of their political direction, and the forces loyal to the Convention moved in. The following day, his jaw shattered by a bullet from a gendarme's pistol fired as he was arrested, Robespierre and his closest allies, including Saint-Just, were guillotined. Although the direction that the Revolution might now take was not clear to anyone (least of all the Thermidorians, the authors of the coup against Robespierre), almost all citizens and officials alike were hoping that the time for normality, for constitutional government, had come at last.

THE PARISIAN EXPERIENCE of revolution, in terms of the fabric of the city and its relationship with its people, was of a different scale to that felt in revolutionary New York and in the struggles of reform politics in London. New York had experienced the terror and exhilaration of revolution and war. As we have seen, New Yorkers had some very intense periods in which revolutionary and wartime mobilisation reached into every neighbourhood and street. The political transformation to a new republican order certainly marked its cityscape. London would, as we shall see, experience the leavening of popular radicalism that reached across the metropolis, trying to join together like-minded people from its far-flung parts. Yet neither city experienced the transformation in its environment as Paris did.

The very depth of the wartime mobilisation in Paris, combined with the attempts to establish a new republican order, ensured that the spatial and physical experience of the revolution in 1793–1794 was particularly severe. It certainly recalled New York in 1775–1776, but the intensity of the struggle against both foreign invasion and domestic turmoil ensured that the scale and depth of the Parisian experience were all the greater. This difference was symptomatic of the divergence between the American and French Revolutions. As it turned out, the Americans were able to do most of the work of building a republican constitutional order in the peacetime years that followed the War of Independence, a project that was bound up with the reconstruction of the country after the conflict – as the post-war experience of New York City showed between 1783 and 1790. The French revolutionaries, however, could only hope that such calmer times for consolidating a republican order would come in the not too distant future. Meanwhile, they had to fight a war for survival on every frontier and on the high seas, confront counter-revolution in the West, master a desperate economic crisis and, eventually, fight a full-blown civil war in many parts of the country. It was precisely for this reason that the French revolutionaries did not pretend that the organs of repression and public mobilisation amounted to anything other than extraordinary unconstitutional government, a state of emergency.

It was unsurprising, then, that the conflicts that arose from the politics of the Terror – between the authority of the central government, on the one hand, and the popular movement, on the other, and between the different factions for control of the popular movement – should have been embedded in the buildings and spaces of the city. To some extent, it was also shaped by its topography, as the central government, the *sans-culottes* and rival factions and organisations struggled for the control of the direction of the Revolution and, in the process, for the physical control of the streets and seats of political activism and authority. This diffusion of power, engagement, conflict and contention across the city, taking root in the chapels, cloisters, churches, offices, barracks and mansions that once characterised the old order, was a very real way in which the people of Paris – in addition to hunger, anxiety, fear, terror, hope and exhilaration – experienced their Revolution.

CHAPTER ELEVEN

RADICAL LONDON: DEMOCRATS, LOYALISTS AND THE REACTION, 1792–1794

WHILE PARIS UNDERWENT the turbulent passage from constitutional monarchy to republic, London had an experience
that in many ways paralleled that of the French capital: the dissemination of radical, popular politics across the metropolis; the
opening of the jaws of government repression and crowd violence;
and the experience of wartime mobilisation. All of this played out
in the city's public spaces, but with very different results, not least
of which was the avoidance of revolution. This, in turn, was partly
a consequence of a struggle for the control of the places where
Londoners engaged with politics and culture – and one of the most
important of these was the city's taverns. These were social places
for London's working people, and they became the venues for a
remarkable attempt to mobilise the artisans and labourers of the
metropolis into a single political movement for reform, a British
equivalent of the network of popular societies in Paris. It was
for this very reason that the taverns became the sites of political

debate, but also of conflict, in this troubled period in the history of British democracy.

THE ATTEMPT TO organise a metropolitan-wide radical reform movement stemmed from the vision of successful Scottish shoe-maker Thomas Hardy, who after work on a chilly January evening in 1792 walked into the Bell Tavern on Exeter Street, just off the Strand, to meet with a small number of fellow artisans. The venue was carefully chosen. Hardy trusted the landlord, Robert Boyd, 'who I knew was a friend to freedom and quite agreeable that a society should meet at his house'. Today's Old Bell Tavern, built in 1835 at the northwest corner of the crossroads with the modern-day Wellington Street, occupies part of the site where the eighteenth-century Bell once stood. Exeter Street itself was discreet, a residential lane narrowing at its western end. Its three- and four-storey brick houses were occupied by artisans, tradesmen and their families, precisely the hardworking sort whom Hardy wanted to recruit, although his ambition was to draw in working people from across the metropolis. The Bell was tucked away from the bustle of the Strand to the south and from the hurly-burly of Covent Garden to the north, with its mix of market stalls, prostitutes, hard-drinking revellers and lovers of drama and music hurrying to the theatre in Drury Lane, the Theatre Royal on Covent Garden's famous piazza or perhaps the English Opera House, which backed up onto Exeter Court. Sandwiched, there-fore, in the very thick of London life, the Bell was a convenient spot for all of those whom Hardy was about to meet. Moreover, the tavern was also a fairly short, pleasant walk home for Hardy, whose comfortable house and shop were at 9 Piccadilly. On this day, Monday, 23 January 1792, Hardy met with eight other London artisans who, 'after the business of the day was ended', had 'retired as was customary for tradesmen to do to a public house', as Hardy himself recalled.[1] Leaning back after supper, smoking their long pipes and taking draughts of hoppy ale or of heavy dark porter from their pewter tankards, 'conversation followed', Hardy wrote later, 'condoling with each other on the miserable and wretched state the people were reduced to, merely as we believed, from the want of a fair, and equal representation in the commons house of parliament'.[2] They did not just vent their spleens, but decided to do something about it.

Hardy was immersed in the reformist literature of the day. He had travelled from Scotland in 1774, having learned his trade from his grandfather, carrying little but a few letters of introduction and eighteen pence in his pocket. He prospered as a boot maker, and within ten years he had opened his own shop on Piccadilly, employing five or six journeymen. Yet like many progressive Britons, he had been fascinated by the debate on the American Revolution, and he read many of the pamphlets then being circulated by the metropolitan Society for Constitutional Information. Hardy reread this material and more besides in November and December 1791 during his leisure hours. 'It was very evident', he wrote, looking back from 1799, 'that a *radical reform in parliament* was quite necessary'. The problem was how to achieve it, but by January Hardy had his solution: to establish a truly popular reform movement in London, one that went beyond the form of protests that had rallied behind John Wilkes (too focused on a popular idol) and the Society for Constitutional Information and the London Revolution Society (either too elitist or too confined geographically). So in the warm, candlelit fug of the tavern, Hardy's friends listened as he presented them with his plan for a far-reaching metropolitan society. After some discussion, they agreed on the name the 'London Corresponding Society' (LCS) as the most 'appropriate to the object of the

Society, which was to correspond with individuals, and societies of men who wished for a reformation, and to collect the opinion and sense of the nation as far as possible by that means'. This was no revolutionary cell: Hardy made clear that he regarded the 'gross ignorance and prejudice of the bulk of the nation' to be the greatest obstacle to obtaining redress. So the London Corresponding Society would dispel 'that ignorance and prejudice as far as possible'.[3]

The eight artisans signed up, and Hardy distributed membership tickets before being elected as the LCS secretary and treasurer, controlling the grand sum of eight pence. Yet the funds would grow as the society grew, meeting each Monday night in the Bell Tavern. By the third meeting, there were twenty-five members, including Maurice Margarot, a lawyer whose father, a wine merchant, had known John Wilkes. The LCS began to correspond with other like-minded organisations across the country and with the Society for Constitutional Information, with which Hardy reconnected in order to ask for help in drafting the LCS manifesto. John Horne Tooke of the SCI (and erstwhile ally of John Wilkes) and Thomas Paine both offered to assist. The society's first address was issued on 2 April: 'Man as an Individual', it proclaimed, 'is entitled to Liberty – it is his Birth-right', and without a share in the government of his country, 'no Man can with Truth call himself FREE'. It finished by promising that 'this Society do express their *Abhorrence* of Tumult, and Violence, and that, as they aim at Reform, not Anarchy, Reason, Firmness, and Unanimity are the only Arms they themselves will employ'. The LCS joined with other radical reform societies that actively sought an artisanal, trades and crafts membership, notably the impressively widespread Societies of the Friends of the People in Scotland and the Sheffield Society for Constitutional Information, all of which took the politicisation of the people further than any of their predecessors. Even the solidly middle-class Society for Constitutional Information began to draw in a more popular membership. Such was its embrace of the democratic impulses that Thomas Paine's copies of *Rights of Man*, police agents reported, were being sold and read at LCS meetings.[4]

Yet the LCS was especially successful because of the way it was organised, transcending the vast space of the metropolis and seeking to bind together members in points throughout the great city. Each division was meant to have thirty members, but when they reached forty-six, the extra sixteen members were to split off to form a new division. The society would eventually boast a total of sixty divisions, although they were not all active at the same time. Every three months, each division elected a delegate to a General Committee that met each Thursday evening and acted as a central executive, responding to correspondence, managing the finances and coordinating the divisions. This structure might have rooted the LCS in the local communities (since its members met in their local tavern), while binding them together in a metropolitan network.[5]

The artisanal delegates to the General Committee who converged once a week onto the Bell Tavern from all parts of the metropolis were fusing together a movement that transcended the problem of London's great urban sprawl, overcoming the distances that otherwise, in a 'walking city', would have prevented them from forging together like-minded people into a metropolitan movement. They engaged with issues of national importance, but they also looked outwards, drawing inspiration from the revolutionary events in France, while refusing steadfastly to countenance that Britain might need such an upheaval itself. Hardy would later say that, although the aims of the London radicals and the Parisian *sans-culottes* were the same, that is, democracy, the great difference was that Britain's revolutions of the seventeenth century had already secured many basic rights and freedoms for British subjects; the French were starting from zero. 'We were men while they were slaves', a radical later opined. So the French Revolution – its egalitarianism, its ideology of the rights of man and its struggle against the despotic powers of Europe in the name of freedom – was an inspiration, but not an example to follow.[6]

Francis Place, one of its members, would later recall that the LCS was 'the very best school for good teaching which probably ever existed'. The society achieved this educational aim by a low membership rate of a penny a week, and by their choice of meeting place. As Hardy noted, 'The Society admitted journeymen treadsmen [sic] of all denominations . . . Many of that description of Men are unmarried, and whose practice it is to go to a public house from their workshops after the labour of the day, to have their supper, and then regale themselves with a pint or pot of Beer, and smoak their pipes, and convers about news of the day'. Taverns, in other words, were the natural places for artisans to socialise, and a report by a police spy named Kennedy in November 1792 lists the meeting places of the LCS divisions, sixteen at the time: the Crown and Thistle, the Marquis of Granby, the Black Dog, the Sun, the Three Herrings, the Crown, Red Lyon, Sign of the Cock and so on, all testifying to the London pub as the meeting place of choice. The divisional structure may partly have been a practical response to the problems of space, since although many inns and taverns had upstairs assembly rooms that could be used for meetings, not all could accommodate large groups of people. Veterans later recalled the pipe smoke, spilled beer, pamphlets strewn across the floor and excitement of political discussion. There was a novelty to this activity for the hundreds of artisans who participated, debated about reform, joined the committee and collected money both for their fellow members (once the arrests were made by the government) and to help supply the French army with shoes as they battled for democracy and liberty.[7]

In reality, the LCS never attracted the mass membership that Hardy had hoped for: active members seem to have fluctuated wildly between 250 and more than 3,500. Yet there was a much larger constituency of people who turned up occasionally: at its height, there were fifty pounds in the LCS treasury each week, which at one pence per member suggests that there was a regular attendance of about 12,000 people. This is a drop in the ocean compared with the 1 million in the teeming metropolis, but the society drew many more people to its open-air meetings, to which thousands of people came, especially in times of economic distress. Importantly, too, the LCS represented a breakthrough in that it was the first political organisation in London to aim explicitly at recruiting from the city's workers. Assessments of membership are tricky because the employment of only 347 members is actually known, but they seem to confirm the claim, made by one of the LCS's leading members, that 'the great mass [were] shopkeepers, artisans, mechanics, and labourers'. There was also strong middle-class membership, but then they, too, were at this time politically disenfranchised: doctors, lawyers, booksellers and an auctioneer. Despite this, at least half of the leadership seems to have been artisans, suggesting that they were no longer simply following the lead of middle-class reformers or rallying around such prominent figures as John Wilkes. This was the great breakthrough, for over 1792, as elite and middle-class reformers were taking fright at the radical and violent turn of events in France and dropping away from the cause of political change, the LCS was only just getting started, its number of divisions reaching thirty before the year was out.[8]

When the LCS printed its first address on 2 April 1792 in the radical newspaper *Argus*, it went public. Yet the only name published was Hardy's. In an ominous sign of the difficulties that popular radicalism would encounter, no one else in the LCS wanted their name published beneath the address, some because, Hardy recognised, 'they were serving Masters who might perhaps discharge them from their employment' or 'they might lose their Customers'. Margarot refused to sign because he was seeking a job with the merchants of the City of London.[9]

Respectable, nonviolent, educational, reformist but not revolutionary, popular but socially moderate, the London Corresponding Society stressed repeatedly that it did not pose a threat to the existing social order, nor did it want any other political change than that of a reform of the House of Commons. Yet few of the elites took all this on trust. The Opposition Whigs around Charles James Fox formed an Association of the Friends of the People (membership dues an eye-watering two and a half guineas). When one of its members, Sir Charles Grey, announced that he would introduce a bill into Parliament for a very mild reform, the association was deeply embarrassed to earn the noisy support of the popular radicals in London and the provinces. Like moderates everywhere in times of crisis, the Whigs were buffeted by a swelling mass of conservative voices on one side and the mobilisation of popular radicalism on the other, but it could not prevail over the one or impose moderation on the other. The government, in fact, began to turn the screws after the publication of part 2 of Thomas Paine's *Rights of Man*, with its vision of a more egalitarian world shorn of poverty. The Royal Proclamation against seditious writings on 21 May 1792 called on all loyal subjects to resist subversion and on all magistrates to uncover those who wrote, published and distributed 'seditious' works. On the same day, the government issued a summons against Paine, calling on him to appear in court charged with seditious libel. Before the trial was held, Paine learned that his fame in France had won him election to the Convention. So the author of *Rights of Man* fled into exile, setting sail in the cross-Channel packet from Dover at dawn on 14 September, pursued by the insults and threats of a mob gathered on the pier.[10]

Yet if all this gave moderate Whig reformers pause, the London Corresponding Society reacted determinedly. It sought to forge closer ties with the Society for Constitutional Information, writing to it to coordinate protests against the Royal Proclamation that, the General Committee of the LCS argued on 24 May, tended to 'alarm & prejudice all ranks of men against certain (asserted to be) wicked, seditious & inflammatory writings'. Before Paine fled, it raised money towards the costs of his defence, and it opened correspondence with other reform societies across Britain, among other things inviting them to subscribe to an address to the French National Convention.[11]

The radicals were under pressure in other ways, and here the struggle for control of the city's public spaces was critical. The authorities, represented by the local justices of the peace who issued the licences for taverns and inns, were well aware of the importance that access to the public meeting rooms was to the operation of the LCS, and they acted accordingly. London's taverns were, one by one, closed to the artisanal reformers. On 7 June 1792, the General Committee complained that magistrates were ignoring 'the Brothels, the Houses, and the receptacles of public depredation' and instead hurried to 'threaten harmless Publicans with putting a stop to their licences, if they admitted into their houses any sober industrious body of Tradesmen, presuming to discuss political subjects'. One hundred publicans from up and down the country bent to the pressure and declared that they would report any activity 'of a treasonable or seditious tendency' to local magistrates. Hardy later described the impact (the spelling is in the original):

They succeeded so far in their alarm that not one publick house – tavern nor Coffee House would recieve a branch of the society that professed a reform in parliament . . . All that hubbub and noice throughout the country disorganized the *London Corresponding Society* very much – Many of the Members were also alarmed and fled to different parts of the country – some went to America – others who were great declaimers in the society slunk into holes and corners and were never heard of more . . . The comparatively few who remained firm and true to their first principles and determined to *persevere* – were obliged to hire private houses and Auction rooms at great expence – the members were obliged to double their weekly pay and also to double their dilligence.[12]

Worse, while the LCS was being squeezed out of the taverns, its opponents moved in, well aware that they at least had the blessing of the authorities. So they took over the very spaces upon which the LCS depended. These opponents to reform took the shape of an Association for the Preservation of Liberty and Property Against Republicans and Levellers, founded by the former chief justice of Newfoundland and now the British government's chief paymaster, John Reeves. Reeves was alarmed by what he saw as a cross-Channel conspiracy to subvert the existing order, calling it 'a systematic design, long since adopted and acted upon by France, in conjunction with domestic traitors . . . to overturn the laws, constitution, and government, and every existing establishment civil or ecclesiastical'.[13] There was no such conspiracy, but the LCS and other radical organisations – and French actions in the European war – had certainly provided some superficial evidence for those who wanted to believe that there was.

The purpose of the joint address from British radical societies to the National Convention in France, first proposed by the LCS in reaction to the Royal Proclamation against seditious writings, was now to soothe French expectations that the British reaction to the radical turn of events in Paris would be a universally hostile one. It was also hoped that thousands of signatures would demonstrate public support against government attempts at further repression. Written by Margarot, the address was circulated among the other reform societies up and down the country, with the radicals in Manchester and Norwich and the Whig Constitutional Society in London eventually subscribing, representing as many as five thousand signatures. Eleven other organisations sent their own addresses between September and December 1792, including the SCI. The joint address spearheaded by the LCS was read at the bar of the Convention on 7 November. Expressing support for the French in their war against the 'foreign robbers' who had invaded their territory, and promising to work to keep Britain neutral in the conflict, the address also assured the Convention that there was a political awakening in Britain:

> Frowned upon by an oppressive system of control, whose gradual but continual encroachments have deprived this Nation of nearly all its boasted liberty, and brought us almost to that abject state of slavery from which you have so gloriously emerged, a few thousands of British Citizens indignant, manfully step forward to rescue their country from the opprobrium brought upon it by the supine conduct of those in power ... Though we appear comparatively so few at present, be assured Frenchmen, that our number increases daily ... Men now ask each other, what is Freedom? What are our Rights? Frenchmen, you are already free, and Britons are preparing to become so.[14]

This was no promise of a British revolution, but the language was dangerously ambiguous, and the timing could barely have been worse. France had been a Republic for six weeks, and the Convention would soon put Louis XVI on trial. Yet there was more: on 19 November, the Convention, in a spin after the dazzling success of the French armies at Valmy and Jemappes, issued the 'Edict of Fraternity', which promised 'fraternity and help to all peoples who wish to recover their liberty'. Although the joint address predated these developments by a few weeks, in the confused and rapid pace of events, it was all too easy for the British government to read it not in the context of British reformism, but against the French backdrop of republicanism, regicide and international revolution. So such ambiguous phrases as 'Frenchmen, you are already free, but Britons are preparing to be so' seemed all too clearly to be a statement of revolutionary intent. The French embassy in London now had a mountain to climb in its attempts to avoid a complete breakdown of relations between the two governments. The French diplomats tried to assure Whitehall that the Edict of Fraternity did not apply to Britain.[15]

As FRANCO-BRITISH DIPLOMATIC relations were fracturing, and as British radicals seemed to be encouraging the spread of the French Revolution to the British Isles, Reeves's loyalist association held its first meeting on 20 November 1792 at the Crown and Anchor Tavern on the Strand (the site is now the corner of Arundel Street). There was no prior publicity, no brochure, and though Reeves had acted on his own initiative, his association quickly attracted the support of the government under Prime Minister William Pitt. Pitt was receptive because he wanted to find a way of channelling public feeling, which he rightly sensed was moving against the French Revolution and radicalism. The choice of venue for this first meeting was apposite: if the radicals could use the assembly rooms in taverns, so too could the loyalists. Reeves aimed to counter the organisation and propaganda of the British radicals by bringing, as he put it, all 'good men' to associate together, 'neither to pull up nor to pull down' but 'only to preserve'. This was, he continued, a critical time in which 'licentiousness and sedition had got to such a head, that treason and rebellion seemed to be the stronger side'. Reeves placed an advertisement in the press on 23 November, three days after the first meeting, whereupon the association secured the support of local squires, justices of the peace and clergymen across the country. With their support and that of the government, and drawing in primarily men of property who would form the association's backbone, the organisation spread rapidly. In London both the lord mayor and the livery companies endorsed it on 6 December 1792 – showing how far the French Revolution and the radical challenge had bundled the once contentious City into the government's camp. The nationwide network of loyalists was exploited to disseminate antiradical propaganda, including Hannah More's work. One of the most successful of all writers to reach the working population, More's *Village Politics*, a journal that first appeared in 1792, appealed to people's religious attachments and connected Britishness to the existing political and social order. Her journalism, written in direct, accessible language, also stressed the benefits of the civil liberties under which Britons lived, in contrast to the 'unparalleled anarchy and impiety' experienced by the French.[16]

The local loyalist associations were led by local notables, which in London often meant employers who drummed in their workers. One wallpaper manufacturer assembled his workers and servants into an association branch, telling them to demonstrate their loyalty 'as becomes good and Carefull Subjects'. As Reeves declared, one of the aims of the original association was 'to encourage persons to form similar Societies in different parts of the Town', ideally with larger gatherings in the City, Westminster and Southwark, supported by 'smaller Societies around them, to assist and cooperate'. Indeed, soon every ward and parish of the City boasted an association of its own. In Westminster each parish association sent a delegate to a central committee, which took its orders directly from Reeves, who had taken the Crown and Anchor as his headquarters. From Kensington and Chelsea to Mile End, from Highgate to Southwark (which had an association in each of its five parishes, coordinated by a central committee), the associations formed what one historian has called 'a ring of repression' around the metropolis. Put another way, it was a network against which the LCS simply could not compete. The numbers and zeal of the loyalist associations did not last for more than a year or two, but this was perhaps because in many instances, their radical opponents had been cowed successfully into silence, so their purpose had been served.[17]

This meant that the London Corresponding Society struggled to put down lasting roots in the multiplicity of London's neighbourhoods. Its divisional structure had shown remarkable success in reaching across the distances that separated artisanal reformer from artisanal reformer, but, confronted by the groundswell of loyalism and denied the social draw of the taverns in which they met, the radicals were overwhelmed locally even as they forged metropolitan-wide bonds among their own relatively small and scattered numbers. This was a contrast to the spatial experience of the Parisian popular movement that – as the experience of the Faubourg Saint-Antoine, Les Halles and the Cordeliers district showed – was first and foremost grounded in the different communities of Paris and then hammered into a citywide movement by political leadership and revolutionary organisation.

At the most local level, British loyalists used a range of tactics against radicalism. This involved pounding the streets to make house-to-house enquiries as to their occupants' loyalties and social ostracism for suspected radicals. Loyalist employers threatened their workers with sacking if they did not toe the line. One member of the LCS was told by his employer either to resign from the society or to lose his job, which put him in an invidious position because he was in fact a government informer who had infiltrated the organisation. Radicals were further intimidated by the threat of violence: there was always the danger that church and king mobs, one of which had utterly destroyed the home and laboratory of reformer and scientist Joseph Priestley in Birmingham in July 1791, could be drummed up to unleash their destructive fury. Effigy burnings – Paine was a favourite victim – rallied working-class loyalists in a bacchanalia of antiradicalism: in Peckham and Camberwell, then both outlying villages not far from the metropolis, processions finished not only with Paine burnings, but also with the incineration of copies of *Rights of Man*.[18]

The radicals lost the battle for reform primarily because they were overwhelmed by the sheer numbers of the loyalist movement, backed by the resources of the government. They were rapidly forced to retreat in the struggle to control the public spaces in which they had met, namely, London's taverns. As government paymaster, Reeves was able to use his connections to ensure that radical clubs were not allowed to use such premises for their meetings. Innkeepers continued to be threatened with having their licences withdrawn, at one point leaving Hardy having to console himself with the observation that at least the radicals made better customers. His own Division 2 was forced to leave the Bell on Exeter Street and meet in a private house at No. 3 New Compton Street. Reeves went so far as to prompt a naval press gang to try to snatch leading LCS firebrand John Thelwall, but he was saved from forced service in the Royal Navy by a fair-minded local magistrate. Hardy and the LCS struggled against these currents: the beleaguered divisions still continued to meet wherever possible, but to do so they had to move from one venue to another. When they did meet, loyalists, Hardy complained, made such a racket and were so intimidating that they disrupted the radical gatherings.[19]

While Reeves's association put the LCS under pressure from without, the latter's divisions were being corroded from within: government agents infiltrated the society. The first report came from a spy named Lynam who had joined Division 2 – Hardy's own – in late October 1792. The atmosphere was such that divisions scrutinised new members suspiciously and, on one occasion, unmasked a government agent. In November the spy named Kennedy tried to attend the meeting of Division 8 in the Sun Tavern on Windmill Street, but, as he later reported, 'on entring into the room was immediately suspected and was very ill treated being not only abus'd by the President but was threatened to be turn'd out if I did not immediately depart'. As Kennedy left, 'I rec'd a Kick in the Side on the Stairs'. Such reports were hardly reliable, and indeed some spies were agents provocateurs, seeking to encourage the radicals into making ale-fuelled contentions that went beyond the nonviolent intentions of the LCS. But this material would find its way to the treasury solicitor as the case was built against the radical leadership. Moreover, the very fact that some spies were able to penetrate the divisions shows that, in a metropolis of the scale of London, it was well-nigh impossible for their members to verify the background and sincerity of everyone, no matter how hard they tried. It was, perhaps, the consequence of being an organisation that had a metropolitan reach, but one that, under intense pressure from the association and from the magistrates, was also struggling to find its feet within the local neighbourhoods of the city.[20]

Events across the Channel also told against British radicalism. The execution of Louis XVI on 21 January 1793 was mourned in Britain – when the news arrived in London, theatre crowds rose spontaneously to bellow out the anthem 'God Save Our Gracious King'. The already tenuous relations between Britain and France finally snapped, as the strategic situation in Europe became ominous with the triumphant French following up their victories of the previous autumn by overrunning Belgium and the Rhineland and pressing hard against the Dutch border. A rampant revolutionary France looming on the North Sea coast was a strategic red flag for the British government, and although it was the French who declared war on 1 February, by that point hostilities were almost unavoidable. With Britain's entry into the European conflict, the stunned radicals found that the French revolutionaries whom they had so recently and so publicly lauded were suddenly the enemy.

Yet this did not deter the radicals, for whom it was axiomatic that parliamentary reform was neither subversive nor treasonous. In Scotland the network of Societies of the Friends of the People organised two reform conventions in Edinburgh, first in December 1792 and then in April 1793. Impressed, the LCS wrote asking for 'a more intimate co-operation', and the Scots replied warmly, citing the common danger to the reform movement and the 'principle of universal benevolence'. Even when the Scottish authorities struck in August and September, trying Scottish radical leaders Thomas Muir and Thomas Fysche Palmer and sentencing them to transportation to Australia, the injustice merely steeled the radicals further. The LCS and the SCI both sent delegates to the third "British convention" in Edinburgh, which opened on 19 November. The authorities again swooped, arresting its leaders, Scots and English alike, on 5–6 December, and in January and March 1794 the Scot William Skirving and two LCS delegates, Margarot and Joseph Gerrald, were sentenced to join Muir and Palmer in Australia.[21]

All this brought the seething political pot to the boil in London, as the metropolitan radicals braced themselves for a similar confrontation with the authorities. On 20 January 1794, the LCS called a massive general meeting at the Globe Tavern in Fleet Street, which attracted so many people that the floor collapsed beneath their weight. Any sign that government or Parliament was about to turn the repressive screws on their own people, the meeting's resolution declared, would be met by the summoning of a 'General Convention of the People'. The LCS then threw down the gauntlet at its first open-air meeting on 14 April, held on the bowling green at Chalk Farm, in North London at the bottom of Primrose Hill, along the Hampstead Road. Deploring the 'late rapid advances of despotism in Britain', the meeting sailed peril-ously close to the revolutionary wind by proclaiming, 'That any attempt to violate those yet remaining Laws, which were intended for the Security of Englishmen against ... Tyranny ... ought to be considered as dissolving entirely the social compact between the English Nation and their Governors; and driving them to an immediate appeal to that incontrovertible maxim of eternal Justice, *that the safety of the People is the SUPREME, and in cases of necessity, the ONLY Law*'.[22]

Everything that was said and done was being reported to the government. The open call for a convention – which of course had strong French revolutionary connotations – and the apparent preparedness of the radicals to resist authority now convinced the ministry that the time had come to strike. The political atmosphere made this a propitious moment for the government to move. With the British entry into the war, it had become increasingly difficult for radicals to voice support for democratic change without sound-ing like the treasonous 'Jacobins' that the government claimed them to be. It did not help that the overheated rhetoric of some radical publicists and the relations between the British reformers and the French revolutionaries had planted enough ambiguity to ensure that conservative alarmist claims would stick. Like Paris, the British capital was now a city at war. As in Paris, the public was reminded daily of the military, political and ideological struggles not only by propaganda, but also by the impact of the war on the fabric of their lives and on their city, and in London the effects were felt in both military and maritime senses.

Naval press gangs roamed the streets around the docklands and the East End in search of recruits. 'Crimps', or agents trading in recruits for the army, set up shop in taverns, which became 'crimping houses'. Here they would sign up desperate men seeking to evade debtors' prison or poverty. Crimps were known to employ the shadiest of methods: they induced sailors between voyages to run up debts in the tavern, which they would then be forced to pay off by a bounty from enlistment. Prostitutes would sidle up to likely recruits and draw them into the tavern, where they would simply be kidnapped. Their presence was so resented by working Londoners that in August 1794, the metropolis would be convulsed by a wave of attacks on notorious crimping houses, riots that the authorities could quell only by putting troops on the streets.[23]

Yet while there was the inevitable mixture of wartime fear, resentment, distress and resistance, the conflict also injected parts of the metropolis with economic energy, particularly the dockyards. Although shipbuilding had shifted away from the old naval dockyards along the Thames – Blackwall, Deptford, Chatham – to Plymouth and Portsmouth, they were still abuzz with activity. The workforce at Deptford Yard, which in peacetime hired nine hundred workers, swelled to twelve hundred, men and boys, as shipwrights, carpenters, sailmakers, riggers, armourers, compass makers, blacksmiths, pitch heaters, caulkers, boys working with oakum and wheelwrights all sawed, boiled, cut, sewed and hammered their way through the war. London's maritime trade was certainly disrupted in the initial crisis of 1793 – and would be in the alarming years of 1797–1798, when the British Isles were threatened with a French invasion – but overall the war saw London's merchant commerce expand as Britain's European rivals were blockaded by the Royal Navy.

At the waterfront on the Thames, this was brought home by the sight of a dense tangle of masts, as an average of eighteen hundred vessels crammed into the 'Upper Pool' of the Thames between London Bridge and Union Hole. These were, it is true, smaller coasting vessels, but that they jostled with each other for mooring space intended for five hundred craft shows how far London's trading activity was booming. Larger vessels moored farther down the river, at the Middle Pool and Lower Pools (Union Hole down to Wapping), while the massive five-hundred-tonne merchantmen would anchor, high-sterned, at places like Greenwich, Blackwall and Deptford, where the jam of shipping was made all the thicker by the barges and lighters that received their cargo, hoisted over the side and lowered into their bottoms.

This jostling life on the river affected the wharves in the City itself, because all the goods off-loaded on the Thames had to be cleared at the legal quays on the north bank of the river between London Bridge and the Tower, after which they would be held in warehouses in streets behind the wharves. The congestion became so bad in the 1790s that Parliament finally acted, and a major expansion of London's docklands began, with work beginning on the West India Docks in 1797 (on the Isle of Dogs, completed in 1802), followed by the London Docks at Wapping, the East India Docks at Blackwall and the Surrey Docks at Rotherhithe opening between 1805 and 1807. It is small wonder, then, that the City, in Wilkes's day so fiercely defensive of its freedoms, became one of the strongholds of loyalism against both radicalism and the French: the very expansion of the metropolis, both physically and commercially, was now bound intimately to the struggle against revolution.[24]

In addition to economic interests, the government and their loyalist supporters were very successful in convincing – or compelling – working men to demonstrate their patriotism and fidelity to the existing order by joining regiments of 'volunteers'; 154 such corps were raised across the country by the end of 1794. The first such unit in London were the 'Loyal London Volunteers' in April 1794, but while this may have been something of a damp squib, other City of London units followed, in the wards of Bishopsgate and Farringdon Within. Resplendent in their red coats, the volunteers were in themselves a propaganda device, a glittering display of British determination to resist revolution – at least in its French shape, if not its domestic radical one. Most volunteers were probably driven more by a patriotic desire to defend the country against foreign invasion than by an urge to suppress the parliamentary reform movement within. Volunteer parade days were occasions for patriotic speeches, and the young George Cruikshank, the cartoonist, was deeply impressed when he saw the London and Westminster Light Horse Volunteers on exercise at Finchley Common: 'A finer regiment of cavalry I never saw, nor have I ever seen regulars more perfect in the evolutions'. The volunteers were intended primarily to defend Britain against the French: while rarely *explicitly* opposed to political reform, they nonetheless also represented a broad consensus of opinion in support of the existing constitutional and social order. The City of London's 'model plan' for these units was for them 'to contribute to the due execution of the Laws, maintenance of Civil Order and Government' and 'the immediate Suppression of all Riots and Tumults'. (In 1797, when the Royal Navy was convulsed by mutinies, including the North Sea Fleet at the Nore, close enough to London to pose a threat, the Common Council called on all wards in the City to raise more volunteers against subversion and disorder.) In a bitter irony, both the membership and the organisation of the corps

were similar to those of the LCS: membership of the volunteers
in urban areas boasted a large proportion of artisans, and officers
were elected by the rank and file. Such a formal mobilisation of
the people was backed up by a myriad of unofficial ways in which
Britons swung behind the war effort and the campaign against
radicalism: through the intimidation, boycott and ostracism of
reformers; through the production and distribution of propaganda;
through effigy burning; and through supporting the association
movement. In all these ways, the loyalist backlash penetrated local
communities up and down the country.[25]

As THE GOVERNMENT was rallying the British public in the war
against revolutionary France, it also moved against the metropolitan radicals. At 6.30 in the morning of 12 May 1794, a king's
messenger, escorted by four runners, marched up Haymarket
and then turned onto Piccadilly. They stopped in front of No.
9, the house and shop of the master shoemaker Thomas Hardy,
and hammered on the front door. Gaining access, they arrested
Hardy on a charge of treason. Having taken hold of the radical
leader, they marched (it was later alleged) into the bedroom where
Hardy's wife, heavily pregnant and still in her nightdress, protested
loudly and asked that they at least have the decency to withdraw
while she dressed, a demand that was refused. While one runner
paced the room with pistol in hand, Mrs. Hardy threw on her
clothes and then remonstrated with the intruders when they went
so far as to search the still warm, unmade bed. Elsewhere in the
house, the lodgers were confined to their rooms, while Hardy was
marched off to the Tower of London – the gaol for political prisoners – and while the runners rifled through drawers, wardrobes
and cupboards looking for papers. They found plenty, for Hardy
threw nothing away.[26]

Elsewhere in the metropolis, Hardy's counterpart in the Society for Constitutional Information, Daniel Adams, was woken up, arrested and led away, along with two trunks of papers found in his bedroom. The next day, messengers swooped on the home of John Thelwall, who owed his arrest primarily to his fiery political lectures and pamphlets on behalf of reform. While his attic study was searched, he was bundled into a carriage to be interrogated before the Privy Council, along with a disordered mass of confiscated papers, which shifted around the interior of the coach as it jolted and twisted its way to Whitehall.

One by one, the messengers found their quarry, thirteen in all, seven from the LCS and six from the SCI, including John Horne Tooke, Thelwall's patron and once the argumentative ally of John Wilkes, and Thomas Holcroft, the dramatist who had seen Newgate incinerated during the Gordon Riots. The prisoners were locked away in the Tower (Hardy in a small cell above the West Gate), leaving only to take their exercise along the ramparts or be interrogated at Whitehall, closely watched in their prison by soldiers with fixed bayonets, stewing in the knowledge that soon they would be on trial for their lives. Tooke, who liked to compare his incarceration with being in the Bastille, spent the time writing a prison diary and watching from his cell window the life of the metropolis unfold in the summer heat: passengers on boats on the Thames waving to each other and a man just beyond the Tower moat selling peanuts from a donkey cart. Hardy was allowed to see his wife twice a week. The prisoners would have a few months to wait in this agonising limbo, for on the day of Hardy's arrest, Prime Minister William Pitt asked for and secured from the House of Commons a 'Committee of Secrecy' tasked with investigating the charges that the radicals were seeking to create a French-style National Convention to subvert the British constitution and to unleash revolutionary bloodshed.[27]

With Pitt and some of his key ministerial allies on the Committee of Secrecy, and helped by the interrogations and evidence put together by the Privy Council, the committee was manoeuvred to the conclusion that a conspiracy was indeed afoot to destroy Parliament and to foment violent resistance to its measures. Five days after Hardy's arrest, Parliament suspended habeas corpus. Two days later, proof of a conspiracy came from Edinburgh, where a search of the cellars of a bankrupt wine merchant named Robert Watt uncovered a cache of pike heads. Watt confessed to being part of a radical organisation aiming to seize Edinburgh Castle and leading members of the Scottish judiciary, in order to force the king to dismiss Pitt and end the war against France. Watt and an accomplice were eventually executed for treason, and during the investigations it was discovered that the conspirators had circulated Thomas Hardy's pamphlet calling for another British Convention. For Hardy, the incarceration was especially wrenching, for after Admiral Lord Howe's naval victory over the French (the battle is remembered as the 'Glorious 1 June'), a loyalist mob celebrating the news churned around Hardy's home in Piccadilly. Although the windows of the house had been patriotically illuminated, they were smashed, and the mob howled for the blood of its occupants, beating on the door. As Hardy's pregnant wife tried to escape, she was so badly hurt that, when her baby finally arrived in August, it was still-born. She herself then passed away on 27 August, leaving her final letter to 'My Dear Hardy' unfinished.[28]

After a long, tortuous debate within the government over the findings of the Committee of Secrecy, the attorney general, Sir John Scott, decided to press charges of high treason (rather than the lesser offence of Sedition), the penalty for which was death. On 6 October, a grand jury indicted twelve of the prisoners. This, wrote William Godwin, the radical intellectual and future husband of Mary Wollstonecraft, 'is the most important crisis in the history of English liberty', for if people could be indicted on such flimsy grounds, then Britons 'certainly have reason to envy the milder tyrannies of Turkey and Ispahan [that is, Persia]'. By 24 October, nine of the prisoners had been transferred to Newgate prison – repaired from the devastation of the Gordon Riots – before being arraigned next door in the Sessions House of the Old Bailey, the central court for London and Middlesex. There, the opposing counsels, Sir John Scott prosecuting for the Crown and the great Scottish advocate Thomas Erskine defending, confronted each other across a vast polished mahogany table beneath the attentive eyes of the judge, Lord Chief Justice Sir James Eyre. Crowded into seats in a gallery behind and above the jurors were members of the public, including journalists, who, as was the custom, had paid for the privilege of watching one of the trials of the century. The court listened as Hardy and the others each entered a plea of not guilty.[29]

The first to be tried was Thomas Hardy. The prosecution's opening argument, delivered by Sir John Scott on Monday 27 October, ran to one hundred thousand words and took nine hours (Scott's original notes are indeed weighty: they are in the National Archives at Kew, stitched together down the spine), defining the charge of treason at length and then presenting all the evidence the prosecution could muster. As Scott spoke, court officials raised long tapers to light the candles in the four brass chandeliers that hung from the ceiling. The trial began as it continued: punishingly. Scott did not finish until midnight, when the court adjourned. The jury had an uncomfortable night trying to sleep on mattresses in the Old Bailey, ready for the questioning of the prosecution's witnesses at eight the following morning.

The exhausted jurors heard the next day's cross-examination, which also went on late into the evening, provoking one of the jurors to plead with the lord chief justice that 'we have been forty hours without taking off our cloaths, we want rest, it is necessary to the preservation of our health, even to enable us to go on with the trial'. The court agreed to accommodate the jurors in the Turkish baths at Covent Garden (an apt choice since they were doubtless desperate for a deep cleanse). Thenceforth, they were carried there and back each day in three coaches through the heaving city, escorted by the court officers and sheriffs. Each night, Hardy was led the short distance from the court back to Newgate, nonchalantly calling out to his fellow radicals as he passed by their cells, 'Farewell, citizens, Death or Liberty!' Meanwhile, Erskine spent the early hours each morning examining the evidence brought by the Crown. And so it continued over the coming week, with Erskine grasping only a few short hours of sleep while, in the daytime, he brutally cross-examined Scott's witnesses and doggedly sought to demolish their credibility. Tempers frayed with exhaustion and nerves: initially polite, the exchanges between Erskine and Scott became vitriolic. The attorney general finished making the Crown's case on Saturday afternoon, 1 November.[30]

The court rose for an hour before returning for Erskine's opening for the defence. He spoke for six hours, and he was brilliant. He started by wholeheartedly endorsing Sir John Scott's praise of the excellence of the British constitution and in sharing his condemnation of the Terror in France, which was the very opposite of the rule of law. Erskine then took apart the prosecution's case: the Crown had no evidence that any of Hardy's actions were treasonous, because there was no suggestion of intent to overthrow the existing government and put the king to death. Even the distribution of arms could be attributed to the need for protection against loyalist 'church and king' mobs. Hardy was not a rabid republican, Erskine argued. Throughout, he had argued only for a democratic reform of the lower chamber in Parliament, leaving the lords and monarchy untouched. His aims differed little in substance and means from the radical programme first proposed back in 1780.[31]

When Erskine finished, he was exhausted. 'Gentlemen', he gasped, 'I have already addressed you beyond my strength'. The spectators in the courtroom saluted him with thunderous applause, which spread out into the courtyard and the streets outside, into which a crowd had crammed to follow the trial's progress. When the proceedings were suspended at midnight, the judge and prosecutors were hissed and booed by the onlookers; only the intervention of the shattered Erskine prevented the situation from getting any uglier. He, in turn, was borne into his coach by the admiring crowd and wheeled to his lodgings at Serjeant's Inn.[32]

The trial continued for another two and a half days, with the press of the crowds outside the Old Bailey becoming so great that the lord mayor called out extra constables to keep the way in and out clear. On 4 November, he summoned the Honourable Artillery Company to cordon the courthouse off. On 5 November, the judge, who had conducted the trial with a remarkably even hand, gave a balanced summing up. After deliberating for three hours, the jury returned to the courtroom at half past three. The foreman stood and delivered the verdict: NOT GUILTY. (In some accounts, he then fainted.) Hardy, exhausted but relieved, turned to the jury and said simply, 'My fellow countrymen, I return you my thanks'.[33]

In the gathering gloom of the November evening, lit by the street lanterns and carriage lamps, Hardy left the Old Bailey and was drawn along in a coach by a jubilant crowd all the way down Fleet Street, through Temple Bar, along the Strand, through Saint James's to his sad, darkened home at 9 Piccadilly. There everyone stood in respectful silence while Hardy was allowed to nurse his sorrow for a few minutes before the coach was wheeled to Lancaster Court, his brother-in-law's home, where he recuperated.

Erskine, the last to emerge from the Old Bailey, was treated to a similar triumphant ride home.[34]

With Hardy's acquittal, the government's strategy of prosecuting the radical movement through the courts began to unravel. The trial of Horne Tooke followed between 17 and 22 November, in which the indefatigable Erskine again conducted the defence and went so far as to put a seething Prime Minister William Pitt on the stand. This time the government handpicked the jury to try to ensure a conviction, so that when Erskine saw it being sworn in, he is said to have turned to his client and gasped, 'By God, they are murdering you'. Yet so lucid was Horne Tooke's own testimony that the jury needed a mere eight minutes to deliberate before acquitting him. When Thelwall's turn came between 1 and 5 December, he appears to have wanted a share of the glory, but Erskine would have none of it. When Thelwall scribbled a begging note – 'I'll be hanged if I don't plead my own cause', Erskine's reply was blunt: 'You'll be hanged if you do'. This trial, too, ended in an acquittal. Ten days later, the government decided to bring no further prosecutions. The remaining prisoners were released.[35]

THE TREASON TRIALS of 1794 are the stuff of courtroom drama. The government had hoped to use prosecutions for treason as a means of intimidating the rank-and-file radicals into silence. Had the trials gone the other way, veteran metropolitan campaigner Major John Cartwright told his wife, 'a system of proscription and terror like that of Robespierre . . . would have been completed and written in innocent blood'. Yet in the entire decade, there were fewer than two hundred prosecutions for treason and sedition up and down the country, and many of them were fairly ad hoc affairs pursued by the local courts for casual abuse of the establishment, often made when the accused had overindulged in ale or spirits.[36]

Yet in many ways, the government was already winning in its fight against the democratic movement. Trials like that of Thomas Hardy were just one part of a much wider strategy to stifle the life out of the radical movement, a strategy that included asserting the control by loyalists of the places where British radicals met. This process was aided by the fact that people across the country, in towns and villages, were drummed into Reeves's association, which in London then took over the taverns and pubs that had provided the assembly rooms for the LCS. In this, the association was backed by the law – by magistrates who threatened publicans with the loss of their licences should they accommodate radical meetings. This was perhaps one reason the London Corresponding Society began to hold great outdoor meetings on open ground, which succeeded in drawing enormous crowds: one held on Saint George's Fields in late June 1795 and another at Copenhagen House on 26 October may each have drawn as many as one hundred thousand people, listening to speeches declaiming on reform and against the war. When, three days later, an angry crowd – driven by hunger in a period of deep economic distress – stoned the king's coach in Palace Yard at Westminster, the government seized on the violence to push the Two Acts through Parliament, which expanded the definition of treason and ruled that any meeting of more than fifty people could be banned at the magistrates' discretion and prior notice of any such meeting had to be advertised in the press. These measures failed to stop the LCS, because its divisional structure allowed its separate groups to sail under the fifty-person bar. It also held its largest-ever political meeting in protest at Copenhagen House on 12 November.[37]

Yet vast public rallies on open fields were a very different beast from closed members-only gatherings in the upper rooms of taverns. Many of the thousands of people who thronged the enormous LCS demonstrations did not necessarily subscribe to its programme of reform, but were there to express their anger at government repression, the dire state of the economy and the war: these months in Britain, as elsewhere in Europe, were a time of desperate food shortages and spiralling prices. In 1795 the LCS was able to harness the social distress of thousands of working Londoners and draw them to their great meetings on Saint George's Fields and at Copenhagen House, but it did not offer the scope for political debate, for artisans to hone their ideas and join in participatory democratic forms of politics or to make new, close political associations and friendships with like-minded people on a weekly basis. The expansion of tactics from tavern meetings to great public rallies, therefore, could not win permanent dedicated members to the cause of reform. Thereafter, the numbers of the LCS dwindled, and it slowly crumpled under the impact of government repression, propaganda and the waves of wartime popular patriotism, all of which chased away the lukewarm, intimidated the moderate and exhausted the devoted. By 1799, when the government finally banned the LCS by name, it was an easy target because its membership had withered to two hundred.

The old order in Britain held on partly because, as we have noted, the popular British radical movement itself was, by and large, committed to legality. This meant that its activities and organisation relied on the habitual spaces of artisanal sociability in cities like London. Because such sites, like the taverns, were subject to the supervision (through the licensing laws) of the magistrates, these places could be easily contested by both the authorities and their loyalist supporters among the people. This was perhaps one of the greatest contrasts with the Parisian experience, where the *sans-culotte* movement had, at its highest mark, taken over perhaps three-quarters of the Parisian sections and with it the apparatus of neighbourhood power, entrenching the local leadership of the popular radical movement in buildings that were dedicated to the purposes of political mobilisation. In Britain, by contrast, loyalists harnessed what was mainly a spontaneous tide of popular conservatism – with its associations, its volunteers, its violence (or threats of violence), intimidation, boycotts and sheer weight of numbers – and in London this became a battle waged in the streets, taverns, coffeehouses and printing shops across the metropolis. This meant that while one of the great achievements of the London Corresponding Society was its creation of an organisation that could reach across the metropolis, overcoming through its divisional structure the problems of the vastness of the urban sprawl, it struggled to keep its footing in the city's scattered neighbourhoods and to recruit the vast ranks of members to which it aspired.

In this context, dramatic though the treason trials were, the victories in securing acquittals for the radicals were simply not enough to stem the stronger tide of popular conservatism that cascaded through the city. Even more significant, perhaps, is that though the radicals might have felt vindicated by the acquittals, outside the courtroom it was the prosecution that had won. Whereas the government's case that the radicals were subversives could not stand up to scrutiny in a court of law, the wider public had deeply imbibed this toxic argument. When it did, it turned its hostility against those very people who claimed to be campaigning on their behalf, and it hounded them out of the public spaces on which they depended. Under the impact of the French Revolution and the war, the radical tide that had first stirred with John Wilkes in the 1760s was stemmed: radical London became loyal London.

CHAPTER TWELVE

NEW YORK CONFRONTS THE FRENCH REVOLUTION, 1789–1795

THE STRUGGLE FOR democracy in London and Paris in the 1790s ended in sharply contrasting results, but New York's experience was different from both. There the ideological and political dilemmas posed by the French Revolution and the ensuing war seeped into a political battle for the future of the young Republic. This was often played out in sites connected with the earlier struggles of the American Revolution, which took on a rejuvenated, emotive meaning. So tumultuous and partisan though the political arguments were, they were, usually, embedded in ritual rather than actual violence, as the protagonists mobilised around the old revolutionary sites of the city, trying to legitimise their own political aspirations by connecting them with the sites of New York's historic struggle in the American Revolution. Yet at the same time, since American republican politics encouraged public debate and the development of civic organisations, and since New York was emerging as one of the Republic's great mercantile and financial centres, so new places emerged out of the fabric of the city to become fresh scenes of political contention.

These developments occurred despite the fact that, in 1790, New York ceased to be the capital of the United States. This arose from a dinner party on 20 June 1790 at the residence of Thomas Jefferson, then secretary of state, at No. 57 Maiden Lane, when the two opposing sides in the politics of the young Republic were brought together. The two antagonistic groups, the Federalists and the Democratic-Republicans, grew out of the conflicts over the post-revolutionary order. The Federalists believed in the necessity of strong, centralised government, which would use its power vigorously to drive the country's commerce, manufacturing and finance as the motor of American power. That power should be concentrated in the hands of the elites as a guarantee of political and social stability. Almost all of this rankled with their Democratic-Republican opponents, led by Thomas Jefferson, who argued that a powerful central government and the concentration of economic wealth would directly threaten the liberties of the citizen. An industrial economy would create a class of rootless workers teeming in the country's cities, where they would fall prey to vice and ignorance: a people without civic virtue was no basis for a democratic republic. The wealth of the United States, Jefferson argued, should rest on its agricultural exports, a prosperity best founded on a rural democracy of independent farmers, alongside some small-scale manufacturing, all driven by the free commerce needed to trade the nation's surpluses. Since they feared the consequences of an overbearing central government, the Democratic-Republicans explicitly placed greater trust than the Federalists in the people and emphasised the power of local and state government as against that of the central government.[1]

These divisions threatened to come to a head and to tear the country apart just as it was finding its feet. Among the many problems at issue in 1790 was, on the one hand, the technical yet vital question of the assumption by the federal government of the states' debts left over from the struggle for independence from Britain. On the other hand, there was the matter of where the permanent capital of the United States should be sited. Jefferson organised his dinner party on 20 June with the aim of bringing the two sides together: the Federalists represented by New Yorker, dapper lawyer and financial expert Alexander Hamilton and the Democratic-Republicans by Jefferson himself and his fellow Virginian James Madison. For Hamilton, the assumption of state debts by a strong federal government would harness the states to his vision for a system of national banking and finance. Meanwhile, Jefferson envisaged the new capital rising somewhere in, or close to, his home state, and far away from the urban, moneyed interests of the North. The dinner at Maiden Lane gave both sides what they wanted. Hamilton walked away with a promise of support for the assumption of states' debts by the federal government; Jefferson retired with an assurance that Hamilton would rally his supporters in Congress to ensure that the new capital, the 'Federal City', would rise somewhere on the banks of the Potomac River. This became Washington, the District of Columbia. Philadelphia would be the interim capital of the United States for ten years while the new city was rising from the river's marshy banks.

The story of a compromise over dinner, historians warn, may be a myth conjured up by Jefferson: neither Hamilton nor Madison left a record of the evening. However it was really constructed, the deal was debated and voted through Congress, which disbanded in New York City on 12 August 1790, leaving its fine accommodation in Federal Hall on Wall Street. At the end of the month, President George Washington embarked on a barge on the Hudson and left, never to return. As politicians and their families prepared to leave Manhattan, they did so with some sadness. Abigail Adams, looking ahead to her sojourn in Philadelphia with her husband (and the vice president), John, sighed, 'And, when all is done, it will not be Broadway'.[2]

NEW YORK WAS no longer the capital, but it was no less affected by the impact of the French Revolution, which added new spirits to the already fiery brew of American political debate. Most Americans had at first welcomed the news from France in 1789. Senator William Maclay, sitting in Congress in New York, had recorded his reaction on 18 September: 'By this and yesterday's papers France seems travailing in the birth of freedom. Her throes and pangs of labor are violent. God give her a happy delivery! Royalty, nobility, and vile pageantry, by which a few of the human race lord it over and tread on the necks of their fellow-mortals, seem likely to be demolished with their kindred Bastile, which is said to be laid in ashes'.[3]

Maclay, a Democratic-Republican from Pennsylvania, naturally found much to celebrate. Federalists gave the French Revolution a more cautious welcome. Hamilton wrote to Lafayette from New York on 6 October: 'I have seen with a mixture of Pleasure and apprehension the Progress of the events which have lately taken Place in your Country. As a friend to mankind and to liberty I rejoice in the efforts which you are making to establish it while I fear much for the final success of the attempts, for the fate of those I esteem who are engaged in it, and for the danger in case of success of innovations greater than will consist with the real felicity of your Nation'.[4]

By erupting in 1789, the very moment that the United States was embarking on its own experiment in constitutional government, the French Revolution would provide affirmation, inspiration and warnings to Americans about the course that they were themselves taking. The fire of the French Revolution, it seemed, had been sparked by the American Revolution. In its celebration of Evacuation Day in 1791, New York's Tammany Society – of which we shall hear more – raised its glasses to 'those heroes of France whose patriotic virtues have caused the Columbian flame to consume the Gallic yoke of despotism'. When Lafayette sent Washington the key to the Bastille, he paid homage 'as a Missionary of Liberty to its Patriarch'. And these connections were made in symbolic ways that, as we shall see, were often played out in the city's own historic sites of revolution.[5]

Yet as in Britain, the stakes were high, and they stacked higher as the Revolution in France took its increasingly radical turn, crystallising the already vitriolic partisanship in American politics. 'Ye gods', exclaimed Maclay in his diary as early as September 1789, 'with what indignation do I review the late attempt of some creatures among us to revive the vile machinery [being abolished in France]', a reference to the Democratic-Republican suspicion that the Federalists still nurtured monarchist and aristocratic aspirations. As the French Revolution passed from constitutional monarchy to republic, executing Louis XVI and then going to war with America's old enemy, Britain, these divisions within American politics became sharper. They became more abrasive not least because the Federalists were Anglophile, openly nurturing an admiration for the checks and balances of the British constitution (hence the suspicions of Democratic-Republicans like Maclay). Commercially minded, the Federalists were conscious of American dependence on trade with Britain. Democratic-Republicans were ideologically more in tune with the French Republic, with its political egalitarianism, its anti-monarchism and its disdain for privilege and hierarchies. In the cities, radical American artisans and mechanics could watch from a distance the progress of the popular movement in Paris, drawing lessons from the *sans-culottes*.[6]

New York was a special political battleground because of its complex political geography. As a commercial city whose mercantile elites, artisans, craft workers and mariners had an interest in a vibrant international trade – and American shipping took full advantage of the opportunities that a neutral flag could offer in wartime – it might be seduced by federalism, neutrality and even a closer relationship with the British. Yet it was also a city where many of the same people, particularly the artisans, sailors and dockworkers, had already shown a readiness to oppose the elites. In the 1790s, New York's artisans were struggling to maintain their economic independence from merchants who were beginning to take control of the manufacturing of the goods that they sold. This economic pressure, together with memories of the revolutionary struggle against the British and a latent hostility towards privilege and hierarchy, made many of New York's artisans and labourers receptive to the Democratic-Republicans. These tendencies were given real adrenaline by the fact that New York, pivotal maritime point of entry that it was, was infused with immigrants from Europe. They were fleeing the same conservative hierarchies in the Old World that Democratic-Republicans suspected the Federalists of wanting to re-impose in the New. With so much at stake, both groups worked hard to galvanise their supporters, to mobilise them and to prevail over – even cow – their political opponents. The great controversies over the French Revolution helped both sides anchor their own political positions for the benefit of a storm-tossed public.[7]

AT THE SAME time, New York had a small but significant group of African Americans. With the enslaved living alongside a population of free men and women, they, no less than their fellow citizens of European origin, made full use of the emergent republican political culture to carve out their place in the public spaces of the city and to press their own claims to emancipation and equal citizenship. Moreover, the impact of the French Revolution may have divided New Yorkers along partisan lines, but ultimately it seems to have helped the city's Democratic-Republicans and Federalists finally agree on the abolition of slavery. With the strong leadership that some Federalists like John Jay and Alexander Hamilton gave to the Manumission Society, there was every chance that a fully emancipated African American vote would swing behind them in elections. Democratic-Republicans sidestepped the awkward question of their slaveholding fellow travellers in the South, while publishing blistering attacks on the institution itself in the press. In this they were encouraged by the radical egalitarian language of the French Revolution. Popular enthusiasm for the brave new dawn in France carried people in New York to demand emancipation of all Americans. In 1789, at the John Street Theatre, one play ended with a call for 'Afric's sable Sons' to be freed, to roars of audience approval.[8]

Yet New York's African Americans played a central part in their own emancipation. The existence of a small but growing population of free African Americans, which expanded in the 1790s along with New York City's population as a whole, from eleven hundred to thirty-five hundred, was perhaps the single most important factor in the demise of slavery there. With this expansion of the free population, the proportion of enslaved African Americans declined from six to four in every ten. Their very presence demonstrated to whites that racial origin was no marker of ability to contribute to the life of the city, or of the Republic. Moreover, the free African Americans developed their own institutions, building their own niches in the fabric of the city, and so engaging in the social life that republican political culture encouraged.[9]

The economic and social history of the free African American

population was, it is true, often one of grinding poverty. Free
from slavery, they were cut loose in the competitive currents of
the labour market. Many were forced to work in low-paid tasks
often eschewed by whites, like oystermen and chimney sweeps.
Many of the African American men and women who formed
part of New York's labouring poor had no choice but to live in
the city's lowest-rent accommodation: leaking garrets, outhouses
and damp cellars, places little different from the lodgings of
slaves. Yet African Americans also prospered as shopkeepers,
tobacconists, butchers, barbers, bakers, carpenters, coopers,
cabinetmakers, upholsterers, tanners, carpenters and cobblers.
While many worked for white employers, some set up their own
businesses, sometimes in partnership with other free blacks. The
range of skills on display was truly staggering, with those recently
manumitted employing the skills that they had been forced to use
in slavery. Many more men still sought to escape the constraints
of prejudice and hard economics by going to sea as mariners.
African American women had fewer options, but they worked
as seamstresses, bakers, washerwomen and domestic servants,
often, by a bitter irony, continuing the same menial service that
they had been compelled to do while enslaved. Like the male
oystermen and sweeps, African American women were a common
sight on New York's streets, only this time as sellers of fruits and
vegetables.[10]

Embedded as they were in the social and economic life of post-
revolutionary New York, free blacks also found ways of claiming
greater enjoyment of republican citizenship, seizing the opportunities that urban life offered to create the nucleus of a community
of their own, and in doing so, they made good use of the fabric
and sociability of the city to forge both educational and religious
establishments. The Free African School, originally founded by the
Manumission Society, prospered in the 1790s (and would stride

forward under the dynamic leadership of John Teasman, a former slave from New Jersey who became the principal in 1799).

New York's African Americans also defended their spiritual independence. In 1794 a group of African American Anglicans who worshipped in Trinity Church on Broadway (although separately from whites in designated 'Negro Pews') learned that the African Burial Ground close to the Collect Pond was going to be built upon. They petitioned the Common Council for a new cemetery. The city responded by setting aside four lots on Chrystie Street for this purpose, and the new site was developed with both city funds and money raised by Trinity. In 1796 New York's African American Methodists would build their own church under the leadership of Sexton Peter Williams, who had been born a slave in a cowshed on Beekman Street. As the African Methodist Episcopal Zion Church, the congregation would rent rooms in a cabinetmaker's workshop on Cross Street (between Orange, now Baxter, and Mulberry Streets), which they fitted up for their services, until (within five years) a new building, 'Mother Zion', rose from the corner of Leonard and Church Streets, a bricks-and-mortar expression of African American initiative that won plaudits from the patricians of the New York Manumission Society.[11]

The establishment of African American institutions shaped another development – the gradual emergence of more distinctly African American neighbourhoods. This was driven primarily by economics: with the rapid expansion of the city and developments in manufacturing, more and more workers, black and white, began to live in rented accommodation of their own, away from their places of work. Because of this spatial separation of work and home, specific neighbourhoods came to be dominated by particular social and ethnic groups. African Americans went to the areas where rents were low, especially the cheap marshy land around the Collect (or Freshwater) Pond, a district malodorous from the nearby tanneries. Yet the location was also strategically close to the Zion church on Cross Street, just a little to the southeast of the Pond. A small African American community built up in this area, called the Five Points (although by the 1830s it would become notorious as an immigrant slum). Both were also not too far from the old African Burial Ground close to the Pond.[12]

The existence of a large, articulate and socially engaged free black community had a profound impact on slavery in New York. The urban environment, and the topography of African American life in New York City, meant that inevitably, free and enslaved blacks encountered one another every day, although it is hard to say how far these daily meetings encouraged slave resistance. Many free blacks certainly aided runaway slaves in their escapes. Whether they were exploiting the opportunities that may have opened up or grinding out an existence on the margins, the services and productivity of free African American New Yorkers made them an essential part of the complex tissue of urban life. And if whites noticed, so too must those who were still bridling at their enslavement.[13]

The role of the free African Americans was pivotal in undermining slavery, but there were other factors. First, there was an economic shift, a shower of pebbles rather than an avalanche: slave-owning artisans were beginning to find that it was cheaper to pay a wage to free labourers. Waged labourers did not, after all, have to be fed, clothed and housed and, since they were also working for pay, were likely to be more productive. Moreover, by 1799 the proportion of artisanal households holding slaves had plummeted to one in seventeen, meaning that enslaved African Americans would account for fewer than 5 per cent of the city's population. Fears that a sudden surge of emancipated labour would undercut the wages of white craftsmen were correspondingly diminished.

Second, there were the global repercussions of the French Revolution, which shook the racial hierarchies in the slaveholding American world, and with that came the revolution in the French colony of Saint-Domingue, or Haiti. Breaking out in August 1791, the Haitian Revolution was the only successful slave uprising in modern history, forcing the French National Convention to proclaim the abolition of slavery on 4 February 1794. Many whites and *gens de couleur* (people of colour, the term applied to free people of mixed race) fled the burning plantations for the United States, some ten thousand by 1793. Among them were many slaves dragged by their owners across the sea, some disembarking in New York. Unsurprisingly, the experience of the revolution in Haiti combined with the strong African heritage – religious, linguistic, ideological – of the West Indian slaves injected a new restiveness in New York's own population of enslaved people. In 1792, for example, an African named Zamor, originally from Guinea, had been brought by a French planter from Port-au-Prince. At the first opportunity, Zamor slipped away, melting away into the city streets, his now former owner complaining that he was 'supposed to be lurking about this city among the French negroes' (the term used for the new immigrants from Haiti). The militancy brought by the Haitians may have translated into action against slaveholders. On 9 December 1796, a fire engulfed the warehouses on Murray's Wharf, at the bottom of Wall Street, before consuming the block along Front Street to the Fly Market. There were alarming reports of Haitian incendiarism, of West Indians wrapping burning coals in oil paper and hurling them into the cellars of New Yorkers' homes. Some slaveholders began to ponder whether slavery itself was worth the risk of provoking resistance, the price of recapturing an absconder or merely the daily cost of the upkeep. New York State voted for the gradual emancipation of slaves in 1799.[14]

THE REPERCUSSIONS OF the French Revolution helped to concentrate New Yorkers' minds on the issue of slavery. Over other questions, however, it divided New Yorkers bitterly, particularly over where the United States should stand in the European war. The question of neutrality tormented American politics. Both the Democratic-Republicans and the Federalists agreed with it in principle, but everyone knew that strict neutrality, in which the United States treated both sides evenly, was impossible. The question was whether Americans should be more favourable in their trade and diplomacy to the British or the French. While Jefferson called for a 'fair neutrality', meaning one in which the United States still honoured its 1778 alliance with France, the Federalists feared that the Francophile Democratic-Republicans aimed to drag the United States into a ruinous war against Britain. After the fall of the French monarchy in August 1792, Federalists began to be truly horrified by the events in France: Hamilton wrote to his old friend Lafayette that the prison massacres in Paris in September 1792 had 'cured me of my goodwill for the French Revolution'. Federalists were beginning to slip into the habit of equating the Jacobins with the Democratic-Republicans, whose artisanal supporters in Boston, Philadelphia and New York were painted as the *sans-culottes*.[15]

It was at this highly charged moment, in April 1793, that the French Republic's first official envoy to the United States, a young diplomat named Edmond Genet, stepped off the mighty French warship *Embuscade* at Charleston, South Carolina. Genet had just turned thirty when he was appointed French ambassador (the republican term was 'minister') to the United States in January 1793. As war loomed with Britain, the then Girondin government knew that the conflict would become global and that France needed allies to face the maritime might of its oldest adversary.

Genet's instructions were written by the Girondin journalist and deputy to the National Convention Jacques-Pierre Brissot, who used his knowledge of the United States and Americans amassed during a trip in 1788. Genet's would be no ordinary diplomatic mission. He was to rouse American public opinion and to forge 'a national pact in which the two peoples would amalgamate their commercial and political interests' and 'promote the extension of the Empire of Liberty'. Genet was to remind the Americans that such an engagement would be 'no more than the just price for the independence which the French Nation won for them'. He also bore secret instructions to arm privateers in American ports and to tow their maritime prizes into US harbours – as the original alliance of 1778 had allowed. This was, of course, to strike at British-American trade, which weighed heavily in Federalist calculations. Genet fulfilled his mission with gusto from the moment he arrived in America. As French privateers then sallied forth from Charleston, President Washington was so alarmed that he issued a formal proclamation of neutrality in April 1793.[16]

The Genet mission proved to be especially sensational in New York. As Genet made his progress up the Eastern Seaboard overland, he was preceded by the man-of-war *Embuscade*, which slid into New York Bay on 10 June and moored alongside Peck Slip. It was a magnificent sight, efflorescent with red, white and blue. Its figurehead wore a red liberty bonnet, its quarter galleries were embellished with gold anchors capped with the Phrygian bonnet and from its foremast fluttered a banner with the warning 'Enemies of Equality, reform or tremble'. The pennant from the mainmast proclaimed, 'Freemen, behold, we are your friends and brethren', and the one on the mizzenmast declared, 'We are armed to defend the rights of man'. At *Embuscade*'s stern, flowing confidently in the breeze, was a massive tricolour: it was the very embodiment of awe-inspiring firepower and combative republicanism.[17]

Among those New Yorkers who could scarcely contain their enthusiasm were the members of a new political and cultural organisation, the Tammany Society, which led the festivities welcoming *Embuscade* and its crew. The Tammany Society of New York, also known as the Columbian Order, had been established in 1787, meeting initially in the Exchange on Broad Street. While these surroundings were redolent of New York's commercial might, they also carried memories of the American Revolution – New York's Convention had assembled there in 1775 – and it was perhaps this that the club members occasionally bore in mind as they discussed politics. Moreover, Tammany was most definitely an organisation that had grown from the civil society of the new American Republic. Its very name reflected the society's aim to be truly 'national' in its identity: 'Saint Tammany' was a distinctively American figure. The name came from Tamamend, the superhuman Native American chief who was said to have created Niagara Falls. The club adopted Native American terms, beginning with its meeting place in the Exchange, which it called the 'Grand Wigwam'.[18]

The organisation and rules of the society also reflected concerns that would later be called 'nativist'. Its constitution, framed by John Pintard, a fourth-generation Huguenot and philanthropist, was published on 10 August 1789. All offices in the society were to be filled only by those who were American born. The officers were (in more Native American terms) the grand sachem and twelve other sachems, each leading one of the 'thirteen tribes, which severally represent a state', and each of which had an honorary post of 'warrior' and 'hunter', the only elevated positions to which 'adopted Americans' – in other words, immigrants – could aspire. The Tammany constitution stated categorically that 'no person shall be eligible to the office of Sachem unless a native of this country'. Moreover, applicants for membership were chosen by vote of all members, and a mere two votes out of every sixteen could veto a candidate. In this way, the Tammany Society sought to limit the influence of immigrants.[19]

This 'national' culture reflected the concerns of Tammany's membership: most were artisans and journeymen alarmed by the influx of economic competition from immigrants, the Irish in particular. Moreover, since these newcomers were Catholic, the old Whiggish fears of 'Popery' re-emerged, sharpened by the fact that, in this Republic secular in law, Catholicism could now be openly practised in New York. The first Catholic chapel – initially a carpenter's workshop on a lot between Barclay and Church Streets – was opened in the summer of 1785; among the congregation was the famous French author of *Letters of an American Farmer,* Hector St John de Crèvecoeur, then acting as French consul-general. Tammany therefore sought to defend what it saw as the American identity of the new Republic against any values that it claimed to be alien to it, 'aristocracy' and 'Popery' among them. Looking back after many years, one of Tammany's founders claimed that the organisation aimed at offsetting those who harboured 'views, deep and dark as the holy Inquisition', a choice of words betraying anti-Catholic anxieties. Its critics were quick to point out that its proto-nativism was distinctly *un-American* in principle: Polish visitor Julian Niemcewicz, watching one of Tammany's Fourth of July parades, remarked of the society that 'it is made up of true and pure Americans. Let it not happen that the rules and feeling of this society should be recognized throughout America'.[20]

Tammany had two purposes, both of which were rooted in the republican culture of the new nation. First, and originally foremost, it aimed at the civic education of the people. Second, it sought to act as a counterweight to the power of the city's elites. In its educational purpose, the society wanted to forge the republican

American identity of citizens, particularly among the city's artisans and journeymen, a goal that pragmatically combined with its role as a mutual society for the benefit of its members. Tammany's educational mission, as Pintard envisaged it, would be achieved by an 'American Museum' that would collect 'everything relating to the natural or political history of America'. The museum never really took off, but more effective was the society's fourteen-foot-high obelisk, painted to look like black marble. Lanterns at its foot cast images of the life of Christopher Columbus, and it was first put on public display in the run-up to New York's first-ever Columbus Day celebration, organised by the Tammany Society on 12 October 1792. In fact, the monument had excited such public interest that, two days beforehand, its creators allowed the public in to see it. Thereafter, it was put on permanent display in the 'American Museum'. Indeed, the Columbus Day parade was one of the most important dates in the Tammany calendar: hundreds of men dressed in buckskin coats, feathers in their hair and faces streaked with war paint, would parade through the city, but they also marched in their 'Native American' costumes on 4 July, Evacuation Day, Washington's Birthday and the anniversary of Tammany's own founding (12 May).[21]

Although the society claimed to be apolitical, educational and benevolent, its second avowed aim was to be 'a political institution founded on a strong republican basis, whose democratic principles will serve in some measure to correct the aristocracy of our city'. This hostility towards 'aristocracy' – meaning ex-Tories and Federalists – meant that the society naturally gravitated towards the Democratic-Republicans, which in turn, later in the decade, actually led it away from its proto-nativism towards recruiting from among the city's immigrants, bedrocks of Democratic-Republican support.[22]

With its artisanal base and its stalwart republicanism, it is hardly

surprising that Tammany's five-hundred-strong membership celebrated the overthrow of the French monarchy in 1792 and toasted,
'May the Union and example of France and America enlighten and
bless Mankind' and 'The Citizen of the World, Thomas Paine'. A
few months later, they paraded in the streets of New York with the
red Phrygian bonnet – by now a distinctively 'Jacobin' symbol –
and raucously celebrated news of the first French victories over
the Austrians and Prussians in the autumn of 1792. Now, with
Embuscade making its spectacular arrival at Peck Slip, Tammany
would have one of its most sensational celebrations yet as its members led the city in welcoming the French crew. In the days that
followed, the Tammany Society, joined by a cross-section of New
Yorkers, exploited the city's public spaces in order to make symbolic connections between the French and American Revolutions.
They did this by celebrating the French Revolution both within
the current existing venues of American republican culture and –
making the ideological affinity between the two revolutions still
more explicit – at the sites that recalled New York's earlier struggle
against Britain. The celebrations began on 10 June 1793, the very
day of *Embuscade*'s arrival, when Tammany Society members led
an enormous crowd of New Yorkers from the Exchange down to
the waterfront, bellowing out the Marseillaise and, on reaching
the wharves, greeting the French crew with tricolour cockades.[23]

Four days later, they went further, by turning the Tontine
Coffee House into a place of political conflict. The Tontine's very
name came from how funds were raised for the construction of
the coffeehouse, a three-storey building on the corner of Wall and
Water Streets. The 'tontine' was a scheme whereby each member
put in a share of the funds, in return for a lifetime annuity.
Opening early in 1793, its investors were the stockbrokers who
had met beneath a buttonwood tree on Wall Street in the previous
year to establish rules of conduct and who were now seeking an

indoor place to trade with each other. Thus, the Tontine Coffee House effectively became the first home of the New York Stock Exchange. A British visitor, the retired clothier Henry Wansey, visiting the city in May 1794, was impressed: 'The Tontine tavern and coffee-house is a handsome large brick building; you ascend six or eight steps under a portico, into a large public room which is the Stock Exchange of New York, where all bargains are made. Here are two books kept, as at Lloyd's, of every ship's arrival and clearing out. This house was built for the accommodation of the merchants, by Tontine shares of two hundred pounds each'.[24] It was, therefore, a building that expressed the thrusting vision of a commercial and financial dynamism – a natural home for the Federalist-leaning, mercantile elites of the city, as another visitor noted: 'The Tontine coffee-house was filled with underwriters, brokers, merchants, traders, and politicians; selling, purchasing, trafficking, or insuring; some reading, others eagerly inquiring the news. The steps and balcony of the coffee-house were crowded with people bidding, or listening to the several auctioneers, who had elevated themselves upon a hogshead of sugar, a puncheon of rum, or a bale of cotton'.[25]

Yet since it also had a large assembly room for meetings, balls and clubs, it also became a place for the contentious politics between Federalists and Democratic-Republicans, between those who were pro-British and those who were pro-French. And it was the Tammany Society that made the first move. On 14 June 1793, as part of the riotous celebrations of the *Embuscade*, one intrepid New Yorker scrambled onto the Tontine's roof and planted a liberty cap there: 'It is a beautiful crimson', noted one eyewitness approvingly, 'adorned with a white torsel, and supported by a staff'. Keeping revolutionary sympathies on the boil, a group of French sailors and American sympathisers then paraded over to the Bowling Green, axes and shovels slung over their shoulders.

Here they connected French republicanism with the historical memory of the American Revolution by prising up the remains of the plinth that had once supported the statue of George III. They smashed up the pieces of masonry, a rerun of the symbolic regicide that had occurred in 1776 and a reminder of the actual regicide in Paris just five months previously.[26]

Embuscade had been in port for a few weeks when, on 28 July, a British frigate, *Boston*, commanded by Captain William Augustus Courtney, hovered nearby off Sandy Hook. Courtney hailed an American customs vessel and handed the captain a note, addressed to the commander of *Embuscade*: 'Tell Captain Bompard that I have come all the way from Halifax, on purpose to take the *Embuscade*, and I shall be very happy to see her out this way'. The French captain replied, 'Citizen Bompard will wait on Captain Courtney tomorrow, agreeably to invitation; he hopes to find him at the Hook'. New Yorkers waited with bated breath for the battle: no fewer than nine vessels were privately chartered to allow eager people to sail out to Sandy Hook to watch the action. The firing started shortly after five thirty in the morning, with the two warships and the civilian boats rolling in the swell. The French man-of-war and the British frigate fired broadsides into each other; the French gunners (as was their habit), firing high to disable *Boston*, succeeded in bringing down the main topmast, which careered downwards into the sea. Courtney and eleven of his crew lay dead on deck, strewn with rigging, but Bompard's men had suffered, too, with ten men killed. While *Boston* made good its escape, heading first for the Chesapeake and then casting northwards back to Halifax, *Embuscade*, while in hot pursuit, having run across a hapless Portuguese merchantman and so taking it as a prize, headed back in triumph to New York.[27]

There Bompard and his crew received heroes' welcomes. Charles Janson, a Briton on business in the city, watched aghast as the French returned: 'The wounded were landed and sent to the hospital ... Nothing but commiseration resounded through the streets while the ladies tore their chemises to bind up their wounds ... I witnessed Bompard's triumphal landing the day after the engagement. He was hailed by the gaping infatuated mob with admiration and received by a number of the higher order of Democrats with exultation. They feasted him and gave him entertainments in honour of his asserted victory'.[28]

Among those who gave the French a rapturous welcome were the sailors and dockworkers of the waterfront, whose rough-and-ready republicanism was piqued by the heroic combat of their Gallic brethren. They mingled with the French sailors, whose pockets were clinking with prize money as they drank in the dockside taverns and, where they could cross the language barrier, told stories of their struggle against tyranny, embodied by both the harsh discipline of the old regime navy and the current despotic enemies of France. They – and the working people of New York who so warmly welcomed the French – were struggling with disruptions to trade and employment from, it was alleged, the British stranglehold on maritime commerce, while New York's mariners had to confront the perpetual threat of impressment by the manpower-hungry Royal Navy. The battle-worn French sailors repaid Tammany's hospitality and support by presenting the society with *Embuscade*'s huge tricolour ensign as a symbol of republican brotherhood and respect.[29]

The sharp antagonisms of the day were witnessed by Janson, who recorded that a British naval officer in the city narrowly escaped being beaten up in the Tontine Coffee House: he vaulted over the fence outside to give his assailants the slip. Meanwhile, the main public room of the tavern was decorated with the interwoven flags of the two republics. The French triumph was amplified when fifteen French ships of the line arrived from Haiti, saluted by cannon firing from the Battery. The Democratic-Republic appropriation of the Tontine Coffee House, intended as a watering hole and place of business for New York's Federalist mercantile elites, was deeply symbolic: it was in itself an aggressive statement of the egalitarian principles that the American radicals and the French republicans shared. Thenceforth, as one visitor complained, 'Whenever two or three people are gather'd together, it is expected there is a Quarrel and they crowd round, hence other squabbles arise'.[30]

Embuscade's duel with *Boston* was the prelude to the long-awaited (or dreaded) arrival of Edmond Genet, whose mission had already stirred up a hornet's nest of partisanship, hostility and heated rhetoric. By the time Genet reached New York City on 7 August, Washington's government had banned French privateering out of American ports and was seeking Genet's recall to Paris. Even as Genet stepped onshore at the Battery, his Federalist opponents in New York had already acted, publishing a story that Genet had declared that President Washington 'was a misled man, wholly under the influence of those inimical to France'. Genet would 'appeal from him to the People, the real Sovereigns'. John Jay, the chief justice, verified the report. It was one thing verbally to scorch, eviscerate and even lie about one's opponents; it was quite another to criticise the president, and Washington in particular, in such terms. The moderate Chamber of Commerce issued a protest against freebooting foreign representatives who failed to observe diplomatic protocol. Even the committee that had gathered to organise Genet's reception, crammed with Tammany members, Democratic-Republicans and delegates from the General Society of Mechanics, was given pause.[31]

The reception laid on for the French minister was triumphant enough: the reception committee sailed out to Paulus Hook on the New Jersey side of the bay to greet him, and they crossed together to the Battery, where he was hailed by an artillery salute before passing through an enthusiastic crowd to the Tontine Coffee House. A banquet in Genet's honour was accompanied by the sound of cheering and the pealing of church bells. That evening, he was led in triumph to his lodgings on Maiden Lane. Even so, the welcome address, while saluting France for its 'great and godlike work' in preparing the universal 'triumph of Liberty', reminded the French minister that the president had declared American neutrality and that, sympathetic though New Yorkers may have been to France, 'we regard this sacred voice with attention'.[32]

Genet's main purpose, however, was to supervise the refitting of the French fleet that had now anchored in the bay and was visible from the Battery, its rigging flying the colours of all nations, although, one observer noted, the British ensign had been hoisted upside down. Genet lingered in New York City, where he supervised the repair and supply of damaged vessels and cemented the loyalties of the crews to the Republic, a task he carried out with some aplomb. The ships, repaired and refitted, took to sea on 5 October, the currents bearing them back to France. By then Genet's days as a diplomat were numbered. He was well aware that there were ominous grumblings against him within the new Jacobin regime in Paris. In the United States, the claim that he had denigrated Washington and threatened a direct appeal to the American people created a groundswell of opinion against him. Federalists mobilised their allies up and down the country in public meetings to express their support for the president and for neutrality. Genet's effusive protests in the press availed him nothing, as even his closest American allies began to desert him. In New York, veteran 'Whig triumvir' Robert Livingston fretted that Genet's 'intemperate warmth' was damaging the 'republican interest' in the city.[33]

On 12 August, Washington had told the American minister in Paris, Gouverneur Morris, to ask the French government to recall

Genet, who learned of this bombshell only in September. Everyone in the US administration knew that to send the Girondin-appointed Genet back to Jacobin Paris would almost certainly be to place him beneath the guillotine. The firebrand French diplomat was saved from such a fate by Alexander Hamilton. The New Yorker, now treasury secretary in Washington's cabinet, quietly advised the president that sacrificing Genet to the Jacobins would be a political gift to the Democratic-Republicans, who could accuse the government of having sent an opponent to his death. Genet was therefore granted asylum in early 1794. His most lasting legacy was his marriage shortly afterwards to the intelligent, strongly political daughter of Governor George Clinton, Cornelia Tappan Clinton, whom he had met in one of the dizzying rounds of receptions and dinners in New York. Genet had renamed one of the refitted French warships *Cornelia* in her honour. Now he would settle down to life with his young bride, as an American citizen.[34]

The French Revolution compelled Americans to contemplate their own revolutionary origins and come up with very different answers about the relationship between '1789' and '1776'. Horrified Federalists did their best to separate the two. Writing to George Washington on 2 May 1793, Hamilton distanced the American from the French Revolution: 'A struggle for liberty is in itself respectable and glorious. When conducted with magnanimity, justice, and humanity, it ought to command the admiration of every friend to human nature. But if sullied by crimes and extravagancies, it loses its respectability'.[35] For Hamilton, the American Revolution had been a '*free, regular* and *deliberate*' act of the nation, one that had found shape in writing, in petitions and in law – in total contrast to the French, which had been 'sullied' by its excesses.

Meanwhile, some of the most adamant expressions of a positive connection came in a wave of Democratic-Republican societies that sprang to life up and down the country; thirty-five were founded in 1793 and 1794 alone. 'The Democratic Society of the City of New York', established in February 1794, drew its members from the Tammany Society, from artisans, tradesmen, less skilled labourers and recently arrived Scots and Irish immigrants. It demanded unambiguous support for France and war against Britain. While shouting their admiration for the French Revolution from the rooftops (perhaps even literally on occasion), the societies also laid claim to the heritage of the American. Those who were veterans of the struggle flaunted their record against their Federalist critics: New York Democratic-Republicans may, like their Vermont counterparts, have thundered, 'Where are your scars?' at their Federalist critics. The concern to return to the true 'spirit of '76', as the Democratic-Republicans saw it, continued to lead them to connect the French Revolution to the earlier American struggle for freedom.[36]

Among the New York society's first public acts was to organise 'expressions of republican Joy' at a rare French victory in 1793: the retaking of Toulon (surrendered to the British during the 'Federalist' uprisings in October 1793) by the forces of the Jacobin Convention on 19 December. When the news arrived in New York on 9 March 1794, the new society had the church bells ring out, while cannon fired off salutes and the French tricolour flew. In the Tontine Coffee House, the Democratic-Republicans drafted an address of congratulation to the Convention and sang the Carmagnole, a *sans-culotte* favourite. The following day some eight hundred New Yorkers paraded, a newspaper reported, with 'the two Flags join'd and the Liberty Cap' to the City Hotel. This was New York's first hotel, recently opened and occupying an entire block on Broadway between Thames and Cedar Streets. Like the Tontine, it was both a repair for merchants and financiers on business and a vast public venue taken over for the occasion by the pro-French festivities. It was, therefore, another new site in the heart of the city that had grown from the soil of American independence and almost immediately became a focal point for political confrontation. Meanwhile, Federalists were aghast to learn that the Tammany Society displayed a guillotine in the American Museum, complete with a wax figure of a prone, beheaded victim. Perhaps that was to take its educational mission too far.[37]

When in May 1794 the administration sent John Jay to London to smooth over American differences with the British – who had pressed American sailors into naval service, harassed American shipping and failed to evacuate frontier forts prescribed by the peace treaty of 1783 – he sailed from New York. The Democratic Society took the opportunity to declare: 'We take pleasure in avowing that we are lovers of the French nation; that we esteem their cause as our own. We most firmly believe that he who is an enemy to the French Revolution cannot be a firm republican; and therefore, though he may be a good citizen in other respects, ought not to be intrusted with the guidance of any part of the machine of government'.[38]

When Jay returned with the 'Treaty of Amity, Commerce and Navigation' in May 1795, he was confronted by furious opposition from Democratic-Republicans. In New York, on 16 July 1795, Alexander Hamilton was stoned during a fracas between rival demonstrations for and against Jay's treaty. Two days later, the Democratic Society organised a parade of veterans of the American War of Independence, 'war-torn soldiers of the late American army', *Greenleaf's New York Journal* reported. They carried interwoven French and American flags, 'with the British flag reversed beneath them', and, once again, they connected the French struggle with the American Revolution by rallying at one of the sites from the American conflict. This time the Democratic-Republican march finished with the burning of a portrait of John Jay at 'Bunker Hill', the remains of one of Charles Lee's forts constructed to defend the city in 1776. The veterans were using the historical association of one place to connect the struggles of the French Revolution with their own almost two decades earlier. In the end, it availed them little: Jay's treaty would be narrowly ratified by the Senate and signed by Washington in August, aligning the United States more closely with Britain and finally, formally, swinging it away from its old French ally.[39]

NEW YORK'S EXPERIENCE when confronted with the French Revolution offers a fascinating contrast to that of Paris and London. Between 1789 and 1794, the built environment of the great French capital was adopted, altered, converted and sometimes scarred as the new civic order tried to establish itself and then was gripped by a struggle for its very survival. The French Revolution also saw an expansion of political engagement and activity in a very tangible, spatial sense. The Parisian experience was that of a city at war and in revolution, a struggle so intense in 1793–1794 that it surged into every public space and building in the city. It was an experience that, as we have noted, recalled that of New York in 1775–1776. London, on the other hand, was a city where the established order successfully defended itself, defeating even the most moderate demands for political change. The London experience was that of a city where social and political stability was partly founded on loyalism's ability to dominate, if not entirely monopolise, the city's public spaces. In New York in these years, however, the political debate was about the future direction of a *post*-revolutionary order, and for no one was this more important than the city's African American population, who took full advantage of the opportunities provided by the cityscape and republican society to forge their independence as citizens and so to undermine slavery.

At the same time, the French Revolution – as an inspiration or as a warning – also compelled New Yorkers to connect their current political collisions with their own revolutionary past. It was no accident, therefore, that New Yorkers' response to the French Revolution was often expressed in demonstrations and festivities that connected, on the one hand, the places associated with their city's struggles in the American Revolution with, on the other hand, the sites that expressed the modern political culture of the new Republic and the economic energy of a great commercial hub of a new nation. In these pivotal years, the spaces and places of Paris were the contentious sites of a people in revolution; those of London, of a people rallying against revolution; and those of New York, of a people debating their revolutionary origins and their post-revolutionary future.

CONCLUSION:
THE REVOLUTIONARY CITY
AND HISTORICAL MEMORY

REVOLUTIONS CAN BE, variously, social upheavals, political overhauls and cultural transformations, but the process of revolution – from the collapse of the old order to the attempts to establish a new one – occurs in a location, a geographical space, an environment. Truism though that may be, it is significant in at least three ways. First, revolutionary resistance to, or violence against, the old regime is partly a struggle for the physical conquest of the places of political authority and power, in a riotously varied way: over the disruption and control of communications, the harassment and ejection of state personnel, the seizure of arms and the consolidation of defensive positions. Second, revolutions that do more than just change the people in power but also seek to make deeper changes in politics and society will also make use of existing public buildings and spaces for the institutions of the new civic order, adapting and embellishing them for practical reasons but also using them to send out political messages – inscribing the buildings with slogans, colours, symbols – in order to forge citizens who are meant to adhere to a new set of political values.

Third, revolutionary movements will try to mobilise supporters and reach citizens not just *in* specific places, but also *across* space, seeking to overcome the challenges of distance (and, in the case of the city, population density) by finding ways of reaching into neighbourhoods, streets and homes.

The American and French Revolutions were both of this magnitude. Their impact was felt in almost every sphere of human experience, in politics, culture and society. Their reverberations shook places from aristocratic mansions to the taverns frequented by working people. Their hopes, fears, aspirations and hatreds were expressed in words, in violence and in the culture of politics: processions, symbols, banners, slogans, songs, music, pamphlets, broadsides, prints, engravings, playing cards, clothing, furniture and even hairstyles. The people living through them felt the emotional swings of fear, hope, exhilaration and despair, the physical pangs of hunger or the buzz of coffee or ale mixed with the fire of debate. The two revolutions also occurred in a myriad of *places*. As with all revolutions, they were struggles for the physical control of space. In New York, there was the defence of the city in the summer of 1776 and the ejection of Loyalists. In Paris, there was fighting for the control of the city in July 1789, for the Tuileries Palace on 10 August 1792 and violence over physical access to the Convention in May 1793. London avoided a revolution in these years, but it was still shaken by the roar of political debate and by collisions – and not always peaceful ones – over the 'people's' rights and political reform. This struggle entailed a battle for space no less than it did in Paris or New York, with metropolitan radicals and loyalists vying with each other over the use of the taverns and the channels of communication and organisation for the city's working population.

Yet just as important was the political transition, inscribed on the bricks, mortar and rooftops and in the city's open public spaces.

In revolutionary New York and Paris, perhaps the most immediately striking feature of the upheaval was the way in which the revolutionaries themselves took over and embellished the buildings and places that had belonged to the old order: in New York, City Hall on Wall Street was transformed into the magnificent Federal Hall. In Paris, the revolutionaries took over a veritable portfolio of real estate, including the old royal riding school, the Tuileries Palace and the Louvre, as well as dozens of convents, monasteries, churches and seminaries, which were all adapted for use by the new civic order. For the revolutionaries, it was not enough merely to assume control of the spaces and places: the presence of the new order also had to be proclaimed. The embellishment of Federal Hall, emblazoned with an American eagle, was not just a means of proclaiming a visual republican message; it was stating in bricks and mortar an aspiration to permanence, a statement that this new order would last. In Paris, during the life-and-death struggle of the Terror in 1793–1794, the massive red Phrygian bonnet above the central entrance of the Tuileries Palace was of course a revolutionary symbol, but its siting above former royal apartments also declared the republican ownership of the building itself, a gritty if (in the circumstances of those months) rather desperate message that the French Republic was in control. The grim determination of the revolutionaries in both cities to show that there would be no going back was also expressed in the destruction of landmarks: both New Yorkers (in 1776) and Parisians (in 1792) toppled statues of royalty, a symbolic regicide that in Paris predated by five months the actual decapitation of the king. Place-names were changed in both cities to erase associations with the past, although the process was more intense and far-reaching in Paris than it was in New York. Moreover, both cities experienced the impact of war and its interconnectedness with revolution. New York in 1775–1776 and Paris, particularly in 1793–1794, felt the combined effects of military preparations in buildings and spaces across the city, alongside efforts at the political mobilisation of the people and the repression of dissent that penetrated into every neighbourhood and street.

Yet the divergence of experience between the three cities is also important because it was symptomatic (though not of course a cause of) the divergent paths taken by the three countries. New York's physical transformation was bound up with the post-war reconstruction of the city, a positive experience made possible by peacetime conditions. Moreover, the relative moderation of the political change after 1783 was expressed in the built environment in the post-revolutionary years. New Yorkers could simply take over the existing buildings dedicated to the political life of the former colony and embellish them because, although democratised and shorn of royal authority, their institutions – the governor, mayor, Common Council and so on – were effectively adaptations from the old colonial system. The most important physical changes to the cityscape after the revolution, in fact, were those related to civil society rather than to formal politics: the Tontine Coffee House and the Tammany Society, for example, or the construction of African American churches, all expressions of the post-war flourish in forms of cultural engagement, economic recovery, sociability and the drive for further emancipation.

By contrast, the physical revolutionary transition in Paris from 1789 took place first against a backdrop of impecunious-ness inherited from the ancien régime and then in a deepening military, social and political crisis from 1792. No matter how ambitious were their plans to construct buildings suited to the new civic order, the revolutionaries could never afford to lay the stones. Instead, they took over and adapted the buildings of the old order – especially churches, convents, monasteries, aristocratic town houses, royal palaces – that were not remotely constructed for the purposes intended by the revolutionaries. What then followed, the physical transformation of interiors, the adaptation of internal spaces and the embellishment of the buildings with revolutionary symbols, reflected the radicalism of the French Revolution in constructing an egalitarian order in an environment that had grown organically out of a corporate society based on privilege and royal absolutism. The efflorescence of tricolours, or the construction of seating and tribunes in buildings that once housed sedate friars and contemplative nuns, was a transformation that not only changed the face of once familiar buildings, but also sent out striking visual signals of revolution to the citizens whose cityscape was being altered. In both revolutionary cities, the cityscape was used to maximum advantage in order to proclaim and encourage public engagement with the values of the new order, be that through, as already noted above, the emblazoning and festooning of buildings with the motifs of the new order or through processions and festivities that made both symbolic and practical use of particular sites (the Grand Federal Procession, the inauguration of President Washington, the Festival of the Federation, the Festival of the Supreme Being). Often, too, loyalties to the new order in both New York and Paris were proclaimed and even cemented by the new symbolic meaning ascribed to sites that, originally, may simply have had a practical or strategic purpose, but took on historic value as sites of revolutionary struggle. These include such places as the Common as the site of New York's embattled Liberty Pole or the Bastille, which from being a store of gunpowder and a forbidding fortress with a grim reputation became a symbol of revolution, a metaphor for the challenges and the resistance to be overcome in the struggle for freedom.

London's experience was different and offers an illuminating contrast. The British capital was not convulsed by revolution because the state and its supporters robustly defended the existing

order, particularly in the surge of patriotism that accompanied the
outbreak of war against the old French enemy in 1793. Moreover,
the British reform movement was no less infused with the progressive ideas of the age than its American and French counterparts,
but it was committed to legal means and moderate change – a
difference reflected in the way that London radicals used the fabric
of their city. British radicals never took over the buildings of the
established order to claim them as their own, but worked within
the habitual places in which London's civil society had always
operated, particularly, as we have seen, the city's coffeehouses
and taverns. Yet it was precisely this that left them vulnerable
to the pressure from loyalists. The latter won not only because
they overwhelmed the radicals with a crushing combination of
government repression, a cascade of propaganda and a muscular
show of popular conservatism, but also because, slowly but surely,
with the backing of the authorities, they were able to lay claim to
the same venues in which metropolitan cultural life and political
debate had flourished.

London did not experience a radical physical transformation in
the cityscape, but all three cities witnessed the impact of political
radicalism in a spatial sense. For one, the American Revolution
in New York, the French Revolution in Paris and metropolitan
radicalism in London witnessed the shift in the very locations
of political initiative, activism and mobilisation. From being the
reserve of the established meeting halls and courts of old regime
politics – London's Guildhall and Mansion House, New York's
City Hall and Fort George, Paris's Palais de Justice – political
discussion and cultural debate had moved into the seats of civil
society and sociability, places like the coffee shops of New York,
the bookshops of London and the cafés and salons of Paris. In
the revolutionary era, politics rippled out even further: into the
taverns of New York and London. In the former, these were the

places where popular leaders mingled with artisans and mariners, acting as the link between the colonial elites and the people in the opposition to the British Crown; in the latter, they were the natural meeting places for artisans and craft workers after a full day's labour. In Paris, the shift in the initiative was characterised in 1789 by a movement of the geographical focal point of the resistance to royal authority from the seat of the Parlement in the Palais de Justice to the arcades, shops and gardens of the Palais-Royal.

These changes in locales reflected the wider *social* embrace of revolutionary or radical politics, as action and debate involved people beyond the elites who had traditionally dominated politics. This spatial expression of ordinary working people entering politics reached its apogee in our period in the most expansive and least exclusive spaces of all, where crowds of people from all social backgrounds could gather to demonstrate, such as Saint George's Fields in London, New York's Common and the Palais-Royal in the Paris of the late 1780s. These sites of political mobilisation represented places where the concerns of national politics – Wilkes and Liberty, the Stamp Act, opposition to Bourbon 'despotism' – engaged people from right across the city. Moreover, popular mobilisation also entailed revolutionary politics intersecting with the concerns and interests of the working population in particular communities and neighbourhoods of the city, such as the waterfront in New York or the Faubourg Saint-Antoine and Les Halles in Paris. As we saw in the case of those Parisian neighbourhoods, their geographical location and the topography could in themselves reinforce the sense of social solidarity that encouraged militancy. They could also determine the shape and direction of revolutionary events, as noted in the case of the collision between the market women and the female militants of the women's political club. In the case of New York, one can speculate that the existence of the waterfront alongside the well-heeled district of Queen's Street may

have determined the topographical course of the protests against
the Stamp Act.

So far, these spatial developments were accidental, symptomatic
of the involvement of more popular social groups in the political
controversies of the period. What was also striking, however,
were the deliberate attempts by revolutionaries and radicals to
find ways of overcoming the distances of the metropolitan sprawl
and of the sheer density of people who lived in the city, in order
to encourage political mobilisation at the most localised of levels.
This was achieved in both Paris and London by the creation of
networks. In Paris, these included the popular societies, many of
them encouraged or even planted by the Cordeliers Club. They
also included the Parisian sections themselves. In London, there
was the divisional structure of the London Corresponding Society,
while during the American Revolution New York saw attempts
to enforce the successive boycotts of British goods or to root out
Loyalists through the active engagement of its citizens, reaching
right down to what households purchased and consumed.

In terms of the formal constitutional structures of politics,
the most impressive and intense experience of this development
came in revolutionary Paris, where the popular societies and the
sections represented the very points at which the initiative 'from
below' met politics 'from above'. The sections, as part of the formal
political structure of the new order – with their assemblies, committees, detachments of National Guards and the justices of the
peace – legally took over, adapted and inscribed and decorated
with political symbols and messages the old buildings, churches,
convents and monasteries, in particular, that studded neighbourhoods right across the city. So the creation of the sections entailed
an expansion of political activity into the local levels of metropolitan life in both constitutional and visual senses, its buildings
a reminder of the revolution at work in every neighbourhood

across the city. By contrast, the achievement of the London Corresponding Society in forging, for the first time, a formal radical organisation that could span the metropolis was especially delicate: meeting as its divisions did in taverns, whose licenses were controlled by hostile magistrates, they were standing on ground that could easily be contested by the loyalists, who had the backing of the authorities. Overwhelmed, too, by the strength of loyalism at the grassroots, in neighbourhoods across the metropolis, the local divisions were never able to put down deep local roots, leaving them all the more vulnerable to the infiltration of government agents and the intimidation of their opponents.

So the revolutionary transformation of the cityscape – as a backdrop, as a place where revolution and radicalism inscribed and transmitted their messages, its buildings and spaces sites of political conflict – made the city itself part of the story. This book has woven the story of the cities' peoples – intrepid individuals, angry or hopeful neighbourhoods – into the history of the urban fabric in these momentous, tumultuous years. It has shown, I hope, the truth of what one historian has said of Paris, that 'the city was a player in its own history'. This matters because cities are restless, ever-changing places. After the wars of the French Revolution – and partly because of them – London emerged as the great smoking metropolis of the British Empire, an ever-changing cityscape that was 'blitzed' by Nazi bombs during the Second World War and then re-emerged as a fascinating patchwork of the old and the modern. New York, thanks in no small part to the westward expansion of the United States and its position as a great commercial centre, grew relentlessly, outwards and upwards, until it would have been virtually unrecognisable to the revolutionaries and Loyalists who had once battled in its streets. Since the Revolution, Paris was also transformed: Napoleon Bonaparte began the process in earnest with his building projects, but it reached its climax with Baron Haussmann, Napoleon III's prefect of the Seine in the 1850s and 1860s, who oversaw the renovation, boulevard construction, sewer digging, market building and park planting that laid the foundations for the modern city. Cities adapt, are destroyed over time and are rebuilt.[1]

ABOUT A HUNDRED years ago, the changing cityscape, the emergence of the modern city and the destruction of the old encouraged contemporaries to appreciate and to make moves to preserve, or at least to record, the material remains of the past. Those who researched and wrote about historical sites for their own sake produced a kind of history that has been unfashionable for many years: 'antiquarianism' seemed to amass a lot of interesting detail, but in itself seemed to do little to illuminate deeper historical concerns, such as what shaped classes, societies, nations and cultures; what drove the great movements for change; and the other big questions that still perplex historians and policy makers. Among its practitioners was French writer Louis-Léon Théodore Gosselin, who wrote as George Lenotre, an historian feverish in his pursuit of sites associated with the French Revolution: the political clubs, the homes of revolutionary leaders, the prisons of the Terror and more. He explored old buildings, meticulously examined documents and then wrote vivid, minutely detailed pen portraits of what they might have been like a hundred years previously. Where the places no longer existed, he reconstructed them on paper with the use of plans, archival records and memoirs. Lenotre was driven – quite rightly – by pure curiosity. In 1894 he wrote, 'How often ... have I tried to reconstruct in my mind ... the chamber in which the Convention sat, the prisons, the Committees ... I wondered: *What was it like?*' Yet there was also a practical motor humming behind his prolific research and writing: 'Du Paris de jadis il reste si peu de chose!' (So little remains of the Paris of yes-teryear). By Lenotre's day, much of old Paris had disappeared, and he was among many concerned citizens who wanted to preserve or at least record the city's ancient heritage before it was gone. Yet Lenotre's richly detailed evocations of revolutionary Paris are no longer incompatible with modern historical writing.[2]

For Lenotre, the purpose was to record what was once there or what was on the verge of disappearing. Yet in doing so, he showed that physical places – in his case, Paris – reveal their past in layers, sometimes in a literal sense, when one looks at the fabric of the city both above ground and its archaeological remains below ground. In a more figurative sense, 'layers' means that historical memories associated with sites in the city are overwritten, erased, forgotten or alternatively actively commemorated, remembered or suddenly recalled after years of obscurity, as surely as the bricks and mortar of a city are demolished, built over and reconstructed. Even indi-vidual buildings that seem to have been there for centuries are rarely unaltered – all buildings have their 'secret lives'. So these layers are both physical, the constructed material relics from the past, and cultural, in the historical memories associated with a par-ticular place and space. Such sites educate and fire the imagination. As the great British historian George Macaulay Trevelyan wrote in 1913, an historical site 'is not mere stone and mortar . . . but an appropriate and mournful witness between those who see it now and those by whom it once was seen. And so it is, for the reader of history, with every ruined castle and ancient church throughout the wide, mysterious lands of Europe'. Historical places help shape our stories about the past.[3]

Yet this raises the question as to *which* places are celebrated, marked or noticed and which events, which historical layers, are connected most readily to a particular site. A city's physical places – buildings, public spaces, geographical features – rapidly become 'realms of memory', *lieux de mémoire* in French, places inscribed by historical memories. Yet especially in the urban environment, the memories associated with any particular event are erasable, like wax tablets: each site can become so closely associated with one particular event or group of people that it overwrites all other associations. Often, this 'forgetting' is a matter of choice, or of political decision. What we mark, commemorate and even regard as an historical site is a choice made by communities, societies and governments. So when it is in the gift of authority to decide which sites are marked and remembered and which are not, then the narrative of a society's history can itself be shaped to suit its purposes. It is for these reasons that historical sites have, in the past and in the present, become places of often fierce political and intellectual contest.[4]

One example directly connected to the subject of this book can be readily cited. The dramatic statue of Georges-Jacques Danton marking the spot where his house once stood (by the present-day Odéon metro station, on the boulevard Saint-Germain) was raised in 1889 by the city of Paris as part of the commemorations marking the centenary of the French Revolution. The choice of subject reflected the sensibilities of the then Third Republic: Danton represented the patriotic republicanism and bullish defiance that the regime wanted to project after the humiliating defeat of France at German hands in the Franco-Prussian War of 1870–1871. Yet when the statue was inaugurated in July 1891, there were protests in the French Senate. The debate reflected the deep disagreements about the meaning of the French Revolution, an argument that, in turn, reflected political tendencies. One senator, Henri Wallon, argued that the statue was an 'outrage and a scandal ... the glorification of one of the most sinister deeds that disgraced the French Revolution', a reference either to Danton's role in founding the Revolutionary Tribunal or, perhaps, to his alleged part in the

September massacres. When another senator rose to declare that, on the contrary, 'Danton had roused in France the feeling which enabled her to defeat a coalition of Kings', there was applause from the Left of the chamber. What we commemorate, what we remember and where we do it reflect our own political and cultural concerns.[5]

This book has been far from neutral in this respect. It has focused on one particular layer of the urban past in three western cities, namely, the struggle for democracy in the late eighteenth century. In making this choice, it has chosen to explore those sites associated with political confrontation and the contentious, often violent politics of revolution. This was a pivotal moment in the history of the Atlantic world, and perhaps of the whole world, as many contemporaries claimed. It was a time when thousands of people, often for the first time, seized the initiative and tried to shape their own political futures. It was a struggle that was inscribed – if only temporarily – on the fabric of Paris, London and New York. In those restless, perennially changing cities, many of the places and spaces described in this book have certainly been destroyed, forgotten or built over. Historical associations with the political collisions of the later eighteenth century have sometimes been overwritten or forgotten as the city itself has changed, a process that has sometimes arisen deliberately, sometimes because other memories have more importance for later generations and sometimes simply owing to the passage of time. Yet most of the sites described in this book can often still be discerned, in whole or in part, or at least their architectural footprint can be remembered. We only need to know where to look.

ACKNOWLEDGEMENTS

This book bears the author's name on its cover, but it is actually the product of considerable support and hard work from many good people. My deep thanks go to my two indefatigable editors, Lara Heimert at Basic Books and Tim Whiting at Little, Brown, whose wisdom, encouragement, ability to see the wheat for the chaff and willingness to give me a steer when needed have played a hefty part in making sure that this book made the long and at times tortuous journey from idea to print. They also displayed immense reserves of patience and good humour as the project at first rose shakily to its feet, staggered drunkenly in various false directions and then, at last, found its balance and jogged towards the finishing line. I also thank Alia Massoud at Basic for her suggestions and cheerful help as well as Sandra Beris and Melissa Raymond for helping to push the production on in the final stages. By their care and their attention to detail, Roger Labrie, the line editor for Basic, Annette Wenda, the copy editor, and Iain Hunt, at Little, Brown, saved me from myself more often than I can enumerate: they detected errors, brought the text back to task when I got carried away and helped me dot the *i*'s and cross the *t*'s. As usual, any remaining mistakes, of grammar, fact or judgment, are my own creatures.

Research trips for this book were generously funded by two research grants, in 2011 and 2012, from the Carnegie Trust for the Universities in Scotland, a beacon of humane values. I should also acknowledge a Small Research Grant from the British Academy/Leverhulme Trust for a later trip (in 2015–2016), although the bulk of the material gleaned from this last mentioned is intended for the next book, which will focus exclusively on revolutionary Paris. My heartfelt thanks go to Bill Doyle and Michael Broers for their doggedness in helping me secure this funding – and for their support in so many other respects.

I secured invaluable assistance at various archives and libraries, particularly the Archives Nationales in Paris and, latterly, just outside the city at Pierrefitte-sur-Seine. I have found the staff in the AN always friendly and willing to help. The same is true of Philip Heslip and Tal Nadan in the Manuscript and Archives Division at the New York Public Library. As this book was being written, I moved from the University of Stirling to the University of Glasgow. The librarians in both places have been exceptionally helpful, particularly in securing materials through the Document Delivery or Inter-Library Loan Services. I would also like to thank John Moore and Julie Gardham of, respectively, the excellent Map Collection and the Special Collections at Glasgow University Library, whose holdings proved invaluable as I drew or photographed the maps needed for this present book.

Over the years, I have benefitted greatly from the friendship, collegiality and knowledge of historians and students at Stirling and Glasgow. At Stirling, conversations with the resident *dix-huitièmistes*, particularly Emma Macleod, Colin Nicolson and Ben Marsh (who has moved on to the University of Kent at Canterbury), have enriched not just my teaching and research, but I am grateful for their friendship. At Glasgow, the same applies to many others, but specifically to Simon Newman (whose work I have ruthlessly plundered in this present volume) and Thomas Munck. Also at Glasgow, I should give a very special thanks to Eileen Ritchie. The past three and a half years have seen me take on a rich if demanding position as convenor of the undergraduate honours programmes in history, which also involves a strong pastoral role when things go wrong for individual students as, sadly, they sometimes do. Eileen has been a constant support here, often taking up the slack when other things have diverted my attention: her contribution to the students' experience at Glasgow (and, by extension, to my ability to complete this book) is incalculable. Thomas Munck's supportive and friendly Early Modern Work in Progress Seminar at Glasgow University gave me an opportunity to present some of my ideas and archival sources: the questions of colleagues, postgraduates and final-year honours students helped to put many points into greater focus. Among my students, those who have taken my junior honours course on France and my special subject on the French Revolution, at both Stirling and Glasgow, have been a real joy to work with, but I also thank my students on Glasgow's second-year 'sources and methods' course on the making of modern societies: their thoughts on semiotics and material culture have been especially inspiring as the argument in this book took shape. The postgraduate students on the taught master's course on Thomas Paine have kept the 'Atlantic' context firmly in mind.

Moving beyond Glasgow, the response from the postgraduate participants of the Modern European History Graduate Conference at Cambridge University to a paper I gave on revolutionary Paris was sparky and stimulating, as was the hospitality afterwards: I record special thanks to Daniel Robinson for organising the session and for inviting me to speak. Also beyond Glasgow, working with Kevin Adamson, Ben Marsh (again) and David Andress on different projects has helped me focus my ideas on revolution and helped shaped the broader context in which to place this book. The same must be said for Ewald Frie and the Threatened Orders (Bedröhte Ordnungen) project at the University of Tübingen in Germany, to which I was allowed to give the keynote address at one of its conferences and to contribute a chapter to one of its edited volumes. I have also enjoyed the friendship, support and ideas of Bill Doyle, Michael Broers, Peter McPhee, Marisa Linton and Mette Harder (who pointed me in the direction of a rich seam of archives in Paris). As ever, I also enjoyed the friendship and hospitality of Ross and Nina Bryson on two of my forays into London. Yvonne and Terry Wisdom have been wonderful in looking after our onetime guide dog, Yulie, in their Highland fastness whenever recent research trips have beckoned (and I appreciated Terry's gentle ribbing about when, if ever, the book was going to be finished). And our excellent friends in Stirling have – perhaps more than they know – helped at critical junctures with playdates, school pickups and more: there are too many to mention, but in particular I must thank Claire McEwan and Scott Henderson, Vicky Myers, Marilena Tsante and John Nikolaidis and, last but by absolutely no means least, Eilidh and Barry Smith.

I also want to record my love and thanks to my parents, namely, Anita and Mike Radford in France and Jane and George Rapport in the United States. My wife, Helen, and daughter, Lily, have lived and breathed this book. Lily has bravely tramped the streets of the three cities with us over the years. Feisty that she is, she could not always hide her bemusement about why Mum and Dad get so carried away, first, with the very act of 'walking the city' and, second, with picking out its many 'realms of memory'. She has also been remarkably understanding of her father's 'busyness' during the writing of this book. Helen is an urban historian (a proper one, unlike an interloper like myself), specialising in eighteenth- and nineteenth-century Glasgow and Edinburgh, though she has many more historical strings to her bow. Helen has readily shared with me her knowledge of cities in the past, their culture and how to 'read' monuments and buildings. She has also been an absolute rock of support whenever the process of writing was tough and has been a fount of enthusiasm and encouragement throughout. She is my best friend, as well as the love of my life. I dedicate this book to her.

Mike Rapport
University of Glasgow,
Scotland
20 September 2016

Author's Note

I came to this subject as an historian of the French Revolution. I am not the most theory-driven of scholars, but since the time of writing, I have encountered a rich seam of thoughtful, theoretical work on place and space in the past. So here I acknowledge the work of Katrina Navickas, William Sewell, Christina Parolin, David Featherstone, James Epstein, Leif Jerram and Steve Poole. All have gone before me, most have travelled by different paths, but we all had the map of space and place to guide us.

NOTES

Notes to Introduction

1. N. Karamzin, *Letters of a Russian Traveller*, translated by trans. A. Kahn (SVEC, 2003:04) (Oxford: Voltaire Foundation, 2003), 256.
2. Quoted in H. C. Rice, *Thomas Jefferson's Paris* (Princeton, NJ: Princeton University Press, 1976), 25–26.
3. P. Jones, *The Great Nation: France from Louis XV to Napoleon* (London: Penguin, 2003), 247; D. Garrioch, *The Making of Revolutionary Paris* (Berkeley: University of California Press, 2002), 163–164, 171–172.
4. Laugier quoted in Garrioch, *Making of Revolutionary Paris*, 200–211.
5. L. Auslander, 'Regeneration Through the Everyday? Clothing, Architecture and Furniture in Revolutionary Paris', *Art History* 28 (2005): 227–247. For an excellent comparative study of the upheavals in seventeenth-century Britain and eighteenth-century America and France as 'cultural revolutions', see also L. Auslander, *Cultural Revolutions: Everyday Life and Politics in Britain, North America, and France* (Berkeley: University of California Press, 2009). Modern scholarship offers a methodology with which to approach the meaning and reception of 'things', 'signs' and symbols, including the city, namely, semiotics. I am currently engaging with this elsewhere; the present volume is not the place to do so. See M. Gottdiener and A. P. Lagopoulos, eds., *The City and the Sign: An Introduction to Urban Semiotics* (New York: Columbia University Press, 1986). On the politics of space and place and on the theoretical and historical debates surrounding it, see Katrina Navickas, *Protest and the Politics of Space and Place, 1789–1848* (Manchester: Manchester

University Press, 2016), especially 1–20 and, for our period, 23–50. This excellent book came out a little too late to be fully absorbed for the present volume.

6. On this Atlantic context, see, for example, A. Jourdan, *La Révolution, une exception française?* (Paris: Flammarion, 2004); and W. Klooster, *Revolutions in the Atlantic World: A Comparative History* (New York: New York University Press, 2009). Good examples of the transoceanic movement of people and ideas are M. Jasanoff, *Liberty's Exiles: The Loss of America and the Remaking of the British Empire* (London: Harper Press, 2011); M. Durey, *Transatlantic Radicals and the Early American Republic* (Lawrence: University Press of Kansas, 1997); F. Furstenberg, *When the United States Spoke French: Five Refugees Who Shaped a Nation* (New York: Penguin, 2014); D. P. Harsanyi, *Lessons from America: Liberal French Nobles in Exile, 1793–1798* (University Park: Pennsylvania State University Press, 2010); and J. Polasky, *Revolutions Without Borders: The Call to Liberty in the Atlantic World* (New Haven, CT: Yale University Press, 2015).

7. As David Armitage puts it, the Atlantic 'provides the link but is not in itself the object of analysis'. Armitage, 'Three Concepts of Atlantic History', in *The British Atlantic World, 1500–1800*, edited by D. Armitage and M. J. Braddick (Basingstoke: Palgrave, 2009), 24.

8. In other words, this book seeks to explore how, as David Garrioch says, 'the city was a player in its own history'. Garrioch, *Making of Revolutionary Paris*, 7.

9. For innovative approaches to how people experienced the revolution, see D. Andress, 'Revolutionary Historiography, Adrift or at Large? The Paradigmatic Quest Versus the Exploration of Experience', introduction to *Experiencing the French Revolution*, edited by D. Andress (Oxford: Voltaire Foundation, 2013), 1.

10. For Mercier quotation: L.-S. Mercier, *Parallèle de Paris et de Londres*, edited by C. Bruneteau and B. Cottret (Paris: Didier-Érudition, 1982), 53.

11. L. Picard, *Dr. Johnson's London: Everyday Life in London, 1740–1770* (London: Phoenix, 2001), 3–4; Defoe quoted in G. Rudé, *Hanoverian London, 1714–1808* (Stroud: Sutton, 2003), 2; 1787 observer quoted in P. Ackroyd, *London: The Biography* (London: Vintage, 2001), 517.

12. For Karamzin quotation: N. M. Karamzin, *Voyage en France, 1789–1790* (Paris: Hachette, 1885), 75.

13. For Adams quotation: Abigail Adams to Mary Smith Cranch, 6 July 1784,

in *Letters of Mrs. Adams: The Wife of John Adams*, by A. S. Adams, 2 vols. (Boston: Little, Brown, 1841), 2:25.

14. T. Fleming, *Duel: Alexander Hamilton, Aaron Burr and the Future of America* (New York: Basic Books, 1999), 31–32.

15. Quoted in E. G. Burrows and M. Wallace, *Gotham: A History of New York City to 1898* (New York: Oxford University Press, 1999), 338.

16. For the Liverpool comparison: T. Cooper, *Some Information Respecting America*, excerpted in B. Still, *Mirror for Gotham: New York as Seen by Contemporaries from Dutch Days to the Present* (New York: New York University Press, 1956), 64.

17. Ackroyd, *London: The Biography*, 43, 72.

18. For Mercier quotation: L.-S. Mercier, *Le tableau de Paris*, edited by J. Kaplow (Paris: Découverte, 1989), 38–39; Lichtenberg quoted in R. Porter, *London: A Social History* (London: Penguin, 2000), 221–222; New Yorkers' complaint from 'Petition of occupants of houses on Vesey Street between Greenwich and Church Streets, to the Mayor, Aldermen and Common Council, c. 1803', New York Public Library, Division of Rare Books and Manuscripts, New York City Miscellaneous Collection, Mss. Coll. 2156, Box 11, Folio 14.

19. Adams quotation: Abigail Adams to Lucy Cranch Greenleaf, 5 September 1784, in *Letters of Mrs. Adams*, by Adams, 2:54–55; Grosley quoted in Porter, *London: A Social History*, 120; Brissot quotation: J.-P. Brissot de Warville, *Mémoires, 1754–1793*, edited by C. Perroud, 2 vols. (Paris, 1912), 1:302, 331.

20. D. Roche, *The People of Paris: An Essay in Popular Culture in the 18th Century* (Leamington Spa, Hamburg, and New York: Berg, 1987), 107.

21. J. Godechot, *Taking of the Bastille: July 14th, 1789* (New York: Scribner's, 1970), 55; C. Abbott, 'The Neighbourhoods of New York, 1760–1775', *New York History* 55 (1974): 46; W. C. Abbott, *New York in the American Revolution* (New York: Scribner's, 1929), 10–11; Garrioch, *Making of Revolutionary Paris*, 60–61.

22. Fielding and von Archenholz quoted respectively in Rudé, *Hanoverian London, 1714–1808*, 9, 10.

23. For the 'rules', see *London Magazine* 49 (May 1780): 197.

24. See T. C. W. Blanning, *The Culture of Power and the Power of Culture: Old Regime Europe, 1660–1789* (Oxford: Oxford University Press, 2002).

25. Raynal quoted in K. M. Baker, 'Public Opinion as Political Invention', in *Inventing the French Revolution: Essays on French Political Culture in the Eighteenth Century* (Cambridge: Cambridge University Press, 1990), 187.

26. H. M. Scott, 'The Seven Years War and Europe's Ancien Régime', *War in History* 18 (2011): 425, 429, 432–433.

27. J. Kaplow, *The Names of Kings: The Parisian Laboring Poor in the Eighteenth Century* (New York: Basic Books, 1972), 128–129, 131; Garrioch, *Making of Revolutionary Paris*, 62.

28. For Sandby's engravings, see J. Bonehill, '"The Centre of Pleasure and Magnificence": Paul and Thomas Sandby's London', *Huntington Library Quarterly* 75 (2012): 378–379. For the Bow Street runners in these years, see J. M. Beattie, *The First English Detectives: The Bow Street Runners and the Policing of London, 1750–1840* (Oxford: Oxford University Press, 2012), 46–48.

29. Quoted in Rudé, *Hanoverian London, 1714–1808*, 191.

30. Ibid., 190–201.

31. Grateful merchant quoted in Burrows and Wallace, *Gotham*, 191; despairing merchant quoted in G. Nash, *The Urban Crucible: Social Change, Political Consciousness and the Origins of the American Revolution* (Cambridge, MA: Harvard University Press, 1979), 250.

32. Quoted in Burrows and Wallace, *Gotham*, 192.

33. D. A. Bell, *The Cult of the Nation in France: Inventing Nationalism, 1680–1800* (Cambridge, MA: Harvard University Press, 2001), 63–68; Jones, *Great Nation*, 260–261, 272.

Notes to Chapter One

1. 'The Colden Letter Books, 1765–1775' (Collections of the New-York Historical Society for the Year 1877) (New York: New York Historical Society, 1878), 47.

2. For the idea of a 'dual revolution', see Nash, *Urban Crucible*, 292 (see introduction, n. 31).

3. S. Conway, 'Britain and the Revolutionary Crisis, 1763–1791', in *The Oxford History of the British Empire*, edited by P. J. Marshall, vol. 2, *The Eighteenth Century* (Oxford: Oxford University Press, 1998), 327–328; E. Countryman, *The American Revolution* (Harmondsworth: Penguin, 1985), 47–48.

4. Conway, 'Britain and the Revolutionary Crisis', 327; Countryman, *The American Revolution*, 11; J. Shy, 'The American Colonies in War and Revolution, 1748–1783', in *Oxford History of the British Empire*, edited by Marshall, 2:306.

5. R. Chopra, *Unnatural Rebellion: Loyalists in New York City During the Revolution* (Charlottesville: University of Virginia Press, 2011), 11.

6. P. U. Bonomi, *A Factious People: Politics and Society in Colonial New York* (New York: Columbia University Press, 1971), 63–64, 71–72.

7. I. N. Phelps Stokes, *The Iconography of Manhattan Island, 1498–1909, Compiled from Original Sources*, 6 vols. (New York: Robert H. Dodd, 1915–1928), 1:187; B. Schecter, *The Battle for New York: The City at the Heart of the American Revolution* (New York: Walker, 2002), 18–19; Chopra, *Unnatural Rebellion*, 8–11; Burrows and Wallace, *Gotham*, 109 (see introduction, n. 15); Abbott, *New York*, 13 (see introduction, n. 21).

8. E. S. Morgan and H. M. Morgan, *The Stamp Act Crisis: Prologue to Revolution* (London: Collier Macmillan, 1963), 56, 58; B. Knollenberg, *Origin of the American Revolution, 1759–1766* (New York: Free Press, 1965), 190–191; H. T. Dickinson, 'Britain's Imperial Sovereignty: The Ideological Case Against the American Colonists', in *Britain and the American Revolution* (London: Longman, 1998), 74, 76, 77; Smith quoted in L. F. S. Upton, *The Loyal Whig: William Smith of New York and Quebec* (Toronto: University of Toronto Press, 1969), 53; Morgan and Morgan, *Stamp Act Crisis*, 121.

9. 'Resolutions of the Stamp Act Congress', reprinted in S. E. Morison, *Sources and Documents Illustrating the American Revolution and the Formation of the Federal Constitution, 1764–1788* (Oxford: Oxford University Press, 1965), 32–34, also quoted in full in Morgan and Morgan, *Stamp Act Crisis*, 142–144.

10. J. Montresor, *The Montresor Journals*, edited by G. D. Scull (New York: New York Historical Society, 1882), 336.

11. Ibid., 336; Phelps Stokes, *Iconography*, 4:752; M. Kammen, *Colonial New York: A History* (New York and Oxford: Oxford University Press, 1975), 349.

12. P. A. Gilje, *The Road to Mobocracy: Popular Disorder in New York City, 1763–1834* (Chapel Hill: Institute of Early American Culture / University of North Carolina Press, 1987), 40; R. J. Champagne, *Alexander McDougall and the American Revolution in New York* (Schenectady, NY: Union College Press, 1975), 11; B. Carp, *Rebels Rising: Cities and the American Revolution* (New York: Oxford University Press, 2007), 62–63; *Vox Populi* note in J. R. Brodhead, B. Fernow and E. B. O'Callaghan, eds., *Documents Relative to the Colonial History of the State of New-York*, 15 vols. (1853–1856), 7:770 (hereafter *New York Col. Docs.*).

13. W. C. Abbott prints the Madeira-tippling participant's testimony in full in *New York*, 54–57.

14. Detail and quotations from Abbott, 'Neighbourhoods of New York', 50–51 (see introduction, n. 21).

15. Nash, *Urban Crucible*, 250–251.

16. P. A. Gilje, *Liberty on the Waterfront: American Maritime Culture in the Age of Revolution* (Philadelphia: University of Pennsylvania Press, 2004), 12–13, 100–101; Gilje, *Road to Mobocracy*, 12; R. M. Ketchum, *Divided Loyalties: How the American Revolution Came to New York* (New York: Owl Books, 2002), 151–152; Champagne, *Alexander McDougall*, 5–10; Bonomi, *Factious People*, 267–268; Burrows and Wallace, *Gotham*, 200–201; G. B. Nash, *The Unknown American Revolution: The Unruly Birth of Democracy and the Struggle to Create America* (New York: Penguin, 2005), 223–232.

17. Abbott, *New York*, 9; Nash, *Urban Crucible*, 300.

18. McEvers letter in *New York Col. Docs*, 7:761.

19. Abbott, 'Neighbourhoods of New York', 43; Ketchum, *Divided Loyalties*, 139.

20. Montresor, *The Montresor Journals*, 336–337; James quoted in Burrows and Wallace, *Gotham*, 199.

21. Colden's testimony in *New York Col. Docs*, 7:771; protester quoted in Abbott, *New York*, 56. For traditions of protest, see S. P. Newman, *Parades and the Politics of the Street: Festive Culture in the Early American Republic* (Philadelphia: University of Pennsylvania Press, 1997), 21; Gilje, *Road of Mobocracy*, 39–40; and Gilje, *Liberty on the Waterfront*, 102.

22. Protester quoted in Abbott, *New York*, 56; Colden's account in *New York Col. Docs*, 7:771. There was almost certainly a social as well as a political protest behind the burning of Colden's carriage. Coaches were one of the most ostentatious displays of wealth. By 1775 they were still the expensive toys of the very rich, their ownership enjoyed by only sixty-nine families (Burrows and Wallace, *Gotham*, 172–174).

23. Protester quoted in Abbott, *New York*, 56; further details in Montresor, *The Montresor Journals*, 337; Abbott, *New York*, 56–57; Schecter, *Battle for New York*, 15.

24. Montresor, *The Montresor Journals*, 337–338; Livingston quoted in Bonomi, *Factious People*, 234.

25. Nash, *Urban Crucible*, 303; Livingston quoted in Champagne, *Alexander McDougall*, 14.

26. *New York Col. Docs*, 7:792; Burrows and Wallace, *Gotham*, 200.

27. *New York Col. Docs*, 7:790; Burrows and Wallace, *Gotham*, 202; Kammen, *Colonial New York*, 345.

28. Parliament quoted in R. Middlekauf, *The Glorious Cause: The American Revolution, 1763–1789* (New York: Oxford University Press, 1982), 117; *New York Post-Boy* in Phelps Stokes, *Iconography*, 4:765; Montresor, *The Montresor Journals*, 368.

29. Schecter, *Battle for New York*, 35; colonial assembly in Phelps Stokes, *Iconography*, 4:766.

30. Newman, *Parades and Politics of the Street*, 25; Schecter, *Battle for New York*, 25; Phelps Stokes, *Iconography*, 4:765.

31. Montresor, *The Montresor Journals*, 385; Phelps Stokes, *Iconography*, 4:802.

32. Phelps Stokes, *Iconography*, 4:800.

33. Champagne, *Alexander McDougall*, 22–23; McDougall's words are taken from the original text of 'To the Betrayed Inhabitants of the City and Colony of New York' (New York, 1769).

34. Quoted in Champagne, *Alexander McDougall*, 24.

35. Phelps Stokes, *Iconography*, 4:803–804; Ketchum, *Divided Loyalties*, 226–228 (anxious New Yorker quoted on 228).

36. Phelps Stokes, *Iconography*, 4:805.

37. Champagne, *Alexander McDougall*, 27–28, 31–34.

38. Ibid., 40–42.

39. Phelps Stokes, *Iconography*, 4:812.

40. Ibid., 813.

41. B. L. Carp, *Defiance of the Patriots: The Boston Tea Party and the Making of America* (New Haven, CT: Yale University Press, 2010), 11–20, 130, 139; Burrows and Wallace, *Gotham*, 213–214.

42. Middlekauf, *Glorious Cause*, 230–231; Countryman, *The American Revolution*, 50; Champagne, *Alexander McDougall*, 53; King George III quoted in Burrows and Wallace, *Gotham*, 215.

43. Nash, *Unknown American Revolution*, 141–144 (New Yorker quoted on 143).

44. M. B. Norton, *Liberty's Daughters: The Revolutionary Experience of American Women, 1750–1800* (Boston: Little, Brown, 1980), 242–250; Charity quoted in Burrows and Wallace, *Gotham*, 216.

45. S. White, *Somewhat More Independent: The End of Slavery in New York City, 1770–1810* (Athens: University of Georgia Press, 1991), 9–10, 90 (McRobert quoted on 3); J. L. Van Buskirk, *Generous Enemies: Patriots and Loyalists in Revolutionary New York* (Philadelphia: University of Pennsylvania Press, 2002), 133; S. Schama, *Rough Crossings: Britain, the Slaves and the American Revolution* (London: BBC Books, 2005), 113.

46. Ketchum, *Divided Loyalties*, 276; Morris quoted in S. Lynd, 'The Mechanics in New York Politics, 1774–1788', *Labor History* 5 (1964): 226.

47. Middlekauf, *Glorious Cause*, 247–248; eyewitness to the delegates' departure quoted in Schecter, *Battle for New York*, 41.

48. Ketchum, *Divided Loyalties*, 308.

49. Abbott, *New York*, 136.

50. Eyewitness, Smith and Willett quoted in Schecter, *Battle for New York*, 51.

51. Abbott, *New York*, 135–136; Smith quoted in Ketchum, *Divided Loyalties*, 322.

Notes to Chapter Two

1. Wilkes quoted in J. White, *London in the Eighteenth Century: A Great and Monstrous Thing* (London: Bodley Head, 2012), 512.

2. P.-J. Grosley, *Londres*, 3 vols. (Lausanne, 1770), 2:9–10.

3. Temple Bar was demolished in 1878 by the Victorians who sought to ease the congestion of this major artery through the heart of the imperial metropolis, but, acutely conscious as they were of its historical significance, they took it down stone by stone. Temple Bar was purchased and reconstructed by a private landowner on his estates before, in 2004, it returned to London and was lovingly rebuilt and can be seen today in all its glory on the northwestern side of Saint Paul's Churchyard. On the Temple Bar and its restoration, see www.thetemplebar.info/.

4. Surviving examples of the old livery halls include Apothecaries' Hall off Black Friars Lane, Vintners' Hall on Upper Thames Street and Skinners' Hall at 8½ Dowgate Hill: all date to the reconstruction of the City after the Great Fire in 1666.

5. G. Rudé, *Wilkes and Liberty: A Social Study of 1763 to 1774* (Oxford: Oxford University Press, 1962), 5–6; Porter, *London: A Social History*, 121, 188–190 (see introduction, n. 18).

6. L. Sutherland, 'The City of London and the Opposition to Government, 1768–74', in *London in the Age of Reform*, edited by J. Stevenson (Oxford: Blackwell, 1977), 33.

7. Grosley, *Londres*, 2:10.

8. A. H. Cash, *John Wilkes: The Scandalous Father of Civil Liberty* (New Haven, CT: Yale University Press, 2006), 7, 276.

9. J. Summerson, *Georgian London* (Harmondsworth: Penguin, 1962), 63, 266; Porter, *London: A Social History*, 120; S. Inwood, *Historic London: An*

Explorer's Companion (London: Macmillan, 2008), 51–52 (coffeehouses), 237–238 (Royal Exchange); R. J. Mitchell and M. D. R. Leys, *A History of London Life* (Harmondsworth: Penguin, 1963), 110.

10. L. Colley, *Britons: Forging the Nation, 1707–1837* (New Haven, CT: Yale University Press, 1992), 61–71 (Burke quoted on 71); J. Flavell, *When London Was Capital of America* (New Haven, CT: Yale University Press, 2010), 121–123.

11. Wilkes quoted in Rudé, *Wilkes and Liberty*, 27.

12. www.historyofparliamentonline.org/volume/1754-1790/constituencies/middlesex#constituency-background-info; J. White, *London in the Eighteenth Century*, 523–524; Rudé, *Wilkes and Liberty*, 79–80.

13. In the 1760s, the King's Bench Prison stood along a new road, the modern-day Borough Road, that had been cut from Westminster Bridge into Southwark. Now demolished, the gaol would have stood just to the north of the junction where Newington Causeway runs into Borough Road, on the site of a modern-day housing estate.

14. Saint George's Fields occupied a site that is today a busy part of central London that includes Waterloo Station and is encompassed by Union Street to the north, Kennington Road to the west, Kennington Lane to the south and Borough High Street to the east. Inwood, *Historic London*, 308.

15. Rudé, *Wilkes and Liberty*, 49–51, 56.

16. Cash, *John Wilkes*, 226; Sutherland, 'City of London', 30; Rudé, *Wilkes and Liberty*, 108 (SSBR quoted on 61–62); J. White, *London in the Eighteenth Century*, 527 (Beckford quoted on 529).

17. Rudé, *Wilkes and Liberty*, 62–65.

18. Lady quoted in ibid., 156.

19. Ibid., 158–159; Cash, *John Wilkes*, 280–282 (Wilkes quoted on 281).

20. Rudé, *Wilkes and Liberty*, 159; George III quoted in Cash, *John Wilkes*, 282.

21. Quoted in Rudé, *Wilkes and Liberty*, 163.

22. Cash, *John Wilkes*, 284–285.

23. Ibid., 287.

24. J. White, *London in the Eighteenth Century*, 511; A. Goodwin, *The Friends of Liberty: The English Democratic Movement in the Age of the French Revolution* (London: Hutchinson, 1979), 43–44; official on the hangings quoted in J. Marriott, *Beyond the Tower: A History of East London* (New Haven, CT: Yale University Press, 2011), 82, 85.

25. Wilkes quoted in J. Cannon, *Parliamentary Reform, 1640–1832*

(Cambridge: Cambridge University Press, 1973), 67; and in Sutherland, 'City of London', 47.

Notes to Chapter Three

1. P. McPhee, *Robespierre: A Revolutionary Life* (New Haven, CT: Yale University Press, 2012), 23.
2. For the Parlements, see especially W. Doyle, *Origins of the French Revolution*, 2nd ed. (Oxford: Oxford University Press, 1988), 69–72.
3. P. R. Campbell, 'The Paris Parlement in the 1780s', in *The Origins of the French Revolution* (Basingstoke: Palgrave, 2006), 97; McPhee, *Robespierre: A Revolutionary Life*, 25.
4. Doyle, *Origins of the French Revolution*, 71; Campbell, 'Paris Parlement', 88–89; J. Swann, 'The State and Political Culture', in *Old Regime France*, edited by W. Doyle (Oxford: Oxford University Press, 2001), 156–157.
5. L.-V. Thiéry, *Guide des amateurs et des étrangers voyageurs à Paris; ou, Description raisonnée de cette ville*, 3 vols. (Paris, 1787), 2:14.
6. Jones, *Great Nation*, 260–261, 272 (see introduction, n. 3).
7. For the Sainte-Chapelle, see C. Jones, *Paris: The Biography of a City* (London: Penguin, 2004), 42.
8. Horace Walpole quotation: letter to Lord Hertford, 10 March 1766, in *Horace Walpole's Letters*, edited by W. S. Lewis et al., 48 vols. (New Haven, CT: Yale University Press, 1974), 39:55.
9. Thiéry, *Guide des amateurs et des étrangers*, 2:32; Walpole quotation: letter to Lord Hertford, in *Horace Walpole's Letters*, edited by Lewis et al., 39:55.
10. Quoted in K. M. Baker, ed., *The Old Regime and the French Revolution* (Chicago: University of Chicago Press, 1987), 49. I have made some minor stylistic changes to this translation.
11. W. Doyle, 'The Parlements of France and the Breakdown of the Old Regime, 1771–88', in *Officers, Nobles and Revolutionaries: Essays on Eighteenth-Century France* (London: Hambledon Press, 1995), 6. This article first appeared in *French Historical Studies* 6 (1970): 415–458.
12. Jones, *Great Nation*, 278–279; Doyle, 'Parlements', 8–9, 13–17.
13. Doyle, 'Parlements', 19.
14. Quoted in J. Lough, *France on the Eve of Revolution: British Travellers' Observations, 1763–1788* (London and Sydney: Croom Helm, 1987), 255.
15. Quoted in A. Farge, *Subversive Words: Public Opinion in Eighteenth-Century France* (Oxford: Polity Press, 1994), 188.

16. Hardy quoted in ibid., 188–189; Walpole quoted in Lough, *France on the Eve*, 255.

17. Mercier, *Tableau de Paris*, 349 (see introduction, n. 18).

18. Quoted in Lough, *France on the Eve*, 259.

19. Doyle, 'Parlements', 23–30; Louis XVI quoted in Jones, *Great Nation*, 295.

20. Doyle, 'Parlements', 31; Campbell, 'Paris Parlement', 102.

21. Thiéry, *Guide des amateurs et des étrangers*, 2:29.

22. Blanning, *Culture of Power*, 379 (see introduction, n. 24); Farge, *Subversive Words*, 187; Jones, *Great Nation*, 269 (Malesherbes), 271 (Danish ambassador).

23. Mercier quotation: Mercier, *Tableau de Paris*, 341, 346; Jefferson quotation: letter to John Brown Cutting, 24 July 1788, in *The Papers of Thomas Jefferson*, edited by J. P. Boyd, 41 vols. (to date) (Princeton, NJ: Princeton University Press, 1950–2014), 13:405.

Notes to Chapter Four

1. For the dilemmas of loyalism, see, among others, C. F. Minty, 'Mobilization and Voluntarism: The Political Origins of Loyalism in New York, c. 1768–1778' (PhD diss., Stirling, 2015); Chopra, *Unnatural Rebellion* (see chap. 1, n. 5); R. Chopra, *Choosing Sides: Loyalists in Revolutionary America* (Lanham, MD: Rowman and Littlefield, 2013); L. S. Launitz-Schürer Jr., *Loyal Whigs and Revolutionaries: The Making of the Revolution in New York, 1765–1776* (New York: New York University Press, 1980); M. Kammen, 'The American Revolution as a *Crise de Conscience*: The Case of New York', in *Society, Freedom, and Conscience: The American Revolution in Virginia, Massachusetts, and New York*, edited by R. M. Jellison (New York: W. W. Norton, 1976), 125–189.

2. Buskirk, *Generous Enemies*, 11 (see chap. 1, n. 45).

3. Phelps Stokes, *Iconography*, 4:877 (see chap. 1, n. 7); Ketchum, *Divided Loyalties*, 342 (see chap. 1, n. 16); Schecter, *Battle for New York*, 53 (see chap. 1, n. 7).

4. Phelps Stokes, *Iconography*, 4:906; J. Keane, *Tom Paine: A Political Life* (London: Bloomsbury, 1995), 128 (including Inglis quotation).

5. Abbott, *New York*, 142 (see introduction, n. 21); Continental Congress quoted in Schecter, *Battle for New York*, 65; Provincial Congress and Convention quoted respectively in Kammen, 'American Revolution', 140, 144. For Smith's dilemma, see Upton, *Loyal Whig*, 106–107 (chap. 1, n. 8).

6. Buskirk, *Generous Enemies*, 20.

7. Schecter, *Battle for New York*, 41, 67, 69–71, 95–96; Champagne, *Alexander McDougall*, 98 ('shilly shally'), 102 (see chap. 1, n. 12); Charles Lee quotation on Paine: letter to Benjamin Rush, 25 February 1776, *The Lee Papers* (Collections of the New-York Historical Society for the Year 1871) (New York, 1872), 1:325; Paine quoted in Keane, *Tom Paine*, 128.

8. Washington's order in Phelps Stokes, *Iconography*, 4:940.

9. I. Bangs, *Journal of Lieutenant Isaac Bangs*, edited by E. Bangs (Cambridge: John Wilson and Son, 1890), 57.

10. Montresor, *The Montresor Journals*, 123–124 (see chap. 1, n. 10). In September 1776 Montresor sent one of his men 'through the Rebel Camp' with a message to the Loyalist tavern keeper of the inn at King's Bridge, not far from Moore's, asking him to steal the head and to bury it. When the British drove the Americans off Manhattan, Montresor had the head dug up and sent to Lord Townshend in London 'in order to convince them at home of the Infamous Disposition of the Ungrateful people of this distressed Country' (124). For the use of the lead, see Phelps Stokes, *Iconography*, 5:992. Years later, surviving parts of the statue, including the horse's tail, were rediscovered buried – possibly by Connecticut Loyalists. They were passed on to the New-York Historical Society. The surviving fragments of the statue can be seen on the NYHS museum collections website. The tail can be viewed at www.nyhistory.org/exhibit/fragment-equestrian-statue-king-george-iii-tail.

11. Champagne, *Alexander McDougall*, 91; Abbott, *New York*, 142–143; Schecter, *Battle for New York*, 54–55, 63 (Adams quoted on 59–60).

12. Schaukirk quotation: E. G. Schaukirk, 'Occupation of New York City by the British', *Pennsylvania Magazine of History and Biography* 10 (1877): 420; New Yorker and army chaplain quoted respectively in Buskirk, *Generous Enemies*, 14, 20.

13. *The Lee Papers*, 1:337–338, 354–356; Schecter, *Battle of New York*, 77–80; Burrows and Wallace, *Gotham*, 228–229 (see introduction, n. 15). Lee's papers reveal different ideas for the defence of the city. See, for example, *The Lee Papers*, 1:286–292, 321, 328–330 (this last from General Horatio Gates).

14. Cresswell quotation: N. Cresswell, *The Journal of Nicholas Cresswell, 1774–1777* (London: Jonathan Cape, 1925), 244. Details of the defences on Long Island in Schecter, *Battle of New York*, 117–119.

15. Bangs, *Journal*, 31 (fatigue duty), 65 (bloody flux); New York lady and Continental soldier quoted respectively in Buskirk, *Generous Enemies*, 14–15, 18; Burrows and Wallace, *Gotham*, 229.

16. Keane, *Tom Paine*, 138; rifleman quoted in Burrows and Wallace, *Gotham*, 231; details on the British foray up the Hudson in Burrows and Wallace, *Gotham*, 234.

17. Schecter, *Battle for New York*, 113–114; H. Bicheno, *Rebels and Redcoats: The American Revolutionary War* (London: HarperCollins, 2003), 45; Schama, *Rough Crossings*, 87 (see chap. 1, n. 45).

18. Champagne, *Alexander McDougall*, 112–113; Schecter, *Battle for New York*, 156–165.

19. Schaukirk quotation: E. G. Schaukirk, 'Occupation of New York City by the British: Extracts from the Diary of the Moravian Congregation', edited by A. A. Reinke, *Pennsylvania Magazine of History and Biography* 1 (1877): 251–252; Serle quoted in Burrows and Wallace, *Gotham*, 241.

20. See, above all, the article by Sung Bok Kim, 'The Limits of Politicization in the American Revolution: The Experience of Westchester County, New York', *Journal of American History* 80 (1993): 868–889. Further details (on the revolution and war across New York State) can be found in the essays in J. R. Tiedemann and E. R. Fingerhut, eds., *The Other New York: The American Revolution Beyond New York City, 1763–1787* (Albany: State University of New York Press, 2005).

21. Burrows and Wallace, *Gotham*, 285; Schama, *Rough Crossings*, 112–113; Buskirk, *Generous Enemies*, 136.

22. E. Homberger, *The Historical Atlas of New York City: A Visual Celebration of 400 Years of New York City's History* (New York: Owl Books / Henry Holt, 2005), 50; Burrows and Wallace, *Gotham*, 241–242 (Schaukirk quoted on 241).

23. Quoted in Schecter, *Battle for New York*, 214.

24. Abbott, *New York*, 208, 213–214; Tryon quoted in Phelps Stokes, *Iconography*, 5:1032.

25. For the archaeology on Staten Island, see 'Relics of the Revolution: Historical Society Unearths Rich Store at Fort Hill Site on Staten Island', *New York Times*, 2 November 1919.

26. S. J. Jaffe, *New York at War: Four Centuries of Combat, Fear, and Intrigue in Gotham* (New York: Basic Books, 2012), 101; Buskirk, *Generous Enemies*, 26, 30 (Anglican minister quoted on 23); Abbott, *New York*, 207–208, 215–216, 248; Schaukirk quotation: Schaukirk, 'Occupation of New York', 255.

27. Schaukirk, 'Occupation of New York', 255, 258, 422, 436; Abbott, *New York*, 208; Buskirk, *Generous Enemies*, 34.

28. Cresswell quotation: Cresswell, *Journal*, 220; Schaukirk, 'Occupation of New York', 424, 426, 435, 439–440; Abbott, *New York*, 250–254.

29. E. Burrows, *Forgotten Patriots: The Untold Story of American Prisoners During the Revolutionary War* (New York: Basic Books, 2008), 22, Thorburn quoted on 24.

30. Ibid., 19, Gage quoted on 37, veteran quoted on 92, figures on 200–201; appalled witness quoted in Jaffe, *New York at War*, 103; gaolers quoted in Abbott, *New York*, 245.

31. Abbott, *New York*, 267–268; Upton, *Loyal Whig*, 143–144; C. S. Crary, 'The Tory and the Spy: The Double Life of James Rivington', *William and Mary Quarterly* 16 (1959): 61–72.

32. Buskirk, *Generous Enemies*, 172, 175.

33. This and the following paragraphs are based on R. Ernst, 'A Tory-Eye View of the Evacuation of New York', *New York History* 64, no. 4 (1983): 391–392; and Burrows and Wallace, *Gotham*, 259–261.

34. For the Loyalist diaspora, see Jasanoff, *Liberty's Exiles*, Loyalist numbers on 357 (see introduction, n. 6).

Notes to Chapter Five

1. Paine quotation: Paine, *Common Sense*, 63–64.

2. Tooke and Boylston quoted respectively in J. Sainsbury, *Disaffected Patriots: London Supporters of Revolutionary America, 1769–1782* (Kingston and Montreal: McGill-Queen's University Press; Gloucester: Alan Sutton, 1987), 32, 33.

3. Flavell, *When London Was Capital of America*, 146–147 (see chap. 2, n. 10); Cash, *John Wilkes*, 321–324 (see chap. 2, n. 8).

4. Sainsbury, *Disaffected Patriots*, 9–10.

5. Westminster Association subcommittee quoted in www.historyofparliamentonline.org/volume/1754-1790/constituencies/westminster.

6. J. Field, *The Story of Parliament in the Palace of Westminster* (London: James & James, 2002), 5–7, 32–35; C. Jones, *The Great Palace: The Story of Parliament* (London: BBC, 1983), 10, 30; *The Houses of Parliament: A Guide to the Palace of Westminster* (London: HMSO, 1988), 3–4; J. White, *London in the Eighteenth Century*, 545 (see chap. 2, n. 1); J. Stevenson, *Popular Disturbances in England, 1700–1832* (Harlow: Longman, 1992), 206.

7. E. C. Black, *The Association: British Extraparliamentary Political Organization, 1769–1793* (Cambridge, MA: Harvard University Press, 1963), 58–80, 178–179; H. T. Dickinson, *Liberty and Property: Political Ideology in Eighteenth-Century Britain* (London: Methuen, 1979), 219;

Goodwin, *Friends of Liberty*, 63 (see chap. 2, n. 24); quotations from *An Address to the Public from the Society for Constitutional Information* (London, 1780), 1, 2.

8. Quoted in Dickinson, *Liberty and Property*, 219.
9. C. Haydon, *Anti-Catholicism in Eighteenth-Century England, c. 1714–80: A Political and Social Study* (Manchester: Manchester University Press, 1993), 204; I. Haywood and J. Seed, introduction to *The Gordon Riots: Politics, Culture and Insurrection in Late Eighteenth-Century Britain* (Cambridge: Cambridge University Press, 2012), 1–2.
10. Protestant Association quoted in Haywood and Seed, introduction to *Gordon Riots*, 2.
11. Stevenson, *Popular Disturbances*, 96.
12. Haywood and Seed, introduction to *Gordon Riots*, 3; Stevenson, *Popular Disturbances*, 96–97.
13. Haywood and Seed, introduction to *Gordon Riots*, 4; Stevenson, *Popular Disturbances*, 97–98 (Holroyd quoted on 97).
14. J. P. de Castro, *The Gordon Riots* (London: Oxford University Press, 1926), 47.
15. Ibid., 64–65, 131–132; Stevenson, *Popular Disturbances*, 98–99.
16. De Castro, *The Gordon Riots*, 74–75.
17. Quoted in ibid., 89–90.
18. T. Hitchcock and R. Shoemaker, *Tales from the Hanging Court* (London: Hodder Arnold, 2006), xiii; P. Linebaugh, *The London Hanged: Crime and Civil Society in the Eighteenth Century* (London: Allen Lane, 1991), 91–98; V. A. C. Gatrell, *The Hanging Tree: Execution and the English People, 1770–1868* (Oxford: Oxford University Press, 1994), 8.
19. E. P. Thompson, 'The Crime of Anonymity', in *Albion's Fatal Tree: Crime and Society in Eighteenth-Century England*, edited by D. Hay (London: Allen Lane, 1975), 267; Linebaugh, *London Hanged*, 105.
20. De Castro, *The Gordon Riots*, 98–99.
21. Stevenson, *Popular Disturbances*, 100.
22. Sancho quotation: I. Sancho, *Letters of the Late Ignatius Sancho, an African*, 2 vols. (London, 1782), 2:180.
23. Quoted in de Castro, *The Gordon Riots*, 144.
24. Quoted in ibid., 146.
25. Wilkes quoted in ibid., 142; Johnson quoted in Cash, *John Wilkes*, 362.
26. For an argument that the riots were a social protest, see G. Rudé, *Paris and London in the Eighteenth Century: Studies in Popular Protest* (London: Collins, 1970), 285–287.

27. On the geography of retribution, see the fascinating, if grim, analysis by M. White, 'Public Executions and the Gordon Riots', in *Gordon Riots*, edited by Haywood and Seed, 204–225.

28. Sancho, *Letters of Ignatius Sancho*, 172, 187.

29. N. Rogers, 'The Gordon Riots and the Politics of War', in *Gordon Riots*, edited by Haywood and Seed, 33; Sainsbury, *Disaffected Patriots*, 157–158.

30. Quoted in Black, *Association*, 67.

31. Sainsbury, *Disaffected Patriots*, 159; Burke quoted in I. Gilmour, *Riot, Risings and Revolution: Governance and Violence in Eighteenth-Century England* (London: Pimlico, 1993), 375.

Notes to Chapter Six

1. M. Linton, 'The Intellectual Origins of the French Revolution', in *Origins of the French Revolution*, edited by Campbell, 151–152 (see chap. 3, n. 3); Baker, *Inventing the French Revolution*, 173–175, Dubois de Launay quoted on 180 (see introduction, n. 25); Mercier quotation: Mercier, *Tableau de Paris*, 318–321 (see introduction, n. 18). For French revolutionary attitudes towards the British, see N. Hampson, *The Perfidy of Albion: French Perceptions of England During the French Revolution* (Basingstoke: Macmillan, 1998).

2. Works on the impact of the American Revolution in France are legion, but a good place to start is the now-classic D. Echeverria, *Mirage in the West: A History of the French Image of American Society to 1815* (Princeton, NJ: Princeton University Press, 1956).

3. For Franklin's mission to France, see S. Schiff, *A Great Improvisation: Franklin, France, and the Birth of America* (New York: Owl Books, 2005). On Franklin's image in France, see J. A. Leith, 'Le culte de Franklin avant et pendant la Révolution française', *Annales Historiques de la Révolution Française* (1976): 543–572; Fars-Fausselandry quoted in S. Schama, *Citizens: A Chronicle of the French Revolution* (New York: Alfred A. Knopf, 1989), 49.

4. J. Félix, 'The Financial Origins of the French Revolution', in *Origins of the French Revolution*, edited by Campbell, 50–51, 58–59; Doyle, *Origins of the French Revolution*, 43–45, 48–49 (see chap. 3, n. 2); Brissot quoted in J. Egret, *The French Pre-Revolution, 1787–1788* (Chicago: University of Chicago Press, 1977), 86.

5. Rice, *Thomas Jefferson's Paris*, 13 (see introduction, n. 2); F.-A. Fauveau de Frénilly, *Souvenirs du baron de Frénilly, pair de France (1768–1828)* (Paris, 1908), 24.

6. Jones, *Paris*, 222–223 (see chap. 3, n. 7); Godechot, *Taking of the Bastille*, 56–58 (see introduction, n. 21).

7. For the most recent and compelling assessment of the duc d'Orléans, which explores his political career, his reputation in word and image and his British connections, see Richard Clarke, 'Between Politics and Conspiracy: The Public Image and the Private Politics of the Duc d'Orléans' (PhD diss., Kingston University, 2014). See also G. A. Kelly, 'The Machine of the Duc d'Orléans and the New Politics', *Journal of Modern History* 51 (1979): 667–684. Jefferson quoted in Rice, *Thomas Jefferson's Paris*, 15.

8. Karamzin, *Voyage en France*, 79–80 (see introduction, n. 12).

9. Thomas Jefferson to David Humphreys, 14 August 1787, *Papers of Thomas Jefferson*, 12:32 (see chap. 3, n. 23).

10. Frénilly, *Souvenirs du baron de Frénilly*, 24, 25; Karamzin, *Voyage en France*, 80.

11. Egret, *Pre-Revolution*, 90–91; for Jefferson's analysis, see, for example, his letter to John Jay, 23 May 1788, *Papers of Thomas Jefferson*, 13:188–189.

12. W. Doyle, *Oxford History of the French Revolution* (Oxford: Oxford University Press, 1989), 85.

13. G. Rudé, *The Crowd in the French Revolution* (New York: Oxford University Press, 1959), 29–30.

14. Egret, *Pre-Revolution*, 87–88, government edict quoted on 190, Parlement quoted on 197.

15. Jefferson to Thomas Paine, 23 December 1788, *Papers of Thomas Jefferson*, 14:375.

16. Jones, *Great Nation*, 396 (see introduction, n. 3); Campbell, introduction to *Origins of the French Revolution*, 31; Egret, *Pre-Revolution*, 190, Sieyès quoted on 192.

17. J.-D. Bredin, preface to *Qu'est-ce que le tiers état?*, by E. Sieyès (Paris: Flammarion, 1988), 10–13.

18. Sieyès, *Qu'est-ce que le tiers état?*, 41, 127.

19. Jefferson to David Humphreys, 18 March 1789, *Papers of Thomas Jefferson*, 14:676.

20. Tennis Court Oath quoted in Doyle, *Oxford History*, 105.

21. A. Young, *Travels in France During the Years 1787, 1788 & 1789* (Cambridge: Cambridge University Press, 1929), 134–135.

22. Louis-Philippe, *Memoirs, 1773–1793*, translated by J. Hardman (New York and London: Harcourt Brace Jovanovich, 1977), 33; Cerutti quoted in D. M. McMahon, 'The Birthplace of the Revolution: Public Space

and Political Community in the Palais-Royal of Louis-Philippe-Joseph d'Orléans, 1781–1789', *French History* 10 (1996): 2.

23. This and the following paragraphs are based heavily on the superb analysis by David Garrioch, *Neighbourhood and Community in Paris, 1740–1790* (Cambridge: Cambridge University Press, 1986), 240–253.

24. R. Monnier, *Le Faubourg Saint-Antoine (1789–1815)* (Paris: Société des Études Robespierristes, 1981), 18, 113.

25. Rudé, *Crowd in the French Revolution*, 33, 251.

26. Jefferson to Madame de Bréhan, 14 March 1789, *Papers of Thomas Jefferson*, 14:656.

27. Godechot, *Taking of the Bastille*, 138–151, draper quoted on 134; Rudé, *Crowd in the French Revolution*, 35–38; Monnier, *Faubourg Saint-Antoine*.

28. *Papers of Thomas Jefferson*, 15:267; C. Desmoulins, *Correspondance inédite de Camille Desmoulins* (Paris, 1836), 21–22.

29. Godechot, *Taking of the Bastille*, 87–90; A.-S. Lambert, *La Bastille; ou, 'L'enfer des vivants'?* (Paris: Bibliothèque Nationale de France, n.d.), 3.

30. See H.-J. Lüsebrink and R. Reichardt, *The Bastille: A History of a Symbol of Despotism and Freedom*, translated by N. Schürer (Durham, NC: Duke University Press, 1997).

31. Rudé, *Crowd in the French Revolution*, 56–59; D. Godineau, *The Women of Paris and Their French Revolution*, translated by K. Streip (Berkeley: University of California Press, 1998), 97.

32. Most of the details on which this account of the fall of the Bastille is based have been distilled from the following sources: J.-S. Bailly and Honoré Duveyrier, *Procès-verbal des séances et délibérations de l'Assemblée générale des électeurs de Paris, réunis à l'Hôtel-de-Ville le 14 juillet 1789*, 3 vols. (Paris, 1790), 1:266ff; J. Flammermont, *La journée du 14 juillet 1789: Fragments des mémoires inédits de L.-G. Pitra, électeur de Paris en 1789* (Paris, 1892); L. Deflue, 'Relation de la prise de la Bastille, 14 juillet 1789, par un de ses défenseurs', *Revue Rétrospective* 4 (1834): 284–298; J.-B. Humbert, *Journée de Jean-Baptiste Humbert, horloger, qui, le premier, a monté sur les tours de la Bastille* (Paris, 1789); D. Andress, *1789: The Threshold of the Modern Age* (London: Little, Brown, 2008), 289–293; Godechot, *Taking of the Bastille*, 220–258; and Godineau, *Women of Paris*, 97.

33. Jefferson to Paine, 17 July 1789, *Papers of Thomas Jefferson*, 15:279.

34. Jefferson to Jay, 19 July 1789, ibid., 289–290.

Notes to Chapter Seven

1. Duane quoted in Burrows and Wallace, *Gotham*, 265 (see introduction, n. 15); Phelps Stokes, *Iconography*, 5:1175 (see chap. 1, n. 7).
2. Phelps Stokes, *Iconography*, 5:1197.
3. *Independent Gazette* quoted in Burrows and Wallace, *Gotham*, 275; Jay quotation: Phelps Stokes, *Iconography*, 5:1201.
4. E. Countryman, *A People in Revolution: The American Revolution and Political Society in New York, 1760–1790* (Baltimore: Johns Hopkins University Press, 1981), 230–231 (Livingston quoted on 230); Clinton quoted in Abbott, *New York*, 231 (see introduction, n. 21).
5. Phelps Stokes, *Iconography*, 5:1191, *Pennsylvania Packet* quoted on 1182.
6. Burrows and Wallace, *Gotham*, 267; Buskirk, *Generous Enemies*, 188 (see chap. 1, n. 45); Countryman, *People in Revolution*, 243.
7. A. C. Flick, *Loyalism in New York During the American Revolution* (New York, 1901), 153–154 (claim about the extent of Tory property quoted on 153). Flick provides an interesting appendix with a full list of all sales of 'attainted' estates in New York State. Phelps Stokes, *Iconography*, 5:1193; Homberger, *Historical Atlas*, 61 (see chap. 4, n. 22); Burrows and Wallace, *Gotham*, 267–268.
8. Phelps Stokes, *Iconography*, 5:1193.
9. Countryman, *People in Revolution*, 241–242; Burrows and Wallace, *Gotham*, 268.
10. Countryman, *People in Revolution*, 241.
11. Buskirk, *Generous Enemies*, 188, 192; Burrows and Wallace, *Gotham*, 278; R. Chernow, *Alexander Hamilton* (New York: Penguin, 2004), 197–199, Hamilton quoted on 184.
12. A. Hamilton, 'A Letter from Phocion to the Considerate Citizens of New-York on the Politics of the Day', in *Writings*, by A. Hamilton, edited J. B. Freeman (New York: Library of America, 2001), 129, 139.
13. Countryman, *People in Revolution*, 244; 'New York City', *Thomas Jefferson Encyclopedia* on the Thomas Jefferson's Monticello website, www.monticello. org/site/research-and-collections/new-york-city.
14. Manumission Society quoted in R. J. Swan, 'John Teasman: African-American Educator and the Emergence of Community in Early Black New York City, 1787–1815', *Journal of the Early Republic* 12 (1992): 334. Details on the Manumission Society in Burrows and Wallace, *Gotham*, 285–286; and S. White, *Somewhat More Independent*, 81–86 (slaveholders quoted on 147) (see chap. 1, n. 45).

15. J. L. Rury, 'Philanthropy, Self Help, and Social Control: The New York Manumission Society and Free Blacks, 1785–1810', *Phylon* 46 (1985): 235–237; school regulations quoted in Swan, 'John Teasman', 339–340.

16. Lynd, 'Mechanics in New York', 237–238 (see chap. 1, n. 46); Burrows and Wallace, *Gotham*, 279–280.

17. Chernow, *Alexander Hamilton*, 221; Burrows and Wallace, *Gotham*, 280.

18. Nash, *Unknown American Revolution*, 448 (see chap. 1, n. 16); Jefferson quoted in M. D. Peterson, *Thomas Jefferson and the New Nation: A Biography* (New York: Oxford University Press, 1970), 359.

19. Washington quoted in Chernow, *Alexander Hamilton*, 241; Greenleaf quoted in Burrows and Wallace, *Gotham*, 289.

20. Chernow, *Alexander Hamilton*, 247–248.

21. Phelps Stokes, *Iconography*, 5:1229.

22. Quoted in P. A. Gilje, 'The Common People and the Constitution: Popular Culture in New York City in the Late Eighteenth Century', in *New York in the Age of the Constitution, 1775–1800*, edited by P. A. Gilje and W. Pencak (London and Toronto: Associated University Press, 1992), 61.

23. Homberger, *Historical Atlas*, 57–58; Clinton quoted in E. W. Spaulding, *New York in the Critical Period, 1783–1789* (New York: Columbia University Press, 1932), 27; New York legislature quotation: Phelps Stokes, *Iconography*, 5:1215.

24. R. G. Kennedy, *Orders from France: The Americans and French in a Revolutionary World, 1780–1820* (New York: Alfred A. Knopf, 1989), 96; Burrows and Wallace, *Gotham*, 294–295.

25. Homberger, *Historical Atlas*, 59.

26. L'Enfant quoted in R. G. Kennedy, *Orders from France*, 96.

27. Phelps Stokes, *Iconography*, 5:1236–1237 (see also 1249). For a useful weighing of different contemporary descriptions, see L. Torres, 'Federal Hall Revisited', *Journal of the Society of Architectural Historians* 29 (1970): 327–338.

28. Torres, 'Federal Hall Revisited', 328; Homberger, *Historical Atlas*, 58–59.

29. Phelps Stokes, *Iconography*, 5:1239 (*Daily Advertiser*), 1240 (Boudinot).

30. Ibid., 1240.

31. The route that the procession followed was broken by later urban development that began with the construction of Brooklyn Bridge from 1870: T. E. V. Smith, *The City of New York in the Year of Washington's Inauguration* (1889) (Riverside, CT: Chatham Press, 1973), 225; Homberger, *Historical Atlas*, 59.

32. Eliza Quincy quoted in Smith, *City of New York*, 232; Maclay quotation:

W. Maclay, *Journal of William Maclay*, edited by E. S. Maclay (New York, 1890), 9.

33. Smith, *City of New York*, 232–233; Phelps Stokes, *Iconography*, 5:1243.
34. Maclay, *Journal of Maclay*, 9.
35. Washington ('culprit') quoted in J. R. Sharp, *American Politics in the Early Republic: The New Nation in Crisis* (New Haven, CT: Yale University Press, 1993), 17; 'Washington's Inaugural Address of 1789', www.archives. gov/exhibits/american_originals/inaugtxt.html.
36. Newman, *Parades and the Politics of the Street*, 39 (see chap. 1, n. 21).

Notes to Chapter Eight

1. Lüsebrink and Reichardt, *Bastille*, 74 (see chap. 6, n. 30); Godechot, *Taking of the Bastille*, 265 (see introduction, n. 21); Jones, *Paris*, 256 (see chap. 3, n. 7); R. Clay, *Iconoclasm in Revolutionary Paris: The Transformation of Signs* (Oxford: Voltaire Foundation, 2012), 166–167.
2. For the reforms of the early Revolution, see Doyle, *Oxford History*, 123–129 (see chap. 6, n. 12); and D. Andress, *French Society in Revolution, 1789–99* (Manchester: Manchester University Press, 1999), 61–63, 69–74. For a brief overview of the ways in which the Revolution as a whole changed France politically and socially, see M. Rapport, 'Revolution', in *The Oxford Handbook of the Ancien Régime*, edited by W. Doyle (Oxford: Oxford University Press, 2012), 467–486. For the Declaration of the Rights of Man and the Citizen, see Doyle, *Oxford History*, 118–119.
3. Doyle, *Oxford History*, 125.
4. Andress, *1789*, 337 (see chap. 6, n. 32).
5. Garrioch, *Neighbourhood and Community*, 215 (see chap. 6, n. 23); Young quotation: Young, *Travels in France*, 81–82 (see chap. 6, n. 21); Jones, *Paris*, 49 (origins of Les Halles).
6. Kaplow, *Names of Kings*, 21, 45 (see introduction, n. 27); Garrioch, *Neighbourhood and Community*, 116–117.
7. O. Hufton, *Women and the Limits of Citizenship in the French Revolution* (Toronto: University of Toronto Press, 1992), 15; Garrioch, *Neighbourhood and Community*, 216, 253.
8. Kaplow, *Names of Kings*, 72–73.
9. On these points, see O. Hufton, 'Women in Revolution, 1789–1796', in *French Society and the Revolution*, edited by D. Johnson (Cambridge: Cambridge University Press, 1976), 148–166. Also available in *Past and Present*, no. 53 (November 1971).

10. Andress, *1789*, 337.

11. The preceding paragraphs on the *journées* of 5–6 October are based on Hufton, *Women and the Limits of Citizenship*, 7–12; Rudé, *Crowd in the French Revolution*, 73–77 (see chap. 6, n. 13); and Andress, *1789*, 337–341. On the royal court at the Tuileries during these brief years of the constitutional monarchy, see the brilliant book by Ambrogio Caiani, *Louis XVI and the French Revolution, 1789–1792* (Cambridge: Cambridge University Press, 2012).

12. G. Lenotre, *Paris révolutionnaire* (Paris, 1912), 62–65; J. Tulard, *Nouvelle histoire de Paris: La Révolution, 1789–1799* (Paris: Hachette, 1971), 170.

13. Clay, *Iconoclasm in Revolutionary Paris*, 43.

14. Doyle, *Oxford History*, 139–142.

15. E. G. Bouwers, *Public Pantheons in Revolutionary Europe: Comparing Cultures of Remembrance, c. 1790–1840* (Basingstoke: Macmillan, 2012), 91.

16. Jones, *Paris*, 233, 249; master of novices quoted in Tulard, *Nouvelle histoire de Paris*, 191.

17. Most of the streets described in these paragraphs still exist today, but the district was utterly transformed when the present-day boulevard Saint-Germain was rammed through here in 1876, a topographical stake driven through one of the historic heartlands of the French Revolution. J.-J. Lévêque and V. R. Belot, *Guide de la Révolution française*, 2nd ed. (Paris: Horay, 1989), 103, 108, 112; Jones, *Paris*, 189.

18. R. B. Rose, *The Making of the* Sans-Culottes: *Democratic Ideas and Institutions in Paris, 1789–92* (Manchester: Manchester University Press, 1983), 19; E. Hazan, *The Invention of Paris: A History in Footsteps* (London: Verso, 2011), 92; J.-P. Bertaud, *La vie quotidienne en France au temps de la Révolution (1789–1795)* (Paris: Hachette, 1983), 131.

19. Rose, *Making of the* Sans-Culottes, 60, 69, 72, 78.

20. Ibid., 60, 67–70.

21. Ibid., 80.

22. Desmoulins quoted in Doyle, *Oxford History*, 124 ('active citizens'); and Rose, *Making of the* Sans-Culottes, 80 ('Oh, my very dear Cordeliers').

23. Rose, *Making of the* Sans-Culottes, 89.

24. Lenotre, *Paris révolutionnaire*, 312–313, 318–320. Almost the entire monastery was destroyed when the new medical school was constructed in the nineteenth century. The refectory still survives. Now an exhibition space, it can be seen just off the rue de l'École de Médécine.

25. A. Mathiez, *Le Club des Cordeliers pendant la crise de Varennes et le Massacre du Champ de Mars* (Paris: Champion, 1910), 6.

26. Ibid., 9–10.

27. For Paris government under the old regime, see Garrioch, *Making of Revolutionary Paris*, 68–69, 95, 128–132 (see introduction, n. 3); Mercier quotation: Mercier, *Tableau de Paris*, 337 (see introduction, n. 18).

28. Doyle, *Oxford History*, 129.

29. J. Robiquet, *Daily Life in the French Revolution*, translated by J. Kirkup (London: Weidenfeld and Nicolson, 1964), 47–49.

30. Tulard, *Nouvelle histoire de Paris*, 197.

31. I. Bourdin, *Les sociétés populaires à Paris pendant la Révolution* (Paris: Recueil Sirey, 1937), 418–420 (Louise Kéralio-Robert quoted on 58).

32. D. Andress, *Massacre at the Champ de Mars: Popular Dissent and Political Culture in the French Revolution* (Woodbridge: Royal Historical Society / Boydell, 2000), 148–153; Paine and Lafayette quoted in Keane, *Tom Paine*, 313 (Lafayette), 319 (Paine).

33. Andress, *Massacre at the Champ de Mars*, 174–180; T. Tackett, *When the King Took Flight* (Cambridge, MA: Harvard University Press, 2003), 145–146.

34. The authority on the massacre is Andress, *Massacre at the Champ de Mars*. See also Mathiez, *Club des Cordeliers*, 146–149; and Tackett, *When the King*, 150.

35. Mathiez, *Club des Cordeliers*, 150; deputy quoted in Tackett, *When the King*, 204.

36. Rose, *Making of the* Sans-Culottes, 154.

37. National Guard quotation: 'Lettre d'un garde national', 11 August 1792, reprinted in M. Reinhard, *La chute de la royauté: 10 août 1792* (Paris: Gallimard, 1969), 583–585 (quotation on 585).

38. McPhee, *Robespierre: A Revolutionary Life*, 125–126 (see chap. 3, n. 1).

Notes to Chapter Nine

1. J. Derry, *Charles James Fox* (New York: St Martin's Press, 1972), 293–296 (quotation on 293); *Times* quoted in N. Schürer, 'The Storming of the Bastille in English Newspapers', *Eighteenth-Century Life* 29 (2005): 76.

2. G. Claeys, *The French Revolution Debate in Britain: The Origins of Modern Politics* (Basingstoke: Palgrave, 2007), 9; Goodwin, *Friends of Liberty*, 76–78 (see chap. 2, n. 24).

3. For the Old Jewry: W. Thornbury, *Old and New London*, 6 vols. (London, 1878), 1:425–435.

4. Adams quotation: Abigail Adams to Mary Smith Cranch, 21 May 1786, in *Letters of Mrs. Adams*, by Adams, 2:139–140 (see introduction, n. 13); Brissot quotation: Brissot de Warville, *Mémoires, 1754–1793*, 1:373 (see introduction, n. 19).

5. *An Abstract of the History and Proceedings of the London Revolution Society* (London, 1789), 7, 42–44; Goodwin, *Friends of Liberty*, 85–86; Black, *Association*, 215 (see chap. 5, n. 7).

6. Quotations from Price: R. Price, *A Discourse of the Love of Our Country* (London, 1789), 28–30, 33, 41–42.

7. *Abstract of the History and Proceedings*, 50–51. The address was enthusiastically received in Paris on 25 November: see *Archives Parlementaires*, 10:257.

8. C. B. Cone, *Burke and the Nature of Politics: The Age of the French Revolution* (Louisville: University Press of Kentucky, 1964), 301, 313; DePont quotation: Charles-Jean-François DePont to E. Burke, 29 December 1789, in *The Correspondence of Edmund Burke*, edited by T. W. Copeland, A. Cobban and R. A. Smith (Cambridge: Cambridge University Press; Chicago: University of Chicago Press, 1967), 6:59, 81 (Burke's response); E. Burke, *Reflections on the Revolution in France* (Harmondsworth: Penguin, 1968), 181 ('half a dozen grasshoppers').

9. Burke quoted in Claeys, *French Revolution Debate*, 15 ('a people').

10. Burke, *Reflections on the Revolution*, 103–104.

11. Cone, *Burke and the Nature of Politics*, 285–286; Burke, *Reflections on the Revolution*, 106, 117.

12. Burke, *Reflections on the Revolution*, 169–170, 174–175, 299.

13. Cone, *Burke and the Nature of Politics*, 341; Claeys, *French Revolution Debate*, 24; Derry, *Charles James Fox*, 203; George III quotation from Keane, *Tom Paine*, 290.

14. These figures are taken from the information in J. Pendred, *The London and Country Printers, Booksellers and Stationers Vade Mecum* (London, 1785).

15. J. Brewer, *The Pleasures of the Imagination: English Culture in the Eighteenth Century* (London: HarperCollins, 1997), 130; J. W. von Archenholz, *A Picture of England*, 2 vols. (London, 1789), 1:60; J. White, *London in the Eighteenth Century*, 253–254, 256 (see chap. 2, n. 1).

16. Archenholz, *A Picture of England*, 2:107–108.

17. Blanning, *Culture of Power*, 156–157 (see introduction, n. 24); Brewer, *Pleasures of the Imagination*, 187.

18. Quoted in Brewer, *Pleasures of the Imagination*, 183–184.

19. J. White, *London in the Eighteenth Century*, 264–265; Brewer, *Pleasures of the Imagination*, 35–36.

20. J. Todd, *Mary Wollstonecraft: A Revolutionary Life* (London: Phoenix Press, 2001), 152; Blake quotation: J. Todd, *The Collected Letters of Mary Wollstonecraft* (London: Allen Lane, 2003), 106n.

21. Todd, *Mary Wollstonecraft*, 4, 59–61, 138; Wollstonecraft quotation: Todd, *Letters of Wollstonecraft*, 139.

22. Todd, *Mary Wollstonecraft*, 162, 164.

23. Claeys, *French Revolution Debate*, 57–58; M. Wollstonecraft, *A Vindication of the Rights of Men in a Letter to the Right Honourable Edmund Burke* (London, 1790), 3, 9, 21, 26, 64, 94.

24. C. Nelson, *Thomas Paine: His Life, His Time and the Birth of Modern Nations* (London: Profile Books, 2007), 176, 179 (quotations on 190, 191).

25. Thomas Paine, *Rights of Man* (1791–1792) (Harmondsworth: Penguin, 1984), 41–42, 47, 83.

26. Ibid., 70, 72, 87, 143.

27. Keane, *Tom Paine*, 304–305, 308–309.

28. H. T. Dickinson, *British Radicalism and the French Revolution* (Oxford: Blackwell, 1985), 20; Keane, *Tom Paine*, 306–307, 310, 319.

29. Goodwin, *Friends of Liberty*, 175–177; Walpole, *Gentleman's Magazine* and *Analytical Review* all quoted in Todd, *Mary Wollstonecraft*, 168; Wyvill quoted in Keane, *Tom Paine*, 329.

Notes to Chapter Ten

1. Rudé, *Crowd in the French Revolution*, 114 (see chap. 6, n. 13).

2. M. Sonenscher, 'The *Sans-Culottes* of the Year II: Rethinking the Language of Labour in Revolutionary France', *Social History* 9 (1984): 301–328, esp. 316–326; R. B. Rose, *The Enragés: Socialists of the French Revolution?* (Melbourne: University of Melbourne Press, 1965), 18. For the place of the *sans-culotte* in the wider currents of eighteenth-century ideas of property, commerce, sovereignty, freedom and more, see M. Sonenscher, Sans-Culottes: *An Eighteenth-Century Emblem in the French Revolution* (Princeton, NJ: Princeton University Press, 2008).

3. D. Andress, *The Terror: Civil War in the French Revolution* (London: Little, Brown, 2005), 163. For examples of sectional premises, see Archives Nationales, Paris F/13/1280 (dossier 2).

4. Rose, *Enragés*, 19.

5. L. Whaley, *Radicals: Politics and Republicanism in the French Revolution*

(Stroud: Sutton, 2000), 125; Pétion quoted in McPhee, *Robespierre: A Revolutionary Life*, 149 (see chap. 3, n. 1).

6. Petition quoted in M. Cerati, *Le club des citoyennes républicaines révolutionnaires* (Paris: Éditions Sociales, 1966), 23.

7. For Robespierre's ideas on the venue for the convention, see McPhee, *Robespierre: A Revolutionary Life*, 152.

8. Gorsas quoted in Godineau, *Women of Paris*, 129 (see chap. 6, n. 31).

9. Hanriot quoted in Andress, *Terror*, 176.

10. Doyle, *Oxford History*, 251 (see chap. 6, n. 12).

11. For Saint-Eustache Church, see Jones, *Paris*, 106 (see chap. 3, n. 7).

12. L.-M. Prudhomme, *Révolutions de Paris, dédiées à la nation* 17, no. 215 (13–20 November 1793): 207–210.

13. Doyle, *Oxford History*, 264–265; Law of Suspects quoted in J. M. Thompson, ed., *French Revolution Documents, 1789–94* (Oxford: Blackwell, 1933), 258–260.

14. A. Soboul, *Les sans-culottes parisiens en l'an II: Movement populaire et gouvernement révolutionnaire (1793–1794)* (Paris: Seuil, 1968), 180–183.

15. Decree in J. M. Thompson, *French Revolution Documents*, 255–258.

16. Archives Nationales, Paris, F/13/309–312a (dossier: 'Usines flottantes installées sur des bateaux places sous les ponts') for the floating workshops; F/13/967 for the Évêché; F/13/890 (dossier: Ateliers d'armes) for the Luxembourg factory; F/13/502 for the Manège; J.-F. Belhoste and D. Woronoff, 'Ateliers et manufactures: Une réévaluation nécessaire', in *À Paris sous la Révolution: Nouvelles approaches de la ville,* edited by R. Monnier (Paris: Sorbonne, 2008), 87–88.

17. R. Bijaoui, *Prisonniers et prisons de la Terreur* (Paris: Imago, 1996), 181–184; Archives Nationales, Paris F/16/581 (report of 19 Vendémiaire Year 3); F/16/585 (complaint of 22 Fructidor Year 7) for prison conditions.

18. Quoted in Clay, *Iconoclasm in Revolutionary Paris*, 217 (see chap. 8, n. 1).

19. Jones, *Paris*, 233; E. Kennedy, *A Cultural History of the French Revolution* (New Haven, CT: Yale University Press, 1989), 304, 347–350; Andress, *Terror*, 306–307.

20. Andress, *Terror*, 240; Doyle, *Oxford History*, 260.

21. Archives Nationales, Paris F/13/967, for the stripping out of Notre-Dame Cathedral; Clay, *Iconoclasm in Revolutionary Paris*, 219; E. Hollis, *The Secret Lives of Buildings: From the Parthenon to the Vegas Strip in Thirteen Stories* (London: Portobello Books, 2009), 237–234; quotation 'superstitious credulity' in Doyle, *Oxford History*, 261.

22. A. McClellan, *Inventing the Louvre: Art, Politics, and the Origins of the*

Modern Museum in Eighteenth-Century Paris (Berkeley: University of California Press, 1994), 155–197.

23. Andress, *Terror*, 241–242; commune delegation quoted in Jones, *Paris*, 231.

24. Doyle, *Oxford History*, 263.

25. Robespierre quoted in R. T. Bienvenu, ed., *The Ninth of Thermidor: The Fall of Robespierre* (New York: Oxford University Press, 1968), 38, 39.

26. Quoted in Doyle, *Oxford History*, 277.

27. M. Ozouf, *Festivals and the French Revolution*, translated by A. Sheridan (Cambridge, MA: Harvard University Press, 1988), 150–152 (Robespierre quoted on 150).

28. H. M. Williams, *Memoirs of the Reign of Robespierre* (London: John Hamilton, n.d.), 95 (clothing); Keane, *Tom Paine*, 408 (tenements).

29. Excellent investigations and discussions into the human dimension, including emotional responses to the crisis, can be read in M. Linton, *Choosing Terror: Virtue, Friendship and Authenticity in the French Revolution* (Oxford: Oxford University Press, 2013); Andress, 'Revolutionary Historiography', 1–15 (see introduction, n. 9).

30. P. Barras, *Mémoires de Barras*, edited by J.-P. Thomas (Paris: Mercure de France, 2005), 122–123; McPhee, *Robespierre: A Revolutionary Life*, 93; Lenotre, *Paris révolutionnaire*, 15–16 (see chap. 8, n. 12). Until recently, one could walk straight into the courtyard where there was a restaurant (called, of course, Le Robespierre) at the end. Today, the whole building, which is privately owned, is now sealed off by a gate. The original wide coach entrance was later narrowed into a passageway, but to the rear of the courtyard some of the apartments, including Robespierre's rooms, still survive.

31. On the revolutionaries' ideas of 'transparency' and personal security, see M. Linton, 'The Stuff of Nightmares: Plots, Assassinations and Duplicity in the Mental World of the Jacobin Leaders, 1793–1794', in *Experiencing the French Revolution*, edited by Andress, 207, 214 (see introduction, n. 9).

32. Lenotre, *Paris révolutionnaire*, 115.

33. Renault quoted in Andress, *Terror*, 321; Robespierre quoted in McPhee, *Robespierre: A Revolutionary Life*, 201. See also Linton, 'Plots, Assassinations and Duplicity', 209.

34. D. Arasse, *La guillotine et l'imaginaire de la Terreur* (Paris: Flammarion, 1987), 96; Sanson quotation: H. Sanson, ed., *Executioners All: Memoirs of the Sanson Family from Private Notes and Documents, 1688–1847*

(London: Neville Spearman, 1958), 173; Danton quotation: G. Walter, ed., *Actes du tribunal révolutionnaire* (Paris: Mercure de France, 1986), 583.

35. The Madeleine Cemetery is now the site of the Chapelle Expiatoire on boulevard Haussmann, a nineteenth-century shrine to the executed king and queen, its gardens also the resting place of the remains of the Swiss Guards who had died defending them on 10 August 1792. The Picpus Cemetery still exists and is in today's 12th arrondissement.

36. McPhee, *Robespierre: A Revolutionary Life*, 206–207.

Notes to Chapter Eleven

1. Hardy quotations: M. Thale, ed., *Selections from the Papers of the London Corresponding Society, 1792–1799* (Cambridge: Cambridge University Press, 1983), 5–6; details on the Old Bell: F. H. W. Sheppard, *Survey of London*, vol. 36, *The Parish of St. Paul Covent Garden* (London: Athlone Press, University of London, 1970), 225–226, 228.

2. Thale, *Papers of the London Corresponding Society*, 6.

3. Goodwin, *Friends of Liberty*, 189 (see chap. 2, n. 24); Thale, *Papers of the London Corresponding Society*, 6–7.

4. Thale, *Papers of the London Corresponding Society*, xxv, 10.

5. Dickinson, *British Radicalism*, 9–10 (see chap. 9, n. 28). On the LCS as a 'subaltern' network, see D. Featherstone, 'Contested Relationalities of Political Activism: The Democratic Spatial Practices of the London Corresponding Society', *Cultural Dynamics* 22 (2010): 87–104.

6. 'We were men', quoted in G. A. Williams, *Artisans and* Sans-Culottes: *Popular Movements in France and Britain During the French Revolution* (London: Arnold, 1968), 8.

7. Thale, *Papers of the London Corresponding Society*, 8, 28–29; Place quotation: F. Place, *The Autobiography of Francis Place (1771–1854)*, edited by M. Thale (Cambridge: Cambridge University Press, 1972), 200; G. A. Williams, *Artisans and* Sans-Culottes, 71.

8. Dickinson, *British Radicalism*, 10; E. P. Thompson, *The Making of the English Working Class* (Harmondsworth: Penguin, 1963), 167 (LCS leader quoted on 168).

9. Thale, *Papers of the London Corresponding Society*, 7–8.

10. Black, *Association*, 218–221 (see chap. 5, n. 7); Goodwin, *Friends of Liberty*, 215.

11. Thale, *Papers of the London Corresponding Society*, 14.

12. Ibid., 14–15, 30; Keane, *Tom Paine*, 338. For similar struggles for the control of space in pubs in northern England in this period, see Katrina Navickas, *Protest and the Politics of Space and Place, 1789–1848* (Manchester: Manchester University Press, 2016), especially 38–45.

13. Quoted in Black, *Association*, 233.

14. Thale, *Papers of the London Corresponding Society*, 21; Goodwin, *Friends of Liberty*, 244–262 (address on 501–503).

15. The accounts of meetings between the French diplomatic team in London and British government officials convey a sense of these attempts to paper over the gaps: Archives du Ministère des Affaires Étrangères, Paris, Correspondance Politique (Angleterre), 584, folios 19–22.

16. M. Duffy, 'William Pitt and the Origins of the Loyalist Association Movement of 1792', *Historical Journal* 39 (1996): 943–962; Dickinson, *British Radicalism*, 30, 33; Reeves quoted in Black, *Association*, 234–235; More quoted in A. Cobban, *The Debate on the French Revolution, 1789–1800* (London: Black, 1950), 423. C. Parolin, *Radical Spaces* (Canberra: ANUP, 2010), 108-122.

17. Reeves quoted in Duffy, 'Pitt and the Association Movement', 957; historian quoted in Black, *Association*, 251 (wallpaper manufacturer quoted on 250).

18. Black, *Association*, 257.

19. Ibid., 266; Thale, *Papers of the London Corresponding Society*, 30–31.

20. Thale, *Papers of the London Corresponding Society*, 24 (Lynam), 29 (Kennedy).

21. LCS quoted in Goodwin, *Friends of Liberty*, 285.

22. Thale, *Papers of the London Corresponding Society*, 106, 107, 133; Goodwin, *Friends of Liberty*, 309n, 328.

23. N. A. M. Rodger, *The Command of the Ocean: A Naval History of Britain, 1649–1815* (London: Penguin, 2004), 442–443; Stevenson, *Popular Disturbances*, 209–212 (see chap. 5, n. 6).

24. Porter, *London: A Social History*, 167 (see introduction, n. 18); Rudé, *Hanoverian London*, 230–231 (see introduction, n. 11).

25. A. Gee, *The British Volunteer Movement, 1794–1814* (Oxford: Oxford University Press, 2003), 11, 19, 95, 99; J. R. Western, 'The Volunteer Movement as an Anti-revolutionary Force, 1793–1801', *English Historical Review* 71 (1956): 603–614; Cruikshank quoted in R. Knight, *Britain Against Napoleon: The Organization of Victory, 1793–1815* (London: Allen Lane, 2013), 270; City of London plan quoted in Rudé, *Hanoverian London*, 244.

26. *An Account of the Seizure of Citizen Thomas Hardy, Secretary to the London Corresponding Society* (London, 1794), 2; P. A. Brown, *The French Revolution in English History* (London: Allen and Unwin, 1918), 118.

27. T. Hardy, 'Memoir of Thomas Hardy', in *Testaments of Radicalism: Memoirs of Working Class Politicians, 1790–1885*, edited by D. Vincent (London: Europa, 1977), 64; Goodwin, *Friends of Liberty*, 342; Brown, *French Revolution in English History*, 122–123.

28. Goodwin, *Friends of Liberty*, 334–336, 342; Brown, *French Revolution in English History*, 118, 123.

29. History of the Old Bailey Courthouse', *Proceedings of the Old Bailey*, www. oldbaileyonline.org; Hitchcock and Shoemaker, *Tales from the Hanging Court*, xvi–xxvii (see chap. 5, n. 18); Godwin quoted in Goodwin, *Friends of Liberty*, 341; *The Proceedings in Cases of High Treason, Under a Special Commission of Oyer and Terminer . . . Taken in Short Hand by William Ramsey* (London, 1794), 30.

30. Goodwin, *Friends of Liberty*, 343–347; jurors' complaints: *Proceedings in Cases of High Treason*, 164–165. Parolin, *Radical Spaces,* 20-31.

31. *Proceedings in Cases of High Treason*, 329–330; Goodwin, *Friends of Liberty*, 347–352.

32. Erskine quotation: *Proceedings in Cases of High Treason*, 582.

33. Goodwin, *Friends of Liberty*, 352–353 (lord mayor's precautions); verdict and Hardy quotation: *Proceedings in Cases of High Treason*, 646.

34. Goodwin, *Friends of Liberty*, 353.

35. Erskine ('murdering you') quoted in C. Emsley, 'An Aspect of Pitt's "Terror": Prosecutions for Sedition During the 1790s', *Social History* 6 (1981): 170; Goodwin, *Friends of Liberty*, 353–357.

36. Cartwright quoted in C. Emsley, 'Repression, "Terror" and the Rule of Law in England During the Decade of the French Revolution', *English Historical Review* 100 (1985): 810; Emsley, 'Aspect of Pitt's "Terror"', 174.

37. Dickinson, *British Radicalism*, 24; Goodwin, *Friends of Liberty*, 372, 385.

Notes to Chapter Twelve

1. F. D. Cogliano, *Revolutionary America, 1763–1815: A Political History* (London: Routledge, 2000), 137–144.

2. J. E. Cooke, 'The Compromise of 1790', *William and Mary Quarterly* 27 (1970): 523–545; Adams quotation: Abigail Adams to Abigail Adams Smith, 21 November 1790, in *Letters of Mrs. Adams*, by Adams, 2:209 (see introduction, n. 13).

3. Maclay, *Journal of Maclay*, 155 (see chap. 7, n. 32).

4. Hamilton, *Writings*, 521 (see chap. 7, n. 12).

5. 'Society of Tammany or Columbian Order: Committee of Amusement Minutes, October 24, 1791 to February 23, 1795', New York Public Library, Division of Rare Books and Manuscripts, 305-C-3; Lafayette quoted in S. Elkins and E. McKitrick, *The Age of Federalism: The Early American Republic, 1788–1800* (New York: Oxford University Press, 1993), 309.

6. Maclay quotation: Maclay, *Journal of Maclay*, 155.

7. A. Gronowicz, 'Political "Radicalism" in New York City's Revolutionary and Constitutional Eras', in *New York in the Age of the Constitution*, edited by Gilje and Pencak, 105–107 (see chap. 7, n. 22).

8. Quoted in Burrows and Wallace, *Gotham*, 348 (see introduction, n. 15).

9. S. White, *Somewhat More Independent*, 26–27 (see chap. 1, n. 45).

10. S. White, '"We Dwell in Safety and Pursue Our Honest Callings": Free Blacks in New York City, 1783–1810', *Journal of American History* 75 (1988): 456, 458; P. A. Gilje and H. B. Rock, '"Sweep O! Sweep O!": African-American Chimney Sweeps and Citizenship in the New Nation', *William and Mary Quarterly* 51 (1994): 507–538; Burrows and Wallace, *Gotham*, 350; Gilje, *Liberty on the Waterfront*, 25–26, 57 (see chap. 1, n. 16).

11. Burrows and Wallace, *Gotham*, 398–400; Rury, 'Philanthropy, Self Help, and Social Control', 237 (see chap. 7, n. 15); Swan, 'John Teasman', 335 (see chap. 7, n. 14); Phelps Stokes, *Iconography*, 5:1326 (see chap. 1, n. 7). In 1809 New York's African American Anglicans would create their own congregation, calling it Saint Philip's Church, originally meeting on Sundays in a room let on William Street, before moving to another room rented above a carpenter's shop on Cliff Street, not far from the Free African School, close to Peck's Slip. Eventually, a dedicated wooden church would rise on Collect (now Centre) Street, between Anthony and Leonard Streets, in 1818. See anglicanhistory.org/usa/misc/decosta_philip1889.html.

12. S. White, *Somewhat More Independent*, 173–175.

13. Ibid., 144.

14. Ibid., 145, 155; quotation about Zamor in S. White, '"We Dwell in Safety"', 450.

15. Peterson, *Jefferson and the New Nation*, 494 (see chap. 7, n. 18); H. Ammon, *The Genet Mission* (New York: W. W. Norton, 1973), 38; Hamilton quoted in Chernow, *Alexander Hamilton*, 434.

16. Ammon, *The Genet Mission*, 2–9, 22, 25–29, 31 (Genet's instructions quoted on 26).

17. C. D. Hazen, *Contemporary American Opinion of the French Revolution* (Baltimore: Johns Hopkins University Press, 1897), 176; Phelps Stokes, *Iconography*, 5:1296.

18. Phelps Stokes, *Iconography*, 5:1217.

19. E. P. Kilroe, *Saint Tammany and the Origin of the Society of Tammany; or, The Columbian Order in the City of New York* (New York, 1913), 144; Phelps Stokes, *Iconography*, 5:1253.

20. Phelps Stokes, *Iconography*, 5:1201; Niemcewicz quotation: J. U. Niemcewicz, *Under Their Vine and Fig Tree: Travels Through America in 1797–1799, 1805, with Some Further Account of Life in New Jersey*, edited and translated by M. J. E. Budka (Elizabeth, NJ: Grassmann, 1965), 127.

21. 'Society of Tammany or Columbian Order: Committee of Amusement Minutes'; Kilroe, *Saint Tammany*, 141, 185–186; Phelps Stokes, *Iconography*, 5:1291; aims of American Museum quoted in Burrows and Wallace, *Gotham*, 316.

22. Tammany's political aims quoted in Kilroe, *Saint Tammany*, 135–136.

23. 'Society of Tammany or Columbian Order: Committee of Amusement Minutes'; Burrows and Wallace, *Gotham*, 318.

24. H. Wansey, *An Excursion to the United States of North America in the Summer of 1794*, excerpt in B. Still, *Mirror for Gotham: New York as Seen by Contemporaries from Dutch Days to the Present* (New York: New York University Press, 1956), 65.

25. J. Lambert, *Travels Through Canada, and the United States of North America, in the Years 1806, 1807, & 1808*, excerpt in Still, *Mirror for Gotham*, 74.

26. Eyewitness quoted in Phelps Stokes, *Iconography*, 5:1297; Burrows and Wallace, *Gotham*, 318 (destruction of the plinth).

27. Jaffe, *New York at War*, 111–112 (Courtney and Bompard quoted on 111) (see chap. 4, n. 26); Phelps Stokes, *Iconography*, 5:1299.

28. Phelps Stokes, *Iconography*, 5:1299.

29. Newman, *Parades and the Politics of the Street*, 141 (see chap. 1, n. 21); Gilje, *Liberty on the Waterfront*, 134; Phelps Stokes, *Iconography*, 5:1299.

30. Quoted in Gilje, *Road to Mobocracy*, 102 (see chap. 1, n. 12).

31. Ammon, *The Genet Mission*, 118; Phelps Stokes, *Iconography*, 5:1299, 1300.

32. Quotations from Ammon, *The Genet Mission*, 116–117; Phelps Stokes, *Iconography*, 5:1299; Burrows and Wallace, *Gotham*, 318.

33. Phelps Stokes, *Iconography*, 5:1300; Ammon, *The Genet Mission*, 123–124, 143.

34. On Hamilton's role, see Chernow, *Alexander Hamilton*, 447.

35. Quoted in ibid., 434.

36. E. P. Link, *Democratic-Republican Societies, 1790–1800* (New York: Columbia University Press, 1942), 18 (quotation on 99); Burrows and Wallace, *Gotham*, 319–320.

37. Phelps Stokes, *Iconography*, 5:1305; Burrows and Wallace, *Gotham*, 320.

38. Quoted in Hazen, *Contemporary American Opinion*, 200.

39. Phelps Stokes, *Iconography*, 5:1323.

Notes to Conclusion

1. Garrioch, *Making of Revolutionary Paris*, 7 ('player in its own history') (see introduction, n. 3).

2. Lenotre, *Paris révolutionnaire*, viii (see chap. 8, n. 12).

3. Hollis, *Secret Lives of Buildings* (see chap. 10, n. 21); G. M. Trevelyan, *Clio, a Muse, and Other Essays Literary and Pedestrian* (London: Longmans, 1913), 27.

4. P. Nora, ed., *Les lieux de mémoire*, 3 vols. (Paris: Gallimard, 1984–1993). Selections from these volumes have been translated as *Rethinking France: Les lieux de mémoire*, 4 vols. (Chicago: University of Chicago Press, 1999–2010).

5. Debate on the Danton statue as reported in the *New York Times*, 26 July 1891. Henri Wallon was an historian of the French Revolution. His hostility to Danton stemmed from the fact that he edited a multivolume edition of the acts of the Revolutionary Tribunal, which had been set up on Danton's initiative in the Convention. For a more modern controversy, this time in New York, see C. J. La Roche and M. L. Blakey, 'Seizing Intellectual Power: The Dialogue at the New York African Burial Ground', *Historical Archaeology* 31 (1997): 84–106.

INDEX

Note: ins. refers to pages in the photo insert.

Mike Rapport is a professor of history at the University of Glasgow in Scotland and a fellow of the Royal Historical Society. The author of numerous books, Rapport lives in Stirling, Scotland.